Politics in North and South K(

Politics in North and South Korea provides students with a comprehensive understanding of the political dynamics of the two Koreas. Giving equal weight to North and South Korea, the authors trace the history of political and economic development and international relations of the Korean Peninsula, showing how South Korea became democratized and how Juche ideology has affected the establishment and operation of a totalitarian system in North Korea.

Written in a straightforward, jargon-free manner, this textbook utilizes both historical-institutional approaches and quantitative evidence to analyze the political dimensions of a wide variety of issues including:

- Legacies of Japanese colonial rule (1910–1945) and the Korean War (1950–1953)
- South Korean democratization and democratic consolidation
- South Korean diplomacy and North Korean nuclear crises
- The economic development of both North and South Korea
- The three-generation power succession in North Korea
- North Korean human rights issues
- Inter-Korean relations and reunification

This textbook will be essential reading for students of Korean Politics and is also suitable for undergraduate and postgraduate courses on East Asian Politics, Asian Studies, and International Relations.

Yangmo Ku is Assistant Professor of Political Science and Associate Director in the Peace & War Centre at Norwich University.

Inyeop Lee is Assistant Professor of Politics and History at Spring Arbor University.

Jongseok Woo is Assistant Professor in the School of Interdisciplinary Global Studies at the University of South Florida.

Politics in North and South Korea

Political Development, Economy, and Foreign Relations

Yangmo Ku, Inyeop Lee, and Jongseok Woo

Routledge
Taylor & Francis Group
LONDON AND NEW YORK

First published 2018
by Routledge
2 Park Square, Milton Park, Abingdon, Oxon OX14 4RN

and by Routledge
711 Third Avenue, New York, NY 10017

Routledge is an imprint of the Taylor & Francis Group, an informa business

© 2018 Yangmo Ku, Inyeop Lee, and Jongseok Woo

British Library Cataloguing-in-Publication Data
A catalogue record for this book is available from the British Library

Library of Congress Cataloging-in-Publication Data
Names: Ku, Yangmo, author. | Lee, Inyeop, author. | Woo, Jongseok, author.
Title: Politics in North and South Korea: political development, economy,
    and foreign relations / Yangmo Ku, Inyeop Lee and Jongseok Woo.
Description: Abingdon, Oxon ; New York, NY : Routledge, 2018. |
    Includes bibliographical references and index.
Identifiers: LCCN 2017033557 | ISBN 9781138647459 (hardback) |
    ISBN 9781138647503 (pbk.) | ISBN 9781315627014 (ebook)
Subjects: LCSH: Korea (South)—Politics and government. | Korea (South)—
    Foreign relations. | Korea (South)—Economic conditions. | Democracy—Korea
    (South) | Korea (North)—Politics and government. | Korea (North)—Economic
    conditions. | Nuclear weapons—Korea (North) | Human rights—Korea (North) |
    Korea (South)—Foreign relations—Korea (North) | Korea (North)—Foreign
    relations—Korea (South)
Classification: LCC JQ1725 .K8 2018 | DDC 320.9519—dc23
LC record available at https://lccn.loc.gov/2017033557

ISBN: 978-1-138-64745-9 (hbk)
ISBN: 978-1-138-64750-3 (pbk)
ISBN: 978-1-315-62701-4 (ebk)

Typeset in Times New Roman
by Apex CoVantage, LLC

To our beloved families

Contents

Figures

Tables

Abbreviations

APT	ASEAN Plus Three
ASEAN	Association of Southeast Asian Nations
AWF	Asian Women's Fund
BDA	Banco Delta Asia
BOK	Bank of Korea
CCP	Chinese Communist Party
CEDAW	Convention on the Elimination of All Forms of Discrimination against Women
CIA	Central Intelligence Agency
CMC	Central Military Commission
CPI	Corruption Perceptions Index
CPKI	Committee for the Preparation of Korean Independence
CRC	Convention on the Rights of the Child
CVID	complete, verifiable, irreversible disarmament
DJP	Democratic Justice Party
DMZ	Demilitarized Zone
DLP	Democratic Liberal Party
DPRK	Democratic People's Republic of Korea
DSC	Defense Security Command
DUP	Democratic United Party
ECOSOC	International Convention on Economic, Social and Cultural Rights
EPB	Economic Planning Board
FDI	foreign direct investment
FTA	free trade agreement
GDP	gross domestic product
GNP	Grand National Party
GSOMIA	General Security of Military Information Agreement
HEU	highly enriched uranium
HRNK	Human Rights in North Korea
IAEA	International Atomic Energy Agency
ICBM	intercontinental ballistic missile
ICC	International Criminal Court
ICCPR	International Covenant on Civil and Political Rights
ILO	International Labour Organization
IMF	International Monetary Fund
JCP	Joseon Communist Party
JSA	Joint Security Area

KCIA	Korean Central Intelligence Agency
KCNA	Korean Central News Agency
KEDO	Korean Peninsula Energy Development Organization
KIC	Kaesong Industrial Complex
KOTRA	Korea Trade-Investment Promotion Agency
KMAG	Korean Military Advisory Group
KPA	Korean People's Army
KPG	Korean Provisional Government
KPR	Korean People's Republic
KWP	Korean Workers' Party
MDP	Millennium Democratic Party
MERS	Middle East respiratory syndrome
MPS	Ministry of People's Security
MSC	Military Security Command
MW	Megawatt
NATO	North Atlantic Treaty Organization
NCDC	National Coalition for a Democratic Constitution
NDC	National Defense Commission
NDRP	New Democratic-Republican Party
NGOs	non-governmental organizations
NIS	National Intelligence Service
NKFC	North Korea Freedom Coalition
NKHRA	North Korean Human Rights Act
NKP	New Korea Party
NPT	Nuclear Non-proliferation Treaty
OECD	Organization for Economic Cooperation and Development
OGD	Organization and Guidance Department
OPCON	wartime operational control
OSS	Office of Strategic Services
PAD	Propaganda and Agitation Department
PCUP	Presidential Committee for Unification Preparation
PDS	Public Distribution System
PPD	Party for Peace and Democracy
ROK	Republic of Korea
SEZs	Special Economic Zones
SMEs	small- and medium-sized enterprises
SSD	State Security Department
THAAD	Terminal High Altitude Area Defense
TPP	Trans-Pacific Partnership
UDP	Unification Democratic Party
ULD	United Liberal Party
UN	United Nations
UNICEF	United Nations Children's Fund
UNTCOK	United Nations Temporary Committee on Korea
UPP	United Progressive Party
USAMGIK	US Army Military Government in Korea
WMD	weapons of mass destruction

Acknowledgments

This book project was conceived in the early 2010s, when Yangmo Ku taught an Asian Politics course at American University and then Norwich University. At the time, Ku had difficulty finding a book suitable to undergraduate and postgraduate students that simultaneously addressed politics in both North and South Korea, while having no problem in adopting books covering politics of other East Asian countries, such as China and Japan. The preexisting literature only addressed either North Korean or South Korean politics, thus failing to provide a comprehensive picture of the political dynamics of the two Koreas. The extant literature regarding South Korean politics was particularly out of date. In this context, he took an initiative to write a wide-ranging book that analyzes domestic politics, economy, and foreign relations of both Koreas at the same time. Rather than working on this extensive project as a single author, he decided to collaborate with two other Korea experts, Inyeop Lee and Jongseok Woo, in order to maximize the quality of the book.

This work is very much a product of close co-authorship. Every chapter was fully drafted by a primary author, and the draft was revised based on two rounds of internal reviews among the three authors. Jongseok Woo is the primary author of Chapters 2, 3, 6, and the conclusion, while Inyeop Lee is the primary author of Chapters 1, 8, and 9. Yangmo Ku is primarily responsible for Chapters 4, 5, 7, 10, and the introduction.

Jongseok Woo acknowledges his mentor and colleague Zoltan Barany who gives him thoughtful advices, encouragements, and criticisms on his research. He is also grateful to fellow scholars at the University of South Florida, including, among others, Peter Funke, Bernd Reiter, Steven Roach, Manu Samnontra, Scott Solomon, Nicholas Thompson, and Steve Tauber. And he expresses his heartfelt gratitude to his wife, Eunjung Choi, and son, Austin Jiwon Woo, who are currently staying in Gwangju, South Korea and have shown great patience and understanding throughout this book project. Eunjung read the chapters he drafted and gave helpful comments and suggestions.

Inyeop Lee would like to express his gratitude to Dr. Han S. Park, his advisor and mentor during his doctoral studies at the University of Georgia, for guiding and inspiring him to study Korean politics. He also would like to thank his colleagues at Spring Arbor University, especially Mark Correll and Mark Edwards for their support. He appreciates his parents for their sacrifices and support. Finally, he expresses his deep gratitude to his wife Dasom for her love and patience.

Yangmo Ku wants to acknowledge Norwich University, which has provided him with generous research support, including the Charles A. Dana fellowship, the Chase research release award, and the publication expenses grant. He is also thankful to the Institute for Far Eastern Studies (IFES) in Seoul for inviting him as a visiting scholar. During his stay at the IFES in summer 2014, 2016, and 2017, he was able to significantly promote his understanding of politics, political economy, and foreign policy in both Koreas through research presentations and scholarly interactions with many researchers. He would especially like to express his deep gratitude to his wife, Min Ku, and three children, Paul Ku, Timothy Ku, and Grace Ku for their affection and patience.

Moreover, we are grateful to Dr. In Tae Yoo at Yonsei University in Seoul and three anonymous reviewers who offered their invaluable insights on Korean politics at the book proposal stage. We would like to acknowledge Dr. Rowly Brucken at Norwich University, who read our full manuscript and gave useful comments with nice edits. Our gratitude also goes to the entire team at Routledge. The editor Stephanie Rogers, the editorial assistant Georgina Bishop, and the project manager Kerry Boettcher all provided good guidance throughout this project.

Introduction

Yangmo Ku

It is common today to see global media covering a variety of issues concerning the Republic of Korea (ROK or South Korea) and the Democratic People's Republic of Korea (DPRK or North Korea). For instance, the news about the impeachment of ROK President Park Geun-hye in March 2017, caused by her role in a corruption and influence-peddling scandal, attracted enormous attention from the international community. Many media outlets also reported on the quick deployment of a US missile defense system, the Terminal High Altitude Area Defense (THAAD), to South Korea in April 2017. This event, which had occurred amidst the ROK's political upheaval, sparked strong opposition from both China and progressive citizens within South Korean society.

Moreover, North Korea's provocative acts have been highly covered and analyzed in the international media. These provocations encompass the regime's frequent nuclear and missile tests banned by the international law, the sudden purge and brutal execution of Jang Song-taek, the DPRK leader Kim Jong-un's uncle in December 2013, and the assassination of Kim Jong-nam, Kim Jong-un's half-brother, by North Korean agents in February 2017. Citizens around the world can also read about the success of South Korea's big conglomerates, such as Samsung and LG, in global smartphone markets, alongside stories describing the changes being made in North Korean economy, particularly the acceleration of marketization and the expansion of trade between North Korea and China in spite of intensifying economic sanctions. North Korea's serious human rights violations, including crimes against humanity that take place within the nation's prison camps, have been an important media topic as well.

Given these globally transmitted issues on North and South Korea, it is necessary to study the two nations' politics, political economy, and foreign policy in a more scholarly, comprehensive, and analytical manner than journalists and political commentators can offer. In practical terms, it is important to understand how the political, economic, and diplomatic dynamics surrounding the Korean Peninsula have unfolded and might unfold, because such dynamics can exert significant influence on the fate of the two Koreas themselves, as well as economic conditions and security in the East Asian region. The Korean Peninsula has been, and could be continually, a flashpoint for strategic rivalries between major powers in East Asia, such as between the United States and China, China and Japan, and Russia and Japan. Continental powers such as China and Russia desire to place the Korean Peninsula into their sphere of influence, as the peninsula serves as a conduit for their reaching out to the North Pacific. On the other hand, for the maritime powers such as the United States and Japan, the Korean Peninsula is a strategic location to promote their interests on the Asian continent.

Furthermore, North Korea's nuclear and missile adventurism, and its longstanding stand-offs with the international community will have great impact on the direct fate of about 75 million Koreans, depending on how those issues proceed. It is almost unimaginable to contemplate how many human casualties and what material destruction could result from military contingencies, triggered by North Korea's nuclear/missile provocations or US preemptive strikes on DPRK's nuclear facilities. In a similar vein, the sudden collapse of the North Korean regime would also bring about serious instability on the Korean Peninsula and in the Northeast Asian region, because it would result in massive refugee flows, China's plausible military intervention, and uncertainty over the DPRK's weapons of mass destruction. In a globalized world, therefore, the future economic and military policies of the North Korean regime will heavily influence East Asian security and economic conditions.

In academic terms, the two Koreas also can work as a useful laboratory in which to apply numerous concepts and theories of comparative politics and international relations. For example, modernization theory (Lipset 1959), which posits that economic development increases the possibility of democratization, can assist in explaining South Korean's modern history. As detailed in subsequent chapters, South Korea achieved miraculous economic growth in the period 1960s–1980s, which significantly contributed to increasing people's education level and the size of middle class. This enlarged, educated middle class actively participated in public campaigns for political liberalization in the 1980s, playing a pivotal role in pushing authoritarian leaders to democratize South Korea's political system. South Korea's successful economic growth also can be explained by the developmental state model (Johnson 1982), which places heavy emphasis on state intervention in economic planning. The South Korean government controlled interest rates and bank loans, masterminding industrial policies alongside of an export-driven strategy. While suppressing the labor movement with its authoritarian fist, the ROK government maintained close collusion with big conglomerates, called *chaebols*, thus spawning crony capitalism fraught with rent seeking and corruption.

Moreover, the international relations theory of realism (Morgenthau 1948; Waltz 1979), which generally assumes that states as unitary and rational actors pursue national interests, like security and prosperity in an anarchic international system, is a simple but useful lens through which to explain the two Koreas' foreign policy toward the United States and China. To deter the North Korean threat and promote its security, the ROK has heavily relied on its alliance with the United States, while the DPRK played its two patrons, the Soviet Union and China, off against each other in order to maximize its own interests. The concept of the rally 'round the flag effect (Mueller 1970) also applies to both Koreas. Top North Korean leaders often used their nuclear/missile standoffs with the United States as an instrument for defusing public complaints toward their regime and for promoting internal solidarity among North Koreans. In a similar vein, South Korean leaders have taken advantage of anti-communist sentiments and/or anti-Japanese sentiments among Koreans to turn people's attention to outside actors or to increase their waning popularity.

To promote understanding of the content of the following ten substantive chapters, subsequent sections in this introduction provide rudimentary information regarding Korea's historical background, geographical and geopolitical environment, and political culture in a succinct manner.

Historical background[1]

According to Korea's founding myth, Korean history dates back to 2333 BC when Korea's first kingdom, Gojoson, was established by Tan'gun, who had been born from a bear-turned-woman and the god Hwanung. Subsequently, three kingdoms, consisting of Goguryeo, Baekje, and Silla, began to control different areas of the Korean Peninsula by the first century BC. Based on Buddhism and a code of laws, Goguryeo was the first of the three kingdoms to establish itself as a sovereign country, dominating most of the current North Korea and Manchuria in China. Baekje, strongly influenced by China's advanced culture, constructed a stable political system that controlled the southwestern part of the Korean Peninsula and areas near the current Han River. While adopting Chinese culture through Goguryeo, Silla occupied the southeastern part of the Korean Peninsula. These three kingdoms competed with each other for hegemonic power. Through its expansionist policy, Goguryeo arose by the fifth century as a powerful kingdom in Northeast Asia.

However, Silla was the nation to unify the peninsula with support from the Chinese Dang Dynasty. The Silla–Dang allied forces defeated Baekje in 660 and conquered Goguryeo in 668, which was at the time weakened by a divisive succession struggle. After the fall of Baekje and Goguryeo, Dang China sought to control the entire Korean Peninsula, including Silla. Responding to this provocative act, Silla waged war against Dang China, successfully evicting all Dang forces from the peninsula in 676. Until the end of the 800s, a unified Silla experienced a long period of stable government, cultural and artistic growth, and economic development, including the vibrant trade relationship with the Dang Dynasty.

It is also necessary to note that in 698, the descendants of fallen Goguryeo, led by a former Goguryeo General Dae Jo-yeong, also established Balhae in Manchuria and the northern part of the Korean Peninsula. Some Korean scholars include Balhae as part of Korean history, defining the history of Balhae and unified Silla as the North–South States Period. When the Khitan Liao Dynasty conquered Balhae in 926, the southern part of its territory and its refugees, led by crown prince Dae Gwang-hyeon, were absorbed into Goryeo Dynasty.

By the late 800s, however, the rule of Silla began to unravel due to an internal struggle for power among the nobility. As a result, leaders of powerful regional factions established their own regimes, and the former three-kingdom system emerged. In 918, the northern state of Goryeo unified the later three kingdoms under its rule. The Goryeo Dynasty continued its rule from 918 to 1392, during which Buddhism, trade with Song China, Central Asia, and Arabia, and the arts, particularly celadon pottery, flourished. The current Western name of Korea originated from Goryeo. The people of Goryeo invented metal printing type about 200 years before Johannes Gutenberg in Europe.

The Goryeo Dynasty, though, suffered from Mongolian invasions seven times between 1231 and 1259. Goryeo strongly resisted these attacks before concluding a peace agreement in 1259 under which Mongolians accepted Goryeo's six conditions for peace, including the continued existence of the Goryeo Dynasty. Despite this agreement, until 1273, a group of Goryeo soldiers, referred to as *Sambyeolcho*, continually fought the Mongols, the world's strongest power at that time. Because of this war, Korean land was devastated, and many people's lives were destroyed. Goryeo finally expelled the Mongolian rulers in 1356. The Goryeo Dynasty's power and cohesion then seriously weakened due to internal power struggles among the nobility and external invasions by bandits and pirates. At that time, General Yi Seong-gye, who had become popular for his role in expelling foreign invaders, toppled Goryeo and established the Joseon Dynasty, also known as the Yi Dynasty, in 1392.

The Joseon Dynasty ruled through a series of kings from 1392 to 1910. During the early period of this dynasty, monarchs stabilized the system of governance by instituting a census, launching six ministries, including the Ministries of Finance, Justice, and Defense, and creating the National Code and a long-lasting legal system. In 1443, King Sejong, one of the most respectful figures among current Koreans, supervised the creation of Korea's own written language, *hangeul*, to replace reliance on Chinese characters. This event contributed greatly to the promotion of communication between the people and the government, thus laying the groundwork for a culturally advanced country. Another significant achievement was the development of science and technology, including the invention of a rain gauge and devices for land surveying and mapping. Joseon also maintained good relations with Ming China by exchanging royal envoys annually and engaging in cultural and economic exchanges. Joseon also facilitated trade with Japan by opening its ports to the neighboring country.

As frequently happened in previous kingdoms, however, the Joseon Dynasty began to decline with the renewal of internal power struggles and factional rivalries in the late sixteenth century. On top of these domestic challenges, Korea suffered from foreign incursions, such as a Japanese invasion in 1592 and the Manchu's invasions of 1627 and 1636. Japanese leader Toyotomi Hedeyoshi, who had ended internal wars and unified Japan, invaded Joseon in 1592 in an attempt to dissipate local lords' power and to stabilize his rule in Japan. Japanese forces marched into the northern provinces of Joseon by using advanced military equipment and organization. However, Japanese troops eventually retreated due to Korean opposition, naval victories by Admiral Yi Sun-shin, and Chinese intervention. In 1597, Japan invaded Joseon again in the wake of failed peace talks between China and Japan, but the nation made little headway because of strengthened Joseon-Ming allied forces. Japan completely withdrew from the peninsula after Toyotomi's death in 1598, but eight years of war had devastated Korean lands and inflicted great sufferings on its people. Unfortunately, the Joseon Dynasty was confronted with additional invasions from the Manchus in Manchuria 30 years later. The Manchus, who were trying to topple Ming China, perceived Ming's vassal Joseon as a threat to its southern border and forced Joseon to become a Manchu vassal. The Manchus eventually ousted Ming China in 1644, and Joseon remained a vassal of the new Chinese empire, the Qing Dynasty.

Geographical and geopolitical environment

Located in the middle of Northeast Asia, the Korean Peninsula covers about 85,000 square miles, which is slightly smaller than the size of New York and Pennsylvania combined. The Yalu and Tumen Rivers demarcate the northern border of the Korean Peninsula from China and Russia. Korea's three other sides are surrounded by the sea. Japan is located to the east of the Korean Peninsula. The peninsula, whose northern end is linked to the Asian continent, comprises about 30 percent flat land and 70 percent mountainous areas. With four distinct seasons, the southern part of the peninsula produces rich agricultural resources, especially rice, while its northern part contains abundant natural resources, such as coal and minerals (Kim 2001, 10–13).

Korea's geographical location has continually exerted significant influence on national security and the fate of its people. Koreans have suffered from numerous foreign invasions over the last two millennia. Whenever China and Japan have achieved internal unity, they had tendencies to expand into the Korean Peninsula. Up until the mid-nineteenth century, Korea's survival strategy was to rely on China as its patron by paying a regular tribute to China.

Starting in the late nineteenth century, the Korean Peninsula became a hotspot where great powers clashed. China's last imperial dynasty, the Qing empire (1644–1912), strove to maintain its longstanding hegemonic status on the Korean Peninsula, although its power notably declined in the wake of the First Opium War (1839–1842). Japan, which had succeeded in modernizing after the 1868 Meiji restoration, sought to expand its influence on the Korean Peninsula and into Manchuria. Acquiring great power status, Russia also made every effort to increase its power in the region surrounding Korea. Korea, surrounded by such major powers, was often referred to as "a shrimp amongst whales." Clashing interests among those powerful nations generated the 1894 Sino-Japanese War and the 1904 Russo-Japanese War. Japan surprisingly defeated China and Russia and became the predominant power on the Korean Peninsula. In 1910, Japan annexed Korea, making it a colony until August 15, 1945, when Japan surrendered to the Allied forces in World War II. The fate of Korean security was for a long time dependent on strategic rivalries on the peninsula among major powers.

The geopolitical struggles involving the Korean Peninsula continued in the wake of World War II. Despite its liberation from Japanese colonial rule in 1945, Korea was not able to become an independent state, because the United States and the Soviet Union decided to construct separate trusteeships. The two great powers originally agreed to establish a unified and independent Korea, but the Cold War rivalry between the United States and the Soviet Union prevented this occurrence. On top of the ideological gap between capitalism and communism, a series of incidents triggered and widened the rift between the two superpowers. Among these events were the placement of a million Soviet troops in Romania and Iran beyond the end of 1945, the "Iron Curtain" speech by Winston Churchill in March 1946, the declaration of Truman Doctrine in March 1947, the Marshall Plan in June 1947, and the Berlin Blockade in June 1948 (Nau 2015, 150–2).

As a consequence, not long after experiencing its dramatic liberation from Japan, Korea had to face another tragic experience, the division of Korea into two nations. In spite of vehement opposition from many Koreans, the United States governed the southern region and helped establish the Republic of Korea in 1948, while the Soviet Union ruled the northern region and supported the construction of the Democratic People's Republic of Korea in the same year. This partition soon led to an unprecedented national tragedy, the outbreak of the Korean War (1950–1953), which caused more than three million casualties and devastated industrial facilities. The Korean War did not end the division. Since the end of the war, the two Koreas have largely remained in a confrontational relationship under an armistice rather than a permanent peace treaty.

Political culture

It is necessary to understand Korean political culture, which influences people's political attitudes and behavior, before delving into the two Koreas' detailed political, economic, and diplomatic dynamics in subsequent chapters. The interplay of the following four factors have had a big impact on the formation of Korean political culture. The first was Confucianism, which places a heavy emphasis on the maintenance of order and harmony, the importance of the community rather than the individual, and hierarchical structures in both the political and social spheres (Liberthal 2004). Second, Japanese colonial rule (1910–1945) played a critical role in shaping a more recent political culture in Korean society. Resistance to external control had become an integral part of Korea's political culture. Japan's militaristic bureaucratic rule also set a precedent for the advent of authoritarian regimes in Korea. Third, the Korean War (1950–1953) and more than 60 years of military confrontation between North and South Korea ushered in strong militarism in both Koreas. This led to the creation of hierarchical and male-dominant societies. Fourth, the rapid modernization process in ROK society prompted Korean culture to move toward individualism, mass consumption, and pluralistic values.

Political culture in Korea largely has three distinctive characteristics: communitarian identity, authoritarian value, and factionalism. Based on homogenous racial, cultural, and linguistic legacies, Koreans hold a strong sense of common destiny, considering themselves as part of a single Korean nation. This communitarian identity enhanced not only a robust social bond and solidarity, but it also promoted mutual cooperation by stressing social obligations and loyalty to the community. On the other hand, the supremacy of a collective identity contributed to the emergence of authoritarian state corporatism, in which individual human rights were frequently violated in the name of state development. Excessive collectivism also promoted exclusive nationalism, which delayed the processes of globalization and liberalization, in addition to preventing the spread of political and social pluralism that is indispensable to a stable democracy. Another significant feature of Korean political culture is an orientation toward authoritarian values, inculcated by Confucian conformity, compliance with authority, and acceptance of a hierarchical political order. Based on these authoritarian values, North Korean leader Kim Il-sung formulated his cult of personality and totalitarian political system, and South Korea's authoritarian leaders maintained four decades of oppressive rule.

Finally, factionalism is a big element of political culture in Korean society. Koreans aspire to associate themselves with the groups to which they belong. Although national unity is an important trait, it is very common to see fierce competition among factions in political parties, firms, schools, the military, and so on. Factionalism in Korea has three types: the *munbol* (kinship clan), the *hakyon* (school ties), and the *Jiyon* (regional and local ties). In the past, family names determined social stratification, and the kinship clan was the most important factor determining social upward mobility. Kinship ties are still important, but their overall impact on political and social life has been weakened by the progress of modernization and urbanization. During the Joseon Dynasty, political power struggles often happened among contending schools of Confucian thoughts. In contemporary Korea, school ties are still important, as which school one attended is a significant factor in determining elite recruitment, social mobility, and business opportunities. For instance, a number of Korea University graduates took core governmental positions during the rule of ROK President Lee Myung-bak (2008–2013), who had also attended the same school. Deeply rooted in Korean society, regional and local ties also have exerted influence on political and social life. Until recently, electoral outcomes in South Korea were heavily affected by localism. Local networks were a prime factor for forming factions in political parties or government circles. Factionalism is a double-edged sword, as it can help in the construction of social networks and promote the flow of information while concurrently causing political underdevelopment and economic inefficiency due to rent seeking, corruption, unreasonable patterns of recruitment, and the politics of exclusion (Kim 2001, 24–8).

Organization of the book

The following chapters deal with comprehensive dynamics of domestic politics, political economy, and foreign policy of the two Koreas. Chapter 1 addresses the history of the Japanese colonial period (1910–1945) and the Korean War (1950–1953), which were crucial foundations for the political and economic development of the two Koreas. The declining Joseon Dynasty was colonized by Japan, which had achieved successful modernization and industrialization. As a result, the Korean people were under Japanese colonial rule for 36 years until 1945. Koreans not only experienced Japanese political oppression and exploitation of human and material resources, but they also underwent modernization initiated by Japanese colonial authorities. Atrocious acts, such as forced labor and sexual slavery, committed by the Japanese military continued to be sources of historical disputes and tensions between Korea and Japan. During the colonial period, sharp divisions between leftists and rightists in their struggle against Japan occurred. Internal division among Korean factional leaders and the arrival of the Cold War divided the country and finally ignited the Korean War. As a consequence of the war, millions of Korean people died, and the country's resources were devastated. The Korean War also generated strong hatreds between the two Koreas, and the leaders of the two regimes consolidated their power based on their experiences in the war.

Chapter 2 explores the origin, process, and consequence of South Korea's democratic transition. Democratization in South Korea represents one of the most successful examples in the world of economic modernization and political development. Although aborted, previous pro-democracy movements from the 1960s provided fertile soil for voluntary civil society activities from different quarters of society, ranging from farmers and urban blue collar workers to college students, religious leaders, white collar workers, and intellectuals. These diverse voices formed a united front for democratization that overwhelmed the seemingly invincible authoritarian governments that had utilized physical violence and terror. The activation of civil society contributed to the nonviolent nature of the democratic transition in South Korea. However, the remarkable political achievement – democratization through political compromise – also had its own adverse effects on consolidating and deepening democracy following the transition process. On the one hand, the compromise-based transition minimized socio-political turmoil and prevented any accompanying physical violence that could have derailed the political route to democracy. On the other hand, such compromises made democratic reforms extremely slow and incomplete, thereby hampering the democratic consolidation process.

Chapter 3 looks into post-democratization politics in South Korea, or the era of democratic consolidation. From a minimal or procedural viewpoint, South Korea is undoubtedly a consolidated democracy, as the nation has achieved two peaceful turnovers of power without interruption, and the possibility of a return to dictatorship does not seem feasible. However, the post-democratization politics in South Korea have been marked by political dysfunction, including extreme political, economic, and ideological polarization, rampant political corruption, constrained civil liberties and rights, and security threats from North Korea. After three decades of democratic trials, both ordinary citizens and experts now express a sense of democratic crisis. This chapter focuses on the political processes during the era of democratic consolidation, which has experienced a full swing from two progressive governments (1998–2008) to two conservative ones (2008–2017). Post-democratization politics have suffered from extreme political polarization and an ensuing crisis in democratic governance.

Chapter 4 examines South Korea's miraculous economic development, economic crisis, and current socio-economic challenges. South Korea achieved rapid economic growth between the 1960s and the 1990s, which shifted the nation's status from a poor nation to a developed nation. This dramatic shift was possible based on a state-led development strategy, export-driven policies, the suppression of the labor movement, the supply of well-educated workers, and strong support from the United States and Japan. After this successful economic development, South Korea underwent a painful economic crisis from 1997 to 1998, which produced massive bankruptcies and high unemployment, due to the crony capitalism and the rapid liquidity of international capital. Under harsh International Monetary Fund (IMF) conditionality, summarized as tight fiscal policy and high interest rates, the ROK government adopted a number of drastic economic reforms in the public, corporate, labor, and financial realms. As a consequence of these reforms, the ROK accomplished a faster economic recovery than expected, and its economic development continued into the 2000s and 2010s. Despite some positive macroeconomic indicators, South Korea currently faces various challenges, including prolonged economic stagnation, a persistently low birth rate, and a worsening income inequality between rich and poor.

Chapter 5 addresses the evolution of South Korean foreign policy since the end of the Korean War through the two analytical lenses – traditional interest diplomacy and middle power diplomacy. The ROK's diplomacy has centered on the maximization of its national interests, which are to protect its security from the North Korean threat, foster inter-Korean reconciliation, and promote economic prosperity. South Korea has also made efforts to promote public goods – development, environment, and international security – in the international community by proactively participating in global institutions since the late 2000s. The chapter also pays special attention to the impact of three influential factors – top leadership, domestic public opinion, and international political structure – on South Korean foreign policy. South Korean presidents usually had ultimate authority to determine the ROK's foreign policy, but they were also constrained by international political events, such as the Cold War, the evolving relationship between the United States and the Soviet Union and between the United States and China. After the ROK's democratization in 1987, foreign policy initiatives were often bounded by domestic public opinion as well.

Chapter 6 explores the political history of North Korea, from its state-building period to the power succession from Kim Jong-il to Kim Jong-un. With Kim Jong-un's assumption of political leadership in December 2011, North Korea completed three-generations of hereditary succession. At the heart of this unexpected survival has been Kim Jong-il's military-first politics, under which he closed the door to the outside world and passed the burdens of such isolation and ensuing economic difficulties onto his people. Kim's priority was not achieving economic prosperity or improving his people's livelihood, but he sought to achieve regime security and his political survival. Kim Jong-il's military-first politics brought about adventurous foreign policies that involved developing nuclear weapons, test-firing of missiles, and dispatching frequent low-intensity armed attacks on South Korea. These belligerent actions led to severe economic sanctions by the international community that only exacerbated the country's crumbling economy. The Pyongyang regime muddled through difficulties resulting from the end of the Cold War, the collapse of the communist bloc, and internal crisis. In the meantime, however, it lost out on opportunities to enact reforms and longer-term strategies for wealth and prosperity.

Chapter 7 explains why North Korea has long suffered economic stagnation, while reviewing some cross-temporal variations in the North Korean economy over the last seven decades. In the 1950s after the Korean War, the DPRK attained a quick economic recovery through the mass mobilization of labor forces under a Soviet-style command economy. However, the North Korean economy continued to decline after the 1960s, because of the inherent ineffectiveness of the centrally planned economy, great emphasis on building heavy industry and militarization, ineffective and expensive construction projects, the decline of Soviet aid, and economic autarky based on the ideology of self-reliance. In the 1990s, the North Korean economy plunged into an unprecedented economic crisis and massive famine. This dismal incident resulted from the collapse of the Soviet Union, natural disasters such as drought and flooding, and the DPRK regime's mismanagement. After this famine, Kim Jong-il adopted some economic reforms, but he often reverted to anti-market policies to regain his grip over society. Unlike his father, Kim Jong-un has quite persistently pursued economic reform measures without reverting to anti-market measures. However, North Korean economic conditions have not notably improved. Nevertheless, North Korea is currently experiencing significant changes, such as the deepening of marketization, the rise of private entrepreneurs, and the symbiotic relationship between the state and markets.

Chapter 8 introduces the historical background of North Korean nuclear development and negotiations over the nuclear issue. Both Koreas have been haunted by the memory of the horror and destruction from the Korean War. They have lived under intense military confrontation throughout the Cold War period. The collapse of the Cold War, diplomatic isolation, and shifting balances of power exacerbated North Korea's security conditions and served as catalysts for its decision to develop nuclear weapons. This chapter will trace the process of negotiations with the 1994 Geneva Agreement and the 2000 DPRK–US Joint Communiqué, both under the Bill Clinton administration, and the process of Six-Party Talks under the George Bush administration. It considers why those talks have failed. The chapter then analyzes the policy of "strategic patience," which represents the lack of actions under the Obama administration and explores whether there is any possibility of new diplomatic efforts to resolve this issue. It will also discuss the implication of North Korean nuclear developments on regional order and stability in Northeast Asia.

Chapter 9 examines North Korean human rights issues that began to receive more attention during the 1990s. With its inefficient economic system, natural disasters, and the international isolation and loss of trading partners after the collapse of the Cold War, North Korea has experienced a serious depression and food shortages. Many refugees escaped the country and spread information on human rights abuses within the secluded country. Under the Kim family's centralized political and economic system, North Korea has violated the basic rights of its own people, such as the right to food and freedom from hunger and the rights to freedom of thought, conscience, and religion. Many North Koreans suffer from arbitrary detention, torture, and executions in prison camps. South Koreans and the global public have discussed how to improve the human rights situation in North Korea. Conservatives, who believe that the collapse of the regime is imminent, blame the North Korean regime and want to implement more political pressure and economic sanctions. Liberals are more focused on humanitarian aid for the North Korean people and seeking diplomatic normalization through negotiation and economic reform. The chapter concludes by comparing and evaluating these different approaches regarding North Korean human rights issues.

Chapter 10 accounts for the evolution and fluctuations in the relationship between South and North Korea, while examining the roles of top leaders, domestic conditions, and international structures in shaping inter-Korean relations. Despite some occasional thaws, the two Koreas usually maintained an antagonistic relationship until South Korean President Kim Dae-jung was inaugurated in 1998. President Kim's Sunshine Policy and President Roh Moo-hyun's continuous engagement policy toward North Korea brought about a considerable relaxation of tensions. Between 1998 and 2007, both President Kim and President Roh held historic summits with North Korean leader, Kim Jong-il. In addition to increased governmental interactions, human exchanges skyrocketed primarily due to the opening of the Mt. Geumgang tourist resort and many events initiated by civil society organizations. With South Korea's generous humanitarian support, the two Koreas have also launched many joint economic projects. In particular, the development of the Kaesong industrial complex played a key role in defusing military tensions between the two Koreas, becoming a symbol of inter-Korean cooperation. However, since conservative forces in South Korea took power in 2008, inter-Korean relations have seriously deteriorated. This was due to the ROK governments' hardline policies as well as North Korea's provocative acts, including nuclear and missile tests, as well as artillery firings. The Conclusion offers succinct summaries and primary findings based on the substantive chapters, and it covers policy and theory implications regarding the future of the Korean Peninsula.

Note

1 This section is mainly derived from the Korean Ministry of Culture, Sports, and Tourism www.korea.net, Cumings (1997, 19–85), and Heo and Roehrig (2010, 4–27).

References

Cumings, Bruce. 1997. *Korea's Place in the Sun: A Modern History*. New York: W. W. Norton.

Heo, Uk, and Terence Roehrig. 2010. *South Korea Since 1980*. Cambridge: Cambridge University Press.

Johnson, Chalmers. 1982. *MITI and the Japanese Miracle: The Growth of Industrial Policy, 1925–1975*. Stanford, CA: Stanford University Press.

Kim, Woon-Tai. 2001. "Korean Politics: Setting and Political Culture." In *Understanding Korean Politics: An Introduction*, edited by Soong Hoom Kil and Chung-in Moon, 9–32. Albany: State University of New York Press.

Liberthal, Kenneth. 2004. *Governing China: From Revolution to Reform*. New York: W. W. Norton.

Lipset, Seymour Martin. 1959. "Some Social Requisites of Democracy: Economic Development and Political Legitimacy." *American Political Science Review* 53: 69–105.

Morgenthau, Hans J. 1948. *Politics Among Nations: The Struggle for Power and Peace*. New York: McGraw-Hill.

Mueller, John. 1970. "Presidential Popularity from Truman to Johnson." *American Political Science Review* 64 (1): 18–34.

Nau, Henry. 2015. *Perspectives on International Relations: Power, Institutions, and Ideas*. Washington, DC: CQ Press.

Waltz, Kenneth. 1979. *Theory of International Politics*. New York: Random House.

1 Legacies of Japanese colonial rule and the Korean War

Inyeop Lee

This first chapter discusses the history of the Japanese colonial period (1910–1945) and the Korean War (1950–1953) as a crucial foundation for understanding the political and economic development of the two Koreas. The chapter explains how the leaders of the Joseon Dynasty were divided and failed to achieve modernization until finally colonized by Japan, who already had successfully modernized and industrialized itself. During the 36 years of colonialism, Korea went through political oppression and exploitation of human and material resources. The future leaders of the two Koreas also rose in this period as part of the sharp division between leftists and rightists in their struggle against Japan. This chapter also explores how the arrival of the Cold War in the Korean Peninsula, the decisions by the two great powers, and the internal division among Korean leaders separated the country into the North and the South, finally igniting the Korean War. The Korean War was marked by massive numbers of casualties and destruction. It generated strong hatred between the two Koreas and left serious trauma among the public. The leaders of the two regimes consolidated their power in spite of their disastrous mistakes and failures.

The declining Joseon dynasty

The Joseon dynasty (1392–1910), the last dynasty of Korea, was firmly rooted in Confucianism. The virtues of Confucianism included harmony, order, and hierarchy in the domestic political and social systems. They were expressed within the traditional Sino-centric tributary system that dominated East Asia for centuries, and Korea positioned itself within the hierarchy (Oh 1999, 12–19). Japan, on the margin of this Sino-centric system, was more flexible and eager to Westernize. After Commodore Matthew Perry forced the Japanese to open to the West (1853), Japan embraced Western technology and began the Meiji Restoration (1868), when imperial rule was restored and modernization and industrialization began. Japanese rulers combined Western technology and industrialization with the ancient system of emperor worship, and this merger became the foundation of expansionist and imperialist policy in Asia. The Joseon dynasty, on the other hand, harshly resisted Western influence and refused to open its door to foreigners. Joseon leaders believed Korea to be the last orthodox Confucian state in Asia after the Manchurian Qing's conquest of the Han Chinese Ming dynasty (1644). It tried to defend its Confucian civilization from so-called Western barbarians, even after the Sino-centric system was crumbling down with the Opium War (1839–1842). In 1863, Regent Heungseon Daewongun came to power and ruled as the de facto regent when his twelve-year-old son was enthroned as King Gojong (later Emperor Gojong). Daewongun implemented an anti-Western, anti-foreign seclusion policy.

He persecuted Christians and defeated a French expedition in 1866, and he also resisted a US expedition in 1871. King Gojong, influenced by his wife, Queen Min (later given the title of Empress Myeongseong) and her family and relatives, tried to assume full political power from his father, and forced him into retirement in 1873. Japan became the most powerful country in Asia at this moment after modernizing and industrializing. The nation then began its intervention in the Korean Peninsula by negotiating a commercial treaty with Joseon (1876). Queen Min then pursued a pro-Qing and later a pro-Russian policy to protect the country from Japanese influence (Cumings 2005, 86–138).

With the rapid international changes and the arrival of the Western influence, various movements emerged within Korean society. The Imo Incident (1882) was an anti-Japanese outbreak against Queen Min in support of Daewongun by the 'old military,' who were resentful about preferential treatment given to newly trained Western-style troops in Joseon. It briefly restored Daewongun to power, but Qing forces quickly quelled it and regained control. The Gapsin Coup (1884) was a three-day coup by small number of elites in Korea backed by Japan. They tried to impose Western-style modernization, constitutional monarchy, and independence from Qing, but the coup was put down by Qing's intervention, and Japan withdrew from Korea. The Donghak Peasant Revolution (1894) was an anti-foreign grassroots uprising ignited by oppressive and exploitative government officials and growing foreign interventions by Japan and the Western countries. Frightened by the initial success of the revolution, the Joseon dynasty requested Qing's intervention, and Japan and Qing started the Sino-Japanese War (1894–95) in the Korean Peninsula. A Japanese victory in the war ended the Sino-centric tributary system and Qing's influence over the Peninsula, and Japan brutally assassinated Queen Min by a plot formed by the Japanese minister to Korea, Miura Goro (1895). Ironically, Japan made Korea declare itself as a 'Korean Empire' for the first time in history, at a time when its power was weakest and Korea almost lost its sovereignty to Japan. Japan simply wanted to end the Qing Empire's domination over the Peninsula by letting Korea declares itself an empire. When Japan defeated Russia, the final competitor for control of the Peninsula, in the Russo-Japanese War (1904–1905), there was no longer an obstacle for Japan's colonization of Korea. Japan forcibly made Korea its protectorate and deprived Korea of its diplomatic sovereignty by the Japan–Korea Treaty (Eulsa Treaty) in 1905. The Japan–Korea Annexation Treaty in 1910 made Korea a formal colony. Both treaties were made under threat of force, and the last Emperor, Sunjong (Gojong's son), refused to sign the document.[1]

Both domestic and international factors contributed to the colonization of Korea. It was a time of changing balance of power in East Asia, as Qing declined and Japan rose with the support of Western powers and its own rapid modernization. Being in the center of the East Asian region, where maritime powers and land powers clashed with each other, the Korean Peninsula became a target of great power rivalry for geopolitical advantage. The Japanese victory in the Sino-Japanese War ended the centuries-long Sino-centric system in East Asia and allowed Japan to also annex Taiwan (1895). In a 1902 alliance, Great Britain recognized Japan's interest in Korea in return for Japan's recognition of British interest in China. Great Britain also tried to check and balance Russia by supporting Japan in East Asia. Japan joined the great powers for the first time as the Asian country and surprisingly defeated Russia in the Russo-Japanese War. The United States also supported Japan with the 1905 Taft–Katsura Agreement, a secret diplomatic memorandum between US Secretary of War William Howard Taft and Prime Minister of Japan Katsura Taro. Under the agreement, the United States recognized Japan's sphere of influence in Korea in exchange for Japan's recognition of American influence in the Philippines. Japan's special interest in the Korean Peninsula was officially recognized in the Treaty of Portsmouth in 1905, which President Theodore Roosevelt brokered between Japan and Russia after the Russo-Japanese War (Oberdorfer 1997, 3–5). The Korean Peninsula soon became a battlefield for great power rivalries and the resulting turmoil and conflicts precipitated Joseon's decline.

The Joseon dynasty also lost its chance to modernize and save its sovereignty by its own domestic divisions and futile attempts to rely upon foreign allies. The Daewongun's seclusion policy delayed Joseon's Westernization, and he lost political power to his daughter-in-law Queen Min. He secretly conspired with the leader of the Donghak Peasant Revolution to return to power and even supported the Japanese assassination of Queen Min. Elitist Western-style reformers (the Gapsin Coup) and grassroots traditionalists (Donghak Peasant Revolution) in Joseon have never been united, and their separate attempts to save Korea ended up inviting more foreign intervention from Qing and Japan (Bae 2007, 217–91). After signing the first modern treaty with Japan in 1876, King Gojong and Queen Min tried to defend Korean sovereignty by making the "Treaty of Amity and Commerce" with the United States in 1882. They also asked for Qing's support after the Gapsin Coup and later begged for Qing's help to suppress the Donghak Peasant Revolution. They also made a treaty with czarist Russia to check Japan's growing influence over the Peninsula. Such diplomatic efforts, without domestic unity and strength, were not very successful. Rather than riding through the tide of great power rivalry unscathed, Korea was engulfed by it. A successful balance of power policy could be accomplished by the powerful, but not the weak.

Japanese colonialism (1910–1945)

The Japanese colonial period was extremely oppressive, exploitative, and militaristic. The Japanese Governor General ruled Korea with almost absolute power with the backing of the military police. Many Japanese citizens came to Korea, and Koreans were treated as second-class citizens and denied their basic rights. The Japanese colonial rule can be divided into three periods: the military rule (1910–1919), the cultural rule (1919–1931), and the militarist-fascist war period (1931–1945) (Oh 1999, 20).

Modernization and industrialization in Korea began under Japanese rule, and Koreans experienced an expansion of commerce and urbanization. These changes, however, did not benefit the Korean people but allowed for the Empire to dominate Koreans and exploit resources more efficiently, while empowering Japan to fight wars in China and the Pacific. Japan established a bureaucracy, police and legal systems, and an education system. It also built infrastructure, such as railroads, ports, and basic industries. Major industries were built in the Northern part of the Peninsula, which had abundant mineral resources and hydroelectric power. The south focused on the production of rice and other food. The infrastructure was essential in sending agricultural products from Korea to meet a growing need in Japan, in dispatching massive numbers of Japanese troops to invade China and in conscripting Koreans for forced labor. Japan encouraged the settlement of Japanese citizens in Korea through land reform. When Japanese authorities reestablished ownership by basis of written proof only, many Koreans with traditional ownership but no legal proof lost their land overnight. Japanese ownership of all arable land increased from 7 percent to 8 percent in 1910 to 52.7 percent in 1932. Japan forced many Korean tenants to pay over half their harvest as rent (Nozaki, Inokuchi and Kim 2006). In 1939, about 94 percent of total capital recorded by factories and about 92 percent of large-scale enterprises with more than 200 employees were Japanese owned (Suh 1978; Song 1997). Distorted and uneven development during the colonial period left a mixed legacy for the future development of the Peninsula. Korea became a part of the 'Great East Asian Co-prosperity Sphere' that was Japan's autarkical political-economic system in Asia built by colonizing and conquering. It included Korea, Manchuria, the northern part of Mainland China, Taiwan, and Southeast Asia. Resources were exploited and redistributed according to the central command of the Japanese Empire in order to perpetuate the Empire as a war machine, to defeat enemies, and to continue territorial expansion.

Japan stepped up its militarist-fascist rule in Korea by starting the Second Sino-Japanese War (1937–1945) and the Pacific War (1941–1945). The period was marked by atrocities, such as forced labor and sexual slavery by the Japanese military. Out of the 5,400,000 Korean workers conscripted, about 670,000 were taken to Japan between 1939 and 1945. They were forced to work under harsh and dangerous conditions, and about 60,000 out of 670,000 workers died. The total number of deaths in Korea and Manchuria was between 270,000 and 810,000. About 150,000 died among the 230,000 drafted into the Japanese military. Many Koreans were also forced into labor in Hiroshima and Nagasaki, and about 70,000 to 100,000 Koreans suffered from the atomic bombs dropped on both cities in 1945 (Hippin 2005; Choe 2016). About 50,000 to 200,000 women from Korea were forced into sexual slavery (the so-called comfort women for Japanese soldiers), and they comprised about 90 percent of all of the victims throughout Asia. They were forced to serve in Japanese military brothels, or 'comfort stations,' located in Japanese-occupied territories, and they experienced beatings and torture. Only a small number of women survived the diseases, mistreatment, and execution by the Japanese soldiers before their defeat, and most survivors experienced lasting trauma and sexually transmitted diseases (Cumings 2005, 178-80; de Brouwer 2005, 8).

Japan also tried to extinguish Korean cultural and historical identity through a cultural assimilation policy by the end of the 1930s. Japan prohibited the use of Korean language in public and did not allow the teaching of Korean history and literature. Japan also forced Koreans to surrender their Korean names and adopt Japanese names. Japan required mandatory participation of all Koreans in worship at Japanese Shinto shrines in order to weaken the nationalistic influences of both traditional religions and Christianity in Korea (Kang 1997, 62).

Korean independence movements during the colonial period

The Korean people resisted Japan's intervention and annexation of Korea by force and its oppressive and exploitative colonial rule. On October 26, 1909, a year before Korea's annexation by Japan, An Jung-geun, a Korean independence activist and a lieutenant general in the Korean resistance army, assassinated Ito Hirobumi, a four-time Prime Minister of Japan and former Resident-General of Korea. The March 1st Movement (Sam-il (3·1) Movement) in 1919 marked an early eruption of Korean resistance. It was influenced by President Woodrow Wilson's famous "Fourteen Points" speech outlining the right of national "self-determination" at the Paris Peace Conference in 1918 (Lee 1984, 340–4). Korean students in Tokyo published a statement demanding freedom from colonial rule. The sudden death of former Emperor Gojong on January 21, 1919, and his subsequent funeral, also catalyzed the movement. After Japan forcibly made Korea its protectorate under the Japan–Korea Treaty in 1905, Emperor Gojong secretly sent representatives to the Hague Peace Convention of 1907 to re-assert his sovereignty over Korea by appealing to international society and exposing Japan's illegal actions. The Japanese delegates and their allies blocked the Korean representatives, and Japan forced Gojong to abdicate to his son Sunjong. When Gojong died suddenly in the Deoksu Palace where the Japanese had confined him, many Koreans believed that the Japanese had poisoned him. On March 1, 1919, thirty-three national representatives who formed the core of the Movement read the Korean Declaration of Independence, signed the document, and sent a copy to the Governor General. They were the leaders representing religious groups such as Christian churches, Buddhists, and Cheondogyo. The remnants of the Donghak renamed themselves as Cheondogyo (Cheondoism), and they played a major role in the independence movement. Christian churches that had experienced population growth after the revival in Pyongyang in 1907 also played a crucial roles in organizing and participating in the movement. About two million Koreans had participated in peaceful demonstration before the Japanese authorities brutally suppressed the protests by opening fire on the unarmed protesters. There were 7,509 persons killed, 15,961 wounded, and 46,948 arrested (Lee 1984, 344).

As a consequence of the March 1st movement, the Korean Provisional Government in exile (KPG) formed in Shanghai on April 13, 1919. Japan thereafter tried to change some policies by replacing military rule with cultural rule. For example, its leaders replaced the military police with a civilian force and allowed limited press freedom between 1919 and 1931. Various independence movements based on different ideologies and foreign supporters developed inside and outside of the Peninsula. The brutal Japanese occupation of Korea made domestic resistance very difficult, and many independence activists left the Peninsula to travel to Manchuria and other parts of China and Russia/the Soviet Union. They formed poorly organized and equipped independence militias that engaged in guerrilla attacks on Japanese forces. They had some notable victories, such as at the Battle of Fengwudong (June 1920) and the Battle of Qingshanli (October 1920), but the Japanese invasion of Manchuria in 1931 and subsequent installation of Manchukuo (Japan's puppet state in Manchuria) deprived many of these groups their bases. Many had to flee to China and join the Provisional Government in Shanghai or the Chinese People's Liberation Army. Others joined the Red Army in the Soviet Union. Mu Chong, who led the Korean Volunteer Army, participated in the Long March with the Chinese Communists and operated in Yanan. Kim Tu-bong and Choe Chang-il also joined the Chinese Communists. Kim Il-sung, the future leader of North Korea, led one of the independent militias. Kim became a member of the Northeast Anti-Japanese United Army, a guerrilla group led by the Chinese Communist Party in 1935 that controlled a few hundred men. He executed a raid on Pochonbo, on 4 June 1937, and it made him famous because it was a rare case of a Korean independence militia attacking and capturing a town within Korea. The North Korean government later exaggerated this incident as a great military victory, but it was a poorly guarded small town, and his men only captured the city for a few hours before withdrawing. When pursued by Japanese forces, Kim and his men escaped to Khabarovsk, Soviet Union in 1940, and he was retrained and commissioned as an officer. Kim became a Major in the Soviet Red Army and served until he came back to Korea at the end of World War II in 1945. His time of guerrilla warfare against Japan became essential in building his political authority and ideology in North Korea (French 2007, 50–1).

With limited resources and under threat by Japan, Kim Koo in the Provisional Government organized the Korean Patriotic Corps in 1931 and encouraged its members to attack Japanese leaders. For example, Lee Bong-chang attempted to assassinate Japanese Emperor Hirohito by throwing a grenade in Tokyo on January 8, 1932, but he failed. At a celebration for the birthday of Emperor Hirohito on April 29 that same year, Yun Bong-gil threw a bomb in Shanghai and instantly killed Gen. Yoshinori Shirakawa and the government minister for Japanese residents in Shanghai, Kawabata Sadaji. The explosion also seriously injured several military leaders and governmental officials.[2] Chiang Kai-shek was impressed by these efforts and began to support the Provisional Government and Korea's independence at the Cairo Conference in 1943. When the second Sino-Japanese war broke out in 1937, the Provisional

Government escaped to Chongqing, where Chiang Kai-shek's Nationalist Government was established. Kim Koo established the Korean Liberation Army and trained between 300 and 3,000 soldiers in cooperation with the American Office of Strategic Services (OSS). When the Pacific War started on December 8, 1941, the Provisional Government declared war on Japan and Germany and planned to advance to Korea in cooperation with the OSS in 1945, but Japan surrendered days before the departure of the leading unit. Many Korean historians consider the Provisional Government as the de jure Korean government from 1919. The preamble of South Korea's 1948 constitution declares that "the Republic of Korea succeeded the legitimacy of the Provisional Government in Shanghai, which was established after the March 1 Movement" (Djun Kil Kim 2014, 153).

The future leaders of the two Koreas emerged with different political ideologies and foreign supporters. They already had experienced factional division and ideological conflict during the independence movement and the power struggle after liberation from Japan intensified such division. Kim Koo, a rightist nationalist, and Kim Kyu-sik, a moderate rightist nationalist represented the Provisional government in exile in China. The government was influenced by Sun Yat-sen's republicanism and supported by Chiang Kai-shek's National Government of the Republic of China. Rhee Syngman, who later became the first president of South Korea, was appointed acting president for the Provisional Government in Shanghai, but he was impeached for misuse of power and exiled to the United States for over thirty years during the colonial period. He focused on diplomatic efforts to gain independence and recognition of the Provisional Government from the United States and other countries. Rhee was educated in the United States and was influenced by the American democratic and capitalist systems. Nationalists and moderates, including many of the Christians in Korea, fit into the rightist category. Leftists were influenced by socialism and communism and supported by Chinese and Soviet communists. Many of the leftists had been disillusioned when the March 1st movement, inspired by Wilson's self-determination, was brutally crushed by Japan, and none of Western powers paid serious attention to colonized Korea. In fact, the United States maintained cooperative relations with Japan by endorsing its control of Korea by the Katsura–Taft Agreement in 1905 and recognition of Japan's special interest in Manchuria in 1915. Good relations lasted until the tension grew after Japan's renewed aggression against China in 1937. Many of the leftists, including the future leader of North Korea, Kim Il-sung, operated in Manchuria and the Soviet Union, and they engaged in guerilla warfare against the Japanese military. Within Korea, Pak Hon-yong tried to organize the Joseon Communist Party (the Korean Communist Party) during the colonial period, and he later set up the Joseon Communist Party organization in the South. Yo Un-hyung was a nationalist and moderate socialist who pursued independence for Korea and tried to instigate Left–Right cooperation after liberation.

Liberation and division of the Peninsula (1945–1950)

Japan surrendered to the Allied forces on August 15, 1945, after the United States dropped atomic bombs on Hiroshima (August 6) and Nagasaki (August 9). The Soviet declaration of war against Japan on August 8 and the invasion of Manchuria on August 9 also impacted the surrender (Lekic 2010; Wilson 2013). The Soviet Army defeated Japan's Kwantung Army in Manchuria and proceeded into Manchuria, Northern Korea, and Sakhalin. The United States and the USSR entered the Korean Peninsula to expedite the surrender and disarmament of the Japanese Army. The United States did not have a well-established blueprint for the future of Korea. Lieutenant Colonel Dean Rusk, who later became Secretary of State under

President John Kennedy and President Lyndon Johnson, and Colonel Charles Bonesteel, with limited knowledge about Korea, proposed the 38th parallel as the demarcation line at a meeting on August 10–11, 1945. The USSR accepted the proposal. Rusk later explained that they "felt it important to include the capital of Korea in the area of responsibility of American troops," even though it was difficult to reach very far north before Soviet troops had entered the area (Goulden 1983, 17; Oberdorfer 1997, 6–7). At least the United States was aware of the geopolitical advantage and was afraid of the USSR stretching too far in Asia and controlling the entire peninsula. This decision to draw an arbitrary line on the map without any relation to geographical, cultural, and historical factors led to the contemporary division of the Peninsula after the establishment of separate regimes and the ensuing Korean War.

In China, the Korean Provisional Government in exile (KPG) had long been fighting for the independence of the country. It had maintained close cooperation with the Republic of China under Chiang Kai-shek and also with the OSS. Chiang proposed to recognize the KPG in April 1942, but American officials ignored him (Seth 2016, 325). Although the United States, China, and Great Britain declared that "in due course, Korea shall become free and independent" at the Cairo Conference in 1943, President Franklin Roosevelt proposed a US–Soviet–Chinese trusteeship over Korea at the 1945 Yalta Conference. Concurrently, Yo Un-hyung, an independence activist in Korea, organized the 'Committee for the Preparation of Korean Independence (CPKI)' for transition to independence. The Korean people, celebrating their liberation and expecting imminent independence, responded by setting up People's Committees in all thirteen provinces throughout the country within two or three weeks after liberation. The delegates from the People's Committees declared the Korean People's Republic (KPR) in Seoul on September 6. Washington refused to recognize KPG, CPKI, or KPR and started direct rule by US Army Military Government in Korea (USAMGIK) below the 38th parallel (1945–1948) when Gen. John R. Hodge arrived on the southern part of the Korean Peninsula on September 8th, 1945.[3]

Once again, Korea's fate was determined by a great power rivalry, now in the name of the Cold War struggle. The long-awaited liberation from Japan led to a period of political instability and confusion in Korea. Cold War tensions had already started before the defeat of Nazi Germany and Imperial Japan. Alperovitz (1995, 281–2) argues that the US decision makers saw the dropping of the atomic bombs as an important tool for intimidating the Soviets after the war. Former US Ambassador to Moscow Joseph Davies wrote in his diary on July 28, 1945, that James F. Byrnes, Secretary of State and Truman's closest foreign policy advisor, believed that the atomic bomb assured ultimate success in negotiation with the Soviet Union.[4] George Kennan also argued in his famous "Long Telegram" from Moscow in 1946 and subsequent 1947 article, "The Sources of Soviet Conduct," that the Soviet regime was inherently expansionist and that its influence had to be "contained" in areas of vital strategic importance to the United States. He inspired the Truman Doctrine (1947) and the containment policy expressed in NSC-68 (1949) (Nitze and Drew 1994, 17–19). The Berlin Blockade and Airlift (1948–1949) was the first major crisis of the Cold War. North Atlantic Treaty Organization (NATO) was created in April 1949 as the US-led military alliance against the Communist bloc. Chiang Kai-shek's nationalist forces were already losing ground to the Communists in 1947 before the Communists won the Chinese Civil War (1946–1949) and formed an alliance with the USSR. Against this backdrop, the United States adopted the 'Reverse Course' in Japan from 1947, which was a major shift in policy from disabling Japan's wartime economy to restoring Japan as an American bulwark against the communist surge. Under this policy, the United States de-purged wartime leaders and allowed them to return to prominent positions within politics and the economy, and these officials then conducted a 'Red Purge' by ousting Communist Party members from political and economic power. Many prewar leaders came back as members of the Liberal Democratic Party that dominated Japan throughout the Cold War period, including Kishi Nobusuke, a former class A criminal suspect who later became prime minister. For similar reasons, the United States also tried to establish a pro-American regime in Korea and took advantage of former collaborators under Japanese colonial rule to fight the leftists.

The United States and the Soviet Union, with the rising tension of the Cold War, tried to establish separate governments on their sides of the Korean Peninsula. There was no serious geographic separation according to political ideology until the imposition of 38th parallel. In other words, communists and capitalists, and leftists and rightists, were not geographically separated in the Peninsula. The North had a number of rightists and Christians, and the South had large numbers of socialists and communists. For example, Pyongyang was once known as 'Jerusalem of the East,' with 25 percent to 30 percent of its adult population being Protestant Christians by the early 1940s (Lankov 2005). On the other hand, the survey conducted in the South by USAMGIK on August 13th, 1946, shows that a large number of South Koreans had positive views of socialism. On being asked their preferred political ideology, 14 percent supported capitalism, while 70 percent chose socialism, and 7 percent supported communism (Donga Daily 1946). Therefore, the three-year period of military rule (1945–1948) on the two sides of the 38th parallel by the United States and the USSR was the process of artificial ideological purification according to the ideology coupled with political persecution. The ideological differences and political competition among the independence movements during the colonial period continued after the liberation, but the communists, headed by Kim Il-sung and backed by the USSR prevailed in the North, and the capitalists and pro-American leaders represented by Rhee Syngman, took over the South. Such process was marked by political violence and bloodshed on both sides and also involved massive movements of political refugees. Socialists and communists who were persecuted in the South went North, and rightists, capitalists, landlords, and Christians came into the South. Such artificial and painful processes of division left excessive hatred and desire to unify the peninsula according to the political ideologies of both sides. When the communists in the North successfully consolidated their power, massive numbers of rightists, landowners, elitists, and Christians lost their status, land, and family members, and they fled to the South. Many of them became strong anti-communists, pro-American, and pro-capitalists in the South. Some of them joined paramilitary organizations, such as *Seobuk* (Northwest) Youth League, which participated in brutal crackdowns of South Koreans labeled as leftists. Many socialists and communists from the South were heavily persecuted by the USAMGIK and Rhee Syngman administration, and they therefore crossed the 38th parallel into North Korea. Pak Hon-yong, the leader of the Workers' Party of South Korea, escaped to North Korea in April 1948 when the USAMGIK put him on a wanted list. His party was merged with the Workers' Party of North Korea under Kim Il-sung to form the Workers' Party of Korea. Pak Hon-yong, played a key role in convincing Kim Il-sung to start the Korean War to invade and 'liberate' the South to regain his political base in the South.

In the North, the Soviet Union established a communist regime headed by Kim Il-sung. At the beginning of the Soviet occupation in the North, looting, theft, and rape were widespread, especially in the first week, when many Soviet soldiers were former prisoners conscripted from the Soviet prison and ill-disciplined. Soviet leaders took measures to improve discipline of the soldiers by late September 1945 (Cumings 1981, 399; Lankov 2002, 6). The Soviets pretended to work with various parties, including well-respected Christian leader Cho Mansik, who led the CPKI local committee in Pyongyang and later the Korean Democratic Party, and Cheondogyo members who organized a Friends Party. But the real power fell into the hands of the communists. Kim Il-sung, who was in the Soviet Union from 1940 to 1945, arrived at Wonsan on September 19th, and the Soviets appointed him as the Communist leader in North Korea. The Soviets carried out several reforms, including the nationalization of Japanese industry, a redistribution of land from landlords to individual farmers, and the mobilization of women, peasants, workers, and other less privileged groups for more economic equality. In this process, existing elites, landowners, Christians, and rightists became more frustrated with Soviet policies and the communist takeover of the North. For example, the Sinuiju Incident of 1945 occurred among students and Christian leaders in Sinuiju in North Pyongan Province on November 23rd, 1945. The protest began as a resistance to the violence committed by the initial Soviet occupation forces, the Soviet Army's food procurement, and the communists' domination of the People's Committees. About 5,000 students demonstrated, and the Soviet and North Korean communist forces opened fired and killed 23 and arrested 1,000 (Cathcart and Kraus 2008, 1–28). Cho Man-sik continued to criticize Soviet soldiers' misbehaviors, the Soviet role in the Sinuiju incident, and Soviet trusteeship over the North. Finally, the Soviets and Kim Il-sung put Cho under house arrest in March 1946, which terminated his political influence in the North.

The South had even harsher ideological confrontations and political confusion in its transition period. Notable leaders in the South included pro-American rightist Rhee Syngman, nationalist rightist Kim Koo, moderate rightist Kim Kyu-sik, moderate leftist Yo Un-hyung, communist Pak Hon-yong, and Kim Songsu and Song Chin-u of the Korea Democratic Party that represented landowners and conservatives. Gen. John R. Hodge distrusted the KPR and declared that it had no authority. After conservatives and moderates left the KPR, Gen. Hodge outlawed it. The USAMGIK persecuted leftists and banned labor unions, causing leftists to start strikes and attempt to disrupt American military rule. Gen. Hodge also endorsed Rhee Syngman because of his English language skills and education in the United States. The USAMGIK established an Interim Legislative Assembly and created the Korean National Police and the South Korean Army, mostly with soldiers who had served in the Japanese military and bureaucracies as collaborators.[5] The United States was more concerned about leftists rather than former collaborators, and they wanted to take advantage of collaborators' skills and experiences to rule the South. Rhee Syngman, who did not have a strong domestic political base, built a coalition with these collaborators in the bureaucracy, police, and military. The Allied Powers discussed a trusteeship over Korea for five years at the Moscow Conference on December 27, 1945, and the idea started fierce debates and political confrontations between left and right in Korea. When Rhee discussed the possibility of establishing a separate government in the South on June 3, 1946, other nationalists feared permanent division of the country, and they started a Left–Right coalition movement represented by moderate leftist Yo Un-hyung and moderate rightist Kim Kyu-sik in July 1946. Concerned about Rhee's extremely authoritarian and anti-leftist attitudes, the USAMGIK temporality supported this Left–Right coalition movement, but it lost momentum when Yo Un-hyung was assassinated on July 1947 and the movement faced criticism from both far leftists such as Pak Hon-yong, and rightists such as Rhee Syngman and Kim Koo.

When the American–Soviet Joint Committee failed to reach any agreement until August 1947, the United States turned the issue over to the UN in September. The UN Temporary Committee on Korea (UNTCOK) was created to hold national elections for a unified National Assembly, but the Soviet Union and the North refused to recognize the UNTCOK. Kim Koo, a former independence leader and nationalist, fiercely opposed the establishment of separate governments in the North and the South. Kim Koo and Kim Kyu-sik decided to visit North Korea on April 19, 1948, with the last hope of building a unified country, but Kim Il-Sung utilized their visit to legitimize his authority in the North. Kim Koo came back to the South without any success, and he was assassinated on June 26, 1949, after both sides had established separate regimes. The UNTCOK finally decided to hold elections in "accessible" areas in the South, and South Koreans elected a National Assembly on May 10, 1948. The new assembly members elected Rhee as the first president and established the Republic of Korea (ROK) on August 15, 1948. North Korea also had elections and proclaimed the Democratic People's Republic of Korea (DPRK) on September 9, 1948.

The poor economic conditions continued in the South, since most of the industries were in the North, and North Korea cut off the electric power supply after the division. Rhee Syngman was generally indifferent to economic development, and his administration barely made economic progress. Rhee's government had to rely upon US aid, which became more than one-third of the governmental budget (Oh 1999, 31–17). Rhee, who had a weak domestic political base, maintained very authoritarian leadership and relied upon the bureaucracy, the police, and the military filled with the former collaborators to Japanese colonialism. The collaborators, who were criticized after the liberation, soon formed a strong political alliance with Rhee and the United States. Thus, the former 'Pro-Japanese' became 'Pro-American and anti-communist' for their political survival, and they soon dominated power in the South. The National Assembly passed the 'Special Act on the Punishment of Collaborationist Activities against the Nation' on September 7, 1948 and established the 'Special Committee for the Investigation of Collaborationist Activities against the Nation' during the colonial period. There were at least 7,000 suspects and 682 investigations, but the Committee tried only 38 cases, and individuals in only 12 cases were found guilty and punished. When his political base was threatened by such investigations, Rhee began to sabotage the Special Committee by arresting assemblymen involved with the Committee and ordering a police raid on the Special Committee building. Rhee then dissolved the Committee and revoked the law. In comparison, after French collaborators had ruled for five years in Vichy France, the postwar French government investigated 990,000 collaborators, 10,000 were executed or sentenced to life in prison, and thousands were killed by the French Resistance without a trial. The South Korean government, on the other hand, punished or purged almost no former Japanese collaborators after 36 years of brutal colonial rule; most of them kept their political and economic power in South Korean society. Many South Koreans were disappointed with the bureaucracy, the police, and the military staffed with former collaborators instead of independence activists. Well-known former collaborators who became notable leaders of South Korea included Park Jung-hee, who became president of South Korea, Chung Il-kwon, the prime minister from 1964 to 1970, and Paik Sun-yup, who served in the Korean War as South Korea's youngest general. Most South Korean military leaders, including these three, were trained and served in the Japanese Imperial military. It was also impossible to discuss the issue of collaborators, when Park Jung-hee himself came to power in a coup in 1961 and stayed in power for 18 years.

Rhee took advantage of various paramilitary organizations such as the *Seobuk* (Northwest) Youth League, whose members tried to take revenge themselves upon any suspected leftists. They perpetrated extreme human right abuses and mass killings in incidents such as the April 3rd Jeju uprising and Yosu-Sunchon incident on October 19, 1948. Those incidents emerged as domestic resistance to the purging of the leftists by the US military and to the UN's decision to hold separate elections in the South. On March 1, 1947, Jeju citizens protested against the election for establishing a divided government in the South. Police opened fire, killing six and injuring eight civilians. In response, 41,211 Jeju people joined the strike, and more police and *Seobuk* Youth group members came to Jeju. They indiscriminately arrested, tortured, and killed the strikers. Left wing groups retaliated against the brutality, leading to a massive military crackdown that killed about 60,000 people, or about one-fifth of the island's population (Merrill 1980; Hum Joon Kim 2014). The Yosu-Sunchon incident on October 19, 1948, occurred when some soldiers in Yosu who awaited their dispatch to Jeju refused to help suppress the uprising. The rebelling soldiers seized weapons, took control of Yosu, and killed some police and officials. After one week, the South Korean army subjugated the rebels, killing them and other civilians suspected of involvement. The South Korean Truth and Reconciliation Commission later claimed that the South Korean government killed about 439 to 2,000 civilians (*The Hankyoreh* 2009). In both incidents, American military forces played a role in suppressing the uprising directly and indirectly. After these massive crackdowns and killings, many Communist leaders either fled to the North or were imprisoned. By the spring of 1950, about 60,000 were in prison for violating the National Security Act (Seth 2016, 340).

The Korean War (1950–1953)

Both Kim Il-sung and Rhee Syngman believed that the territorial division would never be permanent, even after their separate regimes were established. Both leaders claimed that they could easily defeat their enemies and achieve unification by force. The big difference was that Kim Il-sung in the North actually prepared for full-scale warfare, while Rhee Syngman only made political rhetoric without actual military capability and preparedness. North Korea, between 1948 and 1950, built a more stable society under the hegemony of the Korean Workers' Party with about 700,000 members. Kim Il-sung and other communist leaders, mostly former guerilla fighters against Japan, had fewer legitimacy problems like those pertaining to the issue of Japanese collaborators in the South. Sweeping land reforms satisfied tenant farmers and small landowners, while many rich landowners and non-communist leaders were heavily persecuted or fled to the South. The North also carried out economic development based on its Japanese-built infrastructure and abundant mineral resources. Kim Il-sung had many military leaders with skills and combat experiences. Most of them were either trained in the Soviet Union or fought alongside the Chinese Communists during the colonial period (Seth 2016, 340–1). Both the United States and the Soviet militaries withdrew from Korea in late 1948 and 1949, but the Soviets provided a more extensive military buildup in the North with more than 3,000 military advisors, T-34 tanks, and artillery. On the other hand, the American approach toward South Korea before the Korean War was ambiguous. Even though the United States was committed to establish a pro-American, anti-communist government in the South, it did not make a substantial investment in South Korea's military or economy. The United States was concerned that Rhee might invade the North to unify the country. Therefore, President Harry Truman provided limited military funding and equipment before withdrawing and leaving behind only a 500-member Korean Military Advisory Group (KMAG). Secretary of State Dean Acheson excluded South Korea from the US defensive perimeter in his speech in January 1950, when he just mentioned the Philippines and Japan.

Many scholars have debated the origins and causes of the Korean War. The traditionalist view of the Korean War was that Kim Il-sung invaded South Korea with support from Joseph Stalin and Mao Zedong as part of the Cold War communist expansion in East Asia. It was, therefore, an international war between the communist and capitalist blocs rather than a civil war confined to the Korean Peninsula. The traditionalists focused on the immediate war decision by the communist elites and the 'outbreak' of the war. For example, William Stueck

(2002, 65) claims that "the Korean War was not in essence a civil war, that its course cannot begin to be understood without devoting considerable attention to foreign involvement." He argued that Kim would never have fired first without the approval from Stalin and Mao.

On the other hand, the revisionists focus more on the long-term socio-economic and political 'origins' of the war rather than on its immediate outbreak (Cumings 1981). The revisionists are influenced by Marxist orientations that stress class struggle based on socio-economic conditions, and their views also emerged during the anti-Vietnam War movement. The declassified documents in the United States related to the Korean War were the main source of their research. They claim that the Korean War was a civil war. It did not simply begin due to Kim Il-sung's decision to invade, but it grew out of complex historical contexts. Cumings (1981, xx) argues "the Origin of the Korean War must be sought primarily in the events of the period 1945 and 1950 and secondarily in forces descending upon Korea in the period of colonial rule that left their peculiar stamp on the interwar years in Korea." Serious social unrest and resentment came from Japanese colonial rule and exploitation, and social revolution was ripe in Korea already in 1945. Therefore, the war was a continuation of the conflict that began in 1945, which was civil and revolutionary in character, and the Korean War was an "explosion of political participation focusing on a land situation inherited from Japanese rule in which most peasants were enmeshed in a system of tenancy dominated by landlords" (Cumings 1981, xxi).

The Soviet Union and the United States made a decision to divide the Peninsula and establish pro-American and pro-Soviet regimes against Korean people's aspirations for an independent and unified nation. Cumings argues that many Koreans supported socialism or leftist ideology, but the United States oppressed them and artificially established a right-wing government in the South. Cumings (1981, 267) explained,

> the Americans could not withdraw their troops so easily, because they were worried about the viability of the southern regime, its dictatorial tendencies and its oft-stated bluster about marching north. . . . but much more important was Korea's growing importance to American global policy – containing communism and reviving the Japanese industrial economy as a motor of the world economy.

He claims that the reforms in North Korea were more successful, and they provided the North with political legitimacy over the South. The North Korean government cleansed former Japanese collaborators more thoroughly, performed land reform, and enhanced labor conditions and women's rights.

On the other hand, the Rhee Syngman government in the South, backed by the United States, lacked public support and strong administrative capability. So, the Rhee government and US military government tried to use Japanese collaborators to strengthen their control and administration over the country, as Washington decided to revive Japanese heavy industries and end the purges of wartime leaders in Japan by the 'Reverse Course.' Most Koreans were disappointed with this policy. Thus, he emphasizes his long-term analysis of the origins of the war by saying, "There is an unbroken chain of critical events linking August 1945 with June 1950" (Cumings 1981, xxii). He also claims that Kim Il-sung did not have a well-established war plan to invade the South and unify the peninsula. The war developed from small-scale battles, such as the fighting in June 1949 in the Ongjin Peninsula, into a full-scale war. Kim wanted only to attack the Ongjin, move eastward, grab Kaesong, and then see what the South did (Cumings 1981, 267). Starting in the summer of 1948, there were many military clashes along the 38th parallel. The two Koreas had 527 small-scale clashes at

Kaesong and Ongjin in August 1949. South Korean military field commanders started many of them, and Rhee did not choose to control them. In the same year, the North sent about 2,000 guerilla fighters into the South. Both Kim and Rhee wanted to acquire more territory and invade each other.

This context was also complicated by ambiguous US actions in the Korean Peninsula. The US military withdrew from the peninsula, and Secretary of State Dean Acheson excluded South Korea from the American "defensive perimeter" while he mentioned Japan and the Philippines in his speech in January 1950. Intelligence on North Korea's invasion was ignored within the US military chain of command, any alerts were called off before the war began, and military commanders were shuffled. Kim Il-sung could have perceived these signals as a 'green light' to invade the South. Cumings also argued that Korea could have been unified by the North, if the United States had not intervened, and the unified Korea could have developed into a more moderate socialist country before reforming its economy as China or Vietnam has done. Kang Chong-gu (1996) has made similar arguments. He points out that 70 percent of Koreans supported socialism when it was a counterforce against imperialism and fascism at that time, and most of the Korean people understood socialism only through its idealistic nature. Casualties of war could have been limited to 10,000 instead of 4 million if the United States had not intervened. The Korean War was a war for unification similar to that waged by the Silla dynasty (57 BC–935 AD) that tried to unify the three kingdoms of the Korean Peninsula.

The revisionist arguments have some clear limitations. Cumings' research was based on US documents and some North Korean documents captured by the US Army during the war. He did not have access to Soviet and Chinese archival sources at that time. Scholars began to rewrite the history of the war with the post-Cold War opening of important archives in the former Soviet Union and China (Cumings and Weathersby 1995/1996; Weathersby 1995/1996; Zubok and Pleshakov 1997; Weathersby 2002). For example, Zubok and Pleshakov (1997, 275) show that Kim Il-sung played a key role in preparing for the full-scale war and in persistently persuading Stalin and Mao to approve the war. Stalin was afraid that US intervention might trigger World War III, and he did not want Soviet personnel in the front lines. He wanted to make sure that the United States would not intervene in the peninsula, or at least that the North could unify the peninsula before US intervention. Stalin rejected Kim's request 48 times before he finally approved of the war by sending a telegram to the Soviet ambassador in Pyongyang on January 30, 1950. Stalin became more confident after the USSR had detonated its first nuclear bomb in September 1949, and American troops withdrew from the South. In early April 1950, Stalin also made it clear that Soviet forces would not officially join the war so as not to engage with the American military. He told Kim that North Korea could "get down to action" only after his plans were cleared "with Comrade Mao Zedong personally." (Weathersby 2002, 10). So the war was planned and conducted with collaboration among communist leaders even though Stalin was much more cautious than suspected by most of the scholars during the Cold War. Mao was considerably less worried about the possibility of military conflict with the United States than was Stalin, and it was actually China rather than the USSR that intervened when UN forces crossed the 38th parallel.

In a similar vein, Park Myung-lim (1996) argues that a revolution could have developed in a gradual and unintended way, but a full-scale offensive war, such as the Korean War, was initiated by a clear elite decision. Therefore, Kim Il-sung is more responsible than any other leader for the outbreak of the war. Even though the necessary conditions for the outbreak of the war existed, there must be some war decision as a sufficient condition. Park also disputed

Cumings' argument on legitimacy by pointing out that South Korea had also completed land reform before the Korean War. He also claims that the point of Acheson's statement was not to give up Korea but empathizing US commitment to Japan. Rhee did not have any problem with Acheson's statement and even sent him a letter appreciating his commitment toward the defense of Asia. Therefore, the findings from the Soviet archive in terms of Kim Il-sung's active role in the war decision and the collaboration of communist leaders seriously undermined revisionist claims.

The revisionist arguments, however, still have some implications. Their research over the colonial period and US occupation was important to understand the situation on the Korean Peninsula. Their findings provide criticism and reflection on US Cold War foreign policy. Many US decisions, such as the division of Korea, taking advantage of former Japanese collaborators, the Acheson statement, and the withdrawal of US troops, indirectly contributed to the disaster on the peninsula. Some US documents on the Korean War are still classified, and they might shed a new light on the causes of the war. It is also important to note the role of Pak Hon-yong in terms of the effects of division on the outbreak of the War. The Soviet archives show that Pak played a key role in the decision for war. After he and other leftists were persecuted in the South and crossed the 38th parallel to the North, Pak became Deputy Prime Minister and Foreign Minister of North Korea in September 1948 and Secretary of the Korean Workers' Party when the Northern and Southern parties united in April 1950. Pak was the vice chairman of the Politburo of the DPRK from 1949 to 1953. He co-signed Kim Il-sung's letters to Stalin that asked for approval to start a war. Pak joined Kim in visiting Moscow to meet Stalin and discuss the war plan in April 1950. In his conversation with Kim and Stalin, Pak asserted that 200,000 members of South Korean Workers' Party would rise up and support the Korean People's Army when it marched into the South. Kim later blamed Pak when he did not find such a massive number of supporters in the South. Kim arrested Pak in August 1953 after accusing him of being an American spy and executed him later. Kim purged Pak and his South Korean Workers' Party faction to consolidate his own political power and scapegoat Pak for his own disastrous mistakes in war planning.

On June 25, 1950, North Korean forces invaded the South. The North experienced a quick and easy victory in the initial stages of the war. The South Korean military lacked tanks, anti-tank weapons, and heavy artillery. It was no match to the North Korean Army, who had trained and prepared for war with weapons provided by the USSR. Rhee Syngman, who repeatedly said he could conquer the North and unify the country, escaped Seoul on June 27th. He broadcasted via radio from Daejeon as if he was still in Seoul, stating that the South Korean military was defeating the invaders and asking citizens to stay calm in Seoul. The South Korean military detonated the bridge in the Han River on June 28th to stop the North Korean military from crossing the river and marching further down into the South. About 4,000 refugees were crossing the river at that time, and the explosion killed hundreds. The citizens and military units who could not cross the river were trapped in the city. Rhee also ordered the massacre of suspected political opponents or anybody suspected as a leftist out of fears of them joining North Korean forces. South Korean police, military and paramilitary organizations executed about 100,000 to 200,000 South Korean civilians without a trial in summer 1950. Most of them were members of the *Bodo* (National Guidance) League, who had converted from leftist ideology and pledged loyalty to the South Korean government (Tirman 2011, 97).

The United States won the vote in the UN Security Council on June 27th, 1950, to intervene on the peninsula to save South Korea. The Soviet Union could not exercise its veto since it was boycotting the UN Security Council in protest over the occupation of the seat of China by the Republic of China (Taiwan). Twenty-one countries of the UN made contributions to the UN intervention to Korea, and the United States and 15 other members committed their armed forces. The United States provided 88 percent of the UN's military personnel. When the North Korean army occupied most of South Korea except for the Pusan Perimeter, UN forces led by Gen. Douglas MacArthur launched an amphibious landing in Inchon, a port city near Seoul, on September 10, 1950. The successful landing cut off North Korean troops who became either enveloped between Inchon and Pusan or disintegrated and withdrew north, and American bombing destroyed most of North Korean tanks and artillery. South Korean forces recaptured Seoul on September 25, 1950. After Seoul and other territories were recaptured, the South Korean police executed people who were suspected to be sympathetic or cooperative during North Korea's occupation, even though many of them were trapped in their cities and forced to cooperate under North Korean occupation against their will.

The original UN mandate was to recover South Korean territory. Gen. MacArthur and President Truman, though, decided to proceed into the North once UN forces reached the 38th parallel in September. Rhee Syngman also strongly supported this decision, insisting upon taking advantage of the momentum to unify the country. China warned the United States that it would intervene if the UN forces crossed the 38th parallel, but Gen. MacArthur ignored the statements and requested unconditional surrender from the North Korean Army. Kim Il-sung made a frantic request for intervention to his allies. Stalin made it clear that Soviet forces would not intervene, but Mao strongly supported intervention and appointed Peng Dehuai as the commander of the Chinese forces in Korea. Chinese forces crossed the Yalu River and entered the war in October 1950. The UN forces advanced the furthest in November, but they soon had to retreat due to massive Chinese human wave attacks in the middle of an extremely cold winter. In January 1951, the UN forces withdrew from Seoul but recaptured it in March. The last two years of fighting, between July 1951 and July 1953, became a war of attrition with the front line close to the 38th parallel. The two years of stalemate made Gen. MacArthur's decision to invade the North controversial. MacArthur even considered using atomic bombs several times when he could not defeat the Chinese forces. The United States held military exercises to simulate dropping the atomic bomb in Pyongyang in 1951 (Cumings 2004, 21–2). His plan was never implemented since Truman, who worried about the war's expansion into a world war, discharged him on April 11, 1951. The nuclear card was still a viable option, and President Dwight Eisenhower and Secretary of State John Foster Dulles later argued that the threat of nuclear weapons pressured China and North Korea to sign the armistice treaty. With the war prolonged without visible achievements, American public support and Truman's approval rate plummeted, and he decided not to run for reelection. Eisenhower, the Republican candidate, promised to end the war if he won the 1952 election. Internationally, the Cold War system had become more stable, and the United States could not afford to start another world war. The United States, Chinese, and North Korean representatives signed the Armistice Agreement on July 27, 1953. Rhee Syngman opposed peace talks and the armistice treaty and insisted on continuing the war to unify the peninsula. The United Nations Command did not support his position and signed the treaty without Rhee. The Armistice treaty was designed to "insure a complete cessation of hostilities and of all acts of armed force in Korea until a final peaceful settlement is achieved," but it has never been replaced with a peace treaty after 60 years.[6] The belligerents established the Korean Demilitarized Zone (DMZ), which has since been fortified and heavily guarded.

Conclusion: legacy of the Korean War

The Korean War is marked by a massive number of casualties and destruction. It generated strong hatred between the two Koreas and left serious trauma among the public. The leaders of the two regimes consolidated their power in spite of their disastrous mistakes and failures. Three years and one month of war generated a total 3 million casualties, 80 percent of which were civilians. About 200,000 women became widows, 100,000 children lost their parents, and 10,000,000 families were separated between the North and South. Throughout the War, North Korea experienced a massive bombing campaign by the US Air Force, and it accounted for 1,316,579 casualties in the North, which is about two or three times higher compared to the South (595,000). Due to the same reason, China lost between 600,000 and 900,000 soldiers, while 33,000 and 54,000 American soldiers were killed. The number of bombs dropped on North Korea was more than the amount used in the entire Pacific War. They destroyed 80 percent of the infrastructure and 50 percent of the cities in the North. Pyongyang, the capital, was wiped off of the map by 428,000 bombs. Napalm bombing on villages became notorious during the Vietnam War, but it started in Korea by the United States dropping more napalm in three years than the amount used during the entire Vietnam War. The memory of the destruction and killing generated strong anti-American sentiments in the North. Kim Il-sung took advantage of such memories and trauma to consolidate his political power. Kim, who was responsible for the failed war decision and strategies more than anybody, successfully scapegoated and purged most of his political competitors during and after the War. For example, he fired and purged famous military leader Mu Chong for military defeats during the Korean War. Kim accused Pak Hon-yong of being an American spy and executed him. There were massive purges of factions that criticized Kim's policies in 1956 and 1967, allowing Kim to establish a monolithic regime based on his charisma and cult of personality (Person 2013). When North Korea faced a now 60-year period of military confrontation with the United States and South Korea, it became a garrison state that is heavily militarized and centralized.

Rhee Syngman in the South also consolidated his power after the war. He took advantage of strong anti-communist sentiments to strengthen his power. Most of his competitors were either eliminated by Rhee or taken by the North Korean military during the war (Oh 1999, 37–40). When he became extremely unpopular during the war among National Assembly members who elected him, he pushed forward a constitutional amendment for the direct election of the president in order to continue his political power. He served three terms until he had to step down after a massive student demonstration on April 19, 1960, that protested his fraud in his election for a fourth term. He left for the United States, where he died. A military government came to power in a coup in 1961, and its leaders justified the military dictatorship in the name of the North Korean threat and anti-communism. The memories of the Korean War and anti-communism dominated South Korean society throughout the Cold War period and obstructed and delayed its democratization until the 1980s. The Korean War also consolidated the Cold War system in Asia. President Truman dispatched the US Seventh Fleet to the Taiwan Strait on June 27th, 1950, two days after the outbreak of the War, to protect Chiang Kai-shek's Nationalist regime in Taiwan. Thus, China could not invade and conquer Taiwan. China and North Korea built an alliance in blood based on their experiences in the Korean War, which is often described as "lips and teeth." Japan enjoyed an economic boom due to the war, and a strong US–Japan alliance resulted. The US forces have stationed in Korea since the Korean War. The international confrontation between communism and capitalism during the Cold War has been epitomized in the division of the Korean Peninsula for the last 60 years.

Notes

1 Both the protectorate treaty (1905) and the annexation treaty (1910) were declared null and void in the 1965 Treaty on Basic Relations between Japan and the Republic of Korea.
2 Mamoru Shigemitsu, then Japanese Envoy in Shanghai, lost one leg in this attack and walked with an artificial leg and cane when he signed the Japanese Instrument of Surrender at the end of World War II in USS Missouri, September 2, 1945, as the Japanese Minister of Foreign Affairs.
3 Gen. MacArthur's 'Proclamation No. 1' on September 7, 1945 started by saying "the victorious military forces of my command will today *occupy* the territory of Korea south of 38 degrees north latitude" and defined in Article I that "All Powers of Government over the territory of Korea south of 38 degrees north latitude and the people thereof will be for the present exercised under my authority."
4 Joseph Davies wrote in his diary on July 28, 1945, "[Byrnes] was still having a hard time over Reparations. The details as to the success of the Atomic Bomb, which he had just received, gave him confidence that the Soviets would agree as to these difficulties. . . . Byrnes' attitude that the atomic bomb assured ultimate success in negotiations disturbed me more than his description of its success amazed me. I told him the threat wouldn't work, and might do irreparable harm" (Alperovitz 1995, 281–2).
5 Article II of Gen. MacArthur's 'Proclamation No. 1' (September 7, 1945) said "Until further orders, all governmental, public and honorary functionaries and employees, as well as all officials and employees, paid or voluntary, of all public utilities and services, including public welfare and public health, and all other persons engaged in essential services, shall continue to perform their usual functions and duties, and shall preserve and safeguard all records and property."
6 The text of The Korean War Armistice Agreement.

References

Alperovitz, Gar. 1995. *The Decision to Use the Atomic Bomb*, First Vintage Books edition. New York: Vintage Books.
Bae, Kichan. 2007. *Korea at the Crossroads – the History and Future of East Asia*. Seoul, Korea: Happyreading.
Cathcart, Adam, and Charles Kraus. 2008. "Peripheral Influence: The Sinŭiju Student Incident of 1945 and the Impact of Soviet Occupation in North Korea." *Journal of Korean Studies* 13 (1): 1–28.
Choe, Sang-Hun. 2016. "Korean Survivors of Atomic Bombs Renew Fight for Recognition, and Apology." *The New York Times*, May 25.
Cumings, Bruce. 1981. *The Origins of the Korean War*. Princeton, NJ: Princeton University Press.
Cumings, Bruce. 2004. *North Korea, Another Country*. New York: The New Press.
Cumings, Bruce. 2005. *Korea's Place in the Sun: A Modern History*, Updated edition. New York: W.W. Norton & Company.
Cumings, Bruce, and Kathryn Weathersby. 1995/1996. "An Exchange on Korean War Origins." *Cold War International History Project Bulletin* 6–7, Winter: 120–2.
de Brouwer, Anne-Marie. 2005. *Supranational Criminal Prosecution of Sexual Violence*. Antwerp, Oxford: Intersentia.
Donga Daily. 1946. "The Survey Conducted in the South by USAMGIK (US Army Military Government) on Ideological Preferences." August 13. Available at: http://newslibrary.naver.com/viewer/index.nhn?articleId=1946081300209203003&editNo=1&printCount=1&publishDate=1946-08-13&officeId=00020&pageNo=3&printNo=7053&publishType=00020.
French, Paul. 2007. *North Korea: The Paranoid Peninsula – a Modern History*, Second edition. New York: Zed Books.
Goulden, Joseph C. 1983. *Korea: The Untold Story of the War*. New York: McGraw-Hill.
The Hankyoreh. 2009. "439 Civilians Confirmed Dead in Yeosu-Suncheon Uprising of 1948." January 8. Available at: http://english.hani.co.kr/arti/english_edition/e_national/332032.html.
Hippin, Andreas. 2005. "The End of Silence: Korea's Hiroshima, Korean A-Bomb Victims Seek Redress." *The Japan Times*, August 2.

Kang, Chong-gu. 1996. *Pundan kwa chonjaeng ui Hanguk hyondaesa* (Korean Modern History of Division and War), Korean language edition. Seoul: Yoksabipyongsa.

Kang, Wi Jo. 1997. *Christ and Caesar in Modern Korea: A History of Christianity and Politics*. SUNY Press.

Kennan, George. 1947. "The Sources of Soviet Conduct." *Foreign Affairs* 25 (4): 566–82.

Kim, Djun Kil. 2014. *The History of Korea*, Second edition (The Greenwood Histories of the Modern Nations). Santa Barbara, CA: Greenwood.

Kim, Hum Joon. 2014. *The Massacres at Mt. Halla: Sixty Years of Truth Seeking in South Korea*. Ithaca, NY: Cornell University Press.

Lankov, Andrei. 2002. *From Stalin to Kim Il Sung: The Formation of North Korea, 1945–1960*. New Brunswick, NJ: Rutgers University Press.

Lankov, Andrei. 2005. "North Korea's Missionary Position." *Asia Times Online*, March 16.

Lee, Ki-baik. 1984. *A New History of Korea*. Cambridge, MA: Harvard University Press.

Lekic, Slobodan. 2010. "How the Soviets Helped Allies Defeat Japan." *San Francisco Chronicle*, August 22. Available at: www.sfgate.com/news/article/How-the-Soviets-helped-Allies-defeat-Japan-3177012.php.

Merrill, John. 1980. "The Cheju-do Rebellion." *Journal of Korean Studies* 2: 139–97.

Nitze, Paul H., and S. Nelson Drew, eds. 1994. *NCS-68: Forging the Strategy of Containment*. Washington, DC: National Defense University.

Nozaki, Yoshiko, Hiromitsu Inokuchi, and Tae-young Kim. 2006. "Legal Categories, Demographic Change and Japan's Korean Residents in the Long Twentieth Century." *The Asia-Pacific Journal* 4 (9): 1–18. Available at: http://apjjf.org/-Kim-Tae-young – Hiromitsu-INOKUCHI – Yoshiko-Nozaki/2220/article.pdf.

Oberdorfer, Donald. 1997. *The Two Koreas: A Contemporary History*. Indianapolis: Basic Books.

Oh, John Kie-chiang. 1999. *Korean Politics: The Quest for Democratization and Economic Development*. Ithaca, NY: Cornell University Press.

Park, Myung-Lim. 1996. *Hangukjeonjaengui balbalgwa giwon 1, 2 (The Korean War: The Outbreak and Its Origins Vol. 1: The Fatal Decisions and Outbreak of the Conflict)* (Korean language edition). Paju, Korea: Nanam Publishing House.

Person, James. 2013. "Commentary: North Korea's Purges Past." *The National Interest*, December 30.

Seth, Michael J. 2016. *A Concise History of Korea: From Antiquity to the Present*, Second edition. Lanham, MD: Rowman & Littlefield.

Song, Byung-Nak. 1997. *The Rise of the Korean Economy*, Second edition. Hong Kong: Oxford University Press.

Stueck, William. 2002. "Why the Korean War, not the Korean Civil War?" In *Rethinking the Korean War*, edited by William Steuck. Princeton, NJ: Princeton University Press.

Suh, Sang-Chul. 1978. *Growth and Structural Changes in the Korean Economy, 1910–1940: The Korean Economy Under the Japanese Occupation*. Cambridge, MA: Harvard University Press.

Tirman, John. 2011. *The Deaths of Others: The Fate of Civilians in America's Wars*. Oxford: Oxford University Press.

Weathersby, Kathryn. 1995/1996. "New Russian Documents on the Korean War." *Cold War International History Project Bulletin* 6–7, Winter: 30–5.

Weathersby, Kathryn. 2002. "Should We Fear This? Stalin and the Danger of War with America." *Cold War International History Project: Working Paper No. 39*.

Wilson, Ward. 2013. "The Bomb Didn't Beat Japan . . . Stalin Did." *Foreign Policy*, May 29.

Zubok, Vladislav, and Pleshakov, Constantine. 1997. *Inside the Kremlin's Cold War: From Stalin to Krushchev*. Cambridge, MA: Harvard University Press.

2 South Korean democratization

Jongseok Woo

South Korea stands as one of the most successful examples of economic development and democratization among the "third-wave" democratizers around the world. In 1987, South Korea had the first free and competitive presidential election; five years later, for the first time in three decades, South Korean citizens elected their first civilian leader in a free and fair election. Afterward, with the inauguration of Kim Dae-jung as president in 1998, the country officially entered an era of consolidated democracy. Generally speaking, democratization refers to a regime transition from nondemocracy to democracy within a state. Democratization entails major political changes that include eliminating autocratic rule, building working democratic institutions with a new constitution, and electing leaders in free and fair elections.

The democratic transition in South Korea represents an archetype of what Samuel P. Huntington (1991, 114) termed "transplacement" or the *ruptforma* mode of transition, in which "democratization resulted largely from joint action by government and opposition groups." The transplacement mode of democratization commences when the government implements limited liberalization measures to lessen the impact of opposition pro-democracy movements, which gives political momentum to the opposition forces to demand more democratic reforms. Such a democratic transition means that "both the government and the opposition . . . have to be committed to compromise and moderation" to minimize possible physical violence (Huntington 1991, 174). However, the old ruling circle was never reform-minded or pro-democracy; its members merely succumbed to pro-democracy forces' demands for political reform.

This chapter explores the dynamics of regime transition from military dictatorship to democratization in South Korea during the 1980s and 1990s. It explains how a confluence of major forces – pro-democracy movements, limited liberalization in the mid-1980s, and international environments – resulted in successful democratization without backlash from the old regime. This chapter comprises four major sections. The next section reviews authoritarian legacies from 1948 through the 1980s and pro-democracy campaigns. Section two discusses the Chun regime's limited liberalization from 1983 through the June 29th Declaration for democratic reform in 1987, when various opposition forces formed a united front to fight dictatorial rule. Section three discusses the first democratic presidential election and the Roh Tae-woo presidency (1988–1993) as a quasi-military and quasi-civilian government, a period of both democratic adjournment and safeguard for a stable transition to civilian rule. Section four details Kim Young-sam's presidency (1993–1998) as the first true civilian leader who carried out democratic reforms. He paved the road to democratic consolidation by the Kim Dae-jung presidency (1998–2003). The conclusion critically evaluates the political achievements and limitations that the democratization process brought to Korean politics in the era of democratic consolidation.

Legacies of authoritarianism

The political history of the Korean Peninsula in the twentieth century is rife with tumultuous incidents, with Japanese colonial rule and lost chances for modern state-building, US military occupation, territorial division and the Korean War, and democratic breakdown, leading to three decades of military dictatorship. The legacy of a strong state apparatus that overshadowed civil society dates back to the Japanese colonial period in which bureaucratic systems and oppressive and brutal police tactics were used to maintain Japan's rule over the Korean people. Subsequently, the US military occupation force (1945–1948) and the Rhee Syngman government (1948–1960) inherited the colonial instruments in the early period of state-building. Moreover, two military dictators – Park Jung-hee (1961–1979) and Chun Doo-hwan (1980–1988) – intensified the legacy of a strong authoritarian state as they brought the top brass in the Korean armed forces into politics to consolidate their dictatorships. Meanwhile, the brutal Korean War (1950–1953) and subsequent security threats from communist North Korea created an ideology of anti-communism and security-intelligence organs that could effectively suppress civil society movements.

Since its liberation from brutal Japanese occupation in 1945, South Korea had three crucial political junctures for democratic governance: first in 1948 with the First Republic with Rhee Syngman as president, second in 1960 with Jang Myon's Second Republic, and third with the "Seoul Spring" in 1979–1980. These democratic experiments ended in failure and the installation of oppressive authoritarian governments headed by three political strongmen – Rhee Syngman, Park Jung-hee, and Chun Doo-hwan. At the same time, however, such aborted democratic experiments provided Korean society with fertile soil for pro-democracy movements that finally achieved full democracy in the 1990s. This section discusses democratic failure and authoritarian rule in pre-democratization South Korean politics.

The Rhee Syngman presidency

After 36 years of brutal Japanese colonial rule (1910–1945) and three years of American occupation, South Korea became a democratic republic on August 15, 1948. The general elections in 1948 established the first National Assembly, which elected the republic's first president, Rhee Syngman, a prominent leader of the independence movement during Japanese rule. Rhee received political backing from the United States, as he represented the conservative components in the post-colonial power struggle with staunch anti-communism. However, this first attempt at democracy did not even survive the three-year Korean War that resulted in millions of deaths and devastated the entire peninsula. Even before the war erupted, the government retained undemocratic elements as it "strengthened the colonial legacy by building an overdeveloped state through the absorption of Japanese colonial bureaucrats, the police, and the military" (Jun 2001, 122). The Rhee government manipulated anti-communism ideology to both internal and external political advantage. Internally, Rhee justified his authoritarian rule and silenced any political opposition voices; externally, he drew upon American support for the conservative government. Moreover, the National Security Law, enacted in December 1948 to deal with a growing national security crisis, soon became a political tool to suppress political opposition movements. As Oh (1999, 37) points out, the National Security Law "was often applied largely for the purpose of South Korean regime maintenance by curbing press freedom, political activities by religious organizations, labor unions, and anti-American behaviors, among others."

The Korean War enabled Rhee to exploit the dire security environment for his political advantage, setting a precedent for authoritarian politics in South Korea that utilized a security crisis and anti-communism for regime maintenance. On May 15, 1952, at the height of the war, Rhee attempted to amend the constitution to elect the president through popular referendum, not through the National Assembly as required by the 1948 constitution. He pursued the constitutional amendment because he failed to garner broad support from the National Assembly and even from his own party, so he was certain to lose the 1952 presidential election. Therefore, he tried to amend the constitution to bypass the National Assembly and have popular elections. Rhee declared martial law to terrorize political opposition forces, arresting 50 assemblymen and ordering the police to surround the National Assembly building to force passage of the legislation. Two years later, Rhee proposed yet another constitutional amendment to the National Assembly to eliminate the two-term restriction on presidential tenure, which effectively made him president for life. Throughout his presidential tenure, Rhee and his ruling Liberal Party nullified the democratic constitution and political processes by utilizing authoritarian political tactics with declarations of martial law and physical terror against potential challenges to his power. As Hong (2000, 84) notes, "the unprincipled manner in which the Constitution was revised contributed to the political instability of the Rhee regime by eroding its legitimacy." Even worse, Rhee's authoritarian political practices set the precedent for nullifying the constitution on grounds of political expediency, a practice his successors repeated.

The April 19 Revolution of 1960 occurred after Rhee ran for his fourth presidential term through massive electoral fraud, which prompted nationwide protests led by high school and college students and joined by middle-class citizens and intellectuals. Rhee responded by declaring martial law and ordering the armed forces into action. However, the military and the police did not follow his order, and they instead demanded that the president step down. The student-led revolution ousted the Rhee government and marked the second critical juncture for democratic governance in South Korea. Jang Myon's Second Republic restored democracy with a parliamentary system that significantly weakened the presidential office and diffused political power throughout the different branches of government. However, the Jang Myon government was too weak and incompetent to cope with growing social demands emanating mostly from impatient and often violent student protestors. A gap grew between citizens' demands for political participation and the political institutions' inability to absorb them, creating a so-called participation crisis. The Second Republic, a highly democratic but incapable government, created a sense of crisis in every quarter of society due to growing crime rates, degenerating economic conditions, and most critically, a national security crisis. The short-lived attempt at democracy ended with a military coup led by Park Jung-hee in May 1961.

The Park Jung-hee presidency

If Rhee Syngman replaced the nascent democracy with authoritarian civilian rule, General Park Jung-hee's military coup and the 1972 *Yushin* (revitalization) constitution entrenched the military's political dominance through the late 1980s. In the middle of the political chaos that arose after Rhee's removal from office and continued under Jang Myon's Second Republic (1960–1961), Park Jung-hee and approximately 250 young Turks in the Korean army staged a bloodless coup, overthrowing the fledgling democracy on May 16, 1961. Park and his followers justified the coup by "criticizing the Jang regime's pervasive corruption, its inability to defend the country from communist threats, and the absence of a viable plan for social and economic development" (Woo 2011, 70). Furthermore, Park's Military Revolutionary Council presented specific policy packages to the Korean people that included anticommunism, industrial revolution, a continuing security alignment with the United States, and "a spiritual regeneration of the people" (Park 1961, 18–19). Contrary to the Council's pledge that it would transfer political power to civilians as soon as its revolutionary missions were accomplished, Park declared martial law and imposed the *Yushin* constitution that gave him unrestricted political power and made him president for life.

The Park regime made heavy use of security and military agencies and emergency decrees to maintain dictatorial rule. Right after the coup, Park established the Korean Central Intelligence Agency (KCIA) with Kim Jong-pil, one of the coup members and Park's brother-in-law, as the founding director. From the beginning, the KCIA was not a mere intelligence institution but an omnipotent organ for the Park regime's coercive rule. The KCIA's surveillance and purges included not just political opponents, but also the inner circle of the coup forces. Another important mission for the security agency was to organize the ruling Republican Party and prepare it for the 1963 presidential election. The *Yushin* constitution provided Park with a legal basis for his dictatorial rule: Article 54 of the constitution states that

> when the President deems necessary, he shall have the power to take emergency measures which temporarily suspend the freedom and rights of the people as defined in the present Constitution, and to enforce emergency measures with regard to the rights and powers of the Executive and the Judiciary.
>
> (Kim 1978, 367)

The *Yushin* dictatorship became possible in the midst of degenerating security environments for South Korea, with the Nixon Doctrine that brought fear of American 'abandonment' and amidst increasing armed infiltrations by North Korea.

Park Jung-hee's dictatorial rule expanded the armed forces' political influence in Korean politics and ultimately fostered the 1979–1980 coup d'etat by sponsoring a private military fraternity named *Hanahoe* (literally meaning, one mind association). In 1964, Captain Chun Doo-hwan and his alumni from the Korean Military Academy organized a private fraternity within the army, called the *Chilseonghoe* (meaning, Seven Stars Association) and later renamed the *Hanahoe*. The *Hanahoe* recruited politically ambitious army officers from the *Yeongnam* region (the Southeastern provinces), and Park Jung-hee became the patron of the military fraternity. Members of the *Hanahoe* faction occupied the most powerful command posts of the armed forces and, when a power vacuum occurred after Park's assassination, Chun and *Hanahoe* members were strong enough to overwhelm pro-democracy movements and install another military dictatorship.

The Chun Doo-hwan presidency

The third attempt at democracy came after Park Jung-hee was assassinated by one of his closest confidents in October 1979. The October 26 Incident occurred under surging domestic and international pressures on the regime, including anti-*Yushin* demonstrations and criticism from the Jimmy Carter administration. The pressures intensified internal strife between hardliners and reformists within the Park regime that ultimately led to Kim Jae-gyu's assassination of the dictator. Park's death resulted in high hopes for democracy among the Korean people. The so-called *Seoul Spring* came as Choi Kyu-ha, ex-prime minister and acting president, declared that full democracy would be recovered with a constitutional amendment through popular referendum, termination of the emergency decrees of the *Yushin* era, and restoration of political rights of opposition political leaders (including Kim Dae-jung), college professors and students, religious leaders, and journalists who had been arrested for opposing Park's dictatorial rule (Oh 1999, 75).

Against such high hopes for democracy, however, Major General Chun Doo-hwan and his followers executed a two-stage coup: first in December 1979 and then in May 1980. They recalled front-line troops from the demilitarized zone and brutally suppressed pro-democracy demonstrators, most notoriously in Gwangju. Chun Doo-hwan and his military violently suppressed the Gwangju pro-democracy demonstration, which according to official records, resulted in 191 deaths and thousands of injuries, although other estimates report many more casualties (e.g., see Clark 1988; Cumings 1999; Kihl 2005). As a result of the coup, the violent suppression of citizens, and the privatization and militarization of Korean politics, the Chun regime constantly suffered from a legitimacy deficit and faced persistent demonstrations until Chun yielded to opposition demands in 1987. Moreover, the incident brought to pro-democracy protestors in South Korea a sense of American hypocrisy and anti-Americanism due to their feeling of betrayal and neglect by the Carter administration, which had been perceived as the champion of democracy and human rights.

The three attempts at democracy illustrate that building a workable democracy in South Korea was not an easy task due to historical legacies, adverse security environment, and resulting political culture and norms of a strong state and weak civil society. Ending decades-long dictatorial rule and building a democratic regime is by no means simple, as it does not merely involve electing leaders in free and fair elections. Indeed, democracy-building entails a much more comprehensive political overhaul to eliminate the old crooks from the dictatorship, write a new constitution and build political institutions, garner popular support for democratic reform, place the politically dominant armed forces under firm civilian control, and manage national security and order. Furthermore, the institutional and procedural aspects of democratization must entail normative beliefs: both political elites' and ordinary citizens' belief that "the democratic regime is the most right and appropriate for their society, better than any other realistic alternative they can imagine," so that democracy is accepted as "the only game in town" (Diamond 1999, 65). As shown later in the discussion, consolidating and deepening democracy does not become a mono-directional or irreversible political course. This is the case especially when the authoritarian regime brings about economic success followed by a new democratic government that fails to sustain the economy. The following sections detail the democratization processes in South Korea during the 1980s and 1990s and critically evaluate the major accomplishments and notable drawbacks that the democratic transition brought to South Korean society.

Limited liberalization to the June 29th declaration, 1983–1987

In South Korea, political challenges to the dictatorial rule began with the so-called *minjung* (people's) movement of the 1970s and 1980s, which included college students and labor unions, as well as Catholic and Protestant clergies. In an effort to pacify the resistance, the Chun Doo-hwan regime adopted limited liberalization that reinstated anti-regime activists, including college students, professors, journalists, and opposition politicians. However, liberalization unexpectedly provided pro-democracy forces with opportunities to make further political demands, which forced the Chun regime to issue the June 29th Declaration for further democratic reform. The democratic transition in South Korea progressed with dynamic interactions between elites from the old regime and pro-democracy opposition forces that led to political transition through political compromise. Such a compromise-induced transition brought mixed political outcomes to post-democratization politics in South Korea. On the one hand, the transplacement mode of democratization led to a peaceful and step-by-step political transition that did not trigger much physical violence from either side. On the other hand, the political compromise resulted in an incomplete purge of the old authoritarian legacies after democratization and brought back the old elites from the authoritarian era. This authoritarian legacy in post-democratization South Korea became a major stumbling block in the country's march to democratic consolidation, which will be discussed in Chapter 3.

Almost two decades of military rule under Park Jung-hee brought ruthless oppression against political opposition movements, as the state apparatus monopolized the means of physical violence and dominated the civil society. However, significant accomplishments under the Park regime included an unprecedented economic miracle and the management of internal and external security threats, especially from possible armed attacks by North Korea. On average, the entire span of Park's rule (1961–1979) recorded double-digit annual economic growth: At the time of the 1961 coup, per capita income in South Korea was $82; it hit the $1,640 mark in the final year of Park's rule. Park's ruling style refashioned the South Korean government and politics from corruption, inefficiency, and chaos into a machine for efficiency, competence, and economic growth.

The two decades of economic developments brought about considerable changes in the culture and political orientation of the Korean people. Fast industrialization accompanied urbanization: At the time of state-building, more than 75 percent of the people lived in rural areas; in the 1980s, more than 70 percent resided in urban or metropolitan areas. Moreover, continued economic growth made the urban population wealthier and better educated. The number of college students increased from less than 20,000 in 1971 to more than 1 million at the turn of the 1980s (Lee 1990, 2). South Korean economic development and democratization serve as a model case for Martin Lipset's modernization theory that presents a causal connection between a country's level of economic development and the probability of being democratic. According to Lipset, economic development accompanies industrialization, urbanization, wealth, and education to foster a democratic culture (Lipset 1959, 75).

At the same time, such socio-economic changes (i.e., fast industrialization, urbanization, and education) often stimulate political activism by enlarging the size and influence of the middle class. These citizens often express high expectations from politics, and they thereby erode the traditional culture of respect for authority. Furthermore, fast industrialization often widens the inequality gap between the haves and the have-nots. In particular, Park Jung-hee's policies of fast industrialization gave a small number of big conglomerates (called *chaebols*) enormous preferential benefits, creating massive corrupt collusion between the state and the *chaebols*. The Park regime provided the *chaebols* with gigantic policy loans, tax breaks, and other administrative favors at the expense of medium-sized and small businesses, urban laborers, and farmers (Kim 2001, 17). Urban laborers and farmers, along with college students and religious clergies, constituted the forerunners of the anti-dictatorship movement in the early stages of democratization in South Korea.

Pro-democracy protests in the early 1980s

At the turn of the 1980s, demonstrations by labor unions and college students focused on revealing the ruthlessly violent nature of the Chun Doo-hwan dictatorship. Irrefutably, the

Table 2.1 National Assembly election outcomes, 1981–1996

	Parliamentary Seats Captured		Party Name
	Ruling Party	Opposition Parties	
11th National	151		Democratic Justice Party
Assembly election		81	Democratic Korea Party
(March 1981)		25	Korean Nation's Party
		19	Independents/Others
		Total Seats: 276	
12th National	148		Democratic Justice Party
Assembly election		35	Democratic Korea Party
(February 1985)		20	Korean Nation's Party
		67	Democratic Party
		6	Independents/Others
		Total Seats: 276	
13th National	125		Democratic Justice Party
Assembly election		70	Peace and Dem. Party
(April 1988)		59	Unification Dem. Party
		35	New Dem.–Repub. Party
		10	Independents/Others
		Total Seats: 299	
14th National	149		Democratic Liberal Party
Assembly election		97	Democratic Party
(March 1992)		31	Unification National Party
		22	Independents/Others
		Total Seats: 299	
15th National	139		New Korea Party
Assembly Election		79	Natl Congress for New Politics
(April 1996)		50	United Liberal Democrats
		15	Democratic Party
		16	Independents/Others
		Total Seats: 299	

Source: Young Whan Kihl (2005) *Transforming Korean Politics: Democracy, Reform, and Culture*. New York: M.E. Sharpe, p. 16; Republic of Korea, National Election Commission. Available at www.nec.go.kr/engvote_2013/main/main.jsp.

ways in which Chun and his followers seized political power made ordinary citizens in South Korea seriously doubt the legitimacy of the regime. Unlike Park Jung-hee's 1961 coup that did not meet with popular opposition, the Korean people vehemently opposed Chun Doo-hwan's unconstitutional usurpation of power from civilian leadership. After controlling political power through the December 12 coup, Chun and key members of the *Hanahoe* (including Roh Tae-woo, who became the first democratically elected president in 1988) declared martial law over the entire nation and banned any organized political activities. They closed college campuses, controlled the mass media, shut down the National Assembly, and banned several dozen politicians (including Kim Dae-jung). South Jeolla province and the city of Gwangju became the focal points of anti-dictatorship demonstrations, and Chun applied martial law most strictly in that region. The brutal suppression of Gwangju pro-democracy demonstrations resulted in the deaths of several hundred civilians.

Shortly after the violent crackdown on civil demonstrations, the coup forces took peremptory measures to seize political power, forcing Choi Kyu-ha to step down. Chun Doo-hwan rose to the rank of four-star general, retired from the army a few weeks later, and ran in the 11th presidential election. In February 1981, the newly formed "electoral college" for presidential elections (a rubber stamp handpicked by Chun and similar to the *Yushin* era's National Council for Reunification) elected Chun as president. On the surface, the Fifth Republic's constitution looked different from, and less repressive than, the *Yushin* constitution, limiting the president to a single seven-year term and giving more political power to the National Assembly. At the same time, however, the constitution granted predominant power to the executive head, giving the president power to disband the National Assembly, impose special emergency measures, and submit constitutional amendments (Kil 2001, 50). In the 11th National Assembly elections held in March 1981, Chun's ruling Democratic Justice Party (DJP) gained a majority of 151 out of 276 seats, while several opposition parties divided the remaining seats.

Limited liberalization measures

Political manipulation, however, was not sufficient to silence pro-democracy demonstrations by labor unions, farmers, and college students, often supported by Catholic and Protestant clergies, white collar workers, and intellectuals. Chun Doo-hwan came to realize that physical violence alone would not stabilize his rule, so he employed various tactics to mitigate political opposition after 1983. Although Chun did not adopt limited liberalization measures of his own volition, he felt quite confident about his regime's performance in security and economic matters. By 1983, for example, the Korean economy had fully recovered from the second oil shock and resulting economic recession,[1] recording double-digit economic growth in the latter years of his term. In the national security arena, the Chun regime successfully rejuvenated security alliances with the United States under the Ronald Reagan administration and effectively deterred North Korea's security threats. With a strong security commitment from the United States, the Chun regime enjoyed the most favorable security environment for the country since the Korean War ended. Ultimately, Chun felt confident that limited liberalization measures and the lessening of oppressive maneuvers would not destabilize his political base.

Quite contrary to his expectations, however, reform measures in 1983 reactivated civil society movements and provided pro-democracy groups with a crucial window of opportunity to push the Chun regime for further political concessions. The liberalization measures reinstated university professors and students who had been engaged in anti-Chun demonstrations and expelled from campus, rehabilitated more than 200 opposition politicians, and released political prisoners who had been indicted for violations of the National Security Law (Yoon 1997, 156–8). Chun Doo-hwan was confident that he could effectively manipulate the divided opposition political forces and maintain the ruling DJP's hegemonic status in the National Assembly. However, liberalization unexpectedly unified and strengthened those opposition political forces that were united under the political determination to eliminate the Chun dictatorship.

The 12th National Assembly elections in February 1985 created crucial political momentum for democratization. As illustrated in Table 2.1, the ruling DJP occupied 148 out of 276 seats, securing the ruling majority, while the opposition New Korean Democratic Party acquired 67 seats, and the Democratic Korea Party gained 35. Although the ruling DJP managed to maintain its majority status, it did so with a meager 35.2 percent of the popular vote. More importantly, the DJP failed to obtain the two-thirds majority in the National Assembly necessary to pass important legislation, including constitutional amendments and presidential election rules, without an opposition party veto. Moreover, a more powerful and longer-term impact of the 1985 National Assembly elections was "the empowerment of opposition politicians, including two of the most prominent pro-democracy leaders, Kim Young-sam and Kim Dae-jung, as well as civil society groups such as college students, labor unions, and dissident groups" (Woo 2011, 106). The two Kims quickly emerged as powerful political symbols around whom the diverse nationwide campaign for democracy rallied.

The June 29th declaration

Anti-Chun demonstrations gained critical momentum when Chun Doo-hwan reversed his previous pledges and announced, on April 13, 1987, that he would suspend any discussion over constitutional reform for a direct presidential election.[2] With this so-called April 13 measure, the DJP held its national convention in Jamsil Olympic Gymnasium to nominate Roh Tae-woo, one of Chun's cohorts in the 11th Korean Military Academy and a key member of the 1979–1980 military coup, as the DJP's presidential candidate. Chun handpicked Roh Tae-woo as the successor to his presidency, to be elected through an indirect presidential election by the electoral college. The opposition forces – progressives, moderates, and conservatives alike – perceived the April 13 measure as "an outright attempt by the DJP to perpetuate autocratic rule at the cost of democratization," thereby igniting nationwide demonstrations (Billet 1990, 301). On June 10, the same day that Roh Tae-woo was nominated as the DJP candidate, opposition forces formed the National Coalition for a Democratic Constitution (NCDC) as an umbrella organization that encompassed all the opposition forces, including opposition politicians, religious organizations, labor unions, and intellectuals.

Throughout June 1987, the NCDC organized massive demonstrations and formed the People's Rally to Denounce the Cover-Up of the Torture-Murder and the Scheme to Maintain the Current Constitution, a political movement equivalent to the People Power Revolution that had deposed the Ferdinand Marcos dictatorship in the Philippines a year earlier. In addition to its demand for a constitutional revision to authorize a direct presidential election, the NCDC publicized the brutality of the Chun dictatorship by revealing its torture and killing of protesters. On May 26, for instance, a Catholic priest revealed that a college student, Park Jong-cheol, had been tortured to death by the police. As street demonstrations surged to the point that they could not be controlled merely by physical violence, Chun Doo-hwan met with Kim Young-sam to discuss a political compromise. At the meeting, Kim demanded that the government lift the house arrest imposed on Kim Dae-jung, release several hundred protestors who had been arrested by the police during street demonstrations after June 10, and resume discussions of the constitutional revision for direct popular presidential elections. Chun Doo-hwan made important concessions to Kim's demands and emphasized that "all problems should be settled through dialogue and compromise within the bounds of law and order" (Haberman 1987).

In the post-April 13 political crisis, the ruling DJP and army leadership were divided between hardliners and softliners over how to respond to the political demands of the opposition forces. Hardliners wanted the armed forces to crack down on the street demonstrations and restore political order, while softliners were willing to compromise and expand democratic openings. Although Chun Doo-hwan took the hardliners' position and was not willing to make concessions, several internal and external circumstances forced him to accept the softliners' demands. First, favorable domestic and international security environments did not provide convincing justification for forcefully suppressing demonstrations in the name of national security. Second, the protests were joined by white collar, middle-class citizens. The early stages of anti-Chun demonstrations were initiated by college students and blue collar workers who often used physical violence to fight for political demands, and they pursued far-reaching politico-economic reforms with left-leaning ideological convictions. This time, however, the middle class joined the political struggle and became the main driving force for further democratic reforms from 1987 forward (Lee, S. 1993, 359). Third, the army leadership opposed Chun's idea of storming Seoul to trounce street protestors, recalling the time when troops did not follow the Rhee regime's order to fire on protestors in 1960. Finally, international pressure on the Chun regime was growing. International human rights groups raised concerns about the harsh repression of pro-democracy activists, and Western democracies threatened to withdraw from the 1988 Seoul Olympic Games. In the meantime, the Reagan administration, once a strong supporter of the Chun dictatorship, warned against use of military force and demanded that the regime reach a political compromise with opposition forces (Oh 1999, 93).

Democratization in South Korea gained critical momentum when Roh Tae-woo, Chun's handpicked successor and the DJP's presidential candidate, issued the Declaration of Democratization and Reforms (the June 29th Declaration), which included an eight-point plan for democratic reform. The Declaration included (1) a constitutional revision for direct presidential elections, (2) free and fair election management with a revision of election laws, (3) a political amnesty and restoration of civil rights of dissidents, (4) the promotion of human dignity and protection of the basic rights of citizens, (5) freedom of the press, (6) local autonomy (including educational autonomy), (7) dialogue and compromise, and (8) bold social reforms for a clean and honest society (Oh 1999, 99–101; Woo 2011, 107–8). Chun Doo-hwan officially accepted Roh's reform proposals, and Roh and the opposition (represented by Kim Young-sam) reached an agreement for constitutional revision. The National Assembly organized a special commission with an eight-member working group to write a new constitution. On October 12, the National Assembly approved the new constitution, and a national referendum ratified it two weeks later.

The quasi-civilian rule of Roh Tae-woo (1988–1993)

As illustrated in the previous section, democratization in South Korea progressed through the interactions between grassroots pro-democracy movements and elite-level responses. Democratization began with mass protests in which the leading forces included college students and militant labor unions. However, democratization moved toward the next stage with negotiations between the ruling authoritarian elites and the opposition elites who emerged as symbols of freedom and human rights. After the June 29th Declaration, Korean society recovered some measure of tranquility as militant *minjung* movements lost their political charm and the elite-level compromises led to a constitutional revision for a popular and direct presidential election. By August 1987, the struggle for democratization "had shifted from the streets to the National Assembly" (Saxer 2002, 65). This section explores the democratic transition through the first democratic presidential election after the *Yushin* constitution was declared. Roh Tae-woo's Sixth Republic seemed to derail democratization for a short time, but it contributed to a more stable and far-reaching democratic transition in the long term.

The presidential election, the three Kims, and regionalism

The newly written constitution allowed a presidential election through direct popular vote, held in December 1987. The most critical issue before the election was whether the opposition leaders, the two Kims – Kim Dae-jung and Kim Young-sam – would remain united and nominate a single presidential candidate for the pro-democracy opposition. At the time of the June 29th Declaration, neither had openly expressed a strong desire to run for the presidency. Before long, however, the power struggle between the two Kims became intense, as neither was willing to yield the candidacy to the other. Kim Dae-jung had his own strong conviction that he deserved to be the opposition candidate, because he had been the symbol of democracy in Korea under authoritarian dictators. He had also been a symbolic leader who won landslide support from the *Honam* region (i.e., southwestern provinces), which had been politically and economically marginalized. Furthermore, he had run in the 1971 presidential election and lost to Park Jung-hee in a close but seemingly unfair competition: Park Jung-hee gained 53.2 percent of the popular vote, while Kim Dae-jung received 45.3 percent. Meanwhile, Kim Young-sam, also a charismatic and symbolic leader of democracy, had justifiable reasons to claim the opposition presidential candidacy because he had been one of the leading elites who had fought for democracy. He garnered strong support from the *Yeongnam* region, especially in Busan and its surroundings. The stakes were extremely high: If the opposition leaders could successfully find a way to nominate a single opposition candidate, they were certain to win the presidential election and gain a great victory for Korean democracy. If they failed to unify, the opposition votes would be split almost evenly, and they would ultimately lose the election. Even more damaging, the two Kims' fighting would intensify the regional division between *Honam* and *Yeognam*.

The opposition forces made every effort to nominate a single candidate and, at an early September meeting, both Kims agreed to negotiations. By that time, however, both political camps had been formulating their own political strategies for the presidential election, and both demanded that the other acquiesce. Kim Dae-jung's camp argued that Kim Young-sam should step down, because Kim Dae-jung was the elder and had undergone more than two decades of political struggles for Korea's democratization. Kim Young-sam's camp asserted that it was Kim Young-sam who brought about the 1980s electoral revolution and had negotiated with the Chun regime for democratic reforms and a political amnesty for hundreds of pro-democracy activists, including Kim Dae-jung. Kim Young-sam moved first on October 10 to announce his candidacy for the Unification Democratic Party (UDP). Kim Dae-jung's faction members defected from the UDP and formed a new opposition party, the Party for Peace and Democracy (PPD), which, on October 28, declared Kim Dae-jung the PPD's candidate. The 13th presidential election was held on December 16, 1987, with Roh Tae-woo as the ruling DJP candidate and three main opposition candidates – the UDP's Kim Young-sam, the PPD's Kim Dae-jung, and Kim Jong-pil of the New Democratic-Republican Party (NDRP) – the NDRP being a conservative group from the Park Jung-hee era. The two Kims' failure to establish a united front resulted in a heartbreaking electoral outcome, as Roh Tae-woo won the election with only 36.6 percent of the popular vote. Kim Young-sam garnered 28 percent, Kim Dae-jung gained 27 percent, and Kim Jong-pil received 8.1 percent. It was evident that with a single candidate, the opposition would have won the election by a wide margin. After the election results came out, the opposition parties protested, claiming more than 800 cases of election misconduct, such as stealing ballot boxes and forging absentee ballots. Regardless of the election irregularities, voters in South Korea felt disheartened and blamed the loss on the two Kims' inability to compromise (Saxer 2002, 76).

After the election, pro-democracy activists and ordinary citizens became disillusioned and lost their passion for further political fighting. More than a dozen opposition lawmakers demanded that the two Kims retire from politics, suggesting that they "have spoiled the best chance in Korea's 5,000-year history to achieve democratization by failing to field a

Table 2.2 Presidential election outcomes, 1987–1997

Election (Year)	Candidates	Parties	% of Votes
13th presidential election	**Roh Tae-woo**	Democratic Justice Party	36.6
(Dec. 16, 1987)	Kim Young-sam	Unification Democratic Party	28
	Kim Dae-jung	Peace and Democracy Party	27
	Kim Jong-pil	New Dem. Republican Party	8.1
14th presidential election	**Kim Young-sam**	Democratic Liberal Party	42
(Dec. 18, 1992)	Kim Dae-jung	Democratic Party	33.8
	Chung Ju-young	United People's Party	16.3
15th presidential election	**Kim Dae-jung**	Natl Congress for New Politics	40.3
(Dec. 19, 1997)	Lee Hoe-chang	Grand National Party	38.7
	Rhee In-je	New People's Party	19.2

Source: National Election Commission, Republic of Korea. 2013. *Results of Presidential Elections*. Available at www.nec.go.kr/engvote_2013/main/main.jsp.

single presidential candidate" (Lee 1990, 95). Equally troubling was the intensification of regionalism in Korean politics as a result of the three Kims having their own regional bases. Kim Young-sam garnered 56 percent of popular support in his hometown of Busan and 51.3 percent in South *Gyeongsang* province. Meanwhile, more than 90 percent of citizens in Gwangju and North/South Jeolla provinces supported Kim Dae-jung. Finally, Kim Jong-pil received 45 percent of popular support in South *Chungcheong* province (Lee 1990, 84). The regional division was more intense in the 1987 presidential election than in the 1971 presidential election, in which Park Jung-hee actively played on regional divisions. In 1971, Park received 72 percent of the popular vote in the *Yeongnam* region and 28 percent in *Honam*; Kim Dae-jung gained 28 percent in *Yeongnam* and 64 percent in *Honam*. However, in the 1987 election, only 5 percent of voters in *Yeongnam* supported Kim Dae-jung, while less than 1 percent of voters in *Honam* voted for Kim Young-sam.

In general, regional antagonism in Korea has long and deep historical and cultural roots, but the regional division in the late twentieth century emerged as a principal political issue, because of political and economic discrimination against *Honam* during the Park and Chun eras. Throughout almost three decades of military rule, elites from the *Yeongnam* region were overrepresented in high-ranking government positions, the military hierarchy, the ownership of big businesses, professionals and intellectuals in higher education, and higher income earners. Given no dominant political party with nationwide support, the mobilization of regional identities by candidates and parties became the easiest and most efficient political strategy for winning elections (Choi 1994; Choe 2003; Kang 2003). The intensification of regional divisions in elections dominated post-democratization Korean politics; electoral fortunes were determined by regional identities, and political parties became based on these divisions, not on policy agendas and candidate qualities.

Roh Tae-woo and Nordpolitik

As the winner of the first direct presidential election under a new constitution, the Roh Tae-woo government took office in 1988. Although Roh was elected through a free and competitive election (but probably not fair), he never intended to be a democratic president. Roh was a cohort of Chun Doo-hwan at the Korean Military Academy, and the two became politically active as early as 1961, when they organized young officers to support the military coup. They founded a private fraternity group called *Chilseonghoe* that later became the infamous *Hanahoe* faction. Furthermore, Roh played a critical role in Chun's December 12 coup d'état by dispatching his own military unit to control army headquarters and the capital city of Seoul. He retired from the military in 1981 as a four-star general, assumed his role as the number-two man in the Chun dictatorship, and later was handpicked by Chun to be his presidential successor. Like Chun, Roh had never championed democracy and, therefore, pro-democracy groups had no choice but to wait for another five years for the next presidential election scheduled in 1992.

However, the Roh Tae-woo presidency entailed at least a few significant positive steps toward democratization. Although he was by no means a democratic reformer, and therefore any political reforms were bound to be extremely limited, the Roh government did not revert to a dictatorship. In addition, the Roh presidency brought political stability by resolving what Huntington called the "praetorian problem" in which a new civilian leadership must find ways "to reduce military involvement in politics and establish a professional pattern of civil-military relations" and, if the leadership fails, the military might intervene or threaten to intervene in politics when its demands are not met (Huntington 1991, 209). Politically active generals (mostly *Hanahoe* members) openly threatened that they would not remain politically neutral if an unwanted opposition candidate (i.e., Kim Dae-jung) won the presidential election. Under Roh, though, those army officers did not have to worry about losing their political prerogative or facing prosecution for their unconstitutional intervention in politics and human rights violations throughout the 1980s. Right after Roh assumed the presidency, civil society groups and opposition lawmakers fiercely called for the investigation and punishment of suspected politicized military officers, including Chun. However, Roh protected the officers by limiting the investigation and gave them influence in his government.[3] Retired officers' presence in politics was quite pervasive in the Roh government: They occupied 20 percent of the cabinet and 7 percent of the National Assembly. The number was not significantly lower than during the Chun dictatorship.

Another positive legacy of the Roh presidency in post-democratization politics was his vigorous foreign policy approach, called *Nordpolitik*. The Roh government benefited from internal and external structural changes – such as the democratic opening, the Seoul Olympics, and the fall of the communist bloc – in pursuing a diplomatic offensive. Roh took advantage of the Olympics to communicate with countries in the communist bloc. With the collapse of the Eastern bloc at the end of the 1980s, South Korea established full diplomatic relations, starting with Hungary in early 1989 and Poland and Yugoslavia by the end of that year. By the turn of the 1990s, it had established full diplomatic relations with all Eastern European countries. The Roh government also expanded its diplomatic interactions with the Soviet Union and China, two major patrons of North Korea. It persuaded them not to veto the two Koreas' acceptance into the United Nations and to reject Kim Il-sung's plan for a single membership for the two Koreas. The end of the Cold War also meant multifaceted crises for Pyongyang. The Soviet Union, the biggest economic and security supporter providing one-sided trade and roughly 70 percent of North Korea's weapons, demanded hard currency for trade, which Pyongyang could not accept. Loss of diplomatic ties with the former communist comrades negatively affected North Korea's diplomatic relations and economic conditions. Ultimately, by the end of Roh's presidential term, it became evident that South Korea had won the battle with North Korea in the diplomatic, economic, and ideological realms (Gills 1996).

Yeosoyadae and the conservative alliance

While the Roh government was enjoying tremendous accomplishments in foreign policy, domestic politics remained in gridlock with the so-called *yeosoyadae* (ruling minority and opposition majority), which was created as a result of the 1988 National Assembly elections. In the 13th National Assembly elections held just two months after Roh assumed the presidency, the ruling DJP suffered an excruciating defeat to the opposition parties by losing its majority status. As Table 2.1 illustrates, Roh Tae-woo's DJP gained 125 out of 299 seats, while Kim Dae-jung's PPD occupied 70 seats, Kim Young-sam's UDP 59 seats, and Kim Jong-pil's NDRP 35 seats.[4] The electoral outcomes clearly reflect intensification of regional divisions among the parties. The ruling DJP received strong support from Daegu and *Gyeongsang* provinces, taking all seats in Daegu and 80 percent of the seats in North *Gyeongsang* province. The PPD secured all seats from Gwangju and Jeolla provinces. The UDP's regional base was in Busan and South *Gyeongsang* province, while the NDRP represented the *Chungcheong* provinces (Lee 1990, 103).

The opposition parties' victory in the National Assembly elections made them even more politically assertive, and they demanded purges of the Chun family and the inner circle of the Fifth Republic for corruption and other unconstitutional deeds. Chun Gyung-hwan, Chun Doo-hwan's brother, was sentenced to seven years in prison for his corrupt behavior during the Fifth Republic. The opposition parties campaigned for an investigation into the military's massacre in the 1980 Gwangju prodemocracy uprising, aiming to identify the one who was ultimately responsible for the shooting. The nationally televised investigations in the National Assembly badly damaged Roh's image and forced him to make Chun offer a public apology to the people for his dictatorial rule and his family's corruption. He later voluntarily moved to a remote Buddhist temple called *Baekdamsa*. Political attacks on Roh came from all political fronts, from both conservatives and progressives. Political pressure came from the old ruling circle from the Fifth Republic whose members were not happy about the National Assembly's investigation and humiliation of Chun. Meanwhile, the progressive forces kept up the belief that Roh, the number-two man in the Chun dictatorship, had to face punishment too.

The political climate of *yeosoyadae* and the resulting political stalemate suddenly ended with a conservative grand alliance. Roh's ruling DJP, Kim Young-sam's UDP, and Kim Jong-pil's NDRP announced on January 22, 1990, a three-party merger to form a new ruling Democratic Liberal Party (DLP). The newly formed DLP controlled 217 of the 299 National Assembly seats, leaving Kim Dae-jung's PPD as the only opposition party that represented the progressive elements of society. The *Honam* region was now completely isolated and encircled. Kim Dae-jung criticized the alliance by claiming that it was a "coup against democracy" and a rebirth of *Yushin* (Lee 1990, 132). The three-party merger marginalized the progressive political voices in Korean politics and allowed the conservatives to hijack post-democratization politics. On the one hand, the conservative grand alliance provided the Roh government with political stability and effectiveness; on the other, it allowed some of the conservatives from the old regime to return to the post-democratization political scene (Park 1990). The Roh Tae-woo presidency had both positive and negative impacts on the ensuing post-democratization politics in South Korea. At a minimum, his presidency did not reverse democratization and return to a military dictatorship. It did create political stability, without which the nascent democracy would have been more violent and unpredictable, with the possibility that politicized officers in the army and old conservatives might have fought back to maintain their political prerogative. On the other hand, the Roh government delayed democratization by keeping democratic reforms to a minimum, and the compromise-based political transition neutralized the momentum to purge authoritarian political legacies completely. The return of old conservatives to post-democratization politics turned out to be detrimental to democratic deepening, which will be discussed in Chapter 3.

The Kim Young-sam government and democratic reform

The conservative grand alliance, or the three-party merger, was an utter shock to South Koreans in general and to progressive pro-democracy groups in particular, as it was considered to be Kim Young-sam's self-denial of his own political identity and betrayal of his pro-democracy comrades. The three-party merger provided Roh with a breakthrough from *yeosoyadae* and political gridlock; for Kim Young-sam, the alliance was a guaranteed way to win the upcoming presidential election. Kim justified his decision as "a grave decision to save the nation" from political paralysis and claimed that he had to "enter a tiger's lair to capture the tiger" (Lee 1990, 134). Roh and the conservative bloc had to put Kim at the forefront of the party and make him the successor to the president; if not, the alliance would have collapsed and politics would have returned to the previous gridlock. In May 1992, the ruling DLP held its party convention to select its candidate for the upcoming presidential election, and Kim Young-sam was nominated with 66.3 percent of delegate support.

The 1992 election and reform drives

Regardless of the conservative alliance's negative impact on Korea's democratization, the 1992 presidential election served as a crucial turning point for furthering democratization. Prior to the election, President Roh announced two important decisions for a stable power transition (Lee, H. 1993, 35–6). First, he declared that he would resign from his leadership position in the DLP and maintain strict political neutrality during the election campaign to make sure that the election was fair and peaceful. Roh's decision prevented senior army officers and old conservatives from the Chun era from interfering in the electoral process. Second, he adopted strict election campaign laws, including reduced periods for campaigning and limited campaign spending to preclude secret political funds from big businesses entering election campaigns. The presidential election had seven candidates, but three of them – Kim Young-sam, Kim Dae-jung, and Jung Ju-young – divided most of the votes. Kim Young-sam won the election with 42 percent of votes, while Kim Dae-jung captured 33.8 percent and Jung Ju-young, the owner of Hyundai Corporation, 16.3 percent (see Table 2.2 for the election outcomes). Kim Dae-jung had now lost three presidential elections in 1971, 1987, and 1992. After the 1992 election, Kim Dae-jung retired from politics and left to take a visiting scholar position at Cambridge University.

Although Kim Young-sam's electoral victory brought the first true civilian leadership to Korean politics since 1961, and therefore can be considered a historic event, pro-democracy groups did not have much to celebrate. "Because of the way in which he had ascended to power," as Kim (1997, 1140) notes, "most civil society groups remained profoundly suspicious about what he could do and would do to break with the authoritarian past and to further the democratic consolidation of South Korea." To the great surprise of such pessimistic forecasts, the Kim Young-sam government lost no time in carrying out decisive and stormy reform drives that were unprecedented in the history of Korean politics. As a matter of fact, Kim Young-sam was in a better position than his predecessor to carry out extensive reforms in every quarter of society, including the government bureaucracy, the military, and the corrupt connections between politics and businesses (especially *chaebols*). He claimed a sense of political legitimacy as the first civilian president elected through a free and fair election, the first since the Second Republic by Jang Myon. Unlike his predecessor who had suffered from a legitimacy deficit, Kim Young-sam boasted a colorful political career as a pro-democracy activist and one of the main pillars of the political opposition under brutal dictatorship. For that reason, he reaped political support from a wide spectrum of political groups, both progressives and conservatives, so that his approval ratings went above 80 percent during the early years of his term (Woo 2011, 113).

The first reform task Kim Young-sam undertook was to put the politically influential military under firm civilian control and reorganize it into a politically neutral organ. He targeted the *Hanahoe* faction that had been the main source of officers' political activism and the backbone of the Chun Doo-hwan dictatorship. Officers of the *Hanahoe* faction occupied some of the most strategically important positions in the army and even in civilian politics. Immediately after becoming president, Kim received a positive response from several high-ranking army generals regarding his plan to demote politically active officers. Within his first year in office, President Kim conducted a massive reshuffling of officers and promoted non-*Hanahoe* officers, while none of the faction members received promotions (Yoon 1996, 512–13; Oh 1999, 133–4; Saxer 2004, 394–5). Furthermore, the president seized an opportunity for military reform through an anti-corruption campaign directed against the military hierarchy in which bribery was commonly used to acquire promotions. Naturally, most of the officers purged were *Hanahoe* members.[5]

President Kim's reform agenda, often called "clean politics," included important legislation such as the Real-Name Financial Transaction System, the Integrated Election Act, and the Political Fund Act. The latter aimed to put legal limits on campaign funds and required political candidates to disclose their personal assets to the public (Kil 2001, 61, 186). For the clean politics initiative, Kim voluntarily disclosed his and his family's assets only two days after assuming office, and all other high-ranking government officials followed suit. In particular, the Real-Name system aimed to stop tax evasion and corrupt connections between businesses and politics by outlawing anonymous or false-name financial transactions and account holdings. With the new system in place, it became increasingly difficult for *chaebols* to donate large amounts of secret funds to politicians. The original purpose of the law was to crack down on illegal financial activities and real estate deals. However, an unexpected outcome was that the law enabled prosecutors to trace huge sums of secret funds accumulated by former presidents Chun and Roh. On October 19, 1995, opposition legislator Park Kye-dong publicized that he had discovered 40 false-name banking accounts that retained approximately $650 million.

Kim Young-sam quickly seized the political momentum to purge previous dictators when nationwide demonstrations erupted to demand punishment of Chun and Roh. With such strong political backing from the general public and civil society groups, the National Assembly passed a special law to investigate bribery scandals, the 1979 coup d'état, and the 1980 Gwangju massacre (Woo 2011, 113). Charges against Chun and Roh included rebellion, murder of military superiors and guards, and corruption. Chun was sentenced to death, Roh received 22 years in prison, and 13 other former generals were also convicted and sentenced to several years of imprisonment. By this time, it was evident that civilian control over the armed forces in Korea had finally occurred, as the two generals-turned-president and other leading figures of the *Hanahoe* were all eliminated from the political scene without the top brass in the military protesting.

Corruption, financial crisis, and the end of the Kim era

The first few years of efforts to eradicate the authoritarian past and rebuild a democratic society had an enervating effect, as the reform drives often looked as if they were politically motivated. Moreover, some of the anti-corruption policies returned as a boomerang that targeted the president's family and close political aides. The biggest political and moral blow to Kim's clean politics campaign came with the bankruptcy of Hanbo Steel Company, then the second-largest steelmaker in Korea, due to $6 billion in debt. This bankruptcy turned out to be a precursor to the 1997 financial crisis (Heo 2001, 155). The investigation revealed that Hanbo had bribed numerous lawmakers, Kim Hyon-cheol (the president's second son), and Hong In-gil (one of the president's closest political aides), for loans from banking and financial institutions (Kim and Lim 2000, 122). Even worse, the investigation also disclosed that President Kim himself had amassed a huge amount of illegal campaign funds for the 1992 presidential election. In the end, most citizens in Korea viewed Kim's political reform drives as political hypocrisy.

Moreover, an inherent limitation on Kim Young-sam's democratic reforms was that the government designed and implemented the reforms in an authoritarian manner. The Kim government was eager to join the Organization for Economic Cooperation and Development (OECD), which required labor reform in South Korea. The labor reform issue engendered a thorny disagreement between labor and business (represented by *chaebols*), along with ruling and opposition political forces. The labor sector demanded that the government legalize unions and protect the rights of workers, while the business sector focused on revising laws to create a more flexible labor market by making it easier to lay off workers. The opposition parties (and leaders such as Kim Dae-jung and Kim Jong-pil) opposed the reform bills, and opposition lawmakers occupied the National Assembly to physically block the legislation. However, the ruling party held a seven-minute legislative session at 4 a.m. on December 26 to unilaterally pass the law without opposition lawmakers present. The legislation significantly curtailed the rights of workers and gave *chaebols* the upper hand. Although the new law recognized the right of free association (i.e., organizing labor unions), it postponed implementation of the right for three years, making labor unions illegal until 1999. Meanwhile, the law made it easier for *chaebols* to lay off workers (Saxer 2002, 191). This "legislative coup" made the opposition forces and labor sectors to even more militantly oppose the Kim government, paralyzing Kim Young-sam's leadership during his final year as president. In the middle of the 1997 financial crisis, Kim Young-sam ended his presidential term with a staggering 8 percent approval rating.

Kim Young-sam's presidency brought into Korean politics an enthusiasm and high hopes for democratic deepening, and he acutely understood the historical mandate given to him. As a symbol of the decades-long fight for democracy and the first true civilian leader since the 1961 coup, he initially garnered political support from across the ideological spectrum, and he used his immense political capital to carry out extensive reforms in virtually every area of society. However, the ways in which he implemented reforms resembled those of his authoritarian predecessors. He had been a fierce combatant for democracy throughout his career, but he ironically never became accustomed to political compromise with his opponents. Another significant limitation of Kim's democratic experiment was that he used the notorious National Security Law against not just left-leaning activists, but also opposition lawmakers. He used this authority as extensively as his authoritarian predecessors, to the point that even the US Department of State expressed that "the use or threatened use of the National Security Law continues to infringe upon citizens' civil liberties, including the right to free expression" (Steinberg 1996, 194). Finally, the Kim government revealed its incapacity to manage the national economy during the 1997 financial crisis. The economic failure brought authoritarian nostalgia, or the so-called Park Jung-hee syndrome, to South Korean society, which reevaluated Park in a more positive light as the leader who brought an economic miracle and modernization to the country. The Park Jung-hee syndrome contributed to the rise of conservative politics and the conservatives' electoral victories in two of the recent presidential elections in 2007 and 2012.

Conclusion

In its fourth attempt at democratic governance, South Korea finally achieved full democracy with the inauguration of the Kim Young-sam administration. The political dynamics of the late twentieth century brought about a nationwide consensus and aspiration to terminate the three-decades-long military dictatorship. Democratization in South Korea represents one of the most successful examples of economic modernization and political development. In particular, although aborted, previous pro-democracy movements from the 1960s provided fertile soil for voluntary civil society activities from different quarters of society, ranging from farmers and urban blue collar workers to college students, religious leaders, and white collar workers and intellectuals. These diverse voices formed a united front for democratization that overwhelmed the seemingly invincible authoritarian government that had monopolized the means of physical violence and terror. The activation of civil society contributed to the nonviolent nature of the democratic transition in South Korea.

However, the remarkable political achievement – democratization through political compromise – also had its own adverse effects on consolidating and deepening democracy in post-democratization South Korea. On the one hand, the compromise-based transition minimized socio-political turmoil and any accompanying physical violence that could derail the political route to democracy. At the early stage of democratization, militant *minjung* movements propelled anti-authoritarian demonstrations that frequently entailed violent resistance to the oppressive regime. However, subsequent pro-democracy movements gained strength through political compromises between reformists' demands and the ruling elites' concessions that led to orderly political transitions. On the other hand, such compromises made the democratic reforms extremely slow and incomplete, thereby hampering the democratic consolidation process thereafter.

As will be illustrated in the next chapter, political compromise – culminating in the conservative grand alliance in 1990 (the three-party merger) – brought back old conservatives from the authoritarian era into post-democratization politics. The conservatives' political platforms included the issue of national security (often identified with anti-communism and anti-North Korea), the National Security Act that severely limited citizens' freedom, and the emphasis on economic growth vis-à-vis socio-economic justice. First, in the post-democratization era, Seoul's policy toward Pyongyang continued to polarize the domestic politics of South Korea between the conservatives and the progressives, especially after the Kim Dae-jung government implemented the Sunshine Policy, or engagement with the North. Second, South Korean citizens have had limited political freedom and rights, as their anti-government protests were often violently suppressed by the state in the name of national security and order. Finally, the emphasis on economic growth put off the government's effort to break the system of corruption between politicians and businesses (i.e., *chaebols*) that had been created during the Park Jung-hee government's state-led industrialization. The result has been systemic corrupt transactions between the political and business elites in an era of democratic consolidation. Indeed, no president after democratization has been immune to rampant political corruption. Chapter 3 clearly illustrates the incomplete break from the past that still encumbers democratic deepening in South Korea.

Notes

1 In 1980, the South Korean economy recorded a negative growth rate (−4.8 percent) for the first time since the Korean War ended in 1953 (the only year with negative growth was 1956 with −1.4 percent). However, the economy quickly recovered from the recession, recording 7.2 percent growth in 1982 and 12.6 percent in 1983.
2 Chun Doo-hwan's DJP endorsed a constitutional revision for the presidential election through a National Assembly vote, while opposition parties demanded a direct popular vote.
3 Historically, the Korean armed forces as an institution never intervened in politics. Only a small number of politically active officers took over political power via coup d'etat. As a result, except for a small segment of officers who were politically active, most military leaders remained politically neutral even during the Park and Chun dictatorships.
4 Although the PPD and the UDP were launched by Kim Dae-jung and Kim Young-sam, respectively, the two Kims were not the official party leaders. They retired from politics after the 1987 presidential election. Kim Dae-jung returned to the party leadership on May 7, 1988, and Kim Young-sam on May 12 the same year.
5 Some of the notable military officers removed by Kim Young-sam included Army Chief of Staff General Kim Jin-yong and Commander of the Defense Security Command Lieutenant General Seo Wan-su. In 1993, more than 50 generals (including seven of nine 4-star generals) were reassigned. Furthermore, about 73 percent of the lieutenant generals and 68 percent of the major generals were relocated (see Oh 1999, 134).

References

Billet, Bret L. 1990. "South Korea at the Crossroads: An Evolving Democracy or Authoritarianism Revisited?" *Asian Survey* 30 (3): 300–11.
Choe, Yonhyok. 2003. *Social Change and Party Support: A Comparison of Japan, South Korea, and the United Kingdom*. Huddinge: Södertörns högskola.
Choi, Jang-jip. 1994. "Political Cleavages in South Korea." In *State and Society in Contemporary Korea*, edited by Hagen Koo, 13–50. Ithaca, NY: Cornell University Press.
Clark, Donald N., ed. 1988. *The Kwangju Uprising: Shadows over the Regime in South Korea*. Boulder, CO: Westview Press.
Cumings, Bruce. 1999. *Parallax Visions: Making Sense of American-East Asian Relations at the End of the Century*. Durham, NC: Duke University Press.
Diamond, Larry. 1999. *Developing Democracy: Toward Consolidation*. Baltimore, MD: Johns Hopkins University Press.
Gills, Barry K. 1996. *Korea Versus Korea: A Case of Contested Legitimacy*. London: Routledge.
Haberman, Clyde. 1987. "South Korea Chief Meets Key Leader of the Opposition." *New York Times*, May 24. Available at: www.nytimes.com/1987/06/24/world/south-korea-chief-meets-key-leader-of-the-opposition.html?pagewanted=all.
Heo, Uk. 2001. "South Korea: Democratization, Financial Crisis, and the Decline of the Developmental State." In *The Political Economy of International Financial Crisis: Interest Groups, Ideologies, and Institutions*, edited by Shale Horowitz and Heo Uk, 151–64. Lanham, MD: Rowman & Littlefield.
Hong, Yong-Pyo. 2000. *State Security and Regime Security: President Syngman Rhee and the Insecurity Dilemma in South Korea, 1953–1960*. New York: St. Martin's Press.
Huntington, Samuel P. 1991. *The Third Wave: Democratization in the Late Twentieth Century*. Norman: University of Oklahoma Press.

Jun, Jinsok. 2001. "South Korea: Consolidating Democratic Civilian Control." In *Coercion and Governance: The Declining Political Role of the Military in Asia*, edited by Muthiah Alagappa, 121–42. Stanford, CA: Stanford University Press.

Kang, David C. 2003. "Regional Politics and Democratic Consolidation in Korea." In *Korea's Democratization*, edited by Samuel S. Kim, 161–80. New York: Cambridge University Press.

Kihl, Young W. 2005. *Transforming Korean Politics: Democracy, Reform, and Culture*. London: M.E. Sharpe.

Kil, Soong Hoom. 2001. "Development of Korean Politics – a Historical Profile." In *Understanding Korean Politics: An Introduction*, edited by Soong Hum Kil and Chung-in Moon, 33–70. Albany: State University of New York Press.

Kim, Byung-Kook, and Lim Hyun-Chin. 2000. "Labor Against Itself: Structural Dilemmas of State Monism." In *Consolidating Democracy in South Korea*, edited by Larry Diamond and Byung-kook Kim, 111–38. Boulder, CO: Lynne Rienner.

Kim, C. I. Eugene. 1978. "Emergency, Development, and Human Rights: South Korea." *Asian Survey* 18 (4): 363–78.

Kim, Sunhyuk. 1997. "State and Civil Society in South Korea's Democratic Consolidation: Is the Battle Really Over?" *Asian Survey* 37 (12): 1135–44.

Kim, Woon-Tai. 2001. "Korean Politics: Setting and Political Culture." In *Understanding Korean Politics: An Introduction*, edited by Soong Hum Kil and Chung-in Moon, 9–32. Albany: State University of New York Press.

Lee, Hong Yung. 1993. "South Korea in 1992: A Turning Point in Democratization." *Asian Survey* 33 (1): 32–42.

Lee, Manwoo. 1990. *The Odyssey of Korean Democracy: Korean Politics, 1987–1990*. New York: Praeger.

Lee, Su-Hoon. 1993. "Transitional Politics of Korea, 1987–1992: Activation of Civil Society." *Pacific Affairs* 66 (3): 351–67.

Lipset, Seymour M. 1959. "Some Social Requisites of Democracy: Economic Development and Political Legitimacy." *American Political Science Review* 53 (1): 69–105.

National Election Commission, Republic of Korea. 2013. *Results of National Assembly Elections*. Seoul: Republic of Korea. Available at: www.nec.go.kr/engvote_2013/main/main.jsp.

Oh, John Kie-chiang. 1999. *Korean Politics: The Quest for Democratization and Economic Development*. Ithaca, NY: Cornell University Press.

Park, Chung Hee. 1961. "What Has Made the Military Revolution Successful?" *Koreana Quarterly* 3 (1): 18–27.

Park, Jin. 1990. "Political Change in South Korea: The Challenge of the Conservative Alliance." *Asian Survey* 30 (12): 1154–68.

Saxer, Carl J. 2002. *From Transition to Power Alternation: Democracy in South Korea, 1987–1997*. New York: Routledge.

Saxer, Carl J. 2004. "Generals and Presidents: Establishing Civilian and Democratic Control in South Korea." *Armed Forces and Society* 30 (3): 366–88.

Steinberg, David I. 1996. "The Republic of Korea: Human Rights, Residual Wrongs, New Initiatives." *Asian Perspective* 20 (2): 185–209.

Woo, Jongseok. 2011. *Security Challenges and Military Politics in East Asia: From State Building to Post-Democratization*. New York: Continuum.

Yoon, Sanghyun. 1996. "South Korea's Kim Young Sam Government: Political Agendas." *Asian Survey* 36 (5): 511–22.

Yoon, Seongyi. 1997. "Democratization in South Korea: Social Movements and Their Political Opportunity Structures." *Asian Perspective* 21 (3): 145–71.

3 Political conflicts and democracy after democratization

Jongseok Woo

This chapter explores post-democratization politics in South Korea, or the era of democratic consolidation. What does 'democratic consolidation' entail? The term conveys an extremely malleable and illusive concept, so no clear consensus on its definition has emerged (Gunther, Diamandorous and Puhle 1996, 5). The multiplicity of meanings has often made it a catch-all term that does not convey a distinct theoretical concept (Schedler 1998, 101). Generally speaking, a new democracy is considered consolidated when the probability of reverting to an authoritarian regime is low. Adam Przeworski (1991, 26), for example, states that

> democracy is consolidated when . . . a particular system of institutions becomes the only game in town, when no one can imagine acting outside the democratic institutions, when all losers want to do is to try again within the same institutions under which they have lost.

Przeworski's depiction represents a minimalist definition of consolidation that focuses on the procedural aspects of democratic transition; a democracy is consolidated when two peaceful turnovers of power occur without interruption. Huntington (1991, 266–7) labels such procedural aspects the "two-turnover test."

Meanwhile, other scholars go beyond the minimal definition to incorporate political developments that occur in various parts of society, such as civil society, political society, economic society, rule of law, and state apparatuses, with three dimensions – behavioral, attitudinal, and constitutional (Linz and Stepan 1996, 6–15). Diamond (1999, 65) suggests that democratic consolidation refers to

> the process of achieving broad and deep legitimation, such that all significant political actors, at both the elite and mass levels, believe that the democratic regime is the most right and appropriate for their society, better than any other realistic alternative they can imagine.

For Diamond (1999, 69), democratic consolidation entails political developments that incorporate both democratic norms and beliefs and behavioral dimensions at three different levels – elite, organization, and mass public. According to this maximalist definition, democratic consolidation involves not merely political procedures but also both elite and mass beliefs in democratic norms and values and their normative commitment to democratic principles. From a minimalist perspective, democratic consolidation is a dichotomous feature; a political regime is democratically consolidated or it is not. From a maximalist standpoint, democratic consolidation exists on a continuum, with different degrees of democratic deepening.

From a minimal or procedural viewpoint, South Korea is undoubtedly a consolidated democracy, as it has passed the two-turnover test, and the possibility of a return to dictatorship does not seem feasible. However, post-democratization politics in South Korea have been mired by political dysfunction, including extreme political, economic, and ideological polarization, rampant political corruption, constrained civil liberties and rights, and security threats from North Korea, to name a few. After three decades of attempts at democracy, both ordinary citizens and experts now express anxiety about the extent of democratic governance in South Korea. This chapter explores the political processes in the era of democratic consolidation that has experienced a full turn from two progressive governments (1998–2008) to two conservative ones (2008–2017). The following sections explain how post-democratization politics have suffered from extreme political polarization and an ensuing crisis in democratic governance.

The rise and fall of progressive politics (1998–2008)

The political transition in South Korea stands as one of the most successful cases of democratization and economic development among the 'third-wave' democratizers around the world. As illustrated in the previous chapter, democratization in South Korea began with the *minjung* (people's) movement at the grassroots level and progressed through political negotiations between ruling and opposition forces at the elite levels. Such compromise-induced transition minimized the possibilities of political violence and socio-economic upheavals that frequently occur in democratizing states. Furthermore, the stable transition paved the road to democratic consolidation, at least in its procedural aspects, with the inauguration of Kim Dae-jung as president in 1998.

At the same time, however, two major legacies of the compromise-based democratic transition became major impediments to democratic deepening in South Korea. First, Kim Young-sam's strategic alliance with conservative forces significantly curtailed the extent of both democratic reforms and purges of old conservatives for their past human rights violations and extra-constitutional activities, including the 1979–1980 coup d'état. Due to the failure to cleanse authoritarian legacies, post-democratization politics in South Korea were destined to be limited in the scope and content of democratic reform. Second, the Kim Young-sam government's mismanagement of the national economy and the 1997 financial crisis triggered an authoritarian nostalgia, or the so-called Park Jung-hee syndrome. Ironically, the political compromises contributed to the stable democratic transition in South Korea in the 1980s and 1990s, but they later became stumbling blocks to democratic deepening.

As the first true civilian-democratic leadership in post-democratization South Korea, the Kim Young-sam government initiated numerous bold reform attempts. His reform efforts ranged from military and security sector reforms, the purging of two former generals-turned-president and their followers for extra-constitutional behaviors, economic reforms that focused on curbing political corruption, and the establishment of autonomy in local governments (albeit not by his will). Kim's bold reform drives garnered unprecedented popularity among ordinary citizens, giving him more than an 80 percent approval rating in 1993, the first year of his presidential term. However, the concluding year of his presidency recorded miserable single-digit public support in the wake of an unprecedented economic crisis, the extent to which the country had not come close to experiencing since industrialization began in the 1960s. The demise of Kim Young-sam and his ruling coalition significantly contributed to the rise of Kim Dae-jung and the decade of progressive politics that extended into the Roh Moo-hyun administration. The next section will examine the political rise, policy agendas, and political successes and failures of the two progressive presidents.

After his fourth run: the Kim Dae-jung presidency (1998–2003)

After losing three elections in 1971, 1987, and 1992, Kim Dae-jung finally won the 15th presidential election in 1997. In his first presidential race in 1971, he lost to Park Jung-hee, who one year later declared martial law and the *Yushin* constitution that perpetuated his dictatorship. During the dictatorship of Park Jung-hee and Chun Doo-hwan, he emerged as a leader of the pro-democracy movement, and he was persecuted until 1987 with imprisonment, house arrests, and assassination attempts. Furthermore, as the leader from *Honam* (southwestern part of the peninsula), Kim was the victim of regional discrimination employed by military regimes whose elites predominantly came from *Yeongnam* (southeastern part of the peninsula).

Ironically, however, Kim Dae-jung has often been criticized as one of the three Kims (along with Kim Young-sam and Kim Jong-pil) who deepened the regional cleavage during and after democratization. The first democratic presidential election in 1987 highlighted the peak of regionalism, as Kim Dae-jung garnered meager single-digit support from *Yeongnam*, while Kim Young-sam did the same from *Honam*. In 1997, Kim Dae-jung finally won the presidential election mainly due to the political split within the ruling party and his political coalition with Kim Jong-pil and his United Liberal Democrats (ULD), a conservative party based in the *Chungcheong* provinces. The ruling New Korea Party (NKP) split during the presidential primaries, as Lee In-je did not accept his defeat from the presidential primary and instead ran for election as the candidate of the New People's Party, a spinoff from the ruling NKP. Ultimately, Kim Dae-jung took advantage of the division within conservative voters between Lee Hoe-chang (with 38.7 percent) and Lee In-je (with 19.2 percent). It would not have been possible for Kim to win the election without the factional split within the ruling circle and the strategic coalition with Kim Jong-pil's ULD.

The victory of Kim Dae-jung signified monumental progress in South Korean politics, as it was the first peaceful leadership transition to an opposition candidate through a free and fair election. Moreover, the Kim presidency ended almost four decades of conservative rule that included three generals-turned-president and Kim Young-sam, who aligned with the conservative forces from pre-democratization politics. As the first progressive president in post-democratization South Korea, Kim Dae-jung had several major policy agendas: salvaging the failing national economy from the previous government, unifying a South Korean society that had been polarized by region and ideology, and terminating the Cold War legacy and building peace on the Korean Peninsula. This section will examine three of the most important policy priorities of the Kim Dae-jung government: economic reform, national reconciliation, and the Sunshine Policy.

The 1997 financial crisis revealed that the country could no longer sustain the developmental state model of the economy in which the government had played a dominant role in economic policymaking and implementation. Park Jung-hee's model of government-led industrialization had once brought about unprecedented economic growth, but it was now blamed for the crisis. Suddenly, "expedient" government-business relations turned out to be highly "corrupt, inefficient, and backward" (Kang 2002, 3). Although tightly controlled by the authoritarian government, the business sector (and especially *chaebols*) had received preferential benefits with generous policy loans, tax breaks, and other favors at the expense of small and medium-sized businesses, urban laborers, and farmers (Kim 2001, 17). In particular, Park Jung-hee's government-led industrialization provided a small number of *chaebols* with enormous favoritism, while disadvantaging other participants in the market, thereby creating massive systemic corruption between the state and market. Such corrupt collusion between state and market functioned well under the strong authoritarian state. However, the businesses slowly came out of state control during democratization. Free from government control, big businesses pursued adventurous and risky investments to expand their business territory by lobbying politicians for 'easy loans.'

The Kim government's reform initiatives were never comprehensive or effective enough to sever the cozy connections between the government and big businesses. Instead, the Kim government itself was the main source of corruption scandals, as his second son, Hyun-chul, and other close political aides, were convicted of exerting influence and accepting bribes. As domestically driven reform efforts failed, the South Korean economy had to accept the bitter pill of restructuring as imposed by the International Monetary Fund (IMF). The IMF demanded extensive structural reforms, including budget cuts, higher tax rates, the opening up of financial markets to foreigners, and, most importantly, the restructuring of *chaebols* and increased transparent government-business relations (Park 1999, 133–4).

The 1997 financial crisis caused the first major recession in South Korea since the 1960s, and the IMF-imposed restructuring was even more painful to all constituents of society. The restructuring provoked socio-political conflicts among bureaucrats, *chaebols*, and laborers over who to blame for the economic turmoil and who would take on the burden of restructuring. On one hand, there was a strong consensus to promptly comply with the IMF's demands and then return to normalcy. Such general consensus brought about nationwide grassroots movements to rescue the economy by voluntarily selling gold to help pay the nation's foreign debt, which amounted to well over $30 billion. Approximately 3.5 million citizens, or about 10 percent of the entire population, donated more than 227 tons of gold. This voluntary movement for economic recovery touched the everyday lives of citizens, who cut consumption, saved more, and bought products made in South Korea (Pollack 1997). For the Kim Dae-jung government, the IMF-sanctioned reform presented the opportunity for a complete overhaul of the *chaebol*-dominated economy.

At the same time, however, the IMF-imposed economic restructuring brought about intense political fighting over who should bear the burdens of the reform. Big businesses blamed militant labor unions, while workers criticized the family-owned conglomerates' unprincipled and risk-taking managements and their corrupt ties with bureaucrats. The IMF's restructuring package focused on reforming *chaebols* and the financial, public, and especially labor sectors. To build a nationwide consensus over reform, the government launched the Tripartite Commission, called *No-Sa-Jeong Wiwonhoe*, or labor-business-government commission. The Commission aimed to dismantle decades-long corrupt ties between the state and *chaebols* and to scale down *chaebols*' dominance over the South Korean economy. For the first time in modern South Korean history, the labor sector was recognized as an equal partner with the government and business for economic policymaking. The Commission's first priority was to recognize the union rights of labor and to identify fair burden-sharing between business and labor. *Chaebols* would take responsibility for mismanagement and the resulting national economic crisis, while labor would stop a nationwide labor strike that dated back to the final months of Kim Young-sam's presidency.

In a sense, the nationwide consensus, or the so-called social compromise, became possible because the unprecedented financial crisis brought a sense of urgency to all constituents of society. However, the social compromise quickly dissipated when the economy showed signs of improvement in the first few months of the Kim presidency (Kihl 2005, 167). Both the labor and the business sectors became ever more impatient: Labor protested that the government had unfairly imposed the burden of reform on the labor sector, while business wanted freedom from tight government control and a crackdown on illegal labor strikes. Labor disputes continued to grow throughout the Kim presidency: For instance, the number of labor strikes in 1999 was 129, but that number rose to 250 the following year; legal accusations amounted to 262 and 586 for the same years. Meanwhile, the concentration of the economy within the 30 largest *chaebols* intensified after the reforms (Choi 2015, 201–7).

Another pressing agenda item for the Kim government was to terminate the half-century-long animosity between the two Koreas. After the peaceful German reunification, the Korean Peninsula was left as the last bastion of the worldwide military and ideological confrontations of the Cold War. In his presidential inaugural address, Kim Dae-jung proclaimed three policy principles toward South Korea's northern counterpart: no tolerance of armed provocation of any kind, no intention to undermine or absorb North Korea, and the active pursuit of reconciliation and cooperation between the two Koreas. He expressed a willingness to expand economic, cultural, and academic exchanges and stressed that he was ready to hold a summit if Pyongyang wanted (Kim 1998). His Sunshine Policy separated politico-military confrontation from economic relations and focused on expanding economic cooperation to rescue poverty-stricken North Korea. Economic engagement, he hoped, would have a spillover effect to reduce military tensions and build mutual trust (Moon 2001).

The Sunshine Policy culminated in the historic summit between Kim Dae-jung and Kim Jong-il on June 13–15, 2000, the first such meeting since the two separate Korean governments were established in 1948. The summit produced the June 15th North–South Joint Declaration that agreed to resolve humanitarian issues, such as reunions of separated family members, expansion of economic, social, and cultural changes, and ultimately Korean reunification. In the same year, the joint declaration led to two rounds of reunions for families separated between the two Koreas, the first on August 15–18, and the second on November 30 and December 1. Both parties also agreed to regular and institutionalized meetings, including the next summit to be held in Seoul, although it did not happen. Furthermore, surprisingly, Kim Jong-il did not insist on Pyongyang's decades-long demand for the withdrawal of American troops stationed in South Korea, even after a peace treaty had replaced the existing armistice agreement (Kihl 2005, 252). The Sunshine Policy led to Kim Dae-jung winning the Nobel Peace Prize in 2000.

However, the Sunshine Policy and the North–South reconciliation did not progress further due to unfavorable internal and external circumstances. The biggest stumbling block to the Sunshine Policy came from the George W. Bush administration (2001–2009), which was highly critical of Pyongyang from its beginning. Upon inauguration, Bush alleged that Pyongyang had been violating the 1994 Agreed Framework by secretly continuing nuclear projects. The 9/11 terrorist attacks resulted in the Bush administration becoming even more belligerent; in his State of the Union address in 2002, President George Bush called North Korea (with Iran and Iraq) an "axis of evil" that destabilized international security and promoted global terrorism. Bush's 'axis of evil' speech and ensuing invasion of Iraq frightened Kim Jong-il enough to accelerate his nuclear weapons program. In January 2003, North Korea declared its withdrawal from the Nuclear Non-proliferation Treaty (NPT) and reopened the Yongbyon nuclear facilities.

The Kim Dae-jung government made efforts to bring the two nations to the negotiation table to save his Sunshine Policy. During his visit to Washington, DC in 2001, Kim requested that Bush resume talks with Pyongyang, which Bush flatly rejected due to North Korea's 'lack of transparency.' The summit not only failed to alleviate tensions between Pyongyang and Washington, but it also aggravated US–South Korean relations. Feeling humiliated, Kim Dae-jung openly expressed his displeasure and embarrassment toward Bush. Meanwhile, Bush's rhetoric became even more provocative than before, as he called Kim Jong-il a 'pygmy,' expressing a willingness to topple the dictatorial regime (Cumings 2005, 504). The policy discrepancies between Washington and Seoul brought about anti-Americanism among ordinary citizens in South Korea, many of whom believed that Bush's policy destabilized South Korea's security. In a public opinion survey conducted in 2002, a majority of Koreans expressed a belief that the United States posed a greater security threat than North Korea (Woo 2011, 158).

While President Kim fought uphill battles to alleviate hostilities between Washington and Pyongyang, a more direct challenge to his Sunshine Policy came from the domestic political front. Conservatives in South Korea condemned Kim's Sunshine Policy for its lack of reciprocity. The conservative opposition Grand National Party (GNP) utilized Kim's North Korea policy as a platform for political attacks on the Kim government. The opposition GNP became more militant after it defeated the ruling Millennium Democratic Party (MDP) in the 16th National Assembly election held in April 2000, in which the GNP secured 133 of the total 273 seats, while the ruling MDP gained 115, as Table 3.1 indicates. The conservatives' opposition to the Sunshine Policy acquired broader popular support with increasing armed provocations by North Korea. In the year Kim declared the Sunshine principles, North Korea attempted a submarine infiltration into the South and test-fired a multi-stage, long-range missile, called *Daepodong* 1, over the northern islands of Japan. The next year, North Korean patrol boats crossed the Northern Limit Line, a United Nations (UN)-demarcated border across the West Sea, in an attempt to nullify the Armistice Agreement. This so-called Battle of Yeonpyeong entailed armed conflict between the two Koreas. The second Battle of Yeonpyeong in June 2002 involved a larger armed conflict with casualties on both sides. Continuing armed provocations from Pyongyang strengthened the opposition GNP's political standing, while weakening domestic support for Kim's North Korea policy.

The third political priority for Kim Dae-jung was national reconciliation for a country that was ideologically, regionally, and economically polarized. For that purpose, Kim pardoned the two former generals-turned-president – Chun Doo-hwan and Roh Tae-woo – who had each received a death sentence and a long jail term for their 1979–1980 coup, human rights violations, and corruption. Although they were released by Kim Young-sam in December 1997, the decision was made through mutual agreement with Kim Dae-jung. The pardon was Kim Dae-jung's symbolic gesture to alleviate regional divisions, especially between conservative and wealthier *Yeongnam* and progressive and discriminated *Honam* (the president's political stronghold). The three-decades-long military dictatorships and their ruling elites had come from the *Yeongnam* region and they fostered the regional division for their political hegemony. Furthermore, regionalism intensified during the democratization with two Kims representing their regions. Kim Dae-jung was acutely aware that national unity would be possible only by embracing *Yeongnam*, the region he had defeated in the presidential election.

However, his efforts toward reconciliation largely failed, as reflected in the 16th National Assembly election held in April 2000. In a sense, the election was considered a mid-term referendum on the president's performance in fomenting economic recovery and restructuring (Kihl 2005, 210). In the election, the *Honam*-based ruling MDP took all 29 seats from *Honam* (including four independents who later joined the party), while the *Yeongnam*-based opposition GNP swept 64 out of 65 seats assigned to the region. The electoral outcome

Table 3.1 National Assembly election outcomes, 2000–2016

	Parliamentary Seats Captured		Party Name
	Ruling Party	Opposition Parties	
16th National Assembly election (April 13, 2000)	115		Millennium Democratic Party
		133	Grand National Party
		17	United Liberal Democrats
		2	Democratic People's Party
		1	Hopeful of New Korea Party
		5	Independent
		Total Seats: 273	
17th National Assembly election (April 15, 2004)	152		Uri Party
		121	Grand National Party
		9	Millennium Democratic Party
		4	United Liberal Democrats
		10	Democratic Labor Party
		3	Independent
		Total Seats: 299	
18th National Assembly election (April 9, 2008)	81		Democratic United Party
		153	Grand National Party
		18	Liberty Forward Party
		5	Democratic Labor Party
		3	Creative Korea Party
		14	Pro-Park Coalition
		25	Independent
		Total Seats: 299	
19th National Assembly Election (April 11, 2012)	152		Saenuri Party
		127	Democratic United Party
		5	Liberty Forward Party
		13	United Progressive Party
		3	Independent
		Total Seats: 300	
20th National Assembly Election (April 13, 2016)	122		Saenuri Party
		123	The Minju Party of Korea
		38	The People's Party
		6	Justice Party
		11	Independent
		Total Seats: 300	

Source: National Election Commission, Republic of Korea. 2016. Available at www.nec.go.kr/portal/main.do.

succinctly demonstrated deep regional antagonism in the country. Furthermore, the electoral defeat by the ruling MDP precipitated political gridlock and accelerated the presidential lame duck status.

Another source of political polarization was critical media, especially conservative newspapers that included *Chosun Ilbo, Jungang Ilbo*, and *Dong-a Ilbo*, which combined accounted for approximately 70 percent of the total media market in South Korea. These media outlets appealed to conservative constituents who distrusted Kim Dae-jung and his political coalition for their 'pro-North Korean' stance. The Kim government responded by investigating 23 newspaper companies for tax evasion. The media and conservatives criticized the investigation as the government's attempt to censor the mass media and influence the 2002 presidential election. The owners of the above-mentioned three newspapers were arrested for tax evasion amounting to 500 billion *won* (or about $380 million) (Ha 2002, 59–60).

Similar to his predecessor's, the Kim Dae-jung government's final year suffered power-lessness due to his lame duck status. He admitted that his economic reform policies were not much successful, and he offered a public apology for his policy failures. In particular, corruption scandals within his political inner circle, involving two of his three sons, dealt a final blow to President Kim's moral cause as a decades-long pro-democracy activist and recipient of the Nobel Peace Prize. Moreover, his Sunshine Policy suffered even further when news revealed that his government had offered Pyongyang a financial donation in return for holding the 2000 North–South summit. Ultimately, Kim Dae-jung's efforts at economic restructuring, national reconciliation, and peace-building with Pyongyang only further deepened South Korea's regional and ideological cleavages.

A human rights lawyer: the Roh Moo-hyun presidency (2003–2008)

Roh Moo-hyun's presidential inauguration in 2003 marked a new era of democratic politics in South Korea in several ways. The Roh presidency finally ended the old legacy of the three Kims – Kim Young-sam, Kim Dae-jung, and Kim Jong-pil – who had commanded their own region-based parties in the 1980s and 1990s. Furthermore, the Roh government began with a much more positive environment than its predecessor: Inter-Korean relations improved after the Sunshine Policy, democracy became further consolidated, and the economy returned to normalcy. South Koreans expected the Roh presidency to further advance the democratic process, engage Pyongyang more deeply, and continue economic prosperity. Contrary to such high expectations, however, the Roh presidency met with further political polarization, including intensified regional cleavages, increasing economic inequality, and Pyongyang's first nuclear test in 2006. In the end, Roh's progressive politics did not fare well or gain broad-based popular support, and the Korean political pendulum soon swung to the conservative side.

As a long time human rights lawyer, Roh began his political career by winning the 13th National Assembly election held in 1988. Although he was brought into politics by Kim Young-sam, he severed his political ties with him after the 1990 three-party merger. Later he became the protégé of Kim Dae-jung, serving as Minister of the Oceans and Fisheries (August 2000-March 2001). Although he was from *Yeongnam*, he never enjoyed a hometown advantage in his elections, losing the 1995 mayoral election in the city of Busan and the 16th National Assembly election in 2000 in the same city. Early in the presidential primary within the ruling MDP, Roh was one of the minor candidates with single-digit popular support. As had been the case in his early career, Roh was not a frontrunner in his hometown of *Yeongnam* but, ironically, he won the primary by garnering substantial support from *Honam*.

In December 2002, Roh Moo-hyun won the 16th presidential election in a close competition in which he collected 48.9 percent of the popular vote, while his rival, Lee Hoe-chang, from the opposition GNP, received 46.6 percent, as Table 3.2 indicates.

The Roh presidency signified a new era of democratic politics in South Korea. He mobilized support from a younger generation, ended the faction-ridden boss politics of the earlier generation, and overcame regional divisions. Roh's self-proclaimed "participatory democracy" brought about several major policy initiatives that were intended to carry out reforms and foster national unity. They included reshaping the US–Republic of Korea (ROK) alliance, improving inter-Korean relations, curbing political corruption, and expanding the social welfare system (Lee 2004, 132). Following the political paths of his predecessor, President Roh made significant progress in democratic deepening with much improved individual freedoms. However, as a political 'outsider,' his ambitious political initiatives met

Table 3.2 Presidential election outcomes, 1997–2017

Election (Year)	Candidates	Parties	% of Votes
16th presidential election (Dec. 19, 2002)	Lee Hoe-chang	Grand National Party	46.58
	Roh Moo-hyun	Millennium Democratic Party	48.91
	Others	Four Minor Parties	4.47
17th presidential election (Dec. 19, 2007)	Jung Dong-yeong	United New Democratic Party	26.14
	Lee Myung-bak	Grand National Party	48.67
	Lee Hoe-chang	Independent	15.07
	Others	Seven Minor Parties	10.07
18th presidential election (Dec. 19, 2012)	**Park Geun-hye**	Saenuri Party	51.55
	Moon Jae-in	Democratic United Party	48.02
	Others	Four Independents	0.41
19th presidential election (May 9, 2017)	**Moon Jae-in**	The Minju Party of Korea	41.08
	Hong Joon-pyo	Liberty Party of Korea	24.03
	Ahn Cheol-soo	People's Party	21.41
	Ryu Seung-min	Bareun Party	6.76
	Sim Sang-jung	Justice Party	6.17

Source: National Election Commission, Republic of Korea. 2017. *Results of Presidential Elections*. Available at www.nec.go.kr/portal/main.do.

with fierce opposition and further polarized the society along ideological and generational lines on major policy issues.

The new president aimed to restructure South Korea's security alliance with the United States, which had broad implications for the country's political place in East Asia. Even before his presidential inauguration, many observers had expected that the US–ROK alliance would be rocky, considering that the election was held at the height of anti-American demonstrations in South Korea. The alliance had already been strained during the final years of the Kim Dae-jung government, largely due to differences between Seoul and Washington regarding North Korea. During the presidential election campaign, Roh Moo-hyun rode on the growing anti-American demonstrations that swept the country after two middle school girls were killed by an American armored vehicle. President Roh was eager to redefine South Korea's security policy direction from a committed American ally to a balancer in East Asia. Seeking a more 'sovereign' foreign policy stance, Roh repeatedly announced ambitious military modernization programs in air, sea, and land forces to go beyond the one-dimensional force to deter the North Korean threat. The Bush administration responded by announcing its plan to relocate all US troops in the Demilitarized Zone (DMZ) further south and to downsize the overall US military presence in South Korea.

The strained alliance instantaneously affected the domestic politics of South Korea, dividing the country across generations and ideologies. The younger generation (often called the *386 generation*: in their 30s, attended college in the 1980s, and born in the 1960s) generally welcomed a more independent foreign policy, expressed confidence in the country's military strength in deterring North Korean aggression, and therefore supported bringing back the Wartime Operation Control from the United States. Meanwhile, the older generation, more conservative and many with personal memories of the Korean War, fiercely opposed Roh's foreign policy re-direction. In a public opinion survey conducted in 2003, more than 63 percent of the younger generation supported the country's independent foreign policy, while 91 percent of the older generation (50 years or older) called for a restoration of the US–ROK alliance (Cha 2005, 36–7).

Roh's progressive supporters criticized his decision to contribute to the US war on terrorism by deploying its military forces to Iraq and Afghanistan and providing financial support to rebuild those war-ravaged countries. Certainly, the decision was not in line with the majority opinion in the country. In a public opinion poll conducted in 2003, less than 10 percent of respondents in South Korea supported America's war in Iraq, 75.6 percent opposed the deployment of Korean troops to Iraq, and only 16 percent supported the decision (Cha 2005, 38). In another poll conducted immediately after Pyongyang's first nuclear test in 2006, 43 percent of respondents criticized the Bush administration, 36 percent blamed North Korea, and only 13 percent accused South Korea's engagement policy (Kang 2007, 115). Given South Korea's strong opposition to the Bush administration's policies in the Middle East and North Korea, Roh's decision to support the US war on terror further antagonized his own political supporters.

At the same time, political opposition also came from the conservatives who criticized the Roh government's policies as 'political amateurism.' In particular, conservative media outlets emerged as the vanguard of the anti-Roh forces. They criticized the president's inconsistency in his policy decisions, his 'radical left' past (and his father-in-law's pro-North Korean background in the 1940s), and unconditional economic engagement with North Korea. In the first year of his presidency, Roh sued four newspapers – *Chosun Ilbo, Dong-a Ilbo, Jungang Ilbo*, and *Hankuk Ilbo* – for their false allegations that Roh was hiding real estate assets under his brother's name among other reports surrounding his family. He personally declared "a war against misreporting" (Kihl 2005, 303). Throughout his presidency and until his suicide in 2008 amid allegations of corruption surrounding his family, the conservative media served as his most tenacious critics.

In domestic politics, the Roh government initiated the so-called *4-dae gaehyok ipbeop* (four reform legislations) that included the National Security Law, media law, education law (that would affect private schools in particular), and the Truth and Reconciliation Law. After the ruling Uri Party won a majority status with 152 seats in the 17th National Assembly election in 2004 (see Table 3.1), the president and his ruling party pushed for the four reform bills that became politically contentious and ideologically divisive. Since the National Security Law was enacted in 1948, presidents from Rhee Syngman through Roh Tae-woo (and even Kim Young-sam) frequently used the law to curtail freedom of expression and association in the name of national security. Even after democratization, the law continued to function "as a tool to attempt to silence dissidents, and to harass and arbitrarily prosecute individuals and civil society organizations who are peacefully exercising their rights to freedom of expression, opinion and association" (Amnesty International 2012). The ruling Uri Party failed to abolish the law due to fierce opposition from the conservative GNP that obtained support from right-wing civil society groups and conservative media.

Meanwhile, the Truth and Reconciliation Law – the only one of four reform bills passed by the National Assembly – aimed to uncover the truth about pro-Japanese collaborators during the Japanese occupation as well as injustices committed by the military regimes. While it was vital to deepening democracy and reconciliation in South Korea, the Roh administration's and ruling Uri Party's decisions ironically polarized the country even further. In 2005, the government instituted the Truth and Reconciliation Commission, which found more than 1,000 cases of mass executions, including more than 200 cases of innocent civilians killed by US troops during the Korean War. Although it would achieve social justice, the investigation – especially of the Park Jung-hee and Chun Doo-hwan eras – was often criticized as politically motivated (Kim, Y. 2011, 156). Conservatives alleged that it was a political scheme to discredit popular opposition leader Park Geun-hye, the daughter of Park Jung-hee, who had collaborated with Japan as an officer of the Japanese Imperial Army. Furthermore, ironically, it revealed the family history of Shin Ki-nam, chair of the ruling Uri Party, whose father served in the military police during the colonial period. Shin had to resign from his post. While the Commission harmed some of Roh's own political attendants, it immediately became a target of criticism by the opposition GNP. Likewise, the other remaining bills – the Media Reform Law and the Private School Law – brought about further political division between progressives and conservatives.

Roh's presidency suffered from a lack of presidential power, making him perhaps the weakest presidential figure in post-democratization Korean politics. His presidential weakness partially came from his own desire to make his office more democratic by decentralizing political power. At the same time, his political weakness stemmed from his lack of leadership in his own party and a stalwart opposition party that controlled the National Assembly. After just more than a year in office, Roh was impeached by the National Assembly on two counts of illegal campaign funding and openly campaigning for the ruling Uri Party, although the Constitutional Court nullified the impeachment and restored his presidential power immediately. On one hand, the impeachment was a clear testament to how far South Korea's democracy had been consolidated; on the other, it revealed the extent of polarization in the political system that forced the government to stop functioning (Faiola 2004).

One monumental achievement of the Roh administration was the opening of the Kaesong Industrial Complex, which is located just north of the DMZ. With joint investment by the South Korean government and more than one hundred companies that hired about 54,000 workers from North Korea, the industrial park became the first tangible outcome of Seoul's effort to engage Pyongyang economically. Although the Complex effectively reduced military tensions between the two Koreas, it immediately met with opposition from both Washington and the conservatives in South Korea. Opposition conservatives especially attacked Roh's engagement policy after North Korea's first nuclear test in October 2006. President Roh supported UN-led sanctions, but at the same time, he was willing to continue engagement and inter-Korean dialogue. His critics alleged that Pyongyang developed nuclear weapons using the financial gains from economic engagement. They urged Roh to stop all business with Pyongyang and participate in UN-led sanctions (Kim and Lie 2007, 53–4). Although a majority of businesses in South Korea supported economic engagement, the opposition gained popularity during the final years of Roh's presidency. North Korea's nuclear test had resurrected a Cold War mentality and anti-communist feelings in South Korean society that had largely been forgotten for more than a decade.

Another significant accomplishment for Roh Moo-hyun's presidency was holding a second North–South summit in October 2007. The summit produced several agreements to improve inter-Korean relations, including creating a special peace and cooperation zone in the West Sea, expanding the Kaesong Industrial Complex further, reconstructing the railways across the DMZ, and opening a direct flight between Seoul and Mount Baekdu, among other steps. (Oberdorfer and Carlin 2014, 439–40). While ambitious enough to advance inter-Korean relations, few expected the agreement to materialize due to unfavorable domestic and international environments. Given the economic sanctions imposed on North Korea for its nuclear program, the inter-Korean economic cooperation had to be limited. A more direct obstacle to the agreement came from the domestic opposition, as public opinion had become increasingly skeptical about the engagement policy. Lee Myung-bak's landslide victory in the 2007 presidential election demonstrated popular rejection of the Roh government's policy initiatives.

Resurgence of conservative politics (2008–2017)

The decline of progressive politics brought back conservatism and the rise of Lee Myung-bak and his ruling GNP in the 2007 presidential and 2008 National Assembly elections. Lee Myung-bak won the 17th presidential election with 48.67 percent of the popular vote, while ruling party candidate Jung Dong-young gained a meager 26.14 percent. Such a wide margin of victory was remarkable considering that Lee Hoe-chang, another conservative candidate who ran as an independent, split the conservative vote, taking 15.07 percent, as Table 3.2 illustrates. Moreover, in the 18th National Assembly election held in April 2018, only slightly more than a month after Lee assumed the presidency, the GNP won 153 out of 299 seats, while the new opposition Democratic United Party (DUP) took a scant 81 seats. Meanwhile, the Pro-Park Coalition, a conservative political faction that grew out of the GNP, took 14 seats. All combined, conservative parties (including conservative-leaning independents) occupied more than 200 seats in the National Assembly (see Table 3.1 for the seat distribution).

The conservatives' electoral victories demonstrated that the previous two presidents had failed to satisfy the majority of South Koreans with their management of inter-Korean relations and the national economy. The conservatives garnered popularity with the "lost decade" slogan, suggesting that the progressives' engagement of Pyongyang had ended up giving "away too much while asking too little of the North Koreans" (Oberdorfer and Carlin 2014, 441). Citizens' support for the slogan also meant that they had not been satisfied with how progressive governments had handled the national economy, although the progressive decade (1998–2007) had recorded an annual average of 4.8 percent growth in gross domestic product (GDP) (World Bank 2016). While the number looks quite impressive given that it includes a −5.71 percent in 1998 at the height of the financial crisis, it ultimately failed to impress ordinary citizens who remembered three decades of phenomenal economic growth under authoritarian regimes.

Citizens' dissatisfaction gave rise to the so-called authoritarian nostalgia, or the Park Jung-hee syndrome. Many citizens in South Korea yearned for the dictator they had fought fiercely to overthrow in the 1970s. The *Merriam-Webster's Dictionary* defines nostalgia as, "pleasure and sadness that is caused by remembering something from the past . . . a wishful or expressively sentimental yearning for return to or some past period or irrecoverable condition." In South Korea, authoritarian nostalgia always refers to the Park Jung-hee leadership and citizens' desire to repeat the economic modernization that the military dictator brought to the country. At the same time, however, the Park Jung-hee syndrome involves something more than the economy, because the South Korean economy recorded much higher rates of growth during the administrations of Chun Doo-hwan (1979–1988) and Roh Tae-woo (1988–1993), two of the most unpopular political figures in South Korea.

How could Park Jung-hee become the most popular figure among nine South Korean presidents since 1948? Park always comes first as the most admired national leader in numerous public opinion polls conducted since 1997. In a 1997 poll by Gallup Korea, more than 80 percent of respondents positively evaluated Park (Kang 2010). In a Gallup poll conducted in 2015, 93.3 percent of respondents positively evaluated Park's contribution to the economic development of South Korea (Gallup Korea 2015). The same poll asked, "which president did the best job leading the country after liberation?" and 44 percent chose Park Jung-hee, followed by Roh Moo-hyun (24 percent) and Kim Dae-jung (14 percent). Those who chose Park identified economic development, the "New Village Movement" (called *Saemaul Undong*), and improved citizen well-being as his prominent legacies.

Originally, Park Jung-hee had been a popular political figure among a small segment of Koreans, especially those who were older, less educated, relatively poor, and in rural areas. However, the political resurgence of Park Jung-hee was associated with two closely related events: the 1997 financial crisis and the emergence of Park Geun-hye as the iconic leader of the conservative movement in South Korea. The Park Jung-hee syndrome sprang out of ordinary citizens' frustration with Kim Young-sam's mismanagement of the national economy, which was in complete disarray in his administration's final year. The unprecedented economic crisis brought back memories of economic miracles under Park's dictatorship. The reevaluation of Park Jung-hee in the light of financial crisis enabled Park Geun-hye, Park's eldest daughter, to rise as the leader of the conservative movement after a decade of progressive governance. Ordinary citizens, in particular, those who were older, less educated, ideologically conservative, and from rural areas, quickly associated Park Geun-hye's leadership style with her father's. However, it was Lee Myung-bak who first gained electoral success from the Park Jung-hee syndrome.

The "Korea 7–4–7 Plan": the Lee Myung-bak presidency (2008–2013)

The Lee Myung-bak presidency signified the fall of progressive politics and the rise of conservatism in South Korea. In some ways, Lee's early life experiences overlapped with the Park Jung-hee era. He was born and raised in a poor family but became the chief executive officer of the Hyundai construction company at the age of 35. After he began his political career in the ruling Democratic Liberal Party for the 14th and 15th National Assemblies (in 1992 and 1996, respectively), he was charged in multiple corruption cases, including violations of election campaign laws during the 1996 election that had nullified his seat in the Assembly. However, he salvaged his political career by winning the Seoul mayoral election in 2002. While mayor, Lee re-invented his image as the chief executive officer of Seoul, as an effective policy leader who carried out innovative projects such as restoring the *Cheonggyecheon* (a narrow creek that runs through downtown Seoul), reformatting the city's public transportation system, opening the Seoul Forest Park, and successfully hosting the 2002 FIFA World Cup. When he officially declared his run for the presidency, many citizens in South Korea hoped that he would be the one to repeat Park Jung-hee's "Miracle on the Han River."

Such high expectations allowed many voters not to worry about numerous corruption charges against Lee. Immediately after he won the GNP primary, a rumor emerged that Lee owned land in Dogok-dong, Gangnam-gu, under his brother's name. Another corruption rumor involved Lee's relationship with BBK, a company whose owner, Kim Kyung-joon, faced charges of large-scale embezzlement and manipulation of stock prices. Kim and Lee established the LTE Bank in 1999 but, a year later, it went bankrupt, and about 5,500 investors lost their money. Rumors continued to emerge that Lee was involved with the company, although Lee denied the allegation and the Supreme Court declared his innocence on all charges. Such corruption scandals did not bother citizens, as the national economy was their primary concern. In a public opinion survey conducted during the 2007 campaign, approximately 55 percent of respondents identified the economy as the most important issue, while only 11.4 percent believed peace on the Korean Peninsula was most important (Lie and Kim 2008, 123). Lee Myung-bak's campaign slogan focused on the national economy with the *7–4–7 Plan*: 7 percent annual growth in GDP, $40,000 GDP per capita, and elevating South Korea into the world's seventh largest economy by the end of his presidency.

President Lee possessed strong political capital from an unprecedented landslide victory against his presidential rival, with a winning margin of more than 5.2 million votes and his party's dominant legislative majority in the National Assembly election. However, his political power quickly evaporated in the first year of his presidency, largely due to new policy directions and his 'entrepreneur-style' leadership that often clashed with democratic political procedures. The Lee government's major policy initiatives included a revival of the national economy through deregulation, privatization, lower tax rates, and further free trade agreements with major economic partners. Meanwhile, President Lee's foreign policy aimed at a complete overhaul by abandoning the Sunshine Policy and restoring an alliance with the United States that had become tenuous at best.

In less than three months after his presidential inauguration, Lee found himself engaged in a confrontation with his own people. His presidential approval rating plummeted to below 20 percent in June 2008, bounced back to 30 percent in the wake of the Beijing Olympics in August, but went down to mid-20 percent throughout his remaining years in office (Gallup Korea 2013). Criticism from the mass media and citizens began when the president formed his cabinet. The media coined the sarcastic terms, *KoSoYoung*, the name of a famous South Korean actress, but it actually referred to *Ko*rea University (the president's alma mater), *So*mang Presbyterian Church (which the president attended), and the *Yeong*nam Province (the president's hometown), and *Gangbuja*, again, the name of an actress, but meaning "wealthy landowners living in the Gangnam area" (Moon 2009, 123). His cabinet candidates came from a narrow pool based on specific regional, religious, and school ties. Even worse, most of the first-year cabinet members faced a variety of corruption charges. Thirteen out of 15 ministerial candidates that the president had nominated for legislative approval were found to have violated laws pertaining to real estate speculation, tax evasion, academic plagiarism, and false resident registration.

As much as he wanted to be CEO of 'Korea Inc.,' his political leadership style often discounted the democratic process of consensus-building across political parties and the general public. For instance, on a visit to Camp David for a summit meeting with George W. Bush less than two months after his inauguration, the president announced that his government was going to lift the 2003 ban on imports of American beef that had been a precautionary measure after an outbreak of mad cow disease in the United States. He made the announcement two days before the summit as a political gesture to Washington. However, the announcement triggered mass demonstrations against the decision and called for renegotiation of the terms of imports of American beef. The Lee government deployed the police to put down the demonstrations by force, and he criticized the protests as orchestrated by "impure elements," such as radicals and pro-North Korean leftists (Moon 2009, 124). However, the demonstrations continued to grow, and on June 10, more than one million people participated in a protest in the heart of Seoul, calling for renegotiation with the United States and the resignation of MB (i.e., Myung-bak). In the end, President Lee offered an official apology to the people (the second time in the first four months of his presidency), replaced 9 of 10 presidential aides, and sent a delegation to the United States for renegotiation. His CEO-style leadership continued to create political conflicts and further weakened the popularity and democratic legitimacy of his government.

Another contentious program was the so-called *Pan-Korea Grand Waterway* project, which had been one of Lee's ambitious proposals as early as 2006. The Waterway project was a 540km-long canal construction that would connect Seoul and Busan then extend to four major rivers running through the country. This grand construction project would make water flow through dozens of mountains. The president emphasized that the canal would bring immense benefits to the country by greatly improving water quality, serve as an important infrastructure for tourism and transportation for commercial goods, and prevent frequent natural disasters. While the proposal did not receive much public attention during the election campaign, Lee's plan instantaneously met with fierce resistance from opposition parties and civil society groups that raised numerous environmental and economic concerns.

Given that his political position was already weakened by candlelight protests and even some of the ruling party members' opposition to the canal project, Lee modified and renamed it the "Four Major Rivers Restoration Project." It became a five-year construction 'facelift' to better maintain water resources for drought and flooding, improve water quality, and restore river ecosystems. Although the approximately $33 billion construction project ended in October 2011, two years earlier than its original target, his 'bulldozer-style' leadership bypassed legislative oversight and the public's and experts' scrutiny. Thousands of experts pointed out the illegality of the project and filed lawsuits, although the courts rejected them. Contrary to the president's promise, the construction had minimal impacts in creating jobs, while illegal gains of approximately $200 million flowed to major construction companies involved in the project (Park 2011).

Meanwhile, the Lee Myung-bak government's foreign policy, often called the *MB Doctrine*, further polarized politics in South Korea. Highly skeptical of the Sunshine Policy, the president aimed to restore the strained security alliance with the United States and link economic assistance to Pyongyang to its denuclearization effort. The *MB Doctrine* was immediately welcomed by Washington, which had been pursuing deeper engagement with East Asia, the so-called Pivot to Asia, to target fast-rising China. The Obama administration responded to the *MB Doctrine* by calling South Korea the "linchpin," a term that had been used to describe the US–Japan alliance. At the G20 meeting in 2010, Obama declared that the US–ROK alliance "is the linchpin of not only security for the Republic of Korea and the United States but also for the Pacific as a whole" (Glosserman 2012, 3). In return, President Lee supported virtually all of Obama's policies, from climate change, the war in Afghanistan, the non-proliferation of weapons of mass destruction (WMD), and the expansion of free trade agreements.

Despite the Lee administration's success in restoring relations with the United States, its relations with neighboring countries deteriorated further. Almost immediately, the *MB Doctrine* brought back a Cold War mentality and tensions with Pyongyang. The first controversy came when a South Korean tourist was shot and killed by a North Korean soldier during her tour of the Hundai-run Mount Geumgang. The immediate cause remains unclear, and North Korea expressed regret for the incident, although it concurrently blamed the tourist for not following regulations. Already critical of inter-Korean cooperation, conservatives in South Korea demanded that the tour program stop immediately to prevent it from becoming a "money pot for Pyongyang" (Oberdorfer and Carlin 2014, 442). It was immediately shut down. An even more troubling incident occurred in March 2010, when a South Korean naval corvette *Cheonan*, on routine exercises, exploded, with 46 soldiers killed. South Korea launched an investigation by experts from five countries (excluding North Korea, China, and Russia), and they concluded that the incident was the result of a North Korean torpedo attack. This resulted in instantaneous domestic and international divisions. Many citizens in South Korea were skeptical of the government's handling of the incident. National Assembly members could not perform their legislative oversight and, more intriguingly, the Lee government announced the investigation's results on May 20, 2010, the very day the fifth local election campaign commenced. Opposition leaders and progressive civil society groups heavily criticized the Lee government for using the incident to influence the election; conservatives frantically called the opposition voices "pro-North Korean communists."

In addition, the *Cheonan* incident symbolically revealed how Lee Myung-bak's pro-US policies backfired among neighboring countries. After the investigation, Russian naval delegates visited Seoul to examine the records, but they did not release any findings. China went further to suggest that there was no definite evidence to confirm that North Korea had carried out the attack. During the Lee administration, China and North Korea entered into an era of renewed friendship and strategic partnership, even after the North had conducted two nuclear tests (in 2006 and 2009) and several rounds of rocket launchings. China and North Korea signed a number of agreements for economic cooperation along their borders. After Seoul shut down the Mount Geumgang tour program, Chinese–North Korean exchanges expanded greatly, including more interpersonal exchanges through tourism, educational, and other cultural programs. Chinese investments in North Korea's natural resources grew, as did its facelift of rugged roads and bridges that crossed their borders. China's uneasy feelings toward Seoul became even more evident after North Korean artillery forces bombarded the island of Yeonypeong in the West Sea in November 2010. Although the incident involved North Korea's outright shelling of the island, Beijing simply stated that "[w]e hope the relevant parties do more to contribute to peace and stability on the Korean Peninsula" (Foster 2010). Throughout the Lee presidency, Seoul's relations with Beijing remained tenuous at best and helped to foster a renewed Chinese–North Korean partnership.

Lee Myung-bak's political rise was possible due to his successful mobilization of the Park Jung-hee syndrome, or citizens' yearning for economic prosperity. However, the national economy further deteriorated during the five years of Lee's rule. On the one hand, the economic slowdown was inevitable, due to the global recession that began in the first year of his presidency. On the other, the average annual GDP growth during the Lee government was 2.92 percent, 2 percent lower than in the decade of progressive rule and also lower than the average of Organization for Economic Cooperation and Development (OECD) member states for the same period. A more troubling aspect of the Lee government was its authoritarian political leadership that significantly downgraded the quality of democracy in South Korea. After massive anti-government demonstrations in his first year in office, President Lee resorted to the security apparatus to limit the political opposition, including those who participated in nonviolent candlelight protests. The police jailed most of the leading protest figures and strictly applied the National Security Law to silence critics of government policies and the president himself.

An important way to muzzle the political opposition was through passage of a new media law that allowed big corporations to run newspapers and television stations, or so-called cross-media ownership. On the surface, the new media bill looked necessary because it gave the media industries more freedom from governmental control. In reality, however, the law allowed a few of the already influential newspapers to expand their dominance. The three highly conservative newspapers – *Chosun Ilbo*, *Jungang Ilbo*, and *Dong-a Ilbo* – already accounted for about 70 percent of readership, and the law gave them a further monopoly of the media market. Media unions and opposition lawmakers strongly protested, but the ruling GNP unilaterally passed the law. The very year that the new media law was passed, Freedom House downgraded freedom of the press in South Korea to being only 'partly free' due to the increase in government censorship of journalists and the general public, stricter application of the National Security Law, government control over the state-run broadcast media companies, and punishments levied out to more than 160 journalists for critical reporting about government policies (Freedom House 2011). Moreover, the Lee government's authoritarian style and lack of transparency vastly increased the level of perceived corruption in South Korea: The Corruption Perceptions Index by Transparency International ranked the country 39th out of 180 in 2007, but in the final year of the Lee presidency, it was 46th out of 179, becoming one of the most corrupt countries in the OECD. In sum, the Lee presidency brought back Park Jung-hee's authoritarian leadership to post-democratization Korean politics, but not the Park-style economic miracle.

The conservative icon: the Park Geun-hye presidency (2013–2017)

Interesting enough, President Lee's unpopularity did not lead to a transfer of power to the opposition party. In the 19th National Assembly election held in April 2012 and the 18th presidential election in December of the same year, the ruling Saenuri Party (the renamed GNP) defeated the opposition DUP. In legislative elections, the ruling Saenuri secured 152 seats out of 300, while the DUP took 127 seats. In less than eight months, Park Geun-hye won the presidential election with 51.55 percent of the popular vote, while opposition candidate Moon Jae-in received 48.02 percent. If Lee's presidency had been highly unpopular, how could the Saenuri Party and Park Geun-hye win these nationwide elections?

At least a few elements contributed to the electoral victory of Park and her party, but a brief look at Park Geun-hye's personal and political background is necessary first. She was born in 1952 as the eldest daughter of military dictator Park Jung-hee. She began her political career as the *de facto* first lady after her mother was assassinated in 1974. After her father's assassination in 1979, she remained a completely forgotten figure until 1998. She resumed her political career by winning a supplementary election in 1998 and served as a lawmaker until 2012. She quickly emerged as an iconic figure for conservatives largely due to the strong nostalgia for her father after the 1997 financial crisis and her gaining landslide support from Daegu and *Yeongnam*.

While running in the 18th presidential election, Park Geun-hye skillfully escaped a negative coattail effect from her predecessor's unpopularity. Since she was defeated by Lee Myung-bak in the presidential primary in 2007, Park had continuously distanced herself from President Lee and acted as if she had been an opposition political figure throughout Lee's presidential term. One prominent incident was the political battle between Lee and Park over the establishment of a special administrative district officially called Sejong Special Autonomous City. The plan was originally proposed by President Roh in 2003, but Lee Myung-bak wanted to revoke the relocation plan, suggesting that "it would hurt the capital's global competitiveness and result in inefficiency" (Lee 2012). Instead, he proposed Sejong as an industrial, science, and education hub. However, Park Geun-hye criticized the president for betraying the citizens of the *Chungcheong* provinces based on political expediency. Park's victory in this fight reinforced her image among conservatives as a leader of integrity, discipline, and trustworthiness.

Another important reason for Park's political rise was the memory among the older generation of her mother as a caring figure and her father as a strong leader who modernized the country. As a conservative leader, Park Geun-hye had championed neo-liberal policy agendas, often called *Jul-Pu-Se* (meaning tax cuts, deregulation, and the establishment of law and order) that symbolically summarized her market (or more specifically *chaebol*)-friendly disposition. Right before the 18th presidential election, however, Park promptly switched her policy position to the center-left to co-opt progressive policy proposals. Some of her policy promises included a gradual returning of the Wartime Operational Control by 2015, awarding about $180 in monthly support to all citizens aged 65 or older, having government pay the entire medical expenses for four major illnesses, embracing economic democratization and fairness in the market, starting a trust-building process with North Korea, and most importantly, refusing to increase taxes (Mundy 2012). She knew what South Koreans wanted, and they believed that she would be trustworthy enough to keep the above-mentioned policy promises. By the end of her first year in office, however, she had abandoned most of the campaign promises.

A more alarming problem was that Park had won the presidential election in the midst of massive election irregularities committed by the state security apparatus in cyberspace. For instance, a National Intelligence Service (NIS, or the Korean Central Intelligence Agency) agent was found to have posted negative comments on the opposition candidate Moon Jae-in and in support of Park Geun-hye on internet websites with about 40 different internet IDs in an effort to influence public opinion. In early 2013, the opposition DUP revealed that many more NIS agents were involved in cyberspace political campaigns and implicated NIS Director Won Sei-hoon, one of the closest political aides of Lee Myung-bak. Won was indicted on charges of illegal interference in the presidential election. Furthermore, it was later revealed that the psychological warfare unit within the ROK Cyber Warfare Command illegally posted more than 286,000 comments that praised or disparaged specific candidates and parties. Considering that South Korea is one of the most wired countries in the world, with more than 85 percent of people having access to the internet by 2012, the online election irregularities committed by the state security agencies must have influenced public opinion in that competitive presidential election (Kwaak 2013). However, rather than thoroughly investigating the illegal acts by state agencies, the Park government instead treated the opposition lawmakers' and civil society groups' charges as politically motivated criticisms to weaken Park's political legitimacy.

Shortly after her presidential inauguration, many South Koreans and foreign reporters raised concerns about a possible return to the authoritarian era. Foreign media pointed out the government's harsh crackdown on protests, lawsuits against journalists who were critical of the president, and imprisonment of opposition politicians. One event that symbolized the Park government's authoritarian propensity was the disbanding of the United Progressive Party (UPP), a progressive party that had secured four National Assembly seats, for being pro-North Korea. Although anti-communism had been a constant in Korean politics even after democratization, the Park government's mobilization of anti-communist ideology reached a fever pitch. The UPP was disbanded in December 2014 after the Ministry of Justice accused two UPP lawmakers of "planning a rebellion to support North Korea in the event of a war" (Hazzan 2016). Park's anti-communist fervor went further to charge that pro-communist views were deeply entrenched within higher education and middle and high school history textbooks. She, along with other conservatives in South Korea, argued that young students should be educated with "correct historical views and values," although she did not elaborate on how the textbooks were pro-communist or what "correct" views really encompassed. In the middle of harsh criticism from both civil society groups and academia, the Park government pushed the Ministry of Education to draft a single version of the government-written history textbook to replace the existing eight state-approved versions.

Massive demonstrations protested the Park government's resort to authoritarian politics and catastrophic policy debacles. Anger climaxed after the sinking of the *Sewol* ferry in 2014, in which the government did nothing while 304 people (mostly high school students) died. The Park government responded by suing news media that criticized the government failure during the crisis, including the progressive newspaper *Hankyoreh,* the right-wing *Chosun Ilbo,* and the Seoul bureau chief of the Japanese newspaper Sankei Shimbun. Against mass protests demanding a thorough investigation and punishment of public officials responsible for the disaster, the Park government simply criticized the protests as political attacks organized by pro-Pyongyang forces. Therefore, she declared the protests to be illegal and carried out harsh crackdowns. The government's lack of transparency continued to cause policy debacles in 2015 with an outbreak of Middle East respiratory syndrome (MERS) in South Korea, in which 186 people were infected and 36 died. The Park government was consistent in the way it responded to public criticism. Reporters Without Borders (also called Reporters Sans Frontieres, RSF) raised concerns about the continuing deterioration of freedom in South Korea, stating that "[t]he government has displayed a growing inability to tolerate criticism and its meddling in the already polarized media threatens their independence" (Cho 2016). In 2016, the Freedom House Index ranked South Korea 70th out of the 180 countries assessed, the lowest ranking for the country since the index was first released in 2002.

While a majority of citizens voted for Park Geun-hye based on their nostalgia for her father, President Park immediately became a political figure who deepened political polarization across regions, generations, and ideologies. Ordinary citizens realized that she was not like her father, and that they lived not in the 1970s but in a society that has experienced three decades of democratic rule. When voting for Park, citizens might have been willing to sacrifice some of the democratic achievements South Korea had built if the Park leadership had brought renewed economic dynamism and political stability. However, the Park government's performance has been unsatisfactory at best: The national economy lost its engine for growth, inter-Korean relations came to complete gridlock, and the recent 'Choi Soon-sil gate' disastrously revealed how political power without the principle of democratic governance can privatize political power. The conservative turn in South Korea eventually invalidated the deep-rooted belief among South Koreans that the Park Jung-hee-style authoritarian rule is better than democratic governance at bringing about economic growth.

After four years in office, President Park was impeached by the National Assembly for violations of the Constitution and the law, including extortion and abuse of power, leaking confidential government documents and information to her longtime crony, and soliciting bribes from *chaebols* (Choe 2016). On March 9, 2017, the Constitutional Court unanimously confirmed the verdict, which was a remarkable decision considering that all the judges were appointed by recent conservative presidents. The impeachment of Park Geun-hye revealed how much South Korean democracy has frayed and how thoroughly the leader had privatized political power mandated by the people. At the same time, however, the impeachment process demonstrated how much democracy has matured in South Korea. The four-months-long nonviolent candlelight demonstrations, in which more than 17 million citizens participated cumulatively and without a single incident of physical violence, successfully unseated the president.

Conclusion

Since the democratization commenced with the first free and competitive presidential election in 1987, South Korea's march to democratic consolidation has not been disrupted or attempted to return to the pre-democracy era. For the past three decades, conservative and progressive parties have alternated the political power, beginning with the conservative turn (1987–1998), switching to the progressive side (1998–2008), switching back to the conservative (2008–2017) and then back to the progressive (2017) with the May 9 presidential election. Procedurally speaking, South Korean democracy is a praiseworthy case of democratization and democratic consolidation; democracy became "the only game in town" (Przeworski 1991, 26).

On closer look, however, democracy in South Korea reveals many pitfalls, limitations, and malfunctionings. First, the three-decades-long democratic experience resulted in extreme polarization of constituents along ideologies, regions, and generations, such that citizens express a low level of confidence in their elected officials. A lack of political trust will weaken the legitimacy of a democratic government and increase the political cost of implementing policies. Second, the democratization has not deepened enough to guarantee freedom and rights of individuals, as state apparatuses frequently limit or even suppress basic individual rights in the name of national security. Finally, the route to democratic deepening has often been interrupted by scandals of political corruption. Among the six democratically elected presidents from 1987 to 2013, no president (or his or her family or close aides) has been free from corruption charges. In particular, corrupt ties between politicians and businesses have become the main source of political corruption.

In 2017, the impeachment of Park Geun-hye led to the 19th presidential election held on May 9, about seven months earlier than the original schedule. In the election, opposition candidate Moon Jae-in of The Minju Party of Korea won a landslide victory in a five-candidate competition. He garnered 41 percent of the popular vote, while Hong Joon-pyo of the Liberty Party of Korea (a spinoff from previous Saenuri Party) secured 24 percent and Ahn Cheol-soo of the People's Party gained 21 percent. Although Moon failed to win majority support, it was an unprecedented landslide victory with 5.57 million more votes than the next candidate, the widest margin in the history of South Korea's presidential election. One noticeable manifestation of the electoral outcome is that, although still a significant factor, regional division between the east (more conservative *Yeongnam*) and the west (more progressive *Honam*) somewhat slackened compared to previous elections. Moon Jae-in secured the most votes nationwide, except for the *Yeongnam* region. Instead, the electoral outcomes revealed a clear generational difference, as Moon received dominant support from the younger generation in their 40s or younger, while voters in their 60s or older supported the conservative opponent.

A longtime human rights lawyer and ex-President Roh Moo-hyun's close friend, Moon Jae-in, entered the presidential office with a strong dedication to complete overhaul of a South Korea that had fallen into disarray in every quarter of the society. It remains to be seen how the new president will fare and whether he will be able to run a clean government free of corruption scandals and bring reconciliation and national unity to the South Korean society that is polarized along wealth, ideology, region, and generation.

References

Amnesty International. 2012. "The National Security Law: Curtailing Freedom of Expression and Association in the Name of Security in the Republic of Korea." November 29. Available at: www.amnestyusa.org/research/reports/the-national-security-law-curtailing-freedom-of-expression-and-association-in-the-name-of-security-in-the-name-of-security-in-the-republic-of-korea/

Cha, Victor D. 2005. "South Korea in 2004: Peninsula in Flux." *Asian Survey* 45 (1): 33–40.

Cho, Il-joon. 2016. "South Korea Hits All-time Low on Press Freedom Ranking." *Hankyoreh*, April 21. Available at: http://english.hani.co.kr/arti/english_edition/e_international/740709.html.

Choe, Sang-Hun. 2016. "Claims Against South Korean President: Extortion, Abuse of Power and Bribery." *New York Times*, December 8. Available at: www.nytimes.com/2016/12/08/world/asia/south-korea-park-geun-hye-accusations-impeachment.html?action=click&contentCollection=Asia%20Pacific&module=RelatedCoverage&region=EndOfArticle&pgtype=article.

Choi, Jang-Jip. 2015. *Democracy After Democratization: The Origins and Crisis of Conservatism in South Korea*. Seoul: Humanitas. (in Korean)

Cumings, Bruce. 2005. *Korea's Place in the Sun: A Modern History*, Updated edition. New York: W.W. Norton & Company.

Diamond, Larry. 1999. *Developing Democracy: Toward Consolidation*. Baltimore, MD: Johns Hopkins University Press.

Faiola, Anthony. 2004. "Court Rejects S. Korean President's Impeachment." *Washington Post*, May 14. Available at: www.washingtonpost.com/wp-dyn/articles/A25441-2004May13.html.

Foster, Peter. 2010. "North Korea Bombs South Korea's Yeonpyeong Island." *The Telegraph*, November 23. Available at: www.telegraph.co.uk/news/worldnews/asia/southkorea/8153000/North-Korea-bombs-South-Koreas-Yeonpyeong-Island.html.

Freedom House. 2011. "South Korea: Freedom of the Press 2011." Available at: https://freedomhouse.org/report/freedom-press/2011/south-korea.

Gallup Korea. 2013. "Gallup Korea Daily Opinion." *Gallup*, February 18. Available at: www.gallup.co.kr/gallupdb/reportContent.asp?seqNo=391.

Gallup Korea. 2015. "Gallup Korea Daily Opinion." *Gallup*, August 7. Available at: http://gallupkorea.blogspot.ca/2015/08/1742015-8-1.html.

Glosserman, Brad. 2012. "The Lynchpin Grapples with Frustration and Distrust: The Fourth US-ROK Strategic Dialogue." *Issues and Insights* 12 (7): 1–20.

Gunther, Richard P., Nikiforos Diamandorous, and Hans-Jürgen Puhle, eds. 1996. *The Politics of Democratic Consolidation: Southern Europe in Comparative Perspective*. Baltimore, MD: Johns Hopkins University Press.

Ha, Yong-Chool. 2002. "South Korea in 2001: Frustration and Continuing Uncertainty." *Asian Survey* 42 (1): 56–66.

Hazzan, Dave. 2016. "Is South Korea Regressing into a Dictatorship?" *Foreign Policy*, July 14. Available at: http://foreignpolicy.com/2016/07/14/is-south-korea-regressing-into-a-dictatorship-park-geun-hye/.

Huntington, Samuel P. 1991. *The Third Wave: Democratization in the Late Twentieth Century*. Norman: University of Oklahoma Press.

Kang, David C. 2002. *Crony Capitalism: Corruption and Development in South Korea and the Philippines*. Cambridge: Cambridge University Press.

Kang, David C. 2007. *China Rising: Peace, Power and Order in East Asia*. New York: Columbia University Press.

Kang, Won-Taek. 2010. "Missing the Dictator in a New Democracy: Analyzing the 'Park Chung Hee Syndrome' in South Korea." *Political and Military Sociology: An Annual Review* 38: 1–25.

Kihl, Young Whan. 2005. *Transforming Korean Politics: Democracy, Reform, and Culture*. New York: M.E. Sharpe.

Kim, Andrew Eungi, and John Lie. 2007. "South Korea in 2006: Nuclear Standoff, Trade Talks, and Population Trends." *Asian Survey* 47 (1): 52–7.

Kim, Dae-jung. 1998. *The Inaugural Address of the 15th President: 'Let Us Open a New Era for the Nation to Overcome Its Difficulties and Leap Again*. Seoul: Office of the President. (in Korean)

Kim, Woon-Tai. 2001. "Korean Politics: Setting and Political Culture." In *Understanding Korean Politics: An Introduction*, edited by Soong Hoom Kil and Chung-in Moon, 9–32. Albany: State University of New York Press.

Kim, Youngmi. 2011. *The Politics of Coalition in Korea: Between Institutions and Culture*. New York: Routledge.

Kwaak, Jeyup S. 2013. "South Korean Agents Accused of Political Interference." *The Wall Street Journal*, December 20. Available at: http://blogs.wsj.com/korearealtime/2013/12/20/south-korean-agents-accused-of-political-interference/.

Lee, Hong Yung. 2004. "South Korea in 2003: A Question of Leadership." *Asian Survey* 43 (1): 130–8.

Lee, Sun-young. 2012. "Sejong City to Open Sunday." *The Korea Herald*, June 28. Available at: www.koreaherald.com/view.php?ud=20120628001115.

Lie, John, and Andrew Eungi Kim. 2008. "South Korea in 2007: Scandals and Summits." *Asian Survey* 48 (1): 116–23.

Linz, Juan J., and Alfred Stepan. 1996. *Problems of Democratic Transition and Consolidation: Southern Europe, South America, and Post-Communist Europe*. Baltimore, MD: Johns Hopkins University Press.

Moon, Chung-in. 2001. "The Kim Dae Jung Government's Peace Policy Toward North Korea." *Asian Perspective* 25 (2): 177–98.

Moon, Chung-in. 2009. "South Korea in 2008: From Crisis to Crisis." *Asian Survey* 49 (1): 120–8.

Mundy, Simon. 2012. "Park Elected South Korean President: Daughter of Former Ruler Becomes Country's First Female Leader." *Financial Times*, December 19. Available at: www.ft.com/content/bd001118-4982-11e2-b25b-00144feab49a.

Oberdorfer, Don, and Robert Carlin. 2014. *The Two Koreas: A Contemporary History*, Third edition. New York: Basic Books.

Park, Soon Yawl. 2011. "South Korea's Rivers Take Brunt of 'Shoveling' Politics." *Asia Times*, December 2. Available at: www.atimes.com/atimes/Korea/ML02Dg02.html.

Park, Tong Whan. 1999. "South Korea in 1998: Swallowing the Bitter Pills of Restructuring." *Asian Survey* 39 (1): 133–9.

Pollack, Andrew. 1997. "Frugal Koreans Rush to Rescue Their Rapidly Sinking Economy." *New York Times*, December 18. Available at: www.nytimes.com/1997/12/18/business/international-business-frugal-koreans-rush-rescue-their-rapidly-sinking-economy.html?pagewanted=all.

Przeworski, Adam. 1991. *Democracy and the Market: Political and Economic Reforms in Eastern Europe and Latin America*. New York: Cambridge University Press.

Schedler, Andreas. 1998. "What Is Democratic Consolidation?" *Democratization* 9 (2): 91–107.

Woo, Jongseok. 2011. *Security Challenges and Military Politics in East Asia: From State Building to Post-Democratization*. New York: Continuum.

World Bank. 2016. "World Development Indicators." Available at: http://data.worldbank.org/data-catalog/world-development-indicators.

4 South Korean economy

Yangmo Ku

Over the last seven decades, South Korea's economic status has shifted from being one of the poorest countries in the world in the 1950s to the 11th largest economy in the current global community. As described in Chapter 1, Korea suffered exploitative economic policies under Japanese colonial rule and subsequently faced the massive destruction of its infrastructure and industrial facilities during the Korean War. Despite these mishaps, South Korea achieved a rapid economic development that contributed greatly to the nation's successful democratic transition, as explained in Chapter 2. After the period of economic growth, the nation underwent an unprecedentedly harsh economic crisis in the late 1990s, which was triggered by a financial meltdown in Thailand. South Korea, however, recovered from the crisis faster than expected and continued its economic development. This backdrop begs the following questions: How was such a dramatic pace of economic development possible? How did South Korea confront the 1997 financial crisis in order to accomplish a quick economic recovery? What socio-economic challenges does South Korea currently face?

In addressing these questions, this chapter first examines South Korea's economic underdevelopment until the early 1960s and then analyzes the policies that generated economic growth from the 1960s through the 1980s. The chapter explains the main causes of rapid economic development, including the importance of primary education, a state-led developmental strategy, an export-driven economy, and strong support from the United States and Japan due to the Cold War. In the next section, it reviews the origins and consequences of the 1997 financial crisis in South Korea. Finally, the chapter considers the contemporary challenges that South Korea faces in the post-Cold War era, such as prolonged economic stagnation, a lower birth rate, and widening income inequality.

South Korea's economic miracle

After the 1945 Korean liberation, the southern part of Korea experienced a sharp economic downturn for two reasons. One was the sudden and chaotic end of the colonial economic administration. The other was an involuntary separation from its northern half into which the South's economy had been gradually integrated. South Korea's industrial output in 1948 remained at only 15 percent of its 1939 level. Agricultural output (in 1970 Korean *won*) decreased by about 15 percent in the South between 1937 and 1947. The Korean War (1950–1953) further damaged the South Korean economy. The 1949–1951 period witnessed South Korea's real gross national product (in 1955 prices) diminished by more than 20 percent. The nation's per capita income in 1953 was approximately $67, and this amount had increased to only $100 in 1961. At the time, this level of development was similar to India's, lower than Sudan's, and one-third of Mexico's (Eberstadt 2010, 98 and 230–1).

In the 1950s, South Korea suffered from slow economic growth, a high inflation rate, corruption, and heavy dependence on US aid. The Republic of Korea's (ROK's) first president, Rhee Syngman (1948–1960), adopted the import substitution policy that many post-colonial states followed, but the policy was not successful. Instead of opening their markets to foreign countries, especially former colonizers, many post-colonial states focused on fostering their own industries to manufacture imported goods. Following this policy, the Rhee administration refused to accept US advice that South Korea should establish trade relations with Japan, which was achieving rapid economic recovery in the 1950s. Rhee was extremely concerned about the possibility that South Korea would become an economic colony of Japan. Instead of normalizing diplomatic relations with Japan, the Rhee government maintained its antagonistic stance based on deeply rooted anti-Japanese sentiments that Rhee himself and many Koreans shared (Seth 2010, 157).

To sustain his regime, Rhee depended heavily on US financial and military aid. Due to the strategic value of the ROK in the intensifying Cold War rivalry, the United States provided South Korea with approximately $5 billion (in current US dollars) of direct grants between 1946 and 1961, exclusive of America's Korean War-related assistance. This amount was an extremely large sum of money, considering that South Korea's GNP in 1953 was estimated to be about $2 billion (at current prices). Such US aid was roughly equivalent to South Korea's imports from abroad over the entire 15-year period, even surpassing the nation's total allocation for gross domestic investment during those years (Eberstadt 2010, 103–4). Owing to this enormous US aid, by the late 1950s, the Rhee administration was able to rebuild the basic infrastructure destroyed during the Korean War.

The Rhee government also continued the inflated exchange rate of the Korean *hwan* in order to sustain the ROK's economy and therefore his regime. This policy, however, aggravated crony capitalism, in which success in business largely depended on close connections between business people and government officials (Kang 2002). For instance, the Rhee government offered import licenses to favored entrepreneur Lee Byung-cheol, the later founder of Samsung, in return for receiving the company's financial support. Using his government-issued import licenses, Lee purchased imported sugar at low prices and made huge profits, because the overvalued Korean currency did not reflect market reality. Part of the profits went to Rhee's Liberal Party (Seth 2010, 158). Under these circumstances, South Korea was one of the poorest countries in the world in the 1950s and early 1960s.

However, the South Korean economy began to grow rapidly in the mid-1960s. As shown in Figure 4.1, South Korea's real economic growth rate mostly fluctuated between 6 and 15 percent from 1966–1996. Figure 4.2 illustrates that in 1966, South Korea's GDP was approximately $3.81 billion in current US dollars, but this number exponentially increased to $31.35 billion in 1976, $119.77 billion in 1986, and $603.41 billion in 1996. Over three decades, the size of the ROK economy multiplied more than 150 times. South Korea's economic development rate was also miraculous in terms of per capita GDP, as depicted in Figure 4.3. Its per capita GDP was just $129 in 1966, but this figure rose to $875 in 1976, $2,906 in 1986, and $13,254 in 1996. As a result of this astonishing development, in 1996, South Korea joined the club of world's richest nations, the Organization of Economic Cooperation and Development (OECD).

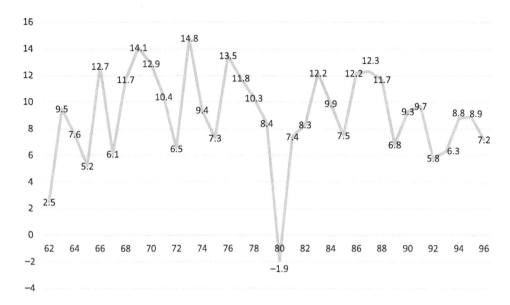

Figure 4.1 South Korea's real GDP growth rate, 1962–1996 (unit: percent)
Source: The World Bank. Available at http://data.worldbank.org/country/korea-rep.

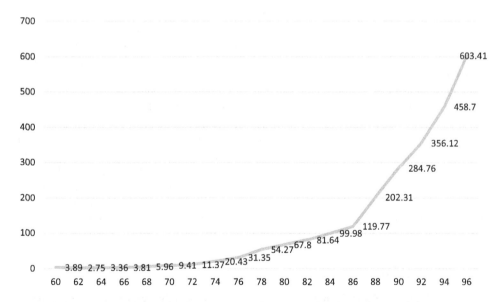

Figure 4.2 South Korea's nominal GDP, 1960–1996 (unit: current US$ billion)
Source: The World Bank. Available at http://data.worldbank.org/country/korea-rep.

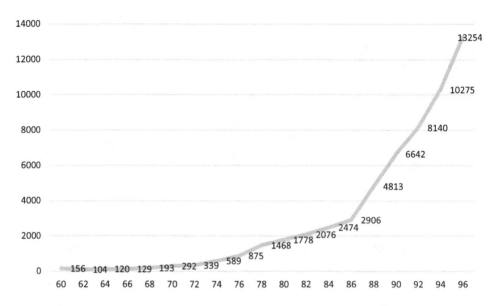

Figure 4.3 South Korea's nominal per capita GDP, 1960–1996 (unit: current US$)

Source: The World Bank. Available at http://data.worldbank.org/country/korea-rep.

Main causes of South Korea's rapid economic development

South Korea's economic miracle was an outcome of various internal and external factors, coupled with some favorable preconditions for industrialization. The former includes the state's deliberate and systematic intervention in the economy, state-business collusion, and a well-educated work force. The latter comprises an intense rivalry with North Korea, a huge amount of financial and military aid from the United States, and a high volume of Japanese investment and technology transfers.

A variety of theories may also be applied to explain such a miraculous economic development in South Korea. The developmental state model (Johnson 1982) places great emphasis on a state-led development strategy, while the hegemonic stability theory (Kindleberger 1973) highlights the role of the United States as the hegemon to provide other states with generous aid and market access. The flying geese model (Akamatsu 1962) pays a special attention to the role of Japan. As the first goose in a V-shaped formation, Japan led other Asian countries toward industrialization by passing older technologies down to the followers as its own income grew and it moved to newer technologies. In addition, cultural explanations (Kahn 1979) emphasize the impact of Confucianism, which give a priority to education, work ethics, and hierarchical structure.

Favorable preconditions for rapid industrialization

As depicted before, South Korea experienced political instability and economic deprivation in the 1950s and early 1960s. However, a few favorable conditions for industrialization existed before the nation's economic takeoff in the mid-1960s. Among them were an increase in the number of entrepreneurs and educators, triggered by land reform, and a strong passion for education.

Land reform, as implemented by the US Army Military Government in Korea (USAMGIK) and then the Rhee administration, laid the groundwork for modernizing the South Korean economy and society. In March 1948, the USAMGIK redistributed 240,000 hectares, which were approximately 11.7 percent of total cultivated land, from former Japanese owners to former tenants. From 1950 to 1952, the Rhee government redistributed 330,000 hectares of farmland while limiting each owner's property holding to three hectares. Furthermore, landlords directly sold about 550,000 hectares to their tenants. This reform brought about a significant change, as tenancy dramatically decreased from 49 percent to 7 percent of all farming households. While 2.7 percent of landowners held 64 percent of all cultivated lands in 1945, the top 6 percent owned only 18 percent by 1956 (You 2014, 203). Peasant unrest ended, and the old landowner class no longer dominated rural society. These changes helped South Korean society to develop two important human resources – business people and educators – for its future economic growth. Due to land reform, conservative landlords redirected their wealth and energy toward business, industry, and education (Lie 1998, 9–18). Some members of the landowner class had first entered the business sector in the 1910s, but the land reform hastened the trend. Many private schools and universities were also founded by former landlords that sought to new opportunities.

Related to the availability of education, South Koreans' strong zeal for intellectual development produced a highly literate population, which served as an essential foundation for the nation's rapid economic growth. In the wake of Korean liberation in 1945, the public's desire for education remarkably increased, as many people believed that education was the primary means of enhancing their status and condition in life. Given this universal desire, the 1948 constitution made primary education a right. In 1949, the Rhee administration copied the US education system: six years of elementary school, three years of middle and high school respectively, and four years of college. The Rhee regime sought to create an open-ended system that expanded access to higher levels of schooling, rather than emphasizing education for elites only. Despite the serious lack of funds and facilities at the time, enrollments grew enormously. Between 1945 and 1960, the number of students who enrolled in elementary schools increased a factor of three, secondary schooling by eight, and higher education by ten (Seth 2010, 174). Most boys and girls attended elementary school by 1960, and they had a marginal dropout rate. Thanks to this improved education system, South Korea was able to produce an educated work force, including a number of high-quality engineers and other technocrats.

State-directed development strategy

In spite of the presence of the above-mentioned favorable preconditions, South Korea could not have achieved such rapid economic growth without the implementation of a state-directed developmental strategy. President Park Jung-hee (1961–1979) took power by a coup in May 1961. Park desperately needed to achieve swift economic development in order to bolster his weak political legitimacy and to address national security threats emanating mainly from North Korea (Heo and Roehrig 2010, 81). As noted above, when he came to power, the South Korean economy suffered from stagnation, high inflation, corruption, and heavy dependence on US aid. To escape these dismal conditions, Park and his administration adopted the developmental state model that was first coined by Chalmers Johnson (1982) to explain Japan's speedy economic progress after 1945. Park respected Japan's success-ful industrialization under the Meiji system in the late nineteenth century, which he studied at the Japanese Military Academy and as a Japanese military officer (Clifford 1994, 50). To achieve economic growth, the ROK government was deeply involved in planning and operating macro and micro economic policies, as Japan had done. Compared to the Japanese developmental state, a distinct characteristic of the Korean version was that ROK military rulers were able to forcibly exercise discipline over the business class and suppress labor movements.

To promote economic growth, the Park administration strongly intervened in the ROK economy in various ways. First, it instituted a powerful bureaucratic organization, the Eco-nomic Planning Board (EPB), for the purpose of directing overall economic development. The EPB, comprised of young talented technocrats, served as a vehicle for designing and conducting a series of economic development plans. To promote the efficiency of technocrat supervision over these plans, Park appointed the EPB head as a deputy prime minister, which therefore outranked all other cabinet members. To accomplish its economic goals, the Park government also effectively utilized many other bureaucratic organizations, including the export department and the department of industrial development. The size of these organiza-tions grew vastly, attesting to the priorities of the Park regime. Between 1960 and 1970, the former increased from one to six divisions, while the latter grew from one bureau and seven divisions to five bureaus and 14 divisions (Huer 1989, 117–18). Given these measures, the Park government invigorated the development of light industries, such as textiles and foot-wear, for export during the First Five-Year Plan (1962–1966). During the Second Five-Year Plan (1967–1971), the administration placed more weight on improving basic infrastructure, including transportation and electric power (Lie 1998, 73). As illustrated in Figure 4.1, South Korea's annual economic growth averaged approximately 7.5 percent under the first plan and more than 11 percent under the second plan. In the 1970s, the role of the EPB declined, and instead an economic secretariat within the Blue House, the presidential residence, took the main authority over the economic decision making. This powerful secretariat took the lead in developing the heavy and chemical industry (Jones and Sakong 1980).

Second, Park nationalized all commercial banks and reorganized the banking system for the purpose of giving the state control over credit. He also reestablished specified banking institutions, including agricultural credit institutions, a bank for small industries, and the Korea Development Bank that administered foreign borrowing. These measures enabled the Park government to lend out money to businesses based on the needs of the state's economic plan (Woo 1991, 84). While exerting pressure on the bureaucrats to diminish corruption, Park prompted them to give credit primarily only to qualified corporations that were effi-cient in the business sense and accepted governmental administrative guidance over what to produce and for whom (Jones and Sakong 1980, 109). In response to a sharp decrease in US aid in the 1960s, the Park regime encouraged high rates of private savings by deliberately increasing interest rates. Toward this end, campaigns to promote thrift and savings were launched as well. Private savings took 6.8 percent of GNP from 1961 to 1965, but this ratio increased to 18 percent from 1976 to 1980 (Kohli 2004, 103). These high rates of savings resulted in high rates of investment, thus contributing to rapid industrialization and economic growth. In addition, the Park government broadened the tax base and improved tax collection through a series of political reforms.

Third, using tight credit control, the Park administration shifted its economic policies from light to heavy industrial development in the early 1970s. This sudden policy transition was made under its enhanced dictatorial power after proclaiming martial law and passing a new constitution in 1972. Park had strong motives to develop heavy industry, although many technocrats and foreign experts advised that South Korea was not prepared or large enough to do so effectively. Park longed to construct a state with strong military and economic capabilities. In addition to furthering economic growth, Park wanted to build most of the nation's own military equipment through the heavy industrial development. This strategy would also enable South Korea to be less dependent on the United States. Even though light industry, such as textiles and wigs, played a critical role in boosting ROK's exports, it was not adequate for the nation to become such a strong and wealthy state. At the time, North Korea's industrial development was farther along than South Korea's, let alone that of Japan, its former colonizer. To compete with its neighbors, it was essential for the Park regime to push for heavy industrial development (Kim 1997, 22).

In this context, the Park regime invested heavily in the steel, shipbuilding, petrochemical, automotive, and electronic industries under the Third Five-Year Economic Plan (1972–1976) (Woo 1991, 132). To administer this new stage of economic development, Park instituted a Corps for Planning and Management of Heavy and Chemical Industries, which was led by a political appointee. This policy shift prompted the government to play an even greater role in aiding and guiding industrial development. Thanks to this policy, heavy industry grew annually at 16 percent during the 1970s. South Korea became a country that exported steel, electronic goods, and even ships. This policy change also led a great deal of economic resources concentrated in huge family-owned conglomerates known as *chaebols*. As mentioned earlier, the Park regime owned all banks after 1961, and they poured credit into a few companies, such as Samsung, Hyundai, and Gold Star (later named LG), to develop industries according to the plan. In order to find favor by the regime, each *chaebol* leader tried to cultivate a good relationship with the government and provide generous political funds. This pattern strengthened the crony capitalism in South Korea.

It is also necessary to note that in 1970, the Park regime launched a massive social mobilization campaign called the *Saemaul Undong* or Saemaul Movement, in order to modernize rural areas that lagged behind in economic development. The ROK government supported the renovation of old houses, the construction of village roads, and the upgrade of irrigation systems for agriculture. Although not directly contributing to the nation's rapid economic growth, this campaign helped rural communities. This movement later expanded into the cities and played a critical role in prompting urban workers to sacrifice and promote production for the sake of national economic development goals. Park desired to consolidate his political legitimacy through this mobilization campaign in rural and urban areas.

Export-driven economy

Export promotion as pursued by the Park regime was another significant contributing factor to the ROK's rapid economic growth. As mentioned before, it was necessary for the Park government to obtain foreign resources, especially foreign currencies, in response to diminishing US aid and increasing national security concerns from North Korea in the early 1960s. The South Korean state thus adopted a variety of policy instruments to promote exports (Jones and Sakong 1980). The first was to devalue the ROK currency multiple times. These currency devaluations helped export promotion by decreasing the prices of South Korean goods in international markets. The second instrument was to provide various forms of government subsidies, including cheap credit, tax exemptions, and discounted transportation and other costs. These subsides also decreased the prices of exported South Korean goods, thus stimulating export promotion.

In addition to such financial incentives, the Park administration took non-financial institutional measures for export promotion. One was to set export targets based on clear government priorities. Following the export targets, the ROK state decided to which countries exports would go as well as sectors and firms within South Korea that would meet such targets. Businessmen usually perceived the targets as equivalent to compulsory orders (Song 1990, 91). The president's office directly examined private companies, so firms that succeeded in meeting the targets received a variety of public supports and gained huge profits. For instance, successful exporters began to receive monopoly rights on export markets in 1967. An export-promotion agency, the Korea Trade Association, also provided successful exporters with such help as discovering markets and training Korean salesmen (Clifford 1994, 57). In addition, the Park regime instituted a national export day and conferred prizes upon and recognized most successful firms as national heroes. The government, furthermore, established several free trading zones to attract foreign investment and promote exports.

The supply of cheap, educated, and disciplined labor was also indispensable to the ROK's successful export-driven economy. As mentioned previously, the Korean people's desire for education increased tremendously after the end of Japanese colonial rule in 1945. The Korean public invested resources in educating their children in order not to transfer poverty to the next generations. Therefore, the ROK government paid much attention to fostering education, especially primary education, in spite of the lack of human and material resources. These efforts paid off, for they yielded a well-educated labor force, which included a large number of highly qualified engineers and technocrats.

The South Korean government attained its successful export-driven economy at the expense of workers' well-being. Under state control and surveillance, South Korean laborers suffered from relatively low wages and long hours of work in the name of national development. The Park regime mainly utilized the Korean Central Intelligence Agency (KCIA) to suppress the labor movement. The KCIA protected rigid, top-down labor-management relations. For instance, the KCIA sought to demobilize labor unions' political ambitions by training their top labor leaders and placing them in power (Choi 1989, 30). Police and intelligence agents kept labor under surveillance by intimidation. According to an American missionary's observation, "each police precinct in an industrial area has an office in charge of labor. It works in close conjunction with the management of the companies. If management reports that there is a troublemaker among its employees, an investigation is begun" (Ogle 1990, 80). Thanks to such state control of labor, workers' wages increased very slowly, and South Korean corporations, especially *chaebols*, were able to gain price advantages in international markets. Park and his administration played a key role in the nation's rapid economic development, but the authoritarian regime left negative legacies, such as political oppression and human rights violations.

As a result of this state-driven export promotion, the volume of South Korea's exports grew dramatically. South Korea's exports of goods and services amounted to only $0.36 billion in 1962, but this number dramatically increased to approximately $22.94 billion in 1982.[1] During the 1962–1982 period, South Korea witnessed about 23 percent gain in its valuation of annual export. Over the same time period, the ratio of foreign trade in the whole ROK economy considerably increased from about 21.4 percent to almost 65 percent. South Korea's primary exports were light industrial goods, such as textiles and footwear in the 1960s, but the items extended to steel products, electric goods, and ships in the wake of the heavy industry drive in the 1970s.

Support from the United States and Japan

In addition to the above-mentioned internal factors, external support from the United States and Japan was also essential to South Korea's successful economic development. The United States provided South Korea with vast amounts of aid and technical assistance. US aid from 1946 to 1976 amounted to $12.6 billion, although the aid was concentrated over the decade after the Korean War, and it began to shrink in the early 1960s. In comparative perspective, the amount given to all of Africa and Latin America over the same time period was $6.85 billion and $14.89 billion, respectively (Woo 1991, 45). Besides massive financial aid, the United States helped a number of South Koreans receive technical training in statistics, economics, and engineering. These aid programs helped the ROK to assemble a large core of highly skilled bureaucrats, engineers, and educators.

Moving beyond this direct aid, the United States contributed greatly to the creation of favorable conditions for the ROK's economic growth. As South Korea's patron, the United States promoted the stability on the Korean Peninsula by making a security alliance and stationing about 50,000 troops within the country. These measures improved security conditions, thus helping promote foreign direct investment and enabling the South Korean government to focus on its economic development plans. Due to Cold War exigencies, the United States also opened its markets to South Korean products without demanding reciprocal actions by South Korea. Thus, the majority of the nation's exports were absorbed into American markets from the early 1960s through the 1980s.

Moreover, American intervention in the Vietnam War (1965–1973) was a special boon to South Korea's economic development. Although he disliked American intervention in South Korean domestic affairs, President Park Jung-hee took advantage of politico-military relations with the United States to advance economic goals. In 1965, Park concluded an agreement with US President Lyndon Johnson to deploy 300,000 South Korean troops to Vietnam in return for substantial benefits. In response, the US government provided South Korean companies with profitable contracts to supply goods and services to the United States and its allied military forces. For instance, Hyundai and other South Korean companies carried out many construction and transportation projects for the United States in Vietnam. These experiences significantly helped South Korean corporations to win numerous contracts later in the Middle East and elsewhere (Seth 2010, 162).

Japanese support was also vital to South Korea's rapid economic growth. Right after its unconditional surrender in World War II, Japan suffered from the wide-ranging destruction of its industrial facilities and infrastructure, as well as a serious lack of food and material resources. However, as the Cold War gained traction in the late 1940s, Japan began to escape its ruined economy. At the outset, the US occupation authorities intended to thoroughly demilitarize and democratize Japanese society, but they soon encouraged reversed policies of remilitarization and economic recovery (Pyle 1996, 223–5). Japan, which had been a dangerously militaristic country, became a bulwark against the Soviet and Chinese communist threats in Asia. Due to its heightened strategic value, Japan received a huge amount of US aid for economic recovery. The outbreak of the Korean War in 1950 considerably helped Japan, because the US and other UN forces procured war-related goods and services. In addition, the United States opened its markets to Japanese exports without requesting reciprocal actions by Japan. Under these favorable conditions, Japan adopted a developmental state model and achieved phenomenal economic growth in the 1950s and 1960s. As a result, the nation became the second-largest economy in the world, only behind that of the United States. In such a burgeoning economy, numerous Japanese corporations looked for foreign countries for investing their surplus capital and gaining cheap labor. For many Japanese companies, South Korea offered a place to maximize their profits on account of its geographical proximity to Japan, provision of cheap and disciplined labor, and existing human networks connecting the two nations that dated from Japanese colonial rule over Korea (Kohli 2004, 116–17).

In this context, the ROK's diplomatic normalization with Japan in 1965 brought about significant changes in the South Korean economy. Under the rule of President Rhee Syngman (1948–1960), South Korea maintained an antagonistic relationship with Japan primarily due to strong anti-Japanese sentiments widely shared among the Korean public, including Rhee. After taking power in 1961, however, President Park Jung-hee, who had had respect for Japan's successful economic development during the Meiji period, made great efforts to normalize the ROK's diplomatic relations with Japan. For the Park regime, Japanese support was advantageous to South Korea's industrialization as American aid was shrinking in the early 1960s. Despite robust opposition from the general public, the Park regime declared martial law and pushed for the ROK–Japan normalization. This finally led to the conclusion of the Treaty on Basic Relations between the ROK and Japan in June 1965. As a result of this treaty, Japan paid $300 million in grants and $500 million in loans, though it did not offer an outright apology for its past colonial rule. These funds were mainly used for constructing infrastructure, including the steel company POSCO and the Gyeongbu Expressway, which played a critical role in boosting ROK economy. After the treaty, furthermore, Japan's investments in the ROK increased significantly. The Park administration discouraged direct foreign investment due to widespread anti-Japanese feelings among the public. Rather, the Park government intently promoted public and commercial loans by guaranteeing foreign loans against both default and foreign-exchange depreciation. These loan guarantees promoted Japan's commercial loans in South Korea. Trade volumes between the two nations also increased more than tenfold over the first decade after the normalization treaty. During the 1962–1981 period, Japan provided South Korea with almost 60 percent of its foreign technology imports as well (Sakong 1993, 276). These technology transfers promoted South Korea's productivity growth and industrial development.

Economic crises and adjustments

The South Korean economy, which had experienced high rates of growth in the 1960s and 1970s, hit bottom due to the second oil crisis in 1979. As shown in Figure 4.1, 1980 saw a negative 1.9 percent in economic growth. As oil prices skyrocketed, South Korea's inflation rate for consumer prices reached almost 28.7 percent in 1980 (IMF 2015). High inflation and decreased international demand caused by the oil shock had negative impacts on the nation's exports. Corporate and foreign debts also rose for two reasons. The *chaebols* borrowed a huge amount of loans to expand their businesses. Heavily dependent on foreign loans, the Park regime pushed for the development of heavy and chemical industries and the construction of social infrastructure. This critical economic condition was further compounded by the assassination of President Park Jung-hee in October 1979 and a decline in the grain harvest due to inclement weather (Seth 2010, 170). In these circumstances, some foreign experts believed that South Korea's export-driven economy, mainly based on cheap labor and foreign investment, was not likely to grow much more in the future.

This pessimistic assessment proved to be wrong, however, as South Korea made a quick economic recovery in 1981 and continued to grow rapidly during the 1980s. As illustrated in Figure 4.1, South Korea's growth rate shifted from negative 1.9 percent in 1980 to 7.4 percent in 1981. The average growth rate between 1981 and 1989 was approximately 9.8 percent. In particular, the 1986–1988 period saw higher than 12 percent economic growth per annum.

This quick recovery and resumption of high growth rates derived from both internal and external factors. Another authoritarian regime, governed by President Chun Doo-hwan (1980–1988), adopted several reform measures in order to deal with the existing economic crisis. To control inflation, the Chun administration increased interest rates, lessened available credit, and implemented a tight fiscal policy by freezing government expenditures in 1984. As a result, the budget deficit decreased by 39 percent in 1985, and the inflation rate did not go beyond 3 percent between 1983 and 1987 (Haggard and Moon 1990, 210–37). The second objective was to restructure the South Korean economy. As noted before, South Korea's economic development was heavily dependent on the performance of the *chaebols*. To diminish this dependence, the Chun government attempted to reduce credit allocation to the *chaebols* and require governmental approval before the *chaebols* launched new businesses. In an effort to make businesses more efficient, furthermore, the Chun regime pushed corporations to improve their performance or face closure. As a consequence, a number of mergers and closures took place. According to Uk Heo and Terence Roehrig (2010, 88), "fifty unprofitable companies were liquidated through acquisition, seventeen companies were merged, and one company was put under legal management." These policy measures were possible to implement because of the authoritarian nature of the Chun regime. Besides these internal reforms, external factors also helped to improve the South Korean economy in the 1980s. Starting in 1982, the US economy improved significantly, thus contributing to an increase in South Korean exports. The decline of international oil prices and rise in foreign investments boosted the South Korean economy as well.

Despite some fluctuations in growth rates, the South Korean economy continued to grow up until the mid-1990s, as shown in Figures 4.1 and 4.2. However, the ROK was hit by a serious financial crisis in 1997. This crisis occurred as a result of a domino effect triggered by a financial meltdown in Thailand. In July 1997, the Thai government, which carried a huge foreign debt, was forced to switch its fixed exchange rate system to a managed floating system after failing to defend its currency *baht* from speculative attack. This action led to the sharp decline of the baht value and the plummeting of stock prices. This financial problem quickly spread to other Southeast Asian countries such as Indonesia and Malaysia, because worried foreign investors in Asian countries withdrew their capital at a rapid pace. Hong Kong was also affected, and its stock market crashed in October 1997. These financial troubles in the Southeast Asian region sent negative signals to the South Korean economy, as approximately one-third of South Korean exports went into that region. Under these circumstances, credit rating agencies, such as Moody's Investors Service and Standard & Poor's, lowered the credit levels of many financial institutions in South Korea. As a consequence, stock prices in the ROK fell, and its exchange rates dramatically increased from 890.5 Korean *won* for $1 in July 1997 to almost 2,000 *won* for $1 in early 1998 (Heo and Roehrig 2010, 96). Due to the lack of foreign-exchange reserves, the South Korean government could not protect the sinking value of the *won*. Facing a critical situation, in November 1997, the Kim Young-sam government asked the International Monetary Fund (IMF) to provide a rescue fund to sustain its economy, and it received an emergency package of $57 billion in loans. With this huge bailout, the IMF prompted the ROK government to adopt tight fiscal policies and high interest rates. Due to these IMF-led austerity measures, South Korea suffered a flood of bankruptcies and high unemployment rates. More than 3,300 companies went bankrupt due to heightened interest rates, and the nation's unemployment rate rose from about 2.6 percent in 1997 to 6.9 percent in 1998.[2] Its economic growth rate plummeted from 5.76 percent in 1997 to a negative 5.71 percent in 1998, as viewed in Figure 4.4.

There are two main arguments that explain the causes of the 1997 financial crisis in South Korea. The first is that the crisis arose as a result of crony capitalism (Krugman 1998; Doucette 2016, 345). A primary element of crony capitalism is extensive political intervention into market processes, including the granting of artificial monopoly rights and government bailouts to politically connected enterprises. Under close collusion between state and business, it was easy for big Korean conglomerates or *chaebols* to receive unchecked loans from banks, most of which were under the ROK government's supervision, although those companies' business performance was not very successful. Since the government provided loan guarantees, the *chaebols* sought to borrow as much as possible from banks, and they invested those monies into other industrial sectors, although few profits resulted. Moral hazard and unprofitable investments became sources of the financial crisis.

The second view places greater emphasis on an immediate cause of the financial crisis, which was the quick and massive inflow of dollar-denominated short-term loans and the lack of foreign-exchange reserves available to defend the Korean *won* (Lee 2016a). In December 1996, South Korea held approximately $3.2 billion in short-term loans, but they exponentially grew to $64.2 billion in March 1997. This sharp increase during such a short period of time was due primarily to the Kim Young-sam administration's financial liberalization. To implement anti-corruption and *segwehwa* (globalization) as his two key policy goals, President Kim Young-sam (1993–1998) actively sought to liberalize the nation's financial system. The Kim administration adopted liberalization measures not only to cope with rising globalization, but also to join the OECD, which required greater economic liberalization. The Kim government first opened the South Korean stock market to foreign investors and then increased the cap on foreign ownership of company shares to 15 percent to animate stock transactions. As a result of these measures, foreign investors

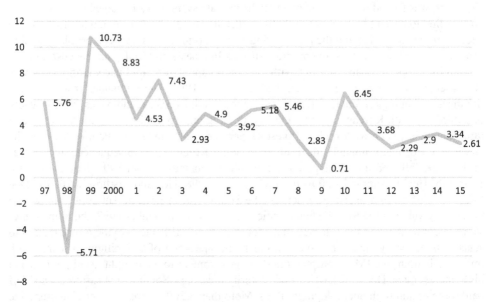

Figure 4.4 South Korea's real GDP growth rates, 1997–2015 (unit: percent)

Source: The World Bank. Available at http://data.worldbank.org/country/korea-rep.

came to retain 14.6 percent of South Korean stocks in 1997, while the rate was merely 5.8 percent in 1993. The Kim administration also tried to stimulate international capital flows by lifting the ban that precluded businesses from acquiring loans from foreign financial institutions. In an eased regulatory environment, South Korean commercial banks and other financial institutions borrowed short-term loans from international financial markets at low interest rates and lent them to domestic firms at high interest rates. This was possible thanks to the ROK government's policy of keeping high interest rates to promote domestic savings. This investment strategy worked well during the period of economic boom, as short-term loans were frequently extended. However, as the economy slowed down and business performance worsened, many loans became non-performing. As economic concerns grew, foreign creditors requested the return of their short-term loans, and this caused a chain reaction of business collapses and the bankruptcies of numerous financial institutions (Heo and Roehrig 2010, 97–9).

To overcome this unprecedented economic crisis, President Kim Dae-jung (1998–2003), who had taken power only a few months after the IMF bailout, conducted a series of drastic reform measures. While downsizing the government, Kim instituted the Planning and Budget Commission under his direct supervision in order to conduct closer oversight of the economy. By enacting the Bank of Korea (BOK) Act, the Kim government tried to transform the BOK into a more autonomous organization that could make politically independent monetary policy decisions, such as managing interest rates. Using the BOK Act, the Kim administration also established an independent regulatory agency, the Financial Supervisory Commission, aimed at supervising financial institutions with consistent standards. In the past, it was quite easy for ROK politicians to manipulate financial regulations for their personal political and economic gains. Another significant reform measure was to promote economic openness to attract foreign investment. An important lesson that the ROK government learned from the IMF crisis was that domestic firms often failed to make necessary adjustments to remain competitive in the globalized market due to governmental protection measures. Given this rationale, the Kim Dae-jung administration adopted a number of neo-liberal economic policy measures. Among them were eliminating most regulations on foreign investment, liberalizing financial transactions and foreign land ownership, providing tax incentives to foreign investors, and allowing local governments to autonomously pursue foreign direct investment (FDI). As a result of these changes, the amount of inward FDI surged from $1.2 billion during the 1991–1996 period to $2.9 billion in 1998, $5.2 billion in 1999, and $9.3 billion in 2000 (Heo and Roehrig 2010, 104–6).

Based on recommendations made by the IMF, the Kim government also conducted drastic reforms in the corporate, labor, and financial sectors. A primary corporate reform was to conduct business swaps, referred to as Big Deals. Based on the perception of "too big to fail," South Korean large conglomerates or *chaebols*, such as Samsung and Hyundai, aspired to expand by purchasing subsidiary companies often unrelated to their main business. This practice brought the *chaebols'* overcapacity and lowered their profitability, as their businesses overlapped in many areas. Thus, the ROK government pushed the top five *chaebols* to shed some of the subsidiaries and to focus on their main businesses. To make management accountability more transparent, the *chaebols* were required to eliminate the group control tower system, in which *chaebol* owners dominated decision making. The Kim administration also forced the *chaebols* to provide transparent financial information and to ban debt payment guarantees among *chaebol* subsidiaries. Moreover, the top five *chaebols* were pressured to decrease their debt/asset rations below 200 percent.

In terms of labor reforms, the Kim government made the labor market more flexible, thus enabling Korean companies to lay off workers to improve their profitability. To reduce their labor costs, many firms were allowed to hire more part-time workers, often called "irregular" workers, whose salaries were less than half those of regular workers. This reform resulted in boosting the number of irregular workers, which accounted for 32.8 percent of the 14.1 million employed in 2003. As addressed in the next section, this pattern worsened income inequality in ROK society over time. In the financial realm, the Kim government sought to overcome crony capitalism by enhancing transparency in lending practices. As part of this effort, the ROK government privatized publicly owned banks to end its involvement in management. The government also allowed many merchant banks to collapse with virtually no support, as these banks had produced huge non-performing loans through aggressive lending practices without proper control and monitoring. Another financial reform measure was to promote credit card usage for elevating domestic consumption and rejuvenating the economy. Credit-based consumption increased aggregate demand in the ROK and exerted a positive influence on economic recovery, but it brought about a significant increase in household debt. As a result of these reform policies, South Korea was able to recover from the economic crisis and to complete the IMF bailout program in 2000 earlier than expected (Heo and Roehrig 2010, 107–18).

Key challenges in the current South Korean economy

South Korea's economic performance after the financial crisis appears to be quite successful, according to some macroeconomic indicators. As shown in Figure 4.5, the nation's GDP in 2015 was approximately $1.38 trillion in current US dollars, which was the 11th largest economy in the world. The amount was about $603.4 billion in 1996 when South Korea became a member of the OECD. South Korea's exports of goods and services amounted to

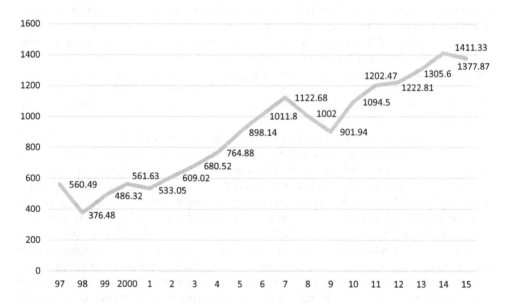

Figure 4.5 South Korea's nominal GDP, 1997–2015 (unit: current US$ billion)

Source: The World Bank. Available at http://data.worldbank.org/country/korea-rep.

approximately $632.5 billion in 2015, which was the 6th largest in the world, while it had been $155.4 billion in 1996.[3] South Korea's life expectancy also increased from 73.9 in 1996 to 82.2 in 2015, whereas its infant mortality rate decreased from 7.7 per 1,000 live births in 1996 to 3 in 2013 (*Chosun Daily* 2016). As Choong Yong Ahn (2016, 29) claims, "among countries with a population above 50 million, South Korea became in 2007 the seventh to have a per capita income above the benchmark of US $20,000." South Korea also joined the prestigious OECD Development Assistance Committee in 2009, marking a unique shift from aid recipient to international donor for the first time in the world (Heo and Roehrig 2014, 183). Despite these positive markers, however, the ROK's economy currently faces a variety of challenges, including low economic growth rates over the last decade, a widening income gap between the rich and the poor, and a continual low birth rate.

First, South Korea has suffered sluggish economic growth since 2000, when it recovered from the IMF crisis, as shown in Figure 4.4. The nation's average economic growth rate was approximately 9.13 percent during the 1982–1996 period, but this rate notably decreased to about 3.94 percent during the 2001–2015 period. In particular, its average economic growth rate remained very low – about 2.96 percent – from 2011–2015 following the 2008–2009 global financial crisis. This pattern continued in 2016, when the growth rate was about 2.8 percent according to the BOK.[4] This economic stagnation has taken place due to a combination of external and internal factors. A key external element was a sharp decline in the export sector's contribution to economic growth. As noted before, the export-oriented strategy was a driving force for South Korea's rapid economic growth, but the nation's recent exports failed to make such big contributions (Kim 2016a). In 2011, South Korea's real export growth rate was 15.13 percent, but the number slid to 5.09 percent in 2012, 4.26 percent in 2013, 2.03 percent in 2014, and 0.78 percent in 2015, as demonstrated in Figure 4.6. These declining export growth rates were due mainly to the overall decrease in consumer

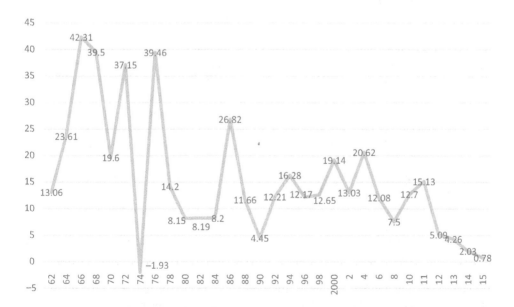

Figure 4.6 South Korea's export growth rates, 1962–2015 (unit: percent)

Source: The World Bank. Available at http://data.worldbank.org/country/korea-rep.

demands in international markets, as triggered by the 2008–2009 global financial crisis. China's recently declining economic growth also had a negative impact on ROK exports, because China has been South Korea's largest trade partner since 2004. According to the World Bank, China's economic growth rate significantly decreased from 10.64 percent in 2010 to 7.86 percent in 2012 and 6.92 percent in 2015.[5] Another external factor was the rise of Chinese companies as competitors in the fields of informational technology, steel, ship-building, automobiles, and electronics. A symbolic example is that "Samsung, which com-manded a 20 percent share of the Chinese cellphone market in 2012, now has only 6 percent. The top four best-selling cellphone brands in China are now made by Chinese companies," as Motoko Rich (2017) reports.

Internal factors for South Korea's continual economic stagnation include the increas-ing ratio of South Korean household debt to disposable income. This ratio increased from 147.7 percent in 2009 to 160.2 percent in 2013 and 173.6 percent in 2016, which was 40 per-cent higher than the average ratio (134 percent) of the 23 OECD members (Lee 2016b). This increase was mainly because of low interest rates, easy bank loans for purchasing houses, and diminished household incomes (Jo and Oh 2016). As larger chunks of incomes were diverted to debt servicing, this pattern became a persistent drain on private consumption, thus contributing to slow economic growth. Another significant internal factor was the lack of investment made by large South Korean companies and the paucity of carrying out a large-scale structural adjustment by non-profitable firms. For five years from 2010–2014, 30 big conglomerates, such as Samsung and Hyundai, increased their internal reserves by about $154.5 billion, while they increased their facility and R&D investments by only $1.8 billion. By the end of 2014, the number of Korean companies that failed to pay bank interests using their profits, reached about 3,300 companies, or about 17 percent of all firms within South Korea (Pyo 2016).

Second, a consistently low birth rate is a big burden on South Korean economy. In 1960 the ROK's fertility rate was as high as six babies per woman, but this number plunged to 1.29 per woman in 2001 and 1.17 in 2016. This rate, the lowest among 35 OECD countries, is well below the "replacement level of 2.1 children, a rate that allows a society to maintain its population without migration," according to Sang-hun Choe (2016). This low birth rate was caused by a mixture of economic, educational, and sociocultural factors. South Korea's rapid economic development significantly promoted education levels, enabling a large num-ber of South Korean women to enter colleges. These college-educated women then moved into the job market and delayed their marriages. A young generation's perception of marriage also changed notably, and many Koreans think that marriage is just an option rather than an essential part of life. In 2008, 68 percent of respondents said that marriage was a "must," but this rate decreased to 56.8 percent in 2014 (Yoon 2016). In addition, many Koreans in their 20s and 30s delayed or even gave up marriage because of unstable employment caused by the nation's continual economic downturn. It is a Korean tradition that before marriage men are expected to prepare a house, and for women to purchase furniture and appliances to fill the home (Ock 2015). High child-rearing costs are another important factor that contributes to the dwindling marriage rate. Even many married women are reluctant to have children, because they would then feel pressure to quit their jobs when they become pregnant. It is very hard for many women working in the private sector to return to work after an extended parental leave, although South Korean law allows them to take up to a year off. Even women who return to work have difficulty finding affordable day care centers, despite the ROK gov-ernment's great efforts to increase their number. In South Korean society, moreover, raising a child is still largely seen as a woman's responsibility, even when they work outside the home. All these factors contribute to declining birth rates. As South Korea becomes a rapidly aging society on account of a low birth rate and longer life spans, the burden of the younger Korean generation to support the elderly grows significantly, and the ROK government must spend more to take care of the elderly. The lack of a young labor force also makes it hard for South Korean companies to recruit able-bodied workers.

Third, the widening income gap between haves and have-nots is another serious problem in South Korean society. According to a study issued by the IMF, South Korea's income inequality is the highest among 22 countries in the Asia-Pacific region, as illustrated in Figure 4.7. Based on the 2013 latest data available, the top 10 percent of the Korean population gained 45 percent of the total income, which had been 29 percent in 1995. The top 1 percent had a 12 percent share of income in 2013, which made South Korea second in the Asia-Pacific region behind Singapore with 14 percent. Between 1990 and 2013, South Korea saw this figure increase by 5 percentage points, which was the biggest surge among the countries studied (Jain-Chadra et al. 2016). The share of the ROK's middle-income class also dropped from 64.8 percent in 1997 to 56 percent in 2010 (Ahn 2016, 30). Furthermore, South Korea suffers generational income inequality, as it is hard for young jobseekers to find quality jobs due to the prolonged economic stagnation. In February 2016, the nation's youth-unemployment rate hit a record high of 12.5 percent (Kim 2016b). Due to this unprecedentedly high youth-unemployment rate, young Koreans coined a self-scorning buzz-phrase, "*Hell Joseon*," which means that "they feel their country is like a hellish version of the medieval feudal kingdom" (Choi 2016). This term reflects young Koreans' resentment and frustration about high unemployment and low job security. These statistics illustrate the worsening of South Korea's income inequality over the last two decades.

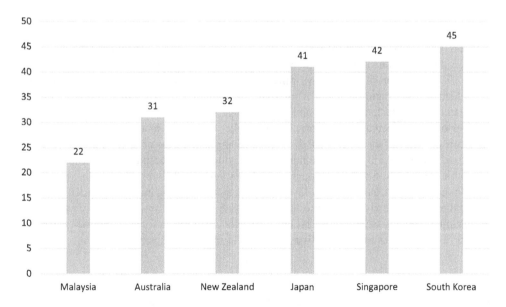

Figure 4.7 Share of income taken by top 10% (unit: percent)

Source: IMF Sonali Jain-Chadra et al. (2016).

A primary reason for increasing income inequality was the sharp distinction between large conglomerates and small- and medium-sized enterprises (SMEs) in terms of productivity, salaries, and the composition of regular/non-regular workers. With strong governmental support, South Korean *chaebols* have gained huge profits through competitive global brand names, technological innovation based on large-scale R&D investments, and overseas networks. In 2016, total sales from four *chaebols* – Samsung, Hyundai Motor, LG, and SK – accounted for 60 percent of the nation's gross domestic product; this figure was 40 percent ten years ago. Although GDP is measured by value added, and not by sales, this pattern shows the concentration of economic power in a small number of *chaebols*. On the other hand, South Korean SMEs, including self-employed and family-based microbusinesses, have been technologically outdated and domestic-oriented as a consequence of the country's rapid *chaebol*-led industrialization. In comparison to the *chaebols*, SMEs have low productivity and low wage levels. In terms of value added per worker, large conglomerates showed three times higher productivity than SMEs. The low productivity of SMEs led to a wide wage gap between *chaebols* and SMEs. Moreover, SMEs hire many more non-regular workers than *chaebols*, and this contributes greatly to income inequality as well (Ahn 2016, 31–2). With this acute dichotomy between *chaebols* and SMEs, the nation's rapid aging and unprecedentedly prolonged economic stagnation also deepen the income inequality between the rich and the poor. It is also worth noting that such widening income inequality has been accelerated by the IMF crisis and the subsequent neo-liberal economic policies, such as privatization and deregulation, which were adopted by the ROK government.

Conclusion

This chapter showed that South Korea achieved miraculous economic growth between the 1960s and the 1990s, which shifted the nation's status from an underdeveloped nation to a developed nation. This dramatic shift was possible due to a state-led development strategy, an export-driven policy, the suppression of the labor movement, the supply of well-educated workers, and strong support from the United States and Japan. After undergoing a successful period of economic development, South Korea experienced a painful economic crisis in 1997–1998, which produced massive bankruptcies and high unemployment, due to the crony capitalism and the rapid liquidity of international capital. Under harsh IMF conditionality, summarized as tight fiscal policy and high interest rates, the ROK government adopted a number of drastic economic reforms in the public, corporate, labor, and financial realms. As a consequence of these reforms, the ROK accomplished a faster economic recovery than expected, and its development continued in the 2000s–2010s. Despite some positive macro-economic indicators, South Korea currently faces various challenges, including prolonged economic stagnation, a persistently low birth rate, and worsening income inequality between rich and poor. The newly elected President Moon Jae-in administration has a big responsibility in simultaneously catching two rabbits – to rejuvenate the nation's economic growth and to improve the fairness of wealth distribution in South Korean society.

Notes

1 The World Bank. Available at http://data.worldbank.org/country/korea-rep.
2 The World Bank. Available at http://data.worldbank.org/country/korea-rep.
3 The World Bank. Available at http://data.worldbank.org/country/korea-rep.
4 The Bank of Korea's Economic Statistics System. Available at http://ecos.bok.or.kr.
5 The World Bank. Available at http://data.worldbank.org/country/china.

References

Ahn, Choong Yong. 2016. "Rising Inequalities in South Korea and the Search for a New Business Ecosystem." *Global Asia* 11 (2): 28–35.

Akamatsu, Kaname. 1962. "Historical Pattern of Economic Growth in Developing Countries." *Developing Economies* 1 (1): 3–25.

Choe, Sang-hun. 2016. "South Korea's Plan to Rank Towns by Fertility Rate Backfires." *The New York Times*, December 30. Available at: www.nytimes.com/2016/12/30/world/asia/south-korea-fertility-birth-map.html.

Choi, Jang Jip. 1989. *Labor and the Authoritarian State: Labor Unions in South Korean Manufacturing Industries, 1961–1980*. Seoul: Korea University Press.

Choi, Sung-jin. 2016. "90% of Young Koreans Sympathize with 'Hell Joseon.'" *The Korea Times*, July 2. Available at: www.koreatimes.co.kr/www/news/nation/2016/07/116_208441.html.

Chosun Daily. 2016. "OECD 20 Years Korea: Really Advanced Country?" October 28.

Clifford, Mark L. 1994. *Troubled Tiger: Businessmen, Bureaucrats and Generals in South Korea*. Armonk, NY: M. E. Sharpe.

Doucette, Jamie. 2016. "The Post-Developmental State: Economic and Social Changes Since 1997." In *Routledge Handbook of Modern Korean History*, edited by Michael J. Seth. New York: Routledge.

Eberstadt, Nicholas. 2010. *Policy and Economic Performance in Divided Korea During the Cold War Era: 1945–1991*. Washington, DC: AEI Press.

Haggard, Stephen, and Chung-in Moon. 1990. "Institutions and Economic Policy: Theory and a Korean Case." *World Politics* 42: 210–37.

Heo, Uk, and Terence Roehrig. 2010. *South Korea Since 1980*. New York: Cambridge University Press.

Heo, Uk, and Terence Roehrig. 2014. *South Korea's Rise: Economic Development, Power, and Foreign Relations*. New York: Cambridge University Press.

Heur, John. 1989. *Marching Orders: The Role of the Military in South Korea's Economic Miracle, 1961–1971*. New York: Greenwood Press.

International Monetary Fund (IMF). 2015. World Economic Outlook Database, April.

Jain-Chadra, Sonali, Kalpana Kochhar, Shi Piao, Tidiane Kinda, and Johanna Shauer. 2016. "Sharing the Growth Dividend: Analysis of Inequality in Asia." *IMF Working Paper*, WP/16/48.

Jo, Gyurim, and Junbeom Oh. 2016. "Causes of the Increase in Domestic Households' Debt and Its Prospects." *Issue Report 16–42*, Hyundai Economic Institute, October 31.

Johnson, Chalmers. 1982. *MITI and the Japanese Miracle: The Growth of Industrial Policy, 1925–1975*. Stanford, CA: Stanford University Press.

Jones, Leroy P., and Il Sakong. 1980. *Government, Business, and Entrepreneurship in Economic Development: The Korean Case*. Cambridge: Council on East Asian Studies, Harvard University.

Kahn, Herman. 1979. *World Economic Development: 1979 and Beyond*. New York: Westview Press.

Kang, David. 2002. *Crony Capitalism: Corruption and Development in South Korea and the Philippines*. Cambridge: Cambridge University Press.

Kim, Jae-won. 2016b. "Korea Worst in Income Inequality in Asia-Pacific." *The Korea Times*, March 16. Available at: www.koreatimes.co.kr/www/news/biz/2016/03/488_200524.html.

Kim, Kyung-rok. 2016a. "Sluggish Exports the Biggest Factor in S. Korea's Weak Economic Growth." *The Hankyoreh*, April 4. Available at: http://english.hani.co.kr/arti/english_edition/e_business/738149.html.

Kim, Linsu. 1997. *Limitation to Innovation: The Dynamics of Korea's Technological Learning*. Boston, MA: Harvard Business School Press.

Kindleberger, Charles. 1973. *The World in Depression, 1929–39*. Berkeley, CA: University of California Press.

Kohli, Atul. 2004. *State-Directed Development: Political Power and Industrialization in the Global Periphery*. New York: Cambridge University Press.

Krugman, Paul. 1998. "What Happened to Asia." January. Available at: http://web.mit.edu/krugman/www/DISINTER.html.

Lee, Jaymin. 2016a. "The Nature and Consequences of the Korean Foreign Exchange Crisis." *Korean Economic Forum* 9 (2): 79–135.

Lee, Ju-young. 2016b. "South Korean Households' Debt to Disposable Income Surpassed 170%." *The Kyunghyang Shinmun*, September 29. (in Korean) Available at: http://biz.khan.co.kr/khan_art_view.html?artid=201609291807001&code=920100.

Lie, John. 1998. *Han Unbound: The Political Economy of South Korea*. Stanford, CA: Stanford University Press.

Ock, Hyun-ju. 2015. "Koreans' Changing Perceptions on Marriage." *The Korea Herald*, March 27. Available at: www.koreaherald.com/view.php?ud=20150327001036%20.

Ogle, George E. 1990. *South Korea: Dissent Within the Economic Miracle*. London: Zed.

Pyle, Kenneth B. 1996. *The Making of Modern Japan*. Lexington, MA: D.C. Heath and Company.

Pyo, Hak-gil. 2016. "Is There a Breakthrough in South Korea's Low Economic Growth?" East Asia Foundation Policy Debate 49.

Rich, Motoko. 2017. "As Leaders Argue, South Korea Finds China Is No Longer an Easy Sell." *The New York Times*, March 8. Available at: www.nytimes.com/2017/03/08/world/asia/china-south-korea-economy.html?_r=0.

Sakong, Il. 1993. *Korea in the World Economy*. Washington, DC: Institute for International Economics.

Seth, Michael J. 2010. *A Concise History of Modern Korea: From the Late Nineteenth Century to the Present*. Lanham, MD: Rowman & Littlefield Publishers.

Song, Byung-Nak. 1990. *The Rise of the Korean Economy*. New York: Oxford University Press.

Woo, Jung-en. 1991. *Race to the Swift: State and Finance in the Industrialization of Korea*. New York: Columbia University Press.

Yoon, Ja-young. 2016. "Korea Faces Rapidly Aging Society." *The Korea Times*, March 23. Available at: www.koreatimes.co.kr/www/news/biz/2016/03/123_201016.html.

You, Jong-Sung. 2014. "Land Reform, Inequality, and Corruption: A Comparative Historical Study of Korea, Taiwan, and the Philippines." *The Korean Journal of International Studies* 12 (1): 191–224.

5 South Korean diplomacy

Yangmo Ku

As a relatively weak nation, Korea has had to survive among powerful neighboring countries over a long period of time. Up until the late nineteenth century, Korea often asked the Middle Kingdom China to help protect its security while paying a regular tribute to China. After then, Japan, which had succeeded in its modernization effort after the 1868 Meiji restoration, defeated China and Russia and became the predominant power on the Korean Peninsula until August 1945, when Japan surrendered to the Allied Forces in World War II. The Korean liberation, however, did not lead to the establishment of a unified and independent country, but culminated into a national division in 1948 and a tragic war in 1950. Given this harsh geopolitical environment, what types of diplomacy has South Korea adopted since the end of the Korean War in 1953? What factors have been most influential in determining the nation's foreign policy? How has South Korean diplomacy evolved over the last seven decades?

To answer these questions, this chapter first examines two types of diplomacy – traditional interest diplomacy and middle power diplomacy – and applies the two concepts to the South Korean context. The chapter then pays great attention to three elements – top leaders, domestic public opinion, and international political structure – as key determinants of South Korea's foreign policy. In the subsequent sections, the chapter explores the evolution of the Republic of Korea's (ROK's) foreign policy since the Korean War, which has largely followed three different phases – focusing on traditional interest diplomacy (1953–1987), tilting toward a more independent traditional interest diplomacy (1988–2007), and mixing traditional interest diplomacy and middle power diplomacy (2008–2017). The chapter ends with a brief summary and some policy implications.

Key goals and determinants in South Korean foreign policy

South Korean diplomacy since the end of the Korean War can be largely divided into two categories – traditional interest diplomacy and middle power diplomacy. In this chapter, traditional interest diplomacy is defined as a state's actions that seek to maximize its narrow national interests, which can be summarized as survival (security) and prosperity. This concept can generally apply to all small, middle, and great powers, as it is natural for all nation states to aim at maximizing their national interests through diplomatic actions. The concept corresponds to general realist principles in the field of international relations: In an anarchic international system, states as unitary and rational actors pursue national interests defined in terms of power (Katzenstein, Keohane and Krasner 658). In the South Korean context, traditional interest diplomacy can be interpreted as follows: South Korea, a relatively weak power, strove to protect itself from the North Korean threat, while effectively managing its relationships with four big giants – the United States, the Soviet Union/Russia, China, and Japan – to enhance its security and prosperity.

While this traditional interest diplomacy has been always a major feature, South Korea, which had ascended to middle power status in the 1980s–1990s, also began to practice so-called middle power diplomacy in the 2000s. The concept of middle power diplomacy has been widely discussed in academic and practical terms since the early 1990s, but there is no general consensus over its meaning in the extant literature. Thus this chapter accepts common principles deriving from the existing literature (Cooper et al. 1993; Soeya 2006; John 2014, 328): (1) Middle powers never attempt to challenge the international political system created by great powers; (2) middle powers make the world a better place by addressing international security, economic, and environmental issues that do not relate directly to the national interest; and (3) middle powers desire to work through multilateral institutions and processes, make a commitment to promoting international legal norms, and use diplomatic, military and economic measures proactively to accomplish selected political purposes. These assumptions are largely compatible with liberalism and constructivism in international relations. The former emphasizes the linkage between institutions and cooperation, while the latter stresses the role of middle powers as "norm entrepreneurs" in diffusing new ideas (O'Neil 2015, 77). In the South Korean context, the concept of middle power diplomacy can be interpreted as the following: South Korea, identified as a middle power, sought to exert significant influence on vital international issues such as the environment, economic development, and nuclear non-proliferation, thereby improving its reputation in the international community. South Korean middle power diplomacy moved beyond traditional interest diplomacy, in that the country paid great attention to transnational issues, which were not directly linked to the nation's narrow national interests such as survival (security) and prosperity.

The following three elements – the nature of top leaders, domestic public opinion, and international political structure – have been extremely influential in determining South Korean foreign policy over the last seven decades. Top political leaders, namely presidents, have worked as the main agents in deciding the nation's foreign policy. ROK's presidential system has enabled presidents to predominantly make foreign policy decision vis-à-vis the National Assembly, political parties, and the bureaucracy (Robertson 2016). Therefore, these leaders' worldviews, ideological orientations, and past experiences have substantially affected South Korea's foreign policy. This also creates a lack of policy continuity, as new leaders make different choices than their predecessors. As further elaborated in subsequent sections, one of the most distinctive examples of foreign policy shifts prompted by top leaders was the move away from South Korea's hardline approach to North Korea to an engagement policy in 1998 before switching back to a hawkish stance in 2008. These changes took place primarily due to the alteration of progressive and conservative leaders.

Despite their preeminent role in the ROK's foreign policy, top leaders have had to operate within both domestic and international constraints. The Cold War largely worked as a restrictive condition for the ROK's foreign policy, in that it was almost implausible for the nation to develop diplomatic relationships with Soviet bloc countries. However, the easing of Cold War confrontation, caused by détente and the US–China rapprochement in the early 1970s, provided the ROK with a window of opportunity to cultivate its relationships with North Korea. Therefore, during the initial Cold War period, South Korean foreign policy was largely decided by the interplay between top leaders and international political structures. Meanwhile, South Korean authoritarian leaders manipulated or suppressed domestic public opinion until they fell from power in 1987. A key example was the diplomatic normalization between South Korea and its former adversary, Japan, in 1965. Under intense Cold

War confrontation, the United States strongly pushed its two key Asian allies, the ROK and Japan, to normalize their relationship in an attempt to unite against the Soviet communist threat. In addition to US pressure, ROK President Park Jung-hee possessed a strong desire to enhance his weak political legitimacy by restoring ROK–Japan relations and thereby gaining economic assistance from Japan. In this context, the authoritarian leader Park pushed for the conclusion of the 1965 ROK–Japan normalization treaty despite powerful opposition from college students and trade union workers. The Park administration cracked down on such civil protests using violent measures and achieved diplomatic normalization with Japan.

The ROK, however, had the opportunity to cultivate relationships with communist countries at the end of the Cold War. Soviet leader Mikhail Gorbachev initiated the New Thinking, including *glasnost* to open up political debate and *perestroika* to modernize the Soviet bureaucracy and economy (Nau 2015, 179). As further elaborated in a later section, ROK leaders utilized the end of the Cold War as a new era in which they could conduct independent diplomatic initiatives. Along with the collapse of the Cold War, South Korean democratization, which began in 1987, significantly changed the dynamics of the nation's foreign policy decision making, as domestic public opinion became another salient element in the nation's foreign policy. Top leaders could not overlook their people's opinions in order to maintain or bolster their political legitimacy and popularity. On the other hand, some ROK leaders took advantage of foreign policy issues for their own political gains. As the rally 'round the flag effect states, the public support for government leaders tends to increase "when a government undertakes a war or foreign military intervention at a time of domestic difficulty to distract attention and gain public support" (Goldstein and Pevehouse 2012, 144).

The evolution of South Korean foreign policy

South Korean foreign policy has largely followed three phases since the Korean War. The first phase was from 1953 to 1987, during which South Korea mainly focused on traditional interest diplomacy to ensure its security and prosperity. During a second phase that lasted between 1988 and 2007, the ROK continually pursued conventional interest diplomacy aimed at not only defending its security from the North Korean threat, but also promoting inter-Korean reconciliation and improving relationships with neighboring countries. During this second period, the nation's foreign policy was more independent than during the Cold War. The third phase, the post-2008 period, saw the rise of South Korean middle power diplomacy, although it was still centered on the traditional interest diplomacy. This chapter's subsequent sections analyze South Korean diplomacy within each phase by outlining and analyzing the most significant diplomatic events, while providing a comprehensive assessment of these initiatives.

Phase I (1953–1987): traditional interest diplomacy

The first phase witnessed South Korea primarily pursuing traditional interest diplomacy to guarantee national security and to promote economic prosperity. During this period, top political leaders played a major role in deciding the ROK's foreign policy without being significantly influenced by the South Korean public. Their diplomatic decisions, however, were largely constrained by the Cold War rivalry between the US-led capitalist and Soviet-led communist blocs. In this context, the ROK had little necessity and capacity to develop relationships with communist nations, including North Korea. The easing of Cold War tensions in the early 1970s, though, provided ROK leaders with a window of opportunity to employ a limited but more independent foreign policy of reconciliation toward North Korea.

Two pillars of South Korea's traditional interest diplomacy during this first phase were to strengthen the ROK–US alliance and to manage ROK–Japan relations. Above all, the ROK–US alliance was the linchpin of South Korean foreign policy during the Cold War period. As the Korean War ended with the armistice, not a peace treaty, the war technically continued. ROK's first president, Rhee Syngman (1948–1960), had strong anti-communist sentiments, and this led to antagonistic relationships with North Korea and other communist countries. Adding to this tension, North Korea often showed its desire to unify the two Koreas under its communist ideology through its military infiltrations into the ROK and the instigation of a communist revolution within South Korean society. To cope with such communist threats, South Korea heavily depended on the ROK–US security alliance, which served to deter the North Korean military threat and more broadly protect South Korean from the Soviet communist threat. As shown in Table 5.1, the deployment of a large number of US military forces inside the South Korean territory played a pivotal role in guaranteeing ROK's security. These American troops functioned as a tripwire, which meant that should North Korea attack the South, the United States would surely enter the war because of its endangered forces in the South. To further deter the North Korean threat, the United States introduced nuclear weapons to South Korea in 1958, and by the mid-1970s, Washington had deployed at least several hundred nuclear warheads (Lee 2009).

By the late 1960s, though, South Korean leaders had a fear of abandonment due to diplomatic initiatives taken by the United States. The United States had reduced its security commitment to the ROK through the 1969 Nixon Doctrine, the withdrawal of US Seventh Infantry Division from South Korea in 1971, and US President Jimmy Carter's pledge to completely withdraw American troops from South Korea (Cha 1999). In response to US disengagement, President Park Jung-hee (1961–1979) sought to reduce South Korea's dependence on the United States. As part of this action, Park secretly pursued developing nuclear weapons and negotiated with France to purchase technology to produce plutonium for these weapons (Whyte 2015). These efforts, however, culminated in failure after the US discovered and forced the end of the clandestine program in 1976. Concurrently, Park tried to defuse inter-Korean tensions following détente and the subsequent US–China rapprochement in the early 1970s. As a result, the fear of abandonment from the ROK's main patron, the United States, served as a vehicle for prompting Park to reach out to North Korea in an attempt to defuse military tensions on the Korean Peninsula.

Moving beyond this security dimension, during the initial Cold War period, it was indispensable for the ROK to receive economic aid from the United States and to foster economic

Table 5.1 US troop deployment in South Korea

Year	1953	1954	1955	1956	1957	1958	1959	1960
Number	326,863	225,590	75,328	68,810	71,043	46,024	49,827	55,864
Year	1961	1962	1963	1964	1965	1966	1967	1968
Number	57,694	60,947	56,910	62,596	58,636	47,076	55,057	62,263
Year	1969	1970	1971	1972	1973	1974	1975	1976
Number	66,531	52,197	40,740	41,600	41,864	40,387	40,204	39,133

Source: The Heritage Foundation. Available at www.heritage.org/defense/report/global-us-troop-deployment-1950-2003.

cooperation with the patron. South Koreans suffered from the Korean War, which destroyed almost all industrial facilities and infrastructure. Under such horrible conditions, it would have been extremely hard for South Koreans to survive without generous American support. During the early years of the Rhee Syngman government, US aid approximately accounted for one-third of the nation's budget (Oh 1999, 40). This number increased to 50 percent in 1963, after Park took power via a military coup. US aid also accounted for 70 percent of defense expenditures at the time (Eckert et al. 1990, 361–2). Although the amount of US aid significantly decreased over time, the opening of the American market to South Korean products without a reciprocal action contributed greatly to ROK's rapid economic growth during the Park Jung-hee and Chun Doo-hwan regimes. In addition, the Vietnam War provided South Korea with an opportunity to boost its economy. As a key US ally, the Park administration dispatched approximately 300,000 ROK troops to Vietnam from 1964 to 1973. In response, the United States paid the salaries of the dispatched troops and offered numerous procurement and construction contracts to South Korean companies such as Hyundai.

In addition to the ROK–US alliance, South Korean leaders placed great emphasis on their nation's economic relationship with Japan in order to reconstruct its devastated economy and promote economic development. President Rhee Syngman had strong anti-Japanese sentiments, because he had actively participated in the independence movement during the period of Japanese colonial rule while staying in Hawaii. As an example of his animosity toward Japan, in 1952, Rhee unilaterally declared the so-called Peace Line, which incorporated the Dokdo Islands as Korean territory. This incident brought about strong opposition from Japan, which had claimed sovereignty over the islands. The 1951 San Francisco Peace Treaty, which officially ended World War II in the Asia-Pacific region, did not clearly address the sovereignty of the Dokdo Islands, which Japan had taken from Korea immediately after the Russo-Japanese War of 1904–1905 (Lee and Van Dyke 2010). Since the declaration of the Peace Line, the Dokdo Islands have been administered by South Korea, although territorial disputes with Japan have frequently erupted. This animosity prevented South Korea from normalizing the relationship with its former colonizer, although the two nations held bilateral talks about diplomatic normalization.

President Park Jung-hee, however, made great efforts to normalize ROK–Japan relations after taking power in a 1961 coup. Park's stance on this issue was starkly different from his predecessor's. Park had formerly served as an officer in the Japanese Imperial Army and held respect for Japan's successful modernization after the 1868 Meiji restoration. His past helped Park to have an affinity for Japan. Moreover, Park was desperate to gain Japan's economic support to promote South Korea's economic development. Since he had weak political legitimacy due to his ascendance to power via a coup, economic development was an extremely important instrument for Park's political rule (Heo and Roehrig 2010, 24). South Korea and Japan held a series of bilateral talks and finally concluded the Treaty on Basic Relations between South Korea and Japan in 1965, despite staunch public resistance in South Korea. The Basic Relations Treaty contributed greatly to the promotion of the South Korean economy through the influx of Japanese capital and the rise of mutual trade. At the signing of the treaty, Japan provided South Korea with $300 million in outright grants and $500 million in loans and credits (Lee 1985; Cha 1999). Using this huge investment, the Park government built the Gyeongbu highway and POSCO, the famous steel company, which played a significant role in the advancement of the South Korean economy. In the process of concluding the treaty, however, the Park regime dropped demands for a sincere apology from Japan and for reparations for its past colonial rule. This diplomatic action left behind negative legacies that later renewed historical disputes between the two nations.

South Korean diplomacy during the Chun Doo-hwan administration (1980–1988) also focused on strengthening ROK–US and ROK–Japan relations. President Chun, who had taken power via another military coup in 1980, desperately needed political and economic support from the United States and Japan both to promote his weak political legitimacy and to deter the North Korean threat. To these ends, in November 1980, Chun prompted the newly elected US President Ronald Reagan to issue an official invitation to Washington. As a result, on February 2, 1981, two weeks after Reagan's inauguration, Chun visited the White House for a summit with Reagan. This event worked as a catalyst for restoring ROK–US relations, which had hit the bottom during President Jimmy Carter's administration (1977–1981). President Carter strongly criticized human rights abuses in South Korea under the military government, and he pushed for the complete withdrawal of US forces from the nation. The Chun–Reagan summit also served as an instrument for legitimizing the Chun government, which had brutally repressed its domestic opposition with the Gwangju Massacre and the imprisonment of dissident leader Kim Dae-jung (Wampler 2010). Reagan's approval of the brutal Chun regime soon became a significant reason for the emergence of anti-American sentiment among the South Korean public.

For authoritarian leaders, achieving successful economic growth is an important source for bolstering weak political legitimacy. In this regard, Chun sought to acquire Japan's economic aid as his predecessor Park Jung-hee had done before. To finance the Fifth Five-Year Socio-economic Plan (1982–1986), Chun asked Japan for a $6 billion loan package in 1981, arguing that South Korea's economic development would contribute to the construction of a 'bulwark' against communism, thus helping to defend Japan too (Bridges 1993, 14–15). Although Japanese Prime Minister Nakasone Yasuhiro denied the link between the loan and security issues, the final $4 billion loan agreement was concluded at the Chun–Nakasone summit in January 1983. The provision of this enormous loan to the Chun government considerably helped South Korea to maintain economic growth. Moreover, the geographical proximity between the two nations also made it easier for South Korea to adopt cutting-edge technologies from Japan in the fields of electronic and machinery industries. On the other hand, South Korea suffered from a large trade deficit with Japan.

In addition, Chun tried to improve inter-Korean relations by providing humanitarian aids to North Korea and by holding a reunion of separated families. However, these conciliatory gestures did not bear fruit due to North Korea's provocative acts, such as the 1983 attempted assassination of President Chun and the 1987 bombing of a South Korean passenger plane. Due to the revival of intense Cold War rivalry, ROK authoritarian leaders had no opportunity to improve relationships with the Soviet Union and China.

Phase II (1988–2007): more independent traditional interest diplomacy

During this second phase, South Korean foreign policy still centered on traditional interest diplomacy aimed at maximizing security and economic interests. The ROK made great efforts to deter North Korean threats while often promoting inter-Korean reconciliation. South Korea also tried to improve its relationships with other countries, particularly with the United States, China, Japan, and Russia. Compared to the first phase, however, this second period clearly saw a more independent foreign policy in South Korea, because the primary structural constraint, the Cold War, ended.

A key example of independent foreign policy was the so-called northern diplomacy, also referred to as *Nordpolitik*. ROK President Roh Tae-woo (1988–1993), who had come to power by a direct presidential election in December 1987, adopted this diplomatic initiative "to induce North Korea to open up and thus to secure stability and peace on the Korean Peninsula" (Lee 2006, 137). To this end, the Roh administration sought to improve the ROK's relationships with Soviet bloc nations, as West Germany had done under *Ostpolitik* in the late 1960s and the early 1970s. This northern diplomacy eventually ushered in the ROK's diplomatic normalization with the Soviet Union in 1990 and China in 1992, in addition to establishing diplomatic relations with East European communist countries, such as Hungary and Poland, in 1989. Moreover, this conciliatory policy produced two important agreements between South and North Korea: The Agreement on Reconciliation, Non-Aggression, Exchanges and Cooperation (Basic Agreement) in 1991 and the Declaration on the Denuclearization on the Korean Peninsula in 1992. These agreements played key roles in alleviating tensions on the Korean Peninsula.

The following two factors particularly served as catalysts for Roh's northern diplomacy. First, the easing of tension at the international level, prompted by Soviet President Mikhail Gorbachev's reforms and the subsequent end of the Cold War, provided a permissive condition for the ROK's independent diplomacy. Under the intense Cold War confrontation, it would have been unimaginable for ROK leaders to encourage the United States and Japan to recognize North Korea in exchange for the Soviet Union's and China's recognition of South Korea. Second, in the late 1980s, South Korea came to have a middle power identity with its rapid economic development and successful democratization. Given the confidence stemming from such economic and political developments, South Korea was able to initiate a relatively independent foreign policy.

The 1993–1998 period, during which President Kim Young-sam ruled South Korea, for the first time witnessed the important role of domestic public opinion in influencing the nation's foreign policy. The Kim administration initially accepted the Asian Women's Fund (AWF), mainly established by Japanese citizens in 1995, as a reasonable way of resolving the comfort women issue.[1] However, South Korean civil society organizations, supported by many Japanese and other foreign non-governmental organizations, pressured the ROK government to decline the AWF's fund since the money did not directly come from the Japanese government's coffers. In response to this civil pressure, the Kim administration generated its own fund to compensate comfort women survivors, as opposed to reaching an agreement with the Japanese government.

A structural factor constrained the Kim government's foreign policy in addressing the first North Korean nuclear crisis (1993–1994). President Kim made every effort to launch the Four-Party talks, consisting of the ROK, the Democratic People's Republic of Korea (DPRK), the United States, and China, to peacefully resolve the North Korean nuclear problem. However, the United States took the initiative in negotiating with North Korea over its nuclear adventurism. As a result of direct US–DPRK negotiations, the two nations reached the so-called Agreed Framework in October 1994. In return for freezing North Korea's nuclear development facilities, the United States promised to construct two light-water nuclear reactors to alleviate the lack of electricity in North Korea. The United States also promised to annually provide 500,000 tons of heavy oils to North Korea until the two reactors were completely constructed. President Kim was upset with ROK's exclusion from the negotiation process. However, he had to join the new Korean Peninsula Energy Development Organization (KEDO), which was in charge of constructing the two light-water reactors along with other nations, including Japan and some Western European countries.

One diplomatic initiative pursued by President Kim was the acceleration of internationalization or *Segyehwa*. To this end, the Kim government established and provided generous support for graduate programs in international studies at major universities in South Korea.

As part of this campaign, President Kim made every effort to have South Korea join other wealthy Western-oriented nations in the Organization for Economic Cooperation and Development (OECD). To meet the standards of OECD membership, the ROK government liberalized economic and financial systems by repealing a variety of regulations, including strict labor-related laws and limits on foreign investment in Korean companies. Ironically, these sudden liberalization measures became one of the main causes of the financial crisis that hit the South Korean economy hard in late 1997, as detailed in Chapter 4.

President Kim Young-sam also used a diplomatic issue, the Dokdo dispute with Japan, as an instrument for rejuvenating his notably declining popularity. As the first civilian president after 30 years of military rule, Kim had a record-high public approval rating of close to 90 percent when he assumed the presidency in February 1993. Given this strong public support, Kim successfully conducted reforms, including the purging of politicized generals and the adoption of the real-name financial transaction system. However, Kim's popularity drastically dropped over time due to corruption scandals and disappointing diplomatic performance on the North Korean issue. In December 1995, the once record-high support rate for Kim plummeted to 33.4 percent. Under these circumstances, the controversy over Dokdo between the ROK and Japan erupted in February 1996, only two months before a general election in South Korea. When the ROK government announced its plan to construct a wharf facility on Dokdo, the Japanese government vehemently objected and claimed sovereignty over the islands. In response, the Kim administration acted decisively. In a press release, the Kim government stated that Japan recently angered our nation by making a groundless claim that Dokdo is its territory, which is obviously South Korean territory in terms of history and international law. The Kim government also cancelled Kim's scheduled meeting with a delegation of Japanese politicians. Kim also said that his government would "sternly deal with" Japan over the issue. These statements infuriated the Japanese people, souring ROK–Japan relations (Koo 2009, 85–90; Choi 2005, 476–82).

In many respects, President Kim Dae-jung (1998–2003) showed a more independent foreign policy than his predecessor, although he was also constrained by domestic public opinion and international political structure. A most important foreign policy goal during his tenure was to achieve reconciliation between the two Koreas. As a longstanding political dissident, Kim maintained a clear vision for inter-Korean reconciliation and peaceful unification. To accomplish his vision, Kim adopted the so-called Sunshine Policy of reconciliation and cooperation with North Korea, in opposition to Cold War rivalry. As addressed in detail in Chapter 10, the Kim administration made every effort to increase humanitarian and economic exchanges between the two Koreas, while seeking to defuse military tensions.

Kim conducted two significant diplomatic initiatives to gain external support for his Sunshine Policy. The first was to improve South Korea's relationship with its former adversary, Japan. As noted before, during the Kim Young-sam government, ROK–Japan relations deteriorated due mainly to the Dokdo and comfort women controversies. Running counter to this trend, President Kim Dae-jung visited Japan in October 1998 for a summit with Prime Minister Obuchi Keizo. At the summit, Kim gladly accepted Obuchi's written apology for the sufferings inflicted on the Korean people during the 1910–1945 period of Japanese colonial rule. Moreover, the two leaders announced a new Korea–Japan partnership toward the twenty-first century. This declaration was not only rhetoric; the ROK government for the first time decided to gradually open the nation's markets to Japanese cultural products. This act was unimaginable before, as many Koreans still believed that any influx of Japanese cultural goods could regenerate Japanese colonization. This agreement worked as a vehicle for augmenting other cultural exchanges and paved the way for the rise of *Hallyu* (the "Korean

Wave" of popular cultural outflows) in Japan after 2003 (Ku 2016b). The 1997–1998 Asian financial crisis was arguably another motive for the Kim administration to take drastic measures. Since the financial crisis had seriously damaged the South Korean economy, the Kim government desperately needed economic assistance from Japan (Cho 2015).

The second diplomatic initiative to spur the Sunshine Policy was for Kim to persuade the United States to adopt an engagement approach to North Korea. Kim and his aides knew that it would be extremely hard for the ROK to promote its cooperative relationship with North Korea if the United States, South Korea's most important ally, preserved a hostile stance toward the North. US President Bill Clinton was actually wary of the Sunshine Policy, as was a hawkish Republican-dominated Congress. In reaction to the DPRK's firing of a long-range missile over Japan in August 1998, Clinton appointed former Secretary of Defense William Perry as his North Korea Policy Coordinator and asked Perry to conduct a comprehensive review of US policy. Perry was a hawkish figure who had in 1994 argued for surgical strikes on North Korean nuclear facilities. The ROK government, therefore, was quite concerned about the possibility that the Clinton administration would adopt a more hardline attitude toward the DPRK than before. America's hawkish stance on North Korea would have resulted in impeding Kim's Sunshine Policy. Thus ROK President Kim Dae-jung and his senior presidential secretary for foreign and security affairs, Im Dong-won, made every effort to persuade Perry to turn away from his confrontational attitude toward North Korea (Im 2015, 305–29).

Successfully persuaded, in October 1999, Perry issued his report recommending a two-path strategy. If the DPRK gave up its missile development, the US would normalize relations with the DPRK, lift sanctions that had long constrained trade with the DPRK, and take other positive steps. Otherwise, the United States and its allies would have to take defensive actions to promote their security and contain the North Korean threat.[2] Under the so-called Perry Process, the two Koreas held their first inter-Korean summit in June 2000. Bill Clinton then invited DPRK Vice Marshall Cho Myung-rok to the White House in October 2000 to discuss improvements in US–DPRK relations. Two weeks later, US Secretary of State Madeleine Albright visited Pyongyang and met with Kim Jong-il. These actions showed that political leaders in South Korea could change the international context from restrictive to favorable conditions for inter-Korean reconciliation. However, the Kim government's Sunshine Policy was significantly limited by the George Bush administration's anti-North Korea stance. After he came to power in January 2001, President Bush discarded his predecessor's engagement policy toward North Korea and identified the nation as part of an "axis of evil" in his 2002 State of the Union address.

It is also important to note that, as the first South Korean leader to envision East Asia as a peaceful community, Kim Dae-jung paid special attention to the promotion of East Asian regionalism. While going through the 1997–1998 financial crisis, Kim realized the significance of regional cooperation in coping with economic crisis and fostering sound economic development. To this end, the Kim government emphasized two strategies. First, it helped consolidate the framework of the ASEAN (Association of Southeast Asian Nations) Plus Three (APT),[3] which was designed in 1995 to develop East Asian regional cooperation. In December 1998, Kim proposed the formation of an East Asia Vision Group and East Asia Study Group to encourage the private sector to research future economic cooperation within the APT. In 2001, Kim also made a proposal to establish a free trade area that would include all APT members, although it was ultimately deemed somewhat premature. Second, the Kim government made great efforts to conclude a free trade agreement (FTA) with its major trading partners, such as China, Japan, the European Union, and the United States. This active FTA policy aimed to prevent economic isolation amidst the global trend of extending regional FTAs and to expand export markets and foreign direct investment into South Korea (Lee 2008, 203–4).

President Roh Moo-hyun (2003–2008) most earnestly adopted an independent foreign policy compared to previous ROK presidents. In December 2002, Roh was elected as the ninth ROK president with strong support from young Koreans of anti-American sentiments. The origin of anti-American sentiment among the Korean public dated back to the early 1980s when President Ronald Reagan tacitly approved President Chun Doo-hwan's brutal suppression of Korean protesters in Gwangju. But the rise of anti-Americanism in the early 2000s was due mainly to the George Bush administration's hawkish approach to North Korea and the accidental death of two Korean school girls by a US military vehicle. Before the presidential election, Roh expressed his own anti-American posture publicly. When he came into power, Roh desired to enhance the ROK's strategic autonomy and enlarge the nation's role in Northeast Asia, while becoming more independent from the United States. One symbolic event that showed this desire was the Roh administration's negotiations with the US government to transfer wartime operational control (OPCON) from the United States to South Korea by 2012.

The Roh government also sought to play a balancing role between regional powers, given the ROK's growing soft power, successful economic development, and democratization (Sheen 2009, 147). Roh perceived that, on top of the DPRK nuclear problem, Northeast Asia was fraught with mutual mistrust and hegemonic rivalries between China and Japan and between China and the United States. Roh delivered a speech in March 2005 in which he stated that "Korea will play the role of a balancer, not only on the Korean Peninsula, but throughout Northeast Asia" (Pastreich 2005). Following this speech, the Roh administration positioned South Korea as a "peace balancer" that could contribute to peace and prosperity in Northeast Asia, rather than as a hegemonic balancer such as the United Kingdom in nineteenth-century Europe. Many senior level policymakers during Roh's presidency consisted of the so-called 386 Generation – a group of people who were in their 30s in the 1990s (accounting for the numeral 3), who went to college in the 1980s (the 8), and who were born in the 1960s (the 6) – who believed strongly that South Korea could be the 'hub' of Northeast Asia by playing the balancer role. This ambitious policy, however, could not bear fruit due to inadequate domestic support and skepticism from neighboring countries. Many conservatives in South Korean society criticized Roh's balancer policy as weakening the linchpin of ROK foreign policy, the ROK–US alliance. The United States and Japan also feared that South Korea was distancing itself from the American security umbrella in the Pacific and moving closer to China. South Korean foreign policy could not operate free from domestic and international constraints.

Another example showing the structural constraints on South Korean foreign policy during Roh's presidency occurred during the debate of the deployment of South Korean troops to Iraq in 2003–2004. A number of South Korean people, particularly progressive civil organizations, opposed sending ROK troops to Iraq, because they perceived the US war against Iraq as illegitimate. As such, Roh personally disliked the deployment, but he had to support the decision for realist reasons. Roh believed that in this instance it was essential for the ROK to maintain strong cooperation with the United States in order to peacefully resolve the North Korean nuclear problem after the Iraq war ended (French 2003). Right before Roh's inauguration, the second North Korean nuclear crisis erupted. In October 2002, a senior US diplomat revealed that North Korea had been pursuing a secret uranium enrichment program. After this incident, the United States stopped the provision of heavy oils to North Korea, and the DPRK declared the annulment of the 1994 Agreed Framework. North Korea also withdrew from the Nuclear Non-proliferation Treaty in January 2003 and evicted International Atomic Energy Agency inspectors. The DPRK also restarted a nuclear reactor that had been frozen under the 1994 agreement. Under this significant deterioration of US–DPRK relations, Roh could not oppose the deployment of ROK soldiers to Iraq in response to an American request. The Roh government desired to use the deployment as a leverage to deal with the aggressive Bush administration, which had already labeled North Korea as part of an "axis of evil" (Jang 2015). During his presidency, Roh actually strove to resolve peacefully the North Korean nuclear confrontation. While basically following the Sunshine Policy adopted by his predecessor, Roh made a 2005 joint statement on North Korea's denuclearization and the related 2007 action plan in the Six-Party talks, which consisted of the two Koreas, the United States, China, Japan, and Russia.

One peculiar aspect of Roh's diplomacy was to conclude a ROK–US free trade agreement. The Roh government was initially reluctant to pursue the FTA, but it suddenly accelerated the negotiating process in June 2006 and signed the ROK–US FTA in June 2007. This decision to proceed was not obvious, considering his original anti-American stance. Furthermore, based on his progressive ideas, it was natural to expect that Roh would oppose the FTA, which could bring huge profits to big conglomerates through free trade, while damaging the interests of economically weaker actors in South Korean society, such as farmers and workers. Despite this oddness, the Roh administration sought the FTA to expand potential economic growth and to respond to rising Chinese power through the promotion of free trade. The Roh government also intended to utilize the FTA as an instrument for promoting structural reforms in ROK economy and for gaining greater access to the American market for autos and other manufactured goods (Williams et al. 2014).

It is also interesting to note that the Roh government showed a firm stance on historical/territorial disputes with China and Japan, but its ultimate responses to these two neighbors notably diverged. The Chinese Academy of Social Sciences launched the so-called Northeast Project in 2002 and claimed that the ancient kingdom of Goguryeo (37 BC–668 AD) was part of Chinese history. Official Chinese media supported this claim as well. Many Koreans, who proudly considered Goguryeo an ancestral Korean kingdom, were enraged over China's distortion of Korean history. On top of the public uproar, the Roh administration issued official protests against the Northeast Project and criticized the PRC Foreign Ministry on its website describing the misleading history. The ROK government also created the Goguryeo Research Foundation to repudiate the claims of Northeast Project. The Roh government, however, quickly tried to prevent this historical controversy from derailing ROK–China progress in the fields of diplomacy, trade, tourism, and education. In early 2004, the South Korean government stated that "the Northeast Project was purely an academic exercise not connected to the Chinese government" (Larsen 2016). In 2006, furthermore, the ROK government changed the name of the Goguryeo Research Foundation, which aimed to counter the Chinese claims, to the Northeast Asian History Foundation with a much broader mandate.

In a more confrontational mode, in March 2005, Roh declared a "diplomatic war with Japan" in response to the nation's sovereignty claims over Dokdo. Japanese governmental approval of nationalist textbooks that contained territorial claims over the islands but omitted Japan's past misdeeds during World War II provided the pretext for a worsening of relations. It seemed that, as with President Kim Young-sam, Roh tried to rebuild his weakened popularity by bashing Japan, although to be fair, Japan's provocative actions triggered the flare-up (Ku 2016b).

Phase III (2008–2017): continual traditional diplomacy plus middle power diplomacy

This third phase saw a mixture of traditional interest diplomacy and middle power diplomacy in South Korea, though the former was more preeminent than the latter. Unlike their two progressive predecessors, conservative presidents Lee Myung-bak (2008–2013) and Park Geun-hye (2013–2017) adopted a hardline policy toward North Korea to resolve that nation's nuclear and missile adventurism. However, their approach was significantly restrained by the rise of US–China rivalry and a sharply divided public opinion in South Korea. Both conservative presidents also made great efforts to promote South Korea's security and economic interests through cooperation with neighbors. Moving beyond traditional diplomacy, during this third phase, South Korea tried to exert significant influence on vital transnational environmental, developmental, and nuclear non-proliferation issues, thereby enhancing its reputation in the international community. The government paid great attention to global public goods, while simultaneously focusing on protecting security interests and maintaining economic prosperity.

As mentioned before, President Lee Myung-bak firmly criticized the Sunshine Policy, taken by his predecessors, for its inability to change North Korean behavior. Instead, Lee adopted a conditional engagement policy toward North Korea, summarized as "Denuclearization, Opening, and 3000." If North Korea gave up nuclear weapons, South Korea would help the DPRK to reach its gross domestic product (GDP) per capita $3,000 within ten years. In contrast to Lee's expectations, North Korea perceived the policy as a means to topple the DPRK regime, and thus inter-Korean relations deteriorated drastically as detailed in Chapter 10. A series of conflictual incidents ensued. The Geumgang Tourist Resort was shut down because of a South Korean tourist shot dead by a North Korean soldier in 2008. A North Korean submarine's torpedo sank a South Korean naval vessel in March 2010, and 46 crew members were killed. In November 2010, North Korea launched artillery attacks on the South Korean island of Yeonpyeong, with 4 people killed and 16 injured.

Another diplomatic focus of President Lee was to strengthen the ROK–US alliance while maintaining ROK–China cooperation. As mentioned above, ROK–US relations significantly weakened during the rule of the two progressive leaders due mainly to disagreement on North Korea policy and the ROK's balanced approach between the United States and China. South Korean public opinion supported the weaker ROK–US relationship. In a 2004 poll, only 26 percent of Korean respondents expressed a favorable view of the United States, while 61 percent favored China (Chung 2008, 98). China seemed to be a very important nation to South Korea, particularly because China was the ROK's largest trade partner in 2003, while the image of the United States deteriorated due to the rise of anti-Americanism among the Korean public. In these circumstances, the conservative Lee administration sought to improve its relationship with the United States. As part of this effort, in May 2008 the Lee government made a decision to import American beef bones by readjusting the terms of the 2007 ROK–US FTA. However, this decision sparked strong public opposition. The fear of "Mad Cow Disease' swept over South Korean society and was a serious impediment to the Lee government's foreign policy. In June 2010, the Lee administration renegotiated with the United States to postpone the OPCON transfer by two-and-a-half years, which had been planned for April 2012. The rationale was that the delayed transfer could strengthen

America's security commitment to South Korea (*Donga Daily* 2013). Following US guidance, the Lee government also made efforts to strengthen the US–ROK–Japan security triangle by making the General Security of Military Information Agreement (GSOMIA) with Japan. Strong public backlash, however, erupted in June 2012, when it was revealed that the Lee government had secretly pursued the GSOMIA with Japan. Since it retained strong mistrust toward Japan, the Korean public disliked the scheme to share classified military intelligence with an unreliable partner, Japan. The government official who had been in charge of pushing for the conclusion of the GSOMIA had to resign from his post (Ahn and Park 2012). These issues demonstrated the strong impact of the public on South Korean foreign policy.

At the outset of his term in office, Lee tried to improve the soured ROK–Japan relationship dating from the Roh administration by emphasizing future-oriented relations, as opposed to focusing on their past unfortunate and troubled history. However, his initially cordial stance on Japan turned harsh over time, particularly after August 2011, when the Korean Constitutional Court issued a ruling that the ROK government had made inadequate efforts in prompting Japan to address the comfort women and forced laborer issues. At a summit with Japanese Prime Minister Noda Yoshihiko in December 2011, Lee strongly urged Japan to come to terms with the longstanding problems. Moving beyond this pressure, Lee suddenly visited the Dokdo Islands in August 2012 in response to the publication of a new Japanese defense white paper a month earlier that reconfirmed Japan's sovereignty over Dokdo. This unprecedented act was also accompanied by Lee's provocative remark, "Japan's influence in the international community is not as powerful as it once was; the Japanese emperor would not be welcomed without a direct acknowledgement of guilt for Japan's colonial rule of the Korean Peninsula from 1910–1945" (Ku 2016b, 68). It appears that Lee, whose popularity was drastically falling amid corruption scandals implicating associates, used Japan as a diversion to boost his political leverage. As a result, ROK–Japan relations hit bottom. According to public opinion polls, the Japanese unfavorable perception of Korea shifted from 36 percent in 2010 to 66.4 percent in 2014.[4]

In conjunction with these examples of traditional diplomacy, President Lee pursued the Global Korea strategy as part of middle power diplomacy. Under this initiative, the Lee administration hosted a series of major international conferences, including the 2010 G20 Summit, the 2011 Busan High Level Forum on Aid, the 2nd Nuclear Security Summit in 2012, and the Seoul Conference on Cyberspace in 2013. By actively participating in those multilateral institutions and trying to influence the agenda in international affairs, the Lee government exerted great efforts to contribute to the global community, particularly in the realms of international security, development, and the environment. Under the Global Korea strategy, for instance, South Korea expanded its peacekeeping operations by establishing a 3,000-strong standing unit committed to overseas deployments. As part of post-conflict stabilization, in 2010 the nation formed a Provincial Reconstruction Team of 336 personnel in Afghanistan and spent approximately $94 million. As the first country that had shifted from an aid recipient to an aid donor in modern history, South Korea gained credibility from the global community in playing a bridging role between the developing and developed nations (O'Neil 2015, 85). At the 2010 G20 Summit, South Korea, as chair of the event, emphasized the needs and priorities of developing countries in global economic policy discussions. At the 2011 Busan High Level Forum on Aid, South Korea played a key role in forging a new paradigm of development partnership. The ROK government also significantly increased ROK's development assistance from $700 million in 2008 to $1.2 billion in 2011. The Lee government, furthermore, served as a vehicle for promoting the idea of 'low-carbon green growth' as a model for sustainable development. To help developing countries in Asia fight global warming and to promote green growth, the ROK government initiated the East Asia Climate Partnership program in July 2008. All these efforts culminated in the establishment of a Global Green Growth Institute in 2010, whose headquarters are located in Seoul. In 2012, this institution became the first Korea-led international organization (John 2014, 333–8). In this regard, it would be safe to say that the scope of Lee's middle power diplomacy was larger than the East Asian regionalism as pursued by the Kim Dae-jung and Roh Moo-hyun governments.

The presidency of Park Guen-hye (2013–2017) left a very unique legacy in ROK foreign policy involving several dramatic policy shifts. The first was to move from the 'ROK's tilting toward China' to 'its siding with the United States.' The second drastic shift was the sudden transition from its anti-Japan stance to a pro-Japan policy. As explained below, it seems that these notable foreign policy changes were heavily influenced by the mixture of the four factors – the US–China rivalry, American pressure, North Korea's relentless provocations, and the Park government's unreasonable decision-making process.

Above all, it is important to understand the international structure in which the Park government pursued its foreign policy. The Park administration was confronted with an intensification of the US–China rivalry. After the 2008–2009 financial crisis, China, due to its rising economic and military capabilities, became more assertive in dealing with maritime disputes with neighboring countries, such as Japan, Vietnam, and the Philippines. In response to this growing threat, US President Barack Obama declared a so-called pivot to Asia, or rebalance to Asia, in December 2011. Since then, the US government has sought to strengthen ties with allies such as Japan, Australia, and the Philippines, while bolstering partnerships with Vietnam, India, and Myanmar in an attempt to balance China. To this end, the United States also increased its military presence in the East Asian region despite massive budget cuts and worked to establish the Trans-Pacific Partnership (TPP) with 11 other Asia-Pacific nations.

Under these circumstances, Park made every effort to strengthen ROK–China ties while maintaining the robust relationship with the United States. This action can be interpreted as a hedging strategy – not putting all eggs in one basket. South Korea desired to work with both great powers – the United States and China – rather than solely siding with either one of them. Seeking closer relations with China seemed indispensable for dealing with North Korea's belligerent acts as well as for addressing South Korea's economic concerns (Stratfor 2016). As the ROK's largest trade partner, China was extremely important in tackling persistent economic stagnation. China held significant leverage over North Korea, which had conducted a rocket launch and its third nuclear test right before Park's inauguration. In response to these challenges, President Park held six summit meetings with President Xi Jinping and visited China three times in her first two and a half years in office (Tiezzi 2015). Particularly striking was Chinese President Xi Jinping's visit to South Korea in the summer of 2014 without first going to North Korea. This was an unprecedented act in the previous seven decades of China's diplomatic relationships with the two Koreas. In September 2015, Park even stood alongside Chinese President Xi Jinping and Russian President Vladimir Putin in Tiananmen Square to observe the military celebration of the 70th anniversary of the end of World War II. The Barack Obama administration was concerned about Park's presence at the military parade, because it perceived the event as South Korea's tilting toward China at the expense of the United States. In 2015, furthermore, South Korea and China concluded a free trade agreement, and South Korea joined the Asian Infrastructure Investment Bank led by China. Therefore, 2015 marked a peak in ROK–China relations.

However, the Park government rapidly shifted to strengthening the US–ROK–Japan triangular relationship that China had disliked. The first significant shift in the Park administration's foreign policy was the conclusion of the comfort women agreement with Japan on December 28, 2015. After taking power in February 2013, President Park actually kept up a critical stance on Japan, believing that the former colonizer had not adequately come to terms with its past misdeeds, particularly on the comfort women issue. Park's domestic political calculations may have worked as a motive for bashing Japan, because she was vulnerable to criticism that highlighted her late father, Park Jung-hee's, pro-Japanese actions (McGill 2014). Until November 2015, Park held no summit with Japanese Prime Minister Abe Shinzo, who had supported a revisionist historical view of World War II. The Park government blamed the Abe administration for not fully addressing the comfort women issue before many of the elderly victims had passed away. Responding to this criticism in June 2014, the Abe government even tried to damage the credibility of the Kono Statement, which for the first time acknowledged Japan's involvement in the forced recruitment of comfort women in 1993. To this end, Abe had a Japanese government panel investigate the creation of the Kono Statement, and the committee claimed that the statement was formed as a consequence of a *political* compromise between the ROK and Japanese governments (*Asahi Shimbun* 2014). The Park government was also concerned about the Abe government's reinterpretation of the war-renouncing article 9 of the peace constitution in July 2014. As a result of this decision, Japan could exercise the right to collective self-defense by using its Self-Defense Forces to defend its allies even if Japan itself was not under attack (*Japan Times* 2014). With the Chinese government, furthermore, the ROK condemned the Abe government for refusing to acknowledge past crimes during World War II. A key symbolic measure was to jointly build a memorial hall in China in January 2014 to honor Ahn Jung-geun, a Korean independence hero. In 1909, he had assassinated Ito Hirobumi, the first Japanese resident-general of Korea, who had forced a protectorate pact on the Korean people (*Korea Times* 2014).

However, soon Park's anti-Japan policy radically shifted to a pro-Japan posture. The Park administration made a surprising agreement with the Japanese government regarding the comfort women issue on December 28, 2015. Under this agreement, Japan acknowledged its responsibility, though not in a legal sense, for the inhumanity of sexual slavery and provided an apologetic statement. The nation also promised to pay $8.3 million to surviving victims through the provision of governmental funds. The Park government in turn admitted that this agreement was a "final and irrevocable resolution" of the issue and agreed to consider moving a statue of comfort women in front of Japanese embassy in Seoul to a different place. Seoul and Tokyo also agreed that they would cease criticizing each other over the issue at the United Nations and elsewhere (Choe 2015). The ROK and Japanese governments had actually sought to resolve the contentious problem through 12 rounds of negotiations since spring 2014, but their views of the issue diverged too much. Thus the agreement's signing was surprising.

It is worth noting that there were three important catalysts for the sudden making of the comfort women agreement.[5] First, the Abe government had yearned to end the controversy over the longstanding, burdensome comfort women issue in order to construct a more positive version of Japanese history and restore its seriously damaged reputation in the international community. Over the last two decades, comfort women victims and civil society groups supporting them had conducted strong transnational campaigns to push the Japanese government to accept legal responsibility for its atrocities and provide official reparations (Ku 2015). A non-governmental organization, the Korean Council for the Women Drafted for Military Sexual Slavery by Japan, had held weekly rallies in front of the Japanese embassy in Seoul every Wednesday since January 1992. To further exert pressure on Japan, the ROK government and civil society organizations often raised the issue in international forums, including the United Nations and the International Labor Organization. These acts brought shame to Japan and seriously damaged the nation's image at a time when Japan desired to take a leadership role in the international community. Furthermore, this contentious issue found its way to the United States. Korean–American communities in the US constructed comfort women monuments in many places, including in Glendale, California, and Palisades Park, New Jersey (Semple 2012). The Japanese government and Japanese-Americans were extremely sensitive to displays of their dishonorable past. Prime Minister Abe replied that Japan's next generations should not continually have to keep apologizing for the actions of past generations (Fifield 2015). The agreement itself, which comprised a "final and irreversible resolution," reflected Abe's intension to push off the historical burden for all time.

Second, President Park stated that it was urgently necessary to resolve the issue because the comfort women survivors were extremely old. Nine out of the 55 remaining survivors passed away in 2015 alone (Cheong Wa Dae 2015). Despite this humanitarian urgency, however, it also seems necessary to consider an economic reason in understanding the South Korean government's decision to sign the agreement. In the wake of former President Lee Myung-bak's visit to the Dokdo Islands in August 2012, Japanese perceptions of South Korea considerably deteriorated. President Park's inflexible stance on the comfort women issue was another factor that aggravated Japanese feelings toward South Korea. Public opinion polls, conducted annually by the Japanese Cabinet Office, reflected this trend. In a poll taken in January 2012, 62.2 percent of Japanese respondents had favorable perceptions of South Korea, but this number sharply decreased to 39.2 percent in November 2012 and to 31.5 percent in December 2014.[6] As a result, the number of Japanese tourists to South Korea considerably decreased from 3,423,218 in 2012 to 1,742,531 in 2015.[7] Japanese investment in South Korea and trade volumes between the two nations notably shrank as well. In 2011, their bilateral trade volume was worth $108 billion. This number decreased to $95 billion in 2013 and to $72 billion in 2015.[8] These consequences may have burdened the Park administration, which had desperately struggled to revitalize the South Korean economy.

Third, despite the importance of the above two reasons, the comfort women agreement would not have been made without strong US pressure. The US government perceived that the comfort women issue prevented its two close allies, South Korea and Japan, from promoting bilateral cooperation. The United States earnestly desired to consolidate the US–ROK–Japan security triangle in order to effectively check and balance China. In response to a more assertive China, especially regarding the territorial disputes in the South/East China Seas, it was necessary for the United States to maintain close cooperation with its two key allies in the region. This was an extremely important pillar within the Obama administration's Asia policy, which was termed the US 'pivot' to Asia. For the United States, for instance, the construction of a missile defense system in Northeast Asia was vital to weaken China's missile capabilities and deter the North Korean nuclear and missile threats. To establish an effective missile defense system, the United States needed close cooperation with both South Korea and Japan, including the sharing of important military intelligence between the two nations. To this end, the US government pushed the two governments to settle historical grievances (Sneider 2016). As a result, the completion of the comfort women agreement played a pivotal role in revitalizing the US–ROK–Japan triangular relationship at the expense of China's interests. By condemning Japan's historical problems jointly with South Korea, China tried to drive a wedge between South Korea and Japan and weaken the US–ROK–Japan security triangle, but its strategy failed due to the sudden conclusion of the agreement.

Another surprising foreign policy taken by the Park government was the July 2016 decision to deploy the Terminal High Altitude Area Defense (THAAD) missile defense system in South Korea. Before this final decision was made, the Park government was very cautious because of strong Chinese opposition and a sharply divided public. The Chinese government vehemently opposed the US rationale that THADD in South Korea was aimed at solely defending against a North Korean missile attack. Chinese leaders firmly believed that THADD would pose a serious damage to China's missile capabilities, because the X-band radar in THAAD system has the capability to detect important military activities within the Chinese territory (Swaine 2017). On top of this Chinese pressure, many progressive Korean citizens were extremely concerned about THAAD deployment, as they predicted that the decision would drastically hurt ROK–China relations and push South Korea into a US–China confrontation. On the other hand, many conservatives in ROK society regarded the THAAD deployment as within the sovereign rights of South Korea, which would contribute to the promotion of its national security.

Despite this external and internal resistance, in July 2016, the Park government made the final decision to deploy THADD in South Korea. North Korea's fourth nuclear test in January 2016 seems to be the most significant reason behind the decision. In response to the nuclear test, the Park administration actually shut down the Kaesong Industrial Complex, one of the last symbols of inter-Korean cooperation. Since 2004, when the Kaesong complex was built, the site had not been largely affected by periods of political tension between the two Koreas, although it was temporarily closed for four months in April 2013 when North Korea pulled out its 54,000 workers out amid military tensions on the Korean Peninsula. The rationale for the ROK government's decision was "to prevent the DPRK regime from using hard currency earned through the venture to fund its nuclear and ballistic missile programs" (*Guardian* 2016). Even so, it was strange that the Park government made the delicate diplomatic decision without making all efforts to persuade the Korean public and the Chinese government to accept the rationale behind THAAD deployment. Park's abrupt decisions may have been influenced by the advice of her old friend, Choi Soon-sil, with an accompanying lack of adequate, effective communications between Park and her official aides. The revelation of Choi's secret involvement in important presidential decisions became a decisive trigger leading to the impeachment of President Park.

Moving beyond the dynamics of traditional diplomacy, the Park government continually sought middle power diplomacy. For instance, the Park government launched the 'Eurasia Initiative' targeted at building a logistics and energy network through North Korea, Russia, Central Asia, and Europe. The Park regime paid special attention to the Northeast Asia Peace and Cooperation Initiative in an attempt "to overcome the 'Asia paradox' of high levels of economic interdependence but low levels of trust and political cooperation" (Robertson 2016). The Park administration also served as a coalition builder by taking an initiative to form MIKTA, an informal 'middle power consultative body,' that included Mexico, Indonesia, South Korea, Turkey, and Australia. The Korean government refers to this initiative as "one between middle-power nations that share core values of democracy and free market economy and have the willingness and capability to contribute to the international community's development" (Shin 2013). However, the pursuit of middle power diplomacy during Park's presidency was less enthusiastic than during the Lee administration. Park discarded her predecessor's Global Green Growth Initiative, which aimed to establish South Korea as a global hub of green growth and sustainable development. Except in the case of MITKA, Park could not fully facilitate the above-mentioned middle power initiatives, because the regime was overwhelmed by the unstable condition on the Korean

Peninsula, caused by North Korea's leadership change and nuclear/missile adventurism (John 2014, 338–9).

Conclusion

This chapter has thus far examined the evolution of South Korean foreign policy since the end of the Korean War through the two analytical lenses – traditional interest diplomacy and middle power diplomacy. The chapter showed that the ROK's diplomacy has been centered on the maximization of its national interests, which are to protect its security from North Korean threats, to foster inter-Koran reconciliation, and to promote its economic prosperity. On top of this traditional diplomacy, South Korea has also made efforts to promote global public goods – on developmental, environmental, and international security issues – in the international community by proactively participating in global institutions since the late 2000s. This chapter also paid special attention to the impact of three factors – top leadership, domestic public opinion, and international political structure – on South Korean foreign policy. South Korean presidents usually had ultimate authority to determine ROK foreign policy, but they were also constrained by international structures, such as the Cold War, the easing/intensification of rivalries between the United States and the Soviet Union and between the United States and China. After the ROK's democratization in 1987, foreign policy initiatives were often bounded by domestic public opinion as well. It is a challenging task for the ROK, having ascended to middle power status, to maintain its security, perhaps even to achieve a peaceful reunification in the future, and to promote prosperity among the recalcitrant North Korea and the four big giants – the United States, China, Japan, and Russia.

Notes

1 The term 'comfort women' is a euphemism for women drafted for military sexual slavery by Japan during the Asia-Pacific War. The term is used in this book because scholars have commonly used it in their works.
2 US Department of State, "North Korea." Available at www.state.gov/outofdate/bgn/northkorea/26220.htm.
3 The ASEAN Plus Three consists of ten members of the Association of Southeast Asian Nations (ASEAN) and the three Northeast Asian countries – China, Japan, and South Korea.
4 Japanese Cabinet Office. Available at http://survey.gov-online.go.jp/index-gai.html.
5 This discussion derives from Yangmo Ku's (2016a) previous work.
6 Japanese Cabinet Office. Available at http://survey.gov-online.go.jp/index-gai.html.
7 Korea Tourism Organization. Available at http://kto.visitkorea.or.kr/kor/notice/data/statis/profit/notice/inout/popup.kto.
8 Korea International Trade Organization. Available at www.kita.org/kStat/byCount_AllCount.do.

References

Ahn, Chang-hyun, and Byong-su Park. 2012. "Security Aid Resigns in Fallout from Military Pact with Japan." *The Hankyoreh*, July 6.
Asahi Shimbun. 2014. "S. Korea Issues Paper Blasting Japanese Study of 'Comfort Women' Statement." June 27.
Bridges, Brian. 1993. *Japan and Korea in the 1990s: From Antagonism to Adjustment*. Cambridge: Cambridge University Press.
Cha, Victor D. 1999. *Alignment Despite Antagonism: The US-Korea-Japan Security Triangle*. Cambridge: Cambridge University Press.

Cheong Wa Dae. 2015. "Address to the Nation on the Agreement on the Comfort Women Issue." December 31. Available at: www.korea.net/Government/Briefing- Room/Presidential-Speeches/view? articleId=136045.

Cho, Se-young. 2015. "50th Anniversary of Diplomatic Normalization: The Analysis of Korea-Japan Relations and Recommendations." Jeju Peace Institute Policy Forum, February 27. (in Korean)

Choe, Sang-hun. 2015. "Japan and South Korea Settle Dispute over Wartime Comfort Women." *New York Times*, December 28.

Choi, Sung-jae. 2005. "The Politics of the Dokdo Issue." *Journal of East Asian Studies* 5 (3): 465–94.

Chung, Jae-ho. 2008. *Between Ally and Partner: Korea-China Relations and the United States*. New York: Columbia University Press.

Cooper, Andrew F., Richard A. Higgott, and Kim R. Nossal. 1993. *Relocating Middle Powers: Australia and Canada in a Changing World Order*. Vancouver: University of British Columbia Press.

Donga Daily. 2013. "National Security Is Key in Determining Delay in OPCON Transfer." July 18. Available at: http://english.donga.com/List/3/all/26/406635/1.

Eckert, Carter J., Ki-Baik Lee, Young Ick Lew, Michael Robinson, and Edward W. Wagner. 1990. *Korea Old and New: A History*. Cambridge, MA: Harvard University Press.

Fifield, Anna. 2015. "Japan's Leader Stops Short of WWII Apology." *The Washington Post*, August 14.

French, Howard. 2003. "Despite Protests, Seoul to Send Troops to Iraq for Reconstruction." *The New York Times*, April 2.

Goldstein, Joshua S., and Jon C. Pevehouse. 2012. *International Relations*. New York: Longman.

Guardian. 2016. "Seoul Shuts Down Joint North-South Industrial Complex." February 10.

Heo, Uk, and Terence Roehrig. 2010. *South Korea Since 1980*. New York: Cambridge University Press.

Im, Dong-won. 2015. *Peacemaker: Inter-Korean Relations and 25 Years of North Korean Nuclear Issue*. Seoul: Changbi. (in Korean)

Jang, Hoon. 2015. "An Analysis of the Decision Making Process of Sending Troops to Iraq (2003~2004): Changing Roles of the President, the Parliament and Civil Society." *Dispute Resolution Studies Review* 13 (2): 105–35. (in Korean)

Japan Times. 2014. "Abe Guts Article 9." July 2. Available at: www.japantimes.co.jp/opinion/2014/07/02/editorials/abe-guts-article- 9/#.WNp4mjui5Oo.

John, Jojin V. 2014. "Becoming and Being a Middle Power: Exploring a New Dimension of South Korea's Foreign Policy." *China Report* 50 (4): 325–41.

Katzenstein, Peter J., Robert O. Keohane, and Stephen D. Krasner. 1998. "International Organization and the Study of World Politics." *International Organization* 52 (4): 645–85.

Koo, Minkyo. 2009. *Island Disputes and Maritime Regime Building in East Asia: Between a Rock and a Hard Place*. New York: Springer.

Korea Times. 2014. "Ahn Jung-geun Hall Worsens Seoul-Tokyo Ties." January 21.

Ku, Yangmo. 2015. "National Interest or Transnational Alliances? Japanese Policy on the Comfort Women Issue." *Journal of East Asian Studies* 15 (2): 243–69.

Ku, Yangmo. 2016a. "What Is it for? Assessing the South Korea-Japan Deal on the Comfort Women Issue." *E-International Relations*, February 18.

Ku, Yangmo. 2016b. "Irreparable Animosity? Centripetal and Centrifugal Force in South Korea-Japan Mutual Perceptions, 1998–2015." *Asian Journal of Peacebuilding* 4 (1): 53–76.

Larsen, Kirk. 2016. "South Korean Views of Chinese History." *The Asan Forum*, August 29. Available at: www.theasanforum.org/south-korean-views-of-chinese-history/.

Lee, Chae-jin. 2006. *A Troubled Peace: U.S. Policy and the Two Koreas*. Baltimore, MD: Johns Hopkins University Press.

Lee, Chong-Sik. 1985. *Japan and Korea: The Political Dimension*. Stanford, CA: Hoover Institution Press.

Lee, Jae-Bong. 2009. "U.S. Deployment of Nuclear Weapons in 1950s South Korea & North Korea's Nuclear Development: Toward the Denuclearization of the Korean Peninsula." *The Asia-Pacific Journal* 8 (3). Available at: http://apjjf.org/-Lee-Jae-Bong/3053/article.html.

Lee, Seokwoo, and Jon M. Van Dyke. 2010. "The 1951 San Francisco Peace Treaty and Its Relevance to the Sovereignty over Dokdo." *Chinese Journal of International Law* 9 (4): 741–62.

Lee, Sook-Jong. 2008. "Korean Perspectives on East Asian Regionalism." In *East Asian Multilateralism: Prospects for Regional Stability*, edited by Kent E. Calder and Francis Fukuyama. Baltimore, MD: Johns Hopkins University.

McGill, Peter. 2014. "Why History Is a Problem for Park Geun-hye in Confronting Japan." *East Asia Forum*, September 23.

Nau, Henry. 2015. *Perspectives on International Relations: Power, Institutions, and Ideas*. Washington, DC: CQ Press.

O'Neil, Andrew. 2015. "South Korea as a Middle Power: Global Ambitions and Looming Challenges." *Council on Foreign Relations* June: 75–89.

Oh, John K. 1999. *Korean Politics: The Quest for Democratization and Economic Development*. Ithaca, NY: Cornell University Press.

Pastreich, Emmanuel. 2005. "The Balancer: Roh Moo-hyun's Vision of Korean Politics and the Future of Northeast Asia." *The Asia-Pacific Journal* 3 (8). Available at: http://apjjf.org/-Emanuel-Pastreich/2041/article.html.

Robertson, Jeffrey. 2016. "An End to South Korea's Middle Power Moment?" *East Asia Forum*, December 30.

Semple, Kirk. 2012. "In New Jersey, Memorial for 'Comfort Women' Deepens Old Animosity." *The New York Times*, May 18.

Sheen, Seong-ho. 2009. "Out of America, into the Dragon's Arms: South Korea a Northeast Asian Balancer." In *Rise of China and International Security: America and Asia Respond*, edited by Kevin J. Cooney and Yochiro Sato, 140–58. New York: Routledge.

Shin, Hyon-hee. 2013. "Korea, 4 Middle Powers Launch Dialogue Body." *Korea Herald*, September 6.

Sneider, Daniel. 2016. "Behind the Comfort Women Agreement." *Tokyo Business Today*, January 10.

Soeya, Yoshihide. 2006. *Japan's Middle Power Diplomacy: Postwar Japan's Decision and Plan*. Seoul: Oreum. (in Korean)

STRATFOR. 2016. "South Korea's Neighbors Brace for a Foreign Policy Shift." December 28. Available at: www.stratfor.com/analysis/south-koreas-neighbors-brace-foreign- policy-shift.

Swaine, Michael. 2017. "Chinese Views on South Korea's THAAD Deployment." Carnegie Endowment for International Peace, February 2. Available at: http://carnegieendowment.org/2017/02/02/chinese-views-on-south-korea-s-deployment-of-terminal-high-altitude-area-defense-thaad-pub-67891.

Tiezzi, Shannon. 2015. "South Korea's President and China's Military Parade." *The Diplomat*, September 3.

Wampler, Robert. 2010. "Seeing Human Rights in the "Proper Manner": The Reagan-Chun Summit of February 1981." *National Security Archive Electronic Briefing Book No. 306*.

Whyte, Leon. 2015. "Evolution of U.S.-ROK Alliance: Abandonment Fears." *The Diplomat*, June 22.

Williams, Brock R., Mark E. Manyin, Remy Jurenas, and Michaela D. Platzer. 2014. "The U.S.- South Korea Free Trade Agreement (KORUS FTA): Provisions and Implementation." Congressional Research Service, RL34330.

6 North Korean ideology and politics

Jongseok Woo

When the falling dominoes of communist regimes swept across all of Eastern Europe and the Soviet Union since 1989, some communist regimes – China, Vietnam, North Korea, and Cuba – did not suffer the same fate, but have proven to be resilient. Communist parties in China and Vietnam not only survived, but also thrived with the adoption of a free market economy, while keeping a one-party dictatorship. Meanwhile, North Korea presents another intriguing model; it did not succumb to the wave of communist collapses in Europe and the Soviet Union, but it did not transform itself to adopt the Chinese or Vietnamese path of reform either. Although still surviving, the Pyongyang regime does not seem to have a long-term solution for the poverty-stricken country. A corollary prophecy has been that the regime will not survive for long and will collapse sooner or later. Such 'collapsist' argument is not new, but it became prevalent after Kim Il-sung died in 1994, followed by a three-year power vacuum, natural disasters and nationwide famines, and massive defections (the so-called *Gonaneui Haenggun*, or Arduous March).

Contrary to the collapsist forecast, however, the Pyongyang regime has proven resilient; it has survived numerous domestic problems and hostile international environments, and it even completed another hereditary power succession from Kim Jong-il to Jong-un in 2011. In the most recent decade, the Pyongyang regime has conducted nuclear tests five times (once in 2006, 2009, 2013, and twice in 2016). Also, even though North Korea's program of weapons of mass destruction (WMD) has resulted in severe economic sanctions by the international community, North Korean leaders have refused to curtail it. What makes the Pyongyang regime resilient? How has the three-generation hereditary succession been possible with little to no political backlash? Does a long-term solution exist for such an anachronistic political system and economy?

This chapter explains the political trajectory of North Korea, from its state-building period to the power succession from Kim Jong-il to Jong-un. The discussion in the ensuing section begins with the rise of Kim Il-sung as the undisputed North Korean leader through power struggles and the emergence of his *Juche* ideology in the 1950s and 1960s. Sections two and three explore the power succession from Kim Il-sung to Kim Jong-il in the 1970s and Kim Jong-il's military-first politics in the 1990s. Section four discusses the most recent hereditary succession to Kim Jong-un and the youngest Kim's consolidation of power as a young and inexperienced *Suryong*.

The rise of Kim Il-sung and *Juche*

The end of the 36-year Japanese colonial rule in 1945 did not lead to the establishment of an independent and unified Korea, as the wartime superpowers – the United States and the Soviet Union – decided to divide the territory along the 38th parallel. It was the Soviet army that first arrived in the northern half of the peninsula after Japan's defeat. Within two weeks of the Japanese surrender, the Red Army had completed its occupation of the northern half, which was long before American soldiers had arrived in Incheon, a major port city immediately west of Seoul. Although the Soviet Union entrenched its dominance over the northern half, it did not have clear strategic objectives, let alone even a basic understanding of the country or the people. However, as the wartime alliance between the two superpowers quickly fell apart and tensions escalated, the Soviet occupation force began to establish a Muscovite communist regime within its own occupation zone, just as its American counterpart was building a pro-American regime in the southern half.

State-building and Kim Il-sung's political rise

During the early period of Soviet occupation, Kim Il-sung was only one of several communist leaders in post-colonial Korea. Kim Il-sung was a former guerrilla leader who had fought with the Japanese army in the 1930s, although reliable documents on Kim's activities prior to 1945 are virtually nonexistent. Kim Il-sung (allegedly, his original name was Kim Song-ju) was born in 1912 in the village of Mangyongdae, located on the southwestern outskirts of the capital city of Pyongyang. His father was a devout Presbyterian Christian who attended an American missionary school and worked as an herbal pharmacist until Japan colonized the Korean Peninsula. Kim spent most of his early life in Manchuria; he began his guerrilla career as early as 1932, when he was just 20 years old, as part of the Northeast Anti-Japanese United Army, which contained several guerrilla organizations led by the Chinese Communist Party (CCP) (Armstrong 2003, 28). Later, North Korean history obliterated Kim's guerrilla activities under the CCP's command and instead eulogized his heroic victories against the Japanese. At the height of Kim Il-sung's guerrilla activity in 1937 through 1940, he commanded as many as 300 men – both Chinese and Koreans (Suh 1988, 14). At the turn of the 1940s, Kim Il-sung became the most wanted guerrilla leader by the Japanese, who carried out military expeditions to eradicate the guerrilla forces operating across Manchuria. The massive 'annihilation campaigns' by the Japanese forced Kim and his followers to cross the border and join the Soviet Red Army. Kim Il-sung entered the Khabarovsk School for Infantry Officers, where he trained as an infantry officer and studied Russian until World War II ended.

When Kim Il-sung and his comrades returned to North Korea as officers of the Soviet Red Army, Kim was not a dominant figure among the communist elites in Pyongyang. One prominent communist leader was Pak Hon-yong, who organized the Joseon Communist Party (JCP) Reconstruction Committee on August 20, only five days after the Japanese surrender. In contrast, Kim Il-sung and his faction returned to North Korea on September 19, 1945, not as national heroes like Rhee Syngman in the southern half, but as Soviet army officers. In September 1945, Pak Hon-yong and his communist followers officially created the JCP with headquarters in Seoul, which was then under occupation by American forces. That the communist party was headquartered in US-controlled Seoul presented the Soviet occupation force with a political dilemma. As a result, in October, the Soviets sponsored a communist party convention in Pyongyang to establish the Northern Branch of the JCP. The convention elected the first secretary of the party (Kim Yong-beom), the second secretary (Oh Gi-seop), and a 17-member executive committee. Kim Il-sung was elected as one of these executive committee members, which implies that he was still not a leading political figure in Pyongyang. Even when the Korean Workers' Party (KWP) was officially inaugurated in

August 1946, Kim was still not the dominant figure; he was elected one of two vice chairmen of the KWP and kept the position until 1949.

However, Kim Il-sung quickly emerged as a prominent leader in Pyongyang for several reasons. The biggest contributor to Kim's political rise was Moscow's support for him as the leader of communist North Korea. In October 1945, Red Army General Andrei Romanenko praised Kim Il-sung as the paramount patriot who had heroically fought against Japan imperialists. The Soviet occupation established a provisional people's committee in early 1946 and appointed Kim as the leader of the committee, which allowed him to expand his influence over the indigenous communist groups in the northern half of the peninsula. Another reason for Kim's political rise was that, in the post-liberation period, Seoul (and not Pyongyang) was considered the political center for the communist leaders, and most of the leading figures (both communists and nationalists) based their activities in South Korea. The departure of prominent communist leaders for the south made it relatively easy for Kim to emerge as a leading figure above the 38th parallel. (Oh and Hassig 2000, 83).

Kim Il-sung quickly expanded his political power base from about 200 partisans into a nationwide organization. Also, at the heart of the power consolidation process was the military, later officially named the Korean People's Army (KPA) in February 1948. The Soviet occupation force opened the Pyongyang Academy in February 1946 to educate Korean elites in the party, the military, and the government. Kim Chaek, one of the core members of Kim Il-sung's guerrilla group, was appointed as principal of the academy, while instructors were recruited from Soviet-Koreans who taught subjects such as the Russian language, communist ideology, political philosophy, and military science. After 1949, the Pyongyang Academy began to focus on educating political officers (or commissars) who later became the primary instruments for partisan control of the KPA. When the KPA officially launched, Kim Il-sung's guerrilla faction members monopolized all the leadership positions in the army, including Choi Yong-gun (Supreme Commander of the KPA), Kim Il (Commander of the Department of Culture), and Kang Kon (Chief of General Staff), among others (Jung 2011, 80–1). These Manchurian guerrilla faction members served as the backbone of Kim Il-sung's power struggle in the 1950s, paved the road for hereditary succession in the 1970s and 1980s, and buttressed Kim Jong-il's military-first politics in the 1990s. The Soviet occupation force helped to consolidate Kim Il-sung's leadership in the KPA by allowing him to disarm other military factions that could challenge him, including the Yanan faction, the Chinese faction, and the Korean Volunteer Corps under Kim Won-bong's leadership (Suh 1988, 68).

On June 25, 1950, with the backing of the Soviet Union and the People's Republic of China, Kim Il-sung initiated the Korean War to reunify the Korean Peninsula by physical force. Both Kim Il-sung and Pak Hon-yong met with Joseph Stalin and Mao Zedong to receive approval and gain support. They suggested that the war would be quick and decisive and, once initiated, the people in the southern half would rise up and welcome the communist liberators. The Korean War did not progress as Kim hoped, but rather it ended in 1953 with an armistice agreement. The unification failure had an immediate impact on political power struggles in Pyongyang, as Kim attempted to pass the war's failure to his political competitors. Only three days after the armistice agreement, Kim Il-sung convened a show trial to prosecute prominent party leaders for "allegedly aiding and abetting the enemy and plotting to replace the Kim regime. . . " (Oh and Hassig 2000, 7). In particular, he purged the southern faction of the JCP and its leader Pak Hon-yong, who was arrested in August 1953 and sentenced to death in December 1955, despite strong opposition from Beijing and Moscow.

For North Korea, the 1950s was a decade of power struggles, massive purges, and the consolidation of Kim Il-sung's leadership and *Juche* ideology. These political developments in

Pyongyang had both domestic and international origins. Domestically, political power struggles within the KWP revolved around the postwar reconstruction efforts and redefining the socialist political-policy lines within the party. Kim Il-sung and his factional leaders prioritized the heavy industry sectors, while other factional leaders dissented. This policy debate later switched to criticizing Kim Il-sung and his faction's monopoly on political power and his cult of personality that grew after the Korean War. Internationally, political changes in Moscow in the 1950s directly affected the political conditions in Pyongyang in general and Kim Il-sung's political position in particular. The external shock began with the death of Joseph Stalin in 1953 and the power succession to Nikita Khrushchev in 1956. After consolidating his power, Khrushchev attempted to de-Stalinize the Soviet Union by denouncing his predecessor at a closed session of the Communist Party convention for "his intolerance, his brutality and his abuse of power." He urged a return to party-centered collective leadership (Khrushchev 1956). The denouncement of Stalin was a huge blow to Kim Il-sung, who had been replicating what some have called "the Stalinization of North Korea" and his cult of personality. Kim Il-sung's purge of Pak Hon-yong and his fellow faction members broke the power balance among the different communist factions within the KWP, allowing Kim's own faction to entrench its hegemonic status. The Soviet-Korean faction (those who stayed in the Soviet Union during World War II) and the Yanan-Korean faction (those who joined Mao Zedong's army during the period) were left weakened and marginalized.

The Soviet and Yanan faction leaders conspired to redirect Pyongyang toward a more moderate policy line similar to that of the post-Stalin Soviet Union (Lankov 2015, 14). These factions, with support from Moscow and Beijing, attempted a coup d'etat to remove Kim Il-sung while Kim was on a trip to the Soviet Union and communist allies in Eastern Europe in June and July of 1956. However, the coup failed and, at the KWP Central Committee plenary in August, most of the leading members of the two factions were expelled from the party. They were accused of having anti-party and factional tendencies and were later executed or sentenced to forced labor, or they fled to China or the Soviet Union. This so-called August Incident brought about massive purges in the party and the military and ended up consolidating Kim Il-sung's totalitarian dictatorship. From then on, the communist party became Kim Il-sung's party, and the KPA became his military.

Juche and the power succession

Kim Il-sung's power struggle in the 1950s occurred in tandem with the fabrication of the *Juche* ideology. Originally, the political system in Pyongyang merely copied Moscow's political system and ideology and, therefore, it was built on Marxism-Leninism. The first constitution of 1948 was written in Russian and later translated into Korean. Furthermore, in the early years of state-building in North Korea, the term *Suryong* (roughly, chieftain) was used to label prominent communist leaders, such as Vladimir Lenin and Joseph Stalin. However, after the power struggle and Kim Il-sung's monopoly of power, *Suryong* referred only to Kim Il-sung in North Korea. Kim Il-sung's power struggle and his *Juche* led to the establishment of a different kind of a communist political and ideological system dissociated from its patrons in Moscow and Beijing. The *Juche* ideology functioned as the backbone of Kim Il-sung's personality cult throughout his life, as it controlled the ruling elite and the people alike as the guiding ideology and spirit of the entire nation. Its principles shaped the country's overall policy lines and provided ideological justification for the hereditary succession of his son and grandson. Although North Koreans claim that Kim Il-sung's *Juche* emerged in the 1930s during his anti-Japanese guerrilla war, the term was first introduced in December 1955 in his speech to the KWP Propaganda and Agitation Department (PAD). In that speech, Kim Il-sung expressed the desire to prevent the de-Stalinization campaign in Moscow from polluting party elites in Pyongyang. At the same time, given that Chinese military forces were still in North Korea, he intended to circumvent Chinese influence through his own ruling ideology. He used *Juche* on behalf of his power struggle against the Chinese and Soviet factions in Pyongyang.

When Kim Il-sung first mentioned *Juche* in the 1950s, the ideology did not have a clear logical or doctrinal structure. Rather, it evolved through North Korea's responses to changing internal and external circumstances thereafter. Domestically, Kim used *Juche* as his ideological platform to purge his political competitors under the banner of anti-factionalism, especially the factions that had ties to the South Korean communists and the party elites tied to Beijing and Moscow. Externally, Kim's *Juche* stressed political and ideological independence from external forces by emphasizing anti-imperialism that commonly referred to the United States and Japan. When the political and ideological split intensified between Moscow and Beijing in the 1960s, North Korea's *Juche* adopted a balancing act between the two communist patrons by stressing "self-identity in thinking, independence in politics, self-support in economy and self-reliance in national defense" (Yang 1994, 183). After the Sino-Soviet split dissipated in the early 1970s, *Juche* began to emphasize constructing a socialist economy in North Korea by mobilizing the masses with slogans, such as the *Cheollima* Movement, the 70-Day Battle, and the 200-Day Battle. The *Cheollima* Movement officially began in 1958 in order to mobilize the entire populace to build an advanced socialist economy, something similar to Mao's Great Leap Forward (1958–1962). The second *Cheollima* Movement was introduced in 1998–2004, after Kim Jong-il officially emerged as the successor to his father. The third *Cheollima* Movement began in 2009. *Juche* has defined North Korea's economic policy as economic autarchy that suppressed foreign trade and investments and resulted in economic isolation.

As a political principle, the *Juche* ideology encompasses four components: (1) A human is the master of his or her fate, (2) the people are the masters of the revolution, (3) the revolution must be pursued in a self-determinant manner, and (4) absolute loyalty to the supreme leader (*Suryong*, or Kim Il-sung himself) is the key to the revolution's success (Cha 2012, 37). During an interview with a Japanese newspaper, Kim stated that

> [t]he idea of *Juche* means that the masters of the revolution and the work of construction are the masses of the people and that they are also the motive force of the revolution and the work of construction. In other words, one is responsible for one's own destiny and one has also the capacity for hewing out one's own destiny.
>
> (Oh and Hassig 2000, 19)

At the same time, *Juche* was a unique combination of Marxism-Leninism, with nationalism (i.e., patriotism) alongside Korean traditional Confucius values, a combination that differs from Maoism and Stalinism. *Juche* provided Kim Il-sung with ideological justification for his personality cult based on the Confucius teachings of filial piety (or *hyo*) (French 2014, 60–4).

The cult of personality is a common characteristic of totalitarian states, but North Korea's *Juche*-based personality cult is unique and pervasive. The personality cult in ordinary totalitarian states focuses on revering a single dictator as an individual, especially the person's individual qualities and political brilliance. However, North Korea's personality cult goes beyond Kim Il-sung, Jong-il, and Jong-un as individual leaders and sanctifies the entire Kim family, including the leaders' ancestors and their wives. In this sense, the personality cult in North Korea is not merely the cult of an individual leader but rather a family cult (Yang 1994, 255). Cumings (1993) defines North Korea's regime as an Asian version of neosocialist corporatism that departs from Marxist-Leninist doctrines and organizes society based on hierarchy, organic connection, and family. The system creates a paternal style that depicts Kim as the benevolent father of the nation and compares the nation to one large family (Cumings 1993, 209). Kim Il-sung's portraits must be hung everywhere in offices and homes and, after Kim Jong-il was officially declared the successor, his were also displayed just next to his father's. Likewise, North Korea's *Juche* ideology rationalizes the three-generation hereditary successions by the three Kims with the blood line of Mount Baekdu, where Kim Jong-il was allegedly born while his father led anti-Japanese guerrilla forces on the mountain.

It was Kim Jong-il who systematized the ideology to make it Kimilsungism, a national cult that governs people's everyday lives and even their souls. Kim Jong-il was born in 1941 in a Soviet military camp in Khabarovsk. He graduated from Mangyongdae Revolutionary Academy and Kim Il-sung University in 1964, majoring in political economy, philosophy, and military science. Kim Jong-il began his political career in the Organization and Guidance Department (OGD) and the PAD, two of the most powerful departments in the KWP. At the OGD, Kim started in the guidance and personnel positions responsible for supervising lower party units. Often called "the party within the party," the OGD is responsible for enforcing party discipline, appointing high-ranking party cadres, conducting ideological indoctrination, and inspecting other state apparatuses (Jeon 2009, 89). In 1966, Kim Jong-il moved to the PAD and led its Movie and Arts Division to make movies and documentaries that glorified Kim Il-sung and his guerrilla group's heroic fighting during the Japanese colonial era. As the PAD director, Kim founded the *Pibada* (meaning "the sea of blood") Theatrical Troupe and directed five operas of revolution that became the official operas of the country. Among the five operas, *Pibada* is considered the best classical opera that personifies the philosophy of *Juche* and the solidarity of communist revolutionaries. While his works at the PAD effectively propagandized his father as a revolutionary hero who fought the imperialists, Kim Jong-il gained substantial benefits by advertising himself as the devoted interpreter and successor of *Juche* and his father's political authority. Kimilsungism became an official state ideology that was not a mere offspring of Marxism-Leninism, but different and separate from Marxism, Leninism, and Maoism.

Furthermore, although originally written by his uncle Kim Yong-ju in 1967, Kim Jong-il pronounced the "Ten Principles for the Establishment of the *Juche* Idea," or principles that regulate the everyday lives of the people in North Korea. They are as follows (Daily NK 2013):

1 We must give our all in the struggle to unify the entire society with the revolutionary ideology of Great Leader Kim Il-sung.
2 We must honor Great Leader comrade Kim Il-sung with all our loyalty.
3 We must make absolute the authority of Great Leader comrade Kim Il-sung.
4 We must make Great Leader comrade Kim Il-sung's revolutionary ideology our faith, and make his instructions our creed.
5 We must adhere strictly to the principle of unconditional obedience in carrying out the Great Leader comrade Kim Il-sung's instructions.

6   We must strengthen the entire Party's ideology and willpower and revolutionary unity, centering on Great Leader comrade Kim Il-sung.
7   We must learn from Great Leader comrade Kim Il-sung and adopt the communist look, revolutionary work methods, and people-oriented work style.
8   We must value the political life we were given by Great Leader comrade Kim Il-sung and loyally repay his great political trust and thoughtfulness with heightened political awareness and skill.
9   We must establish strong organizational regulations so that the entire Party, nation, and military move as one under the one and only leadership of Great Leader comrade Kim Il-sung.
10 We must pass down the great achievement of the revolution by Great Leader comrade Kim Il-sung from generation to generation, inheriting and completing it to the end.

Furthermore, the Ten Principles contain 65 sub-clauses that detail how to establish *Juche*. All North Koreans, elites and ordinary people alike, must memorize the clauses and perform self-criticisms regularly.

Kim Jong-il's political career arrived at a critical juncture in 1973 when he was appointed party secretary in charge of organization, propaganda, and agitation of the Central Committee of the KWP. One year later, he was appointed a member of the Politburo. Now, it became clear that Kim Jong-il was going to succeed his father. There was virtually no opposition within the KWP given that, by the end of the 1960s, the party and the military were all controlled by Kim Il-sung and his Manchurian guerrilla comrades. Finally, the hereditary succession became official in 1980 at the 6th Congress of the KWP, in which Kim Jong-il was elected a member of the Politburo Standing Committee and the Central Military Commission (CMC). From then on, Kim Jong-il became the *de facto* leader of North Korea, as his father deferred most political decisions to his son until his death. After consolidating his leadership in the KWP, Kim Jong-il also established his authority over the KPA. He was elected vice chair of the National Defense Commission (NDC) in 1990; one year later, he became the Supreme Commander of the KPA. In 1992, he rose to the rank of marshal and the next year he was elected chair of the NDC (Kim I. 2006, 60). After this, the NDC's political authority increased immensely, and it became the most powerful political institution once Kim Jong-il made his leadership official in 1997. As a result, when Kim Il-sung died in 1994, virtually no political turmoil or succession crisis occurred in Pyongyang. However, it took three years for Kim Jong-il to declare himself the undisputed leader of North Korea. The following section discusses why the three-year leadership gap occurred, and why the younger Kim introduced the slogan of military-first politics for his regime's survival.

Kim Jong-il and military-first politics[1]

Challenges to the party-state

The defining characteristic of North Korea under Kim Jong-il was *songun jeongchi* (military-first politics), in which the ultimate aim was to build a *gangseongdaeguk* (a powerful and prosperous nation). These catch words signified the multifaceted problems that threatened the regime's survival. Kim Jong-il's military-first politics was formulated as a strategic response to international structural changes that occurred at the end of the Cold War and the accompanying domestic problems. Complex challenges came from three quarters:

the collapse of the communist regimes in the Soviet Union and Eastern Europe, natural disasters and famine, and Kim Il-sung's death and the ensuing power vacuum.

With the collapse of the Soviet Union in 1991, North Korea lost its biggest security and economic benefactor. Until the end of the 1980s, the Soviet Union, as Pyongyang's largest trade partner, furnished the country with one-sided trade that amounted to $3.5 billion per year (McEachern 2010, 67). However, this amount plummeted at the turn of the 1990s, when both the Soviet Union and China demanded that North Korea use hard currency for trade. Approximately 5 percent of the population was estimated to have perished in a famine that hit North Korea. Although frequent droughts and floods in the 1990s hit the country's already fragile economy and resulted in famine, North Korea faced much more serious structural ills that came from the rigid state-controlled socialist model of economy and the loss of opportunities for reform (Haggard and Noland 2009, 4). The economic hardship threatened the Pyongyang regime, as the state could not continue to provide food and other necessities to its people (probably the only rationale for dictatorial rule). As a result, massive defections to neighboring countries occurred.

Still, the worst disaster came when Kim Il-sung's death in 1994 created a power vacuum in Pyongyang. Despite being a brutal dictator who purged numerous potential rivals and political opponents, Kim Il-sung had enjoyed the "unquestionable acceptance of authority" as the "beloved leader" from ordinary North Koreans for more than four decades (Kim S. 2006, 93). The late Kim legitimized his rule through the glorification and mystification of his leadership in anti-Japanese guerrilla warfare in the 1930s and 1940s and through *Juche*, which his son Jong-il endeavored to develop into a national ideology throughout his political career. Kim Il-sung was revered by North Koreans as the founder of the nation and the *Juche* ideology. When he died, the loyalty vacuum could not be filled, as no one, not even his son, could compare to the "Great Leader."

Faced with multiple challenges to the regime's survival, the KWP as the highest political organ of the state proved incompetent: The party itself was plagued with bureaucratic indolence, arrogance, and rampant corruption. With the collapse of the former communist regimes, communism as a utopian political ideology lost its charm worldwide. The KWP, as the vanguard of Kim Il-sung's *Juche* ideology, failed to win popular loyalty; instead, the party organ continued to rely on the suppression of information and communication, as outside information streamed in to its people. There was a growing discrepancy between the party's propaganda for a utopian society and popular disenchantment. The KWP's inability to govern became evident as the economy continued to deteriorate into the mid-1990s, and the party's control over the people slackened during the Arduous March period. Kim Jong-il certainly realized that the party was unable to offer remedies for the country's troubles; mere attempts to revamp party organizations or reshuffle senior leadership positions would not solve these problems.

Another reason for Kim Jong-il's increasing reliance on the KPA stemmed from his own conviction that the communist regimes in the Soviet Union and Eastern Europe had collapsed not because of their economic difficulties, but because of their "failure to establish and maintain a firm ideology to manage their societies" (Jeon 2009, 183). Kim Jong-il emphasized that

> socialist countries have collapsed, with no shots fired, because they did not have strong troops. There will be no people, no socialist country, and no communist party if they do not have a strong army at a time when they are constructing a socialist society under siege and threat of imperialists.
>
> (Kim 1999, 267)

Certainly, Kim Jong-il's military-first politics derived from lessons on regime survival learned from the experiences of former communist compatriots. Until his death, Kim Jong-il struggled to build the KPA as the vanguard of the *Juche* ideology and guarantor of his regime.

A more deep-seated reason for Kim Jong-il's decision to demote the KWP and align with the KPA was that he lacked his father's leadership qualities and charisma. Kim Jong-il did not possess his father's credentials as a revolutionary. He had not fought a guerrilla war for independence (not to mention not having an active military service career), did not invent a governing ideology, and was not even a good communicator. One of Kim Jong-il's most cherished political endeavors was to enforce party discipline through the OGD, which was responsible for the appointment of high-ranking party cadres, ideological instruction, and the inspection of other state apparatuses (Jeon 2009, 89). However, Kim Jong-il's efforts to enforce discipline and competence in the party were met only with the declining efficiency of the pivotal political organ by the end of the 1980s. In sum, Kim Jong-il's military-first politics emerged in response to internal and external problems that the KWP proved incapable of solving.

Power shift from the party to the military

The ascendance of the KPA under military-first politics was a clear deviation from the orthodox Leninist party system found in traditional totalitarian regimes. In a communist regime, the party as the vanguard of the proletariat commands the highest authority; the party envisions the state ideology, controls the lives of government officials and ordinary citizens, and formulates government policy. Supposedly, the party maintains unity through its leadership of the Politburo (Standing Committee), elected by the Central Committee, which in turn is elected by the Party Congress, while local party cells elect Party Congress members (Scobell 2006, 18). In a party-state, the party administers the organs that represent the proletariat and fulfill the revolutionary mission. In North Korea, however, the party's authority is identified with *suryong*, because it merely carries out *suryong*'s instructions. Rather than becoming the source of political and ideological authority, the KWP functioned as a servant to the single dictator. Simply put, the relationship between the party and the leader is reversed in North Korea.

Kim Jong-il's military-first politics clearly shifted the locus of power and authority from the party to the military, such that North Korea's political system was no longer a party-state in the traditional sense. The question is how much of a power shift occurred under Kim Jong-il. The North Korean political system was still intact, as the party remained the highest political authority that enforced the dear leader's will. At the same time, military-first politics resulted in the institutional autonomy of the military from the party and the "institutional differentiation" between the two, so that the former was not only the vanguard of state apparatuses, but also provided the nation's spirit and morale (Kim, S. 2006, 81). At the expense of the KWP's power and prestige, Kim Jong-il mobilized the KPA beyond its traditional role in national defense and expanded into social, economic, and political areas. However, expansion of the military's role did not translate into building the KPA's political power to the point that officers acquired the ability to veto important decisions by the party or the leader. Kim Jong-il's primary objective with military-first politics was to safeguard his political leadership in the face of domestic and foreign security challenges. As a result, Kim's control over the military tightened, as the military's subordination to its master became ever more resolute. The 1998 constitution of North Korea, which codified the military's vital role in the country, stipulated that all state activities must be conducted under the leadership of the KWP; this was reaffirmed in the 2010 constitution.

The KPA's role expansion into non-military areas under military-first politics was not a new phenomenon due to inter-institutional penetration between the party and the military. The expansion of the military's role is traceable to the 1960s, when Kim Il-sung launched the *4-dae gunsanoseon* (fourfold military line) that comprised "(1) arming the entire nation, (2) training all KPA soldiers to assume higher responsibilities than their rank and position would dictate, (3) turning the entire country into a fortress, and (4) modernizing the KPA" (Koh 2005). From the early years of state-building, the KPA's roles were extensive in the political systems (especially in the party and cabinet), economic development, and the mobilization of the civilian population for political indoctrination and military training.

However, the 1960s were saw the KWP's institutionalized control over the KPA. After eliminating different factions (especially the Soviet-Koreans and the Yanan faction), the KWP installed the party committee at all levels of the KPA in 1958 so that political officers shared command with commanding officers to maintain the party's supervision over the officer corps. Furthermore, the party also instituted the Military Committee in the KWP's Central Committee. The Rules of the Korean Workers' Party, revised in each of the Fourth (1961) through Sixth (1980) Congresses, stipulated that the KWP Central Committee reserved the right to organize the revolutionary forces (Article 23) and lead the country's military forces and defense industries (Article 27). The 1980 version of the Rules of the KWP dedicated all of Chapter Seven to explaining the party's control over the KPA. Likewise, the party rules made it impossible for top brass to exist outside the control of or to supersede the authority of the party (Korean Workers' Party 1981). The party's control over the military was consolidated in 1969 under the political commissar system, under which political commissars were employed at the corps through regiment levels and political guiding officers at the lower military units. These commissars were recruited from high-ranking party cadres, and they shared the leadership role with military commanders by cosigning all military decisions (Lee 2003, 155–168). After Kim Jong-il was officially introduced as the successor to his father at the Sixth Party Congress in 1980, he strengthened the KWP's control over the KPA by reinforcing the party's ideological discipline in the military through his leadership of the OGD of the KWP. Until Kim Il-sung's death, the party and the military were interwoven, as high-ranking officers were party elites and party members also penetrated the military through the political commissar system, which in turn reinforced the KWP's control over the KPA.

Such party-army relations drastically changed after Kim Jong-il assumed political leadership and launched military-first politics in the 1990s. Although the KPA had been the party's army, military-first politics separated the two institutions, and the KPA was now the people's army and the guardian of the Kim Jong-il regime. The institutional separation freed the KPA from the KWP's supervision and made the military not only the defender of the nation, but also the ideological vanguard that sustained the nation's highest spirit and morale. Although military-first politics officially launched in 1997, Kim Jong-il's desire to mobilize KPA forces for non-security-related purposes had emerged earlier in the decade. In 1991, Kim insisted that the country "needs to value the military . . . the state will collapse if it does not honor the military . . . the party organs should put priority on taking care of the problems in military-related industries" (Kim 1999, 24). He reiterated the military's role a year later: "[T]he party can be protected and prosper only when there is a strong military. Accomplishing the *Juche* revolutionary mission first and foremost requires the strengthening of the military" (Kim 1999, 6–7). Military-first politics became state ideology in March 1997, when Kim Jong-il delivered his speech at the KWP Central Committee, declaring that the KPA was "the main driving force of revolution and the pillar of the country" and that the people should firmly grasp the military's revolutionary fervor (Jeon 2009, 190).

Kim Jong-il's employment of military-first politics put the KPA at the fulcrum of power, which elevated the military's prestige and political influence vis-à-vis the party. At the institutional level, military-first politics separated the military from the party and resulted in the latter's loss of control over the former. The KPA's institutional autonomy enabled Kim Jong-il not only to use the military in times of national crisis, but also to safeguard his political power by ruling the party and the military separately. The power shift from the party to the army was manifested in 1998 constitutional revision, which removed two state apparatuses – the state's president and vice president and the Central People's Committee – and elevated the NDC to the highest state institution to orchestrate national security and economic policies (Mansourov 2006, 45).

Military-first policies were also apparent in several governing schemes, including Kim's frequent "guidance inspection" tours to military bases and defense industries, massive increases in defense spending at a time of economic distress, and empowerment of the NDC. In 1994, Kim Jong-il made only one military-related trip out of 21 guidance visits. However, between 1995 and 2006, more than 50 percent of these guidance inspections were related to the military and defense-related facilities, although the number slightly decreased after his stroke and ensuing serious health problems in 2008 (Jung 2011, 127). Key military generals escorted Kim Jong-il closely on these visits, while party officials were marginalized.

The growing influence of the KPA under Kim Jong-il was also reflected in the country's defense spending. North Korea's official defense budget revealed a modest increase during the Kim Jong-il era. It accounted for 11.4 percent of all government spending in 1994 and 14.6 percent in 1998, when Kim Jong-il formally embraced military-first politics. However, the numbers drastically change when one looks at other sources. For example, the Ministry of National Defense in South Korea estimated Pyongyang's defense spending to be above 50 percent throughout Kim Jong-il's rule (Moon and Lee 2009, 88). Despite wide variations in these sources, Kim Jong-il clearly gave the KPA priority in allocating scant domestic resources during and after the Arduous March period. Kim Jong-il mobilized the armed forces to survive the multifaceted challenges to his regime and consolidated his political power by counterbalancing the power of the party. In this process, the military emerged as the most influential governing tool in Kim Jong-il's North Korea.

The politics of regime survival

While Kim Jong-il augmented the power and prestige of the military at the expense of the party as a political tactic, his political priority was to maintain tight control over high-ranking elites in the party and the military. For that purpose, Kim adopted three major strategies for his regime security: (1) granting 'carrots' to his selectorates and using 'sticks' on dissenters, (2) strengthening security and intelligence units to counterbalance the military, and (3) creating a complex system of checks and balances within and among key government units (Jeon 2000; Mesqueta et al. 2003; Byman and Lind 2010).

More often than not, a dictatorship's survival is based on political support not from the ordinary people, but from a small number of key elite groups that buttress the regime. A dictator will provide goods to members of the inner circle in the form of political power, prestige, and material benefits such as luxury goods, cozy housing, vacations, and management rights for lucrative industries (Mesqueta et al. 2003). Given that such provision of goods to the general public is simply not feasible in poverty-stricken North Korea, keeping the small number of key selectorates loyal is vital for regime survival. Equally important is the ruthlessly efficient suppression of all organized challenges to the dictator's political authority.

Upon his succession, Kim Jong-il consolidated his political power base by fashioning a core stratum of new elites, while making sure not to alienate the aging revolutionaries of his father's generation. He kept the old revolutionaries in their positions until they retired or died and, when they died, he kept their positions vacant in their honor. For example, when the venerable Oh Jin-u (one of the core members of the Kim Il-sung regime from the partisan guerrilla era and the second most powerful elite after Kim Il-sung's death) died in 1995, Kim left his post as minister of the KPA vacant for more than seven months until appointing Choe Gwang, general chief of staff of the KPA, to fill the position. When Choe died two years later, the position was again left vacant until 1998, when Kim Il-cheol, commander of the Korean People's Navy, succeeded him. Kim Jong-il did not need to alienate his father's supporters, as they simply occupied honorary posts (Jeon 2000, 766–7).

Such inclusive politics were possible due to Kim's crafty design of a dual-power system in the cabinet and the military, in which the highest-ranking leader kept nominal leadership while a number-two (or number-three) officer typically wielded real power. Kim Jong-il received reports from, and gave orders directly to, the second- or third-highest officers, so that the top brass maintained a system of checks and balances within the hierarchy. Because of this, the official hierarchy and rankings did not accurately reflect the power relations in the system; the top leaders who showed up at state ceremonies might not necessarily have been the actual power brokers within Pyongyang's political system. For instance, Kim Yong-nam, chair of the party's Standing Committee, and Foreign Minister Baek Nam-sun were the Head of State and minister, respectively, but each performed only ritual activities, such as delivering ceremonial speeches and accepting foreign diplomats. In contrast, Kang Sok-ju, a lower ranking official as first Vice Foreign Minister, was one of the key inner circle members of the Kim regime and wielded real decision-making power in important foreign policy areas (Kim S. 2006, 103).

Kim Jong-il secured unwavering allegiance from the top brass in the army and the party with extravagant rewards, including massive promotions and luxury goods. After being elected to the post of Supreme Commander of the KPA in 1992, Kim conferred generous promotions on military officers; about 1,200 general grade officers were promoted during the 1990s (Kim 2009, 178). As the first generation of old revolutionary officers died or retired, Kim replaced them with generals from his alma mater, the Mangyongdae Revolutionary Academy, or officers who had studied in Moscow or Eastern Europe in the 1960s and 1970s. During the mourning period of 1994–1997, about 50 Kim Il-sung era generals died and were replaced with handpicked junior officers whose allegiance to the younger Kim was beyond question. As a result, Kim completed the generational shift from his father's inner circle to his own in both the party and the military.

While conferring material benefits and promotions upon members of his inner circle, Kim Jong-il also resorted to purges and harsh punishments for those whose allegiance was uncertain. As early as 1957, North Korea devised the *songbun* (class) system with three major groups: (1) The 'core' class, comprising those who fought the anti-Japanese guerrilla war or the war with South Korea and turned into high-ranking party cadres, (2) the 'wavering' class, which included the majority of the population, and (3) the 'hostile' class that included landowners, traditional elites, priests, lawyers, doctors, merchants, and Japanese collaborators. The *songbun* system was introduced as a tool for massive purges and tight control and determined "where people lived and worked and even what they ate. Most marriages were also concluded between people of the same or similar *songbun*" (Lankov 2012).

Furthermore, as a way of controlling both elites and ordinary people, Kim Jong-il relied on security agencies and army units that were responsible for Kim Jong-il's regime security. One of the agencies responsible for regime security was the State Security Department (SSD). The SSD, with approximately 50,000 to 70,000 personnel, was the most powerful secret police agency in North Korea. It conducted policing missions from provinces down to *inmanban* (people's groups), as well as with companies of more than 1,000 workers. Kim Jong-il continued to directly control the SSD when director Yi Jin-su died in the 1980s. The SSD reported to Kim over "surveillance and ideological investigations of high-ranking officials within the KWP, the SSD, the Cabinet, and Ministry of People's Armed Forces" (Gause 2012, 25). Another virtually omnipotent security institution was the Ministry of People's Security (MPS, previously the Department of Public Security), which was in charge of maintaining law and order, investigating criminal cases and non-political prisoners, and protecting key governmental facilities. Moreover, with more than 200,000 personnel, the MPS's role extended to the surveillance of public officials in the government and military officials in order to verify their political allegiance to Kim Jong-il. The third security institution was the Military Security Command (MSC), which was responsible for preventing coup attempts by monitoring and investigating high-ranking army officers for corruption, political crimes, and disloyalty. The MSC, relatively small at about 10,000 personnel, was under the direct control of the NDC and Kim Jong-il.

Inasmuch as Kim Jong-il empowered the aforementioned security institutions, he astutely invented a system of checks and balances among them to preclude coup attempts or other challenges to his authority. He compartmentalized the security institutions so that there would be no possibility of inter-organizational collusion, which facilitated inter-agency competition, as officials became preoccupied with their own bureaucratic interests and political survival. Meanwhile, Kim Jong-il monopolized political power, and inter-agency coordination was possible only through the single leader.

Hereditary succession to Kim Jong-un

Kim Jong-il's health concerns and the succession

Surprisingly enough, the Kim Jong-il regime withstood multiple challenges to its survival, but this happened at the expense of opportunities for economic reform and the well-being of the people. Kim's military-first politics brought about an overexpansion of the military and aggressive and often adventurous foreign policies. Against its southern counterpart, the Pyongyang regime used a delicate mixture of conflict and cooperation. While Seoul launched an economic engagement policy, called the Sunshine Policy under the Kim Dae-jung and Roh Moo-hyun presidencies, Pyongyang responded with several rounds of low-intensity armed conflicts along the border. At the same time, it positively answered back with two summits with Kim Dae-jung and Roh Moo-hyun, respectively, and opened the Kaesong Industrial Complex. Concurrently, Kim Jong-il carried out a brinkmanship strategy against the United States, with the nuclear weapons program and medium- to long-range missile firings designed to bring the United States to the negotiation table, which resulted in heavy economic sanctions and further isolation from the international community. Kim Jong-il's military-first politics – closing the door to the outside world and mobilizing the KPA to secure the regime from possible rebellious movements – could not be a long-term solution for the poverty-stricken country.

The problem of power succession emerged when Kim Jong-il experienced a stroke in late 2008. However, the succession planning seems to have begun as early as 2002, when the North Korean media began to idolize Ko Yong-hui, one of Kim Jong-il's wives and the mother of current leader Kim Jong-un, as the respectable mother of the nation who led the military-first revolutionary mission. She was born in Osaka, Japan, went to North Korea in the early 1960s, and became a dancer of the Mansudae Art Troupe until she met Kim Jong-il in the early 1970s. It was ironic that she became the mother of the nation with her *songbun* from the 'hostile' class, as her ancestors had collaborated with the Japanese during the Japanese colonial rule. The idolization of Kim Jong-un's mother coincided with the fall of Jang Song-taek, Kim Jong-il's brother-in-law and the second most powerful figure in Pyongyang. Jang had been expanding his presence in the party, the cabinet, and the security agencies. According to Hwang Jang-yeop's estimation, the purge of Jang and his close aides in 2004 was intended to remove any obstacle to the power succession to one of Kim Jong-il's sons (Jung 2011, 138). However, Jang returned to Pyongyang a few years later and fully restored his power by 2010 when he was elected vice chairman of the NDC.

The power succession process accelerated after Kim Jong-il suffered a stroke in 2008. In early 2009, word began to spread among key elites in the party and the military of a new genius leader called "Young General Kim" and "New Star General," although most ordinary North Koreans had little idea to whom that referred. The following year, however, it became clear that the target was Kim Jong-un, who was born in 1984 as the third and youngest son and became the designated successor to his father in his mid-20s. Kim Jong-un was promoted to the rank of four-star general in September 2010 and, in the same year, became vice chairman of the CMC and member of the Central Committee of the KWP. From then on, he appeared in public alongside his father at major political events, including his father's guidance inspection tours. Kim Jong-un's political rise was sweeping and peremptory after his father's death: He became supreme commander of the KPA on December 30, 2011, was appointed first secretary of the KWP in April 2012, and two days later, was designated chairman of the NDC. He finalized his grip on the political leadership in Pyongyang when he rose to the rank of marshal of the KPA (Armstrong 2014).

Consolidating the Kim Jong-un leadership

The hereditary succession process concluded with Kim Jong-un's assumption of leadership positions in the party and the cabinet, including as first secretary of the KWP, member of the Politburo Standing Committee, chair of the CMC, and chair of the NDC (until June 2016). As first secretary, he controls the Central Committee of the party, which is in charge of buttressing the *Juche* revolutionary ideology and defining the state's policy lines. In turn, the Central Committee elects key leadership positions, including the first secretary, the Politburo (and its Standing Committee), and members of the CMC (Woo 2016b, 257). Furthermore, the first secretary directly controls the OGD, which appoints, inspects, and purges high-ranking officials in the party, the cabinet, and the military.

Second, Kim Jong-un assumed the chair of the CMC, a partisan organ that coordinates policies between the party and the military. The CMC is a collective decision-making institution within the party that defines Pyongyang's security policies and military doctrines. Originally, the CMC was created in 1962 (called the Military Committee) as a subcommittee of the Central Committee but later was elevated to the highest military organization in the party. The CMC's elevation coincided with Kim Jong-il's political rise in the 1970s and 1980s, as Kim used the CMC to tighten his partisan control over the KPA throughout the succession process. Later, Kim Jong-il's military-first politics made the CMC virtually non-functioning throughout his reign, as he used the NDC as the highest decision-making body and bypassed the partisan institutions. However, during the final years of Kim Jong-il's rule, he restored the CMC's political authority and, at present, it includes the most powerful leaders of the military and security-related organizations. The strengthening of the CMC is a clear indication that Kim Jong-un has been trying to alter his father's legacy of military-first politics and restore partisan control over the military.

Kim Jong-un was elected first chair of the NDC in April 2012. The NDC was often misunderstood as a mere military organization due to its name, often called it "the supreme military organization" (Oh and Hassig 2000, 118) and used it as evidence of the military's political dominance to suggest that the NDC turned Pyongyang's political system into "a military garrison state" (Kim, I. 2006, 61). In reality, however, the NDC was the highest political organ, according to the constitution revised in 1998, and it included a small number of key elites from the party, the cabinet, and the military. Originally, the NDC was a mere subcommittee within the Central People's Committee when it was created in 1972, but it gained its current political status in the early 1990s when Kim Jong-il became its vice chair in 1991 and chair in 1993. The 1998 constitution made the chair of the NDC the highest political figure in the political system by assigning Kim Il-sung the title of "Eternal President" and declaring that the NDC was "the supreme national defense guidance organ of the state sovereignty" (Woo 2016b, 260). However, after the power succession to Kim Jong-un, the NDC's political power has significantly declined, and instead other party apparatuses – especially the Central Committee, the Politburo (and its Standing Committee), and the CMC – were given more decision-making authority. In June 2016, the Supreme People's Assembly officially abolished the NDC and created the State Affairs Commission (SAC) as the highest political authority, and as a result, Kim Jong-un is currently chair of the State Affairs Commission (SAC).

In addition to assuming the aforementioned leadership positions, Kim Jong-un made various political decisions to control the elites in the political system, the first of which was to curb the KPA's political clout. Kim Jong-il's funeral ceremony in December 2011 included eight leading figures of Pyongyang's power structure, including four KPA commanders led by Ri Yong-ho (the Vice Marshal and KPA General Chief of Staff) and four party leaders, including Kim Jong-un and his uncle Jang Song-taek (the Vice Chair of NDC and second most powerful figure at the time of the funeral). Less than two years after the funeral, five of the figures had been removed from their posts. Kim Jong-un's massive purges began with Ri Yong-ho and a number of KPA officers behind him, for his opposition to transferring the military's economic management to the cabinet, because the military officers saw it as counter to military-first politics. Three other KPA commanders followed the same path, and dozens of second-tier military commanders also lost their positions. In less than two years of Kim Jong-un's reign, Pyongyang had four ministers of defense and three chiefs of the general staff of the KPA (Lankov 2015, 148). The same pattern of frequent purges and reshuffling of key positions has continued throughout Kim's rule.

Kim Jong-un's political purges culminated in the execution of his uncle, Jang Song-taek, the second most powerful figure and the designated caretaker for the hereditary power succession. In December 2013, the Politburo of the KWP meeting presided over by Kim Jong-un criticized Jang for "anti-party, counter-revolutionary factional acts." More specifically, the meeting identified three major crimes committed by Jang: insubordination (not sincerely accepting the line and policies of the party and disobeying the order issued by the supreme commander of the KPA), jeopardizing security (bringing harmful consequences to the social system, policies, and people), and corruption (being affected by the capitalist way of living and having improper relations with several women, using drugs, and squandering foreign currency at casinos) (NK Leadership Watch 2013). The world was horrified by the brutal character of the young leader revealed by the execution of his uncle.

On closer look, however, the purge of Jang occurred in the context of internal power struggles over management rights of the profit-generating industries under the new leader. Kim Jong-il's military-first politics brought about an expansion of the KPA's control of industries that generated profits from trading with Chinese counterparts. Upon assuming leadership, Kim Jong-un attempted to switch the locus of political power from the KPA to the KWP and the cabinet by limiting the military's role in economic management. He weakened the Defense Security Command (DSC) of the KPA that had been an omnipotent security agency under Kim Jong-il and instead elevated the SSD by transferring the Border Guard from the DSC to the SSD. This was a significant decision, because the Border Guard controls smuggling, defections by North Koreans, and other economic transactions that involve massive bribes and, as a result, is considered a highly lucrative institution. Jang Song-taek rode on the younger Kim's attempt to curb the KPA's power and transfer the economic rights from the military to the cabinet. However, resistance to Jang's policies emerged from both the military and the party. In the military, hawkish army leaders came to the political forefront by initiating a series of armed provocations, such as the test-firing of long-range missiles, nuclear weapons tests, and temporary shutdown of the Kaesong Industrial Complex in 2013. In the party, the OGD and PAD also fought back to check Jang and his group's political dominance. Jang's purge occurred because he lost the power struggle with the party and the military (Park et al. 2014).

Overall, Kim's power consolidation process reduced the military's presence within key decision-making institutions in the party. For instance, in the April 2013 reshuffle of the Central Committee of the KWP, only five members and six alternates out of 17 members and 15 alternates were from the military and security sectors. Three years later, Pyongyang held the 7th Congress of the KWP, presumably the most important and symbolic party event, which had not been held for more than three decades after the 6th Congress of the KWP in 1980 in which Kim Jong-il was officially designated as the successor to his father. The 7th Congress was a formal declaration that Kim Jong-un had firmly established his undisputed leadership of the party, the military, and the cabinet. The decisions made at the 7th Congress clearly reflected Kim Jong-un's new ruling style and intended policy directions. First, the party convention allowed Kim Jong-un to come out of his father's shadow and stand as the undisputed leader, removing the position of first secretary of the KWP, a title that was hurriedly given after his father's death, and instead calling him the chairman of the KWP. Second, in addition to revamping the partisan institutions, the convention introduced massive generational changes in the party organs. About 45 percent of the Central Committee members was newly elected, while a number of old high-ranking generals retired (Woo 2016a, 6). Finally, the party congress reconfirmed its commitment to *Juche* and the *byongjin* policy line, tying its economic development to its nuclear weapons capabilities. Clearly, the Kim regime wants to advance its nuclear program and carry out economic development projects concurrently, although the policy line seems doubtful at best given the severe economic sanctions from the international community.

Conclusion

With Kim Jong-un's assumption of political leadership in December 2011, North Korea completed three-generations of hereditary succession. The first succession from Kim Il-sung to

Jong-il took more than two decades, during which the younger Kim consolidated his author-ity over the party, the military, and the cabinet. Kim Jong-il emerged as the de facto leader after the early 1980s, as the father granted decision-making authority to his son. In contrast, the second hereditary succession from Kim Jong-il to Jong-un occurred somewhat hastily without sufficient time for preparation. To make matters worse, Kim Jong-un was chosen as successor in his mid-20s, and had virtually no political career or experience in the military. When Kim Jong-il died in December 2011, the young and inexperienced son inherited the leadership surrounded by old elites in the party and the military. Naturally, similar to the first succession in the 1990s, numerous outside observers contemplated the possibilities of leadership failure and power struggles. To date, however, there has been practically no sign of regime collapse in Pyongyang, and Kim Jong-un seems to have consolidated his authority over the party, the military, and the cabinet.

What explains this anomalous political path in Post-Kim Il-sung North Korea? At the heart of this unexpected survival has been Kim Jong-il's military-first politics, in which he closed the door from the outside world and passed on the economic burdens of such isola-tion to the people. Kim's priority was not economic prosperity of the country or the people's livelihood, but his regime security and political survival. Kim Jong-il's military-first politics brought about adventurous foreign policies that involved the development of nuclear weap-ons, the test-firing of missiles, and frequent low-intensity armed attacks on South Korea. These belligerent actions led to severe economic sanctions by the international community that exacerbated the country's crumbling economy. The Pyongyang regime muddled through manifold difficulties resulting from the end of the Cold War, the collapse of the communist bloc, and internal crises. In the meantime, however, it lost the chance for reforms that might have placed the nation on a path toward wealth and prosperity.

The 7th Party Congress, held in May 2016, unambiguously revealed the Kim Jong-un regime's desire for economic breakthrough, but with no intention of giving up its nuclear weapons and long-range missile programs. The Congress restored a 'political normalcy' by revamping the party's leadership tasks and downgrading the military's politico-economic roles, thereby going back to the pre-military-first politics era. The institutional modifications accompanied a five-year economic development plan intended to focus on improving food, energy, and consumer goods and expanding economic exchanges with foreign countries. However, as long as Kim Jong-un develops weapons of mass destruction (WMD), North Korea's economic difficulties are likely to continue.

Note

1 An earlier version of this section was published in 2014 as "Kim Jong-il's Military-First Politics and Beyond: Military Control Mechanisms and the Problem of Power Succession." *Communist and Post-Communist Studies* 47 (2): 117–25.

References

Armstrong, Charles K. 2003. *The North Korean Revolution, 1945–1950*. New York: Cornell University Press.

Armstrong, Charles K. 2014. "One-Family Rule: North Korea's Hereditary Succession." *World Politics Review*. Available at: http://www.worldpoliticsreview.com/articles/13573/one-family-rule-north-korea-s-hereditary-authoritarianism.

Byman, Daniel, and Jennifer Lind. 2010. "Pyongyang's Survival Strategy: Tools of Authoritarian Con-trol in North Korea." *International Security* 35 (1): 44–74.

Cha, Victor. 2012. *The Impossible State: North Korea, Past and Future*. New York: Harper-Collins.

Cumings, Bruce B. 1993. "The Corporate State in North Korea." In *State and Society in Contemporary Korea*, edited by Hagen Koo, 197–230. Ithaca, NY: Cornell University Press.

Daily NK. 2013. "What Are the 'Ten Principles?'" August 9. Available at: www.dailynk.com/english/read.php?cataId=nk02900&num=10829.

French, Paul. 2014. *North Korea: State of Paranoia*. New York: Zed Books.

Gause, Ken. 2012. *Coercion, Control, Surveillance, and Punishment: An Examination of the North Korean Police State*. Washington, DC: The Committee for Human Rights in North Korea. Available at: www.hrnk.org/uploads/pdfs/HRNK_Ken-Gause_Web.pdf.

Haggard, Stephan, and Noland, Marcus. 2009. "Sanctioning North Korea: The Political Economy of Denuclearization and Proliferation." *Working Paper Series 09-14*, Peterson Institute for International Economics, Washington, DC.

Jeon, Jei Guk. 2000. "North Korean Leadership: Kim Jong-il's Balancing Act in the Ruling Circle." *Third World Quarterly* 21 (5): 761–79.

Jeon, Miyeong. 2009. "The Kim Jong-il Regime's 'Military-First Politics': Structure and Strategy of Discourse." *Review of Korean Studies* 12 (4): 181–204.

Jung, Sung Jang. 2011. *Contemporary North Korean Politics: History, Ideology, and Power Structure*. Seoul: Hanul. (in Korean)

Khrushchev, Nikita S. 1956. "Speech to 20th Congress of the C.P.S.U." Speech delivered on February 24. Available at: www.marxists.org/archive/khrushchev/1956/02/24.htm.

Kim, Ilpyong J. 2006. "Kim Jong Il's Military-First Politics." In *North Korea: The Politics of Regime Survival*, edited by Young Whan Kihl and Hong Nak Kim, 59–74. Armonk: M.E. Sharpe.

Kim, In Soo. 2009. "State-Elite Cohesion, Intra-Military Cohesion, and Regime Stability in North Korea." *Korean Journal of Military Art and Science* 56 (1): 171-192. (in Korean)

Kim, Jong-il. 1999. *On Strengthening the People's Army*. Pyongyang: Korean Workers' Party. (in Korean)

Kim, Sung Chull. 2006. *North Korea Under Kim Jong-il: From Consolidation to Systemic Dissonance*. New York: SUNY Press.

Koh, Byung Chul. 2005. "'Military-first Politics' and Building a 'Powerful and Prosperous Nation' in North Korea." Available at: http://nautilus.org/napsnet/napsnet-policy-forum/military-first-politics-and-building-a-powerful-and-prosperous-nation-in-north-korea/.

Korean Worker's Party. 1981. *Collection of the Sixth Party Congress of the Korean Worker's Party*. Pyongyang: Korean Worker's Party. (in Korean)

Lankov, Andrei. 2012. "North Korea's New Class System." *Asia Times*, December 2. Available at: www.atimes.com/atimes/Korea/ML03Dg01.html.

Lankov, Andrei. 2015. *The Real North Korea: Life and Politics in the Failed Stalinist Utopia*. New York: Oxford University Press.

Lee, Dae Geun. 2003. *Why Doesn't the Korean People's Army Make a Coup?* Seoul: Hanul. (in Korean)

Mansourov, Alexander Y. 2006. "Emergence of the Second Republic: The Kim Regime Adapts to the Challenges of Modernity." In *North Korea: The Politics of Regime Survival*, edited by Young Whan Kihl and Hong Nak Kim, 37-58. Armonk: M.E. Sharpe.

McEachern, Patrick. 2010. *Inside the Redbox: North Korea's Post-Totalitarian Politics*. New York: Columbia University Press.

Mesqueta, Bruce B., Alastair Smith, Randolph M. Siverson, and James D. Morrow. 2003. *The Logic of Political Survival*. Cambridge, MA: MIT Press.

Moon, Chung-in, and Sangkeun Lee. 2009. "Military Spending and the Arms Race on the Korean Peninsula." *Asian Perspective* 33 (4): 69–99.

North Korea Leadership Watch. 2013. "Expanded KWP Political Bureau Meeting Removes Jang Song Taek from Office." December 9. Available at: https://nkleadershipwatch.wordpress.com/2013/12/09/expanded-kwp-political-bureau-meeting-discusses-anti-party-counterrevolutionary-factional-acts-of-jang-song-taek/.

Oh, Kongdan, and Ralph C. Hassig. 2000. *North Korea Through the Looking Glass*. Washington, DC: Brookings Institution Press.

Park, Hyeong Jung, Dae Seok Choe, Hak Sung Ki, Young Ja Park, and In Suk Jang. 2014. "The Dynamics of the Competition for Power and Interest Under Suryong Dictatorship and the Purge of Jang Sung-taek." *Bukhan Yeonguhakhoebo (North Korean Studies Review)* 18 (1): 1–26. (in Korean)

Scobell, Andrew. 2006. *Kim Jong Il and North Korea: The Leader and the System*. Carlisle: Strategic Studies Institute.

Suh, Dae-Sook. 1988. *Kim Il Sung: The North Korean Leader*. New York: Columbia University Press.

Woo, Jongseok. 2016a. "The 7th Party Congress in Pyongyang: Institutional Adjustments, Policy Priorities, and Future Prospects." *RINSA Forum* 44: 5–8.

Woo, Jongseok. 2016b. "Songun Politics and the Political Weakness of the Military in North Korea: An Institutional Analysis." *Problems of Post-Communism* 63 (4): 253–62.

Yang, Song-chol. 1994. *The North and South Korean Political Systems: A Comparative Analysis*. Boulder, CO: Westview Press.

7 North Korean economy

Yangmo Ku

It is a well-known fact that South Korea, one of the poorest countries in the world in the 1950s, achieved miraculous economic development and recently became the 11th largest economy in the world, as addressed in Chapter 4. It is less commonly known, however, that North Korea also experienced successful economic growth in the 1950s and early 1960s, making it more affluent than South Korea until the early 1970s. This economically animated nation at the time then went into an economic decline up until the late 1980s before plunging into serious economic crisis and famine in the 1990s. Since its last period of moderate recovery in the late 1990s, North Korea has experienced economic stagnation. How could North Korea achieve a quick economic recovery after the Korean War (1950–1953)? Why did the North Korean economy decline from the 1960s and eventually fall into a harsh crisis? Why could North Korea not rejuvenate its economy after the crisis, despite its frequent adoption of economic reform measures? What changes has North Korea experienced since those reforms began in the early 2000s?

To answer these questions, this chapter pays attention to a variety of variables, including the inherent defects of a centrally planned economy, individual leaders' economic initiatives, the political system and ideology, and the international environment – all of which have affected the North Korean economy over the last seven decades. The chapter begins with the 1950s–1980s, during which North Korea quickly recovered economically before experiencing a continual decline. It then analyzes the causes and consequences of the 1990s economic crisis and resulting massive famine. The chapter then explains the primary similarities, differences, and results regarding economic reforms adopted by Democratic People's Republic of Korea (DPRK) leaders Kim Jong-il and Kim Jong-un. Finally, the chapter provides a comparative analysis of the Vietnamese and North Korean economy, and ends with a brief summary of the chapter and some implications.

Quick postwar recovery, but subsequently declining economy (1950s–1980s)

By the end of Japanese colonial rule, the northern part of Korea had better economic conditions than its southern part. In 1939–1940, the former's per capita commodity product, or value added in agriculture and industry, was almost 70 percent higher than the latter's (Suh 1978, 132–7). However, during the Korean War (1950–1953), North Korea's industrial facilities, most of which Japan had constructed for its imperial expansion to Manchuria in the 1930s and 1940s, lay devastated due primarily to US airstrikes. This bombing was so intensive that virtually every city and sizable town in North Korea was leveled. Most of the nation's industry and infrastructure lay in ruins. Human casualties, including North Korean civilians and soldiers, were enormous as well, ranging from 700,000 to 2 million out of a population of 10 million (Koh 1993, 57–8).

Despite this massive destruction, North Korea rapidly reconstructed its economy in the 1950s and early 1960s. Immediately after the war, the DPRK state focused on economic reconstruction by instituting a Three-Year Plan (1954–1956). Kim Il-sung, the founder of North Korea, laid out main features of this plan in his speech in 1953, a week after a ceasefire agreement. Kim Il-sung stated, "In postwar economic construction, we must follow the line of giving priority to the rehabilitation and development of heavy industry simultaneously with development of light industry and agriculture" (Lee 2001, 24). To achieve state-directed goals, the regime adopted mass mobilization, through which people were organized military-style in mass campaigns to reconstruct economy. This strategy worked quite successfully in the initial rebuilding project after the Korean War. Due to the highly mobilized labor force, North Korea was able to escape the destruction by reconstructing houses, schools, factories, and other facilities (Seth 2010, 119).

Foreign aid from the Soviet bloc was also very helpful to the North Korean economy. In 1954, 33 percent of North Korea's revenues derived from such aid. The Soviet Union and its East European communist allies provided North Korea with technical help and material on a large scale. This assistance enabled the nation to rebuild some of the prewar infrastructure, including the chemical fertilizer complex at Heungnam, the Suping hydrolectrical power plant, and the port of Nampo (Kotlin and Armstrong 2006, 110–25). As a result, it was not until 1956, at the completion of the postwar Three-Year Plan, that North Korea reached prewar per capita production levels in basic agricultural and industrial output (Goto 1982, 146).

In the wake of this initial recovery, North Korea launched the Five-Year Plan of 1957–1961, which was designed for constructing a socialist system. Emulating the Stalinist economic model, the DPRK adopted a centrally planned economy directed by the state. Private industry or agriculture was not allowed. By the end of 1956, the DPRK had nationalized all North Korean industry, while the state completed the forced collectivization of agriculture in late 1957. As a consequence of these efforts, North Korea accomplished rapid rates of economic growth during the Five-Year Plan. Gross agricultural product increased at an annual rate of almost 7.5 percent, while gross industrial output grew by more than 35 percent a year (Eberstadt 2010, 42).

In the mid-1960s, however, the North Korean economy began to decline and plunge into a long period of economic stagnation. Since the DPRK government stopped releasing statistical data on its own economy in the early 1960s, it is extremely hard to find reliable information regarding the nation's economic status. Nevertheless, United Nations data, though incomplete and poorly collected, demonstrates that the North Korean economy continued to stagnate, as shown in Table 7.1. The DPRK's per capita GDP was higher than the ROK's up until 1973. However, North Korea's per capita GDP only increased from $477 in 1973 to $811 in 1989, while South Korea's grew from $414 to $5,724 during the same period of time.

These miserable results recorded by the North Korean economy resulted from various factors. First, a centrally planned economy under the communist system was extremely ineffective at scoring sustainable growth rates in the long run. As noted above, a massive input of labor temporarily worked for postwar economic recovery. However, the centralized command economy spawned serious problems over time. As found in other communist nations, a key defect of the Soviet-style command economy was the lack of incentives for workers to toil productively. North Koreans had few motives to work hard in state-run industries and

Table 7.1 Per capita GDP of both Koreas at current prices in US dollars

Year	70	71	72	73	74	75	76	77	78	79	80	81	82	83	84
DPRK	384	413	443	477	515	558	571	587	604	622	639	653	808	794	745
ROK	286	308	331	414	571	625	844	1068	1422	1805	1735	1904	2011	2215	2420

Year	85	86	87	88	89	90	91	92	93	94	95	96	97	98	99
DPRK	722	805	836	764	811	735	663	593	503	384	222	479	462	456	452
ROK	2476	2814	3514	4680	5724	6501	7513	8009	8773	10275	12454	13301	12311	8207	10570

Year	2000	01	02	03	04	05	06	07	08	09	10	11	12	13	14
DPRK	462	476	468	471	473	548	575	597	551	494	570	638	643	666	696
ROK	12155	11465	13022	14466	16164	18866	21122	13290	20660	18480	22296	24363	24649	26192	28166

Source: United Nations. Available at *https://unstats.un.org/unsd/snaama/dnllist.asp*.

collectivized agriculture, as the returns to labor applied equally to all workers regardless of the quality of their labor. This system significantly lowered labor productivity, causing an economic downturn.

Second, following the Soviet model, the DPRK regime placed too much focus on heavy industry rather than nurturing light industry, which was essential to people's daily lives. This pattern was closely linked to North Korea's overemphasis on the military. Due to competition from South Korea, the DPRK regime allocated too many resources on the development of military industry, which produced an imbalanced economic structure. The military expenses in the state budget dramatically increased from 7.5 percent in 1964 to 32.4 percent in 1968 (Eberstadt 2007, 139). The nation's limited resources were, therefore, distributed in a distorted and ineffective manner. Third, the DPRK wasted its scant resources by conducting a number of large-scale, expensive construction projects. Among these projects were political monuments, high-rise buildings, and broad streets in Pyongyang for propaganda purposes.

Fourth, the reduction of Soviet aid was detrimental to the North Korean economy as well. Starting in the early 1960s, the relationship between North Korea's two patrons, the Soviet Union and China, drastically deteriorated due to ideological friction and border disputes. This prompted the DPRK to adopt a more equidistant line of diplomacy between Moscow and Beijing. This posture helped North Korea to have more political autonomy, but it also resulted in a decrease of Soviet aid.

Finally, based on the ideology of self-reliance, referred to as *Juche*, the Kim Il-sung regime placed great emphasis on economic autarky, which seriously hampered North Korea's economic development. Running counter to modern economic principles like the division of labor and specialization, the DPRK expected each industrial enterprise and administrative unit to produce most of what it needed without requesting the central government's assistance. This policy helped to alleviate the burden of the central government to provide adequate industrial machinery and raw materials, but it eventually led to greater inefficiency and wastage. Moreover, despite the slogan of self-reliance, North Korea became one of the most economically dependent nations of the Soviet bloc, and this made the nation's economy very vulnerable to external shocks, such as the demise of the Soviet Union and other Eastern European communist nations (Lankov 2016, 223–9).

Unprecedented economic crisis and famine (1990s)

The continually declining North Korean economy plunged into a serious crisis in the 1990s. Dramatic shifts in macroeconomic indicators demonstrate the severity of the crisis. North Korea's GDP plummeted from $15.8 billion in 1989 to $4.8 billion in 1995 (United Nations 2015). As shown in Table 7.1, its GDP per capita was $811 in 1989, but this number drastically decreased to $222 in 1995. During the 1990–1998 period, the nation's average economic growth rate was about negative 4.2 percent, as illustrated in Figure 7.1. As a result of this harsh economic crisis, a huge number of people, ranging from 600,000 to 1 million, or 3 to 5 percent of the nation's population, starved to death between 1995 and 1998 (Noland 2016, 239–40). In recent world history, this was an unprecedented famine in a previously industrialized nation like North Korea. Various factors caused this humanitarian catastrophe.

First of all, the demise of the Soviet Union and East European communist countries in the early 1990s posed a fatal blow to the already stagnant North Korean economy. As North Korea's primary patron, the Soviet Union had provided the DRPK with a huge amount of aid and credits, amounting to $2.2 billion between 1948 and 1984 (Eberstadt 2010, 91). The Soviet Union was also North Korea's largest trade partner, accounting for more than half of

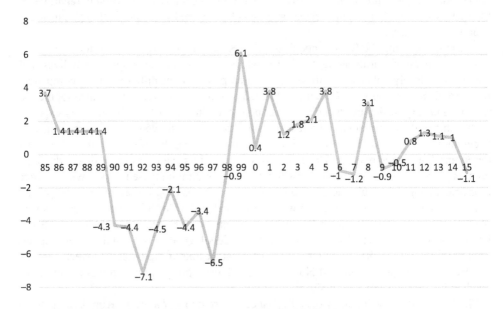

Figure 7.1 North Korea's real GDP growth rate, 1985–2015 (unit: percent)

Source: The United Nations. Available at https://unstats.un.org/unsd/snaama/dnllist.asp.

North Korea's trade, including most of its oil imports. North Korea was able to import cheap, below-market-priced oil and weaponry from the Soviet Union. As such, North Korea's economy was highly dependent upon aid from and trade with the Soviet Union; the collapse of the patron had a devastating effect on the North Korean economy. The fall of East European communist nations with which North Korea had long had trade relationships further worsened the DPRK economy. Along with aging equipment, the severe lack of energy sources brought about a sharp decline in industrial output.

The end of cheap oil from the Soviet Union also aggravated North Korea's agricultural productivity. The nation's agricultural equipment, such as tractors, lay idle for lack of oil. Chemical fertilizers essential to the growth of crops were not produced adequately as well. Furthermore, the DPRK built a number of irrigation systems in order to overcome its geographical handicaps, such as limited farmland and a short growing season. To operate the pumps required for the irrigation systems, North Korea needed to have imported fuel oil, but the facilities no longer worked effectively once the supply of cheap Soviet oil terminated (Seth 2010, 220).

China tried to offset some of the drop in trade with the Soviet Union by exporting food to North Korea on concessional terms. In 1994 and 1995, however, Chinese leaders were very concerned about rising domestic discontent over increasing grain prices stimulated by tight international market conditions. China thus lessened its food exports to North Korea in order to check internal inflation, and this move significantly worsened North Korea's food conditions (Haggard and Noland 2009). Moreover, China, which had been pursuing market-oriented economic reforms, was far more interested in improving its economic relationship with South Korea than North Korea for the purpose of gaining more trade with the vibrant

South Korean economy. Therefore, Chinese support was not enough to save the plummeting North Korean economy (Seth 2010, 215).

Second, natural disasters, such as severe drought and floods, markedly damaged North Korea's agricultural products, especially its key rice crop. North Korea suffered damage due to cold weather in 1993, floods in 1995–1996, and drought in 1997. In particular, the amount of damage caused by the 1995 flooding amounted to approximately \$15 billion (Lee 2014, 167). Deforestation was a main cause of the disastrous flooding. To plant as many crops as possible, North Korean authorities encouraged the clearing of forested hillsides of the mountainous country, although many areas were too steep for proper farming (Natsios 2001, 12). The DPRK also launched a campaign to raise livestock, such as goats, poultry, and pigs, in an attempt to address the scarcity of meat. This policy further contributed to soil erosion, because raising livestock decreased the size of North Korea's already limited grazing land (Park 2002, 93).

It is necessary to note that the above-mentioned factors played a crucial role in bringing about the North Korean famine, but the DPRK regime could have minimized the scope of human casualties with an effective response. According to testimonies by North Korean refugees, North Korea's significant food insecurity already emerged by the late 1980s, as proven by the launch of the "let's eat two meals a day campaign." In response to this food shortage, the DPRK government chose not to address supply constraints, either by increasing exports to finance imports or requesting external assistance. Instead, the DPRK regime decided to repress consumption by cutting rations conveyed by the public distribution system (PDS) from which urban residents, roughly two-thirds of the nation, acquired their food. Although the famine was already underway in 1994, the North Korean regime waited to appeal for international aid until the spring of 1995. The DPRK first approached Japan, its former colonial ruler, whose contributions could be depicted as a kind of reparation. North Korea also asked its rival, South Korea, and ultimately the United Nations. The summer 1995 and 1996 floods were utilized as an instrument for portraying the famine as the outcome of natural disasters, though the inception of the famine had preceded the floods (Noland 2016, 235–6).

Moreover, when international aid arrived, the DPRK government hindered humanitarian relief organizations from distributing food and medical supplies effectively and from monitoring the distribution process. For instance, such organizations were prohibited from using Korean speakers in their relief activities and from having access to certain geographical areas, such as ones suspected to be the worst affected. A large extent of 'aid diversion,' defined as aid not reaching its intended recipients, also occurred due to the weak monitoring of aid distribution. Stephen Haggard and Marcus Noland (2007) estimated that at least 30 percent of aid was diverted to military and/or government officials. Another deplorable aspect of North Korea's handling of the famine was to reduce commercial grain imports as external assistance increased over time. The DPRK utilized then resources freed up by humanitarian aid in order to import advanced weaponry (Noland 2016).

A most significant change in the North Korean economy caused by the famine was the emergence of private entrepreneurs and markets, referred to as *Jangmadang* among North Koreans. Amidst such a harsh economic crisis, North Korea's ration system, the PDS, fell apart, because the DPRK regime could no longer provide its people with food and daily necessities enough to sustain their survival. North Korean refugees gave testimonies that the rations had stopped in most areas by the mid-1990s, and even residents in Pyongyang received a limited amount of food (Kim 1997, 14). Given this context, many average workers, housewives, and even children engaged in profit-seeking activities by becoming traders.

Extreme economic hardships and the collapse of the ration system, particularly in urban areas, prompted common people to take part in commercial activities to provide their households with access to food. Prior to the famine, the DPRK government had strictly controlled its people's movement through residential restrictions, but the government permitted local residents to travel around in search of food and other daily necessities during the food crisis. Most travelers sought to look for food and other goods for their own families, but others intended to gain profits through trade (Natsios 2001, 99).

In addition, the number of private entrepreneurs who dealt with grain products and consumer goods significantly increased during the second half of the 1990s. About 700,000 to 800,000 people, roughly one out of every 30 people, were estimated to have engaged in private entrepreneurial activities at the end of the 1990s (Jeong 2000, 189). Using their household plots, a number of people cultivated crops and sold them in newly emerging *Jangmadang*. For a long time prior to the famine, the DPRK had partially permitted farmers to exchange materials at so-called farmers' markets, or people's markets, but these markets just played a supplementary role within the nation's planned economy (Choi 2016, 53). Numerous markets that emerged amidst the famine, though, have become indispensable to North Korea's economy. Many workers in local enterprises became private entrepreneurs as well. During the crisis, most small-and medium-sized local enterprises ceased their operations due to the lack of state subsidies, energy shortages, and resource deficits. By extracting labor, technology, facilities, and materials from their workplace, many experienced and innovative workers produced various consumer goods, such as garments, shoes, and furniture, and they made profits at the expense of officially assigned products. Managerial officials allowed these experienced and innovative workers to mobilize the enterprises' resources, as they served the role of welfare providers for other workers by sharing profits with their enterprises. These entrepreneurial activities were technically illegal, but the DPRK government tacitly approved them, as the regime was extremely hard to find an alternative to survival in the famine-stricken society of the 1990s (Kim 2006, 150–3).

Moderate recovery but consistent economic stagnation (late 1990s–2011)

The most devastating stage of the famine terminated around 1998, and the North Korean economy began a moderate recovery in 1999 due to external aid, improved agricultural harvests, and some positive effects of *Jangmadang*. Since then, no large-scale famine has occurred, although the lack of food and malnutrition have persisted. As illustrated in Figure 7.1, in 1999 DPRK's GDP growth rate rebounded to 6.1 percent, ending its long years of severe negative growth that began in 1990. Despite some reform measures, however, the DPRK economy stagnated between 2000 and 2011, which coincided with the rule of Kim Jong-il. Between 2000 and 2011, North Korea's average economic growth rate was approximately 1.12 percent, swinging between 3.8 percent and negative 1.2 percent. Figure 7.2 demonstrates that during that period, the nation's trade volume grew slowly as well. The size of North Korean trade began to notably increase in 2008, but this change was not enough to boost its economic growth rate. Nevertheless, it is noteworthy that the marketization, which had been initiated during the famine, continually made a progress in spite of anti-market measures adopted by the DPRK government.

Kim Jong-il emerged as North Korea's leader in 1997, when a three-year period of mourning ended after his father Kim Il-sung's death. Kim Jong-il sought to maintain the North

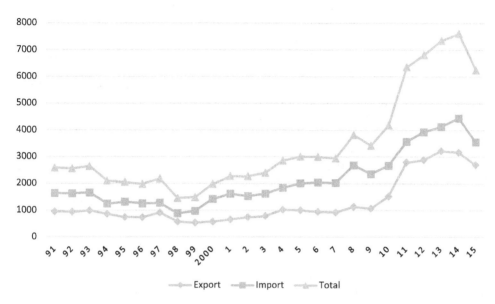

Figure 7.2 North Korea's trade volume, 1991–2015 (unit: US$ million)
Source: KOTRA (2016). *2015 North Korean Trade*. Seoul: KOTRA.

Korean regime's security based primarily on a military-first policy. Amidst the unprecedent-edly severe economic crisis, Kim Jong-il positioned the Korean People's Army (KPA) at the forefront of economic reconstruction and national defense. The supreme leader stated that "without the army, there exist no people, no state, and no party" (Kim 2006, 91). Actually, the North Korean military played a pivotal role in cultivating crops and constructing infra-structure such as power plants. While complimenting the military's economic contributions, many North Korean documents and slogans also placed great emphasis on the revolutionary spirit of the military. In this context, the National Defense Commission (NDC), which Kim Jong-il chaired, and the KPA came to have ultimate authority over the nation's economy.

Within the military-first policy, Kim Jong-il also adopted a series of economic reform measures, although North Korea has never used the term 'reform,' as the word implies that the DPRK government had employed prior incorrect policies. In 1997, the North Korean government tried to reduce the size of working units at public enterprises from 15–20 peo-ple to 7–8 people, and it permitted workers to freely handle surplus products made after meeting quotas set by the government. In 1998, the DPRK allowed technocrats charged with economic management to operate independently from the Central People's Committee. Managing light industries and cooperative farms now became the responsibility of local gov-ernments, while cabinet ministers oversaw the heavy industrial sector (Stradiotto and Guo 2007, 201). In 1998, the North Korean government expanded the Rajin-Sonbong Special Economic Zone and enacted a People's Economic Plan Act in 1999. In the next year, Kim Jong-il had a summit with ROK President Kim Dae-jung to improve inter-Korean relations. As a result, Mt. Geumgang tourism started in 2000, and the Kaesong Industrial Complex was established in 2003 (Choi 2016, 59–61).

Moving beyond these measures, the Kim Jong-il regime in 2002 adopted the most comprehensive set of economic reforms in North Korean history, referred to as "July 1st Measures." First, official prices for food, transportation, and other goods and services increased, often by tenfold or more, in order to bring official prices closer to informal market prices. A most striking example was the increase of rice prices from 0.08 to 44 North Korean *won* per kilogram. Official wages for North Korean workers also increased about 15- to 20-fold. Second, the North Korean currency was considerably devalued, from 2.15 to 150 *won* per dollar, in an attempt to bring it much closer to the informal rate of about 230 *won* per dollar. Third, state-owned enterprises now had to cover their own expenses and be self-sustaining. Limited price-setting authority was given to factories that produced daily necessities and retail products. State enterprise managers also now held enhanced power and independence in managing state-owned companies. They were authorized to purchase materials for production from the open market, to make autonomous investments out of retained profits, and to sell finished goods. Finally, the social security system was radically revamped. The DPRK government eliminated large portions of social security benefits, including food and clothing rations, housing, and other benefits that the government had provided for free. Along with these measures, in 2002 the Kim Jong-il regime designated more special economic zones such as Sinuiju, a northwestern city on the Chinese border, and the Mt. Geumgang tourist resort. Furthermore, in 2003, the North Korean government formally established "general markets," called *Jonghap Sijang*, and built an infrastructure for these markets in main cities (Lankov 2015, 122; Stradiotto and Guo 2007, 201–2).

Many South Korean government officials and scholars, who had supported ROK President Kim Dae-jung's Sunshine Policy, responded positively to the July 1st Measures and associated policies since they indeed incorporated more capitalist components compared to North Korea's previous reforms. The measures were described as "epoch-making measures to push forward reforms and opening simultaneously" and "a severance from the past, significant institutional reforms" (Park 2009, 536). International media also depicted the measures as signs of long-awaited reforms. For instance, a *New York Times* article reported that

> the changes, which were officially started in 2002 and have gradually gained momentum, have undone many of the most basic tenets of North Korea's Communist system, where private commerce was banned, private property circumscribed, and an all-powerful state the universal employer and provider.
>
> (French 2005)

Despite these optimistic prospects, the July 1st Measures and accompanying policies were only temporary remedies for a desperate economic situation, rather than a long-term pursuit of far-reaching economic reforms. Under Kim Jong-il, there was little significant change to forms of ownership in the means of production. The North Korean central government still had ultimate authority to set prices. The July 1st Measures were an acknowledgement by the DPRK government that its economic system had been flawed. In the name of "improvement," the DPRK decided to loosen its control over factories and enterprises, because the government had little financial ability to assist them from the early 1990s. The elimination of social security benefits was a concession that the DPRK government could not afford to provide them any longer. In a similar vein, the legalization of general markets in 2003 acknowledged that the government was incapable of eliminating them. At the time, a vast majority of North Koreans were already participating in market-based commercial activities (Park 2009, 538).

This claim is further supported by the fact that, not long after the adoption of these reform measures, the DPRK government began to take counter-reform measures aimed at reviving the pre-crisis system. North Korean leaders became concerned about the rise of adverse effects caused by its reforms, especially widening income inequality and weakened state authority over local officials and newly emerging capitalists. In this context, the North Korean government often returned to restrictive policies to restore its grip over society. In October 2005, the DPRK announced the full restoration of the long-defunct PDS and the prohibition of private grain sales. However, only a small segment of the population, including residents in Pyongyang, actually received full or near-full rations. The majority of North Koreans received partial rations at best or often none at all. The ban on private grain sales did not last long. By late 2006, private sales of rice and corn resumed, as police and low-ranking officials, who had gained bribes from private sellers, were reluctant to enforce the new regulations. In December 2006, the DPRK banned all men from participating in commercial trade, but this regulation failed since North Korean men were not originally active in trade activities. In December 2007, North Korea prohibited women below 50 years old from engaging in market trade. This ban did not continue long either on account of weak enforcement and people's resistance, such as riots in the cities of Chongjin and Hamheung. In November 2008, the DPRK government even planned to ban the sale of all industrial goods, such as fans and rice cookers, though the plan was cancelled at the last moment.

Above all, the 2009 currency reform was the most notorious anti-market policy taken by North Korean authorities. The confiscatory reform wiped two zeroes off of the value of the North Korean currency *won*, so 10,000 "old" *won* became equivalent to 100 "new" *won*. Each person was allowed to exchange only about 100,000 to 150,000 old *won* for the new notes, and this exchange had to be completed within a week. This reform clearly aimed at cracking down on people who had been actively involved in informal market trading. The measure decimated private stores of cash wealth in local currency, because 100,000 *won* was worth only $35 at the black market rate. This currency reform thus sparked panic among many North Koreans who had a significant amount of cash holdings. In May 2010, however, the DPRK government implicitly admitted that active markets had become essential, and its leaders therefore eliminated all restrictions that had been adopted during the 2005–2009 anti-market campaign (Lankov 2015, 123–33).

Moreover, the Kim Jong-il regime did not enact extensive economic reforms as the military-first policy continued to be the core national policy until Kim's death in December 2011. The North Korean regime's main priority was to maintain regime survival and security through its military, as opposed to the promotion of economic efficiency. While positioning the North Korean military as the model for society to emulate, supreme leader Kim Jong-il assigned a large portion of the nation's limited resources to the military. Kim Jong-il also provided the military with the authority to keep close surveillance over his people's movements at all levels of North Korean society. As South Korean scholar Park Yong-soo (2009, 539) claims, "in such a political atmosphere, in which the military is emphasized over all other aspects of state and society, economic policy has inevitably been considered secondary, and hence the road towards economic reforms has faded away markedly." It would be fair, therefore, to argue that North Korea under the rule of Kim Jong-il underwent a moderate recovery from an unprecedented economic crisis, but the nation suffered continual economic stagnation due primarily to the lack of political will to carry out comprehensive economic reforms.

It is also necessary to note that the rise of a market economy after the severe economic crisis engendered various forms of adverse consequences within North Korean society. The first was widening income inequality between the "new capitalists" and underprivileged groups, and between Pyongyang and other local areas, thus stimulating social instability (*Radio Free Asia* 2013). Related to this, financial contributions by parents became the primary source of income to most schools, so it was common to witness discrimination against the children of poor families. The second phenomenon was widespread corruption as a result of economic struggles and relaxation of social controls. Members of elite groups and middle-level managers often siphoned off external humanitarian aid for personal gains. These practices not only intensified ordinary citizens' distrust of DPRK authorities, but they also weakened central control over local managers and cadres, because the latter could gain a substantial amount of secondary income independently of the government (Szalontai and Choi 2012, 231–2).

Sluggish growth but significant socio-economic changes (2012–present)

The North Korean economy has witnessed continually sluggish growth in the post-Kim Jong-il period. Between 2012 and 2015 under the new leader Kim Jong-un, North Korea's average economic growth rate was approximately 0.58 percent, fluctuating from 1.3 to negative 1.1 percent, as illustrated in Figure 7.1. Starting in 2011, the nation's trade volume notably increased, but this failed to revitalize its overall economic growth, as Figure 7.2 shows. Despite persistent economic stagnation, however, Kim Jong-un has prioritized economic development since he assumed power in 2012. He has conducted a series of economic reform measures and has maintained market-friendly approaches, albeit not full-fledged ones, without reverting back to the anti-market policies of his father. Under these reforms, North Korea has undergone significant socio-economic changes, including the coexistence of centrally planned and market economies, the central position of markets in people's lives, and the symbiotic relationship between state managers and capitalists. The progress of marketization became an almost irreversible pattern in North Korea, although this phenomenon has taken place in a very abnormal manner.

In April 2012, Kim Jong-un officially took over power following his father's death four months earlier. The new supreme leader inherited from his father a crippled economy, which had been in a dire condition with constant shortages of food, foreign currency, and energy resources. Compared to his father, Kim Jong-un also had a much weaker power base, as he became the leader at the age of 27 with no prior military or political experience. In this regard, many expected that it would be extremely difficult for the young leader to maintain the North Korean regime. However, it appears that Kim Jong-un has consolidated his power through the robust support of his relatives, such as his aunt Kim Kyong-hui and uncle Jang Song-taek, at the initial stage of his rule and through ruthless purges later (Snyder 2013; Kwon and Westcott 2016). Since he took power in 2012, Kim Jong-un has ordered about 140 executions of senior officers in the nation's government, military, and ruling Korean Workers' Party (KWP).

Kim Jong-un had employed notably different economic policies than those adopted by Kim Jong-il. A most significant difference was that Kim Jong-un attempted to reassert party control over the military and to scale back his father's military-first policy. Kim Jong-un put the military's senior leadership under party control, purged high-ranked military commanders such as Vice Marshal Ri Young-ho, and greatly reduced the military's policymaking influence. As addressed before, Kim Jong-il pursued the military-first policy to maintain regime stability amidst the unprecedentedly harsh economic crisis. This military-first policy was evidently detrimental to North Korean economy, because limited resources were allocated for military purposes and not for economic development. Running counter to this policy direction, the Kim Jong-un government tried to promote economic efficiency by enhancing the authority of the KWP and Cabinet leaders who had expertise in economic policymaking. As a symbolic event toward this end, in March 2013 Park Bong-ju, who had been ousted for pushing market-oriented policies in the 2000s, was reappointed as a prime minister and placed in charge of managing North Korea's economy (Shin 2013). Paradoxically, with the restoration of Park Bong-ju as a prime minister, Kim Jong-un declared the so-called *byongjin* policy, which meant the simultaneous development of the economy and nuclear weapons. As addressed later, this *byongjin* approach has been a serious roadblock to North Korea's economic development, although the policy seems to have bolstered the DRPK's regime security.

Another difference that Kim Jong-un initially made was to cooperate more closely with China in order to attract more foreign investment, particularly through the development of special economic zones (SEZs) in North Korea's Hwangeumpyong, Wiwhado, and Rajin-Sonbong (Rason) areas. North Korea and China shared common interests in jointly developing such SEZs. The DPRK desperately needed Chinese capital to rejuvenate its economy, because it could not receive any support from the United States, South Korea, and Japan due to its nuclear and missile adventurism. It was necessary for China to develop those areas, because Rason's ports provided China with easy access to the Pacific Ocean, and joint development projects helped the nation to procure the DPRK's natural resources (Ku 2013, 78–9). As part of the *byongjin* policy, in November 2013, the Kim Jong-un government also announced the establishment of 14 new economic development zones to attract foreign investment. By 2015, North Korea had 26 SEZs and economic development zones, and 21 of them were newly established during the rule of Kim Jong-un (Ministry of Unification 2017).

Moreover, the Kim Jong-un regime adopted a series of economic reform measures, although the DPRK government preferred the phrase "economic management in our own style" rather than "market-oriented reforms." Their core, which embraced the principles of the July 1st Measures and expanded the prior scope of reform, was to grant more autonomy to factories, companies, and collective farms (*Daily NK* 2015). The so-called June 28th Measures, announced in June 2012 and carried out on a trial basis for two years, included following elements. The North Korean government allowed state-owned enterprises to make decisions on how to fulfill the state's production targets and meet market needs. Managers of public enterprises had to take responsibility for the results, although the state continued to own the means of production and appoint the heads of the enterprises (Park 2013). In the agricultural sector, the size of each work team on collective farms fell from 15 to 5–6 persons. Work teams had to make decisions on crop productions, and they could keep 30 percent of their production quota plus any surplus over the quota. This meant that the state took 70 percent of the quota, while before this change, DPRK farmers were obliged to deliver their entire harvest to the state. In May 2014, the North Korean government promulgated the so-called May 30th Measures, which further shrank the work teams to "family size" (Ireson 2015). Enhanced autonomy, triggered by the June 28th Measures, now expanded to all factories, companies, and collective farms, rather than a select number. Unlike the July 1st Measures, taken by Kim Jong-il in 2002, the June 28th and May 30th Measures have essentially continued.

Despite these reform measures, the North Korean economy has failed to grow much due mainly to the fear of regime collapse and its nuclear/missile adventurism. The DPRK regime, governed by brutal dictators over the last seven decades, has little ruling legitimacy, as many North Koreans have suffered from political suppression, harsh human rights violations, and dismal economic failure. In this regard, top leaders and their cohorts have been very reluctant to adopt full-fledged, market-oriented economic reforms that other communist nations, particularly China and Vietnam, have done, as detailed in the next section. Such drastic liberalization could accelerate the influx of external information into the DPRK, thus prompting North Koreans to realize how miserable their lives have been compared to people in other nations. This situation would constitute a big threat to the Kim dynasty's survival (Cha 2012).

Relatedly, the DPRK has clung to the development of nuclear weapons and missiles to enhance its regime security, particularly after the nation witnessed the fall of two dictators, Iraq's Saddam Hussein and Libya's Muammar Gaddafi. These two autocratic leaders originally pursued nuclear weapons, but they gave up their nuclear ambitions. After doing so, external powers intervened, hastening the collapse of their regimes and their individual deaths. Hussein was executed after the United States invaded Iraq in 2003, and Gaddafi was killed by rebels in 2011 after the United States and its European allies helped opposition forces expel him from power (Myre 2017). It would have been very hard for the United States and other powers to have taken such aggressive acts if Hussein and Gaddafi had developed nuclear weapons. Based on this conviction, North Korea's top leaders have made every effort to develop such weapons of mass destruction for their regime's survival. This approach has prompted the international community to impose harsh economic sanctions on North Korea. The UN Security Council has passed a number of resolutions to punish the DPRK whenever the nation has violated the international law by conducting nuclear and missile tests.

These international sanctions have seriously prevented the DPRK from developing its economy. North Korea's economic reforms, such as the July 1st Measures and the June 28th Measures, helped the country escape from its desperate economic crisis and to slightly improve people's living conditions. However, such reforms cannot be ultimately successful without the receipt of large amounts of foreign capital from the international community. Due to North Korea's provocative acts, many international organizations, especially the International Monetary Fund and the World Bank, have banned the provision of any developmental loans necessary to revitalize the DPRK's stagnant economy. In addition, the DPRK's nuclear/missile ambitions have generated confrontational relationships with the United States, South Korea, and Japan. These developed nations could potentially provide enormous economic support, but because of North Korea's provocations, these countries have instead imposed economic sanctions. Under these circumstances, North Korea has little capacity to resolve its serious economic problems, including shortages of food, energy resources, and modern technology and equipment. Moreover, foreign investors have little incentive to invest their capital in North Korea's recently established SEZs thanks to the unstable security conditions stemming from the nuclear/missile standoff, in addition to the nation's poor infrastructure and lack of legal protections for private enterprises (Abrahamian and Melvin 2015).

Despite these unfavorable conditions, since the late 1990s, China has been an extremely important nation on which the DPRK has depended. China has recognized North Korea's strategic and even economic importance. From a strategic viewpoint, North Korea has functioned as a buffer zone between China and the United States' sphere of influence, which includes South Korea. From an economic viewpoint, it has been also necessary for China to take advantage of North Korea's natural resources and ports for its rapidly advancing economic development in the three provinces nearest the DPRK. In this regard, North Korea has been more dependent on Chinese support for its economic development and regime survival than the reverse. More than 90 percent of the oil used by the DPRK has been imported from China. In 2005, North Korea's trade with China, approximately $1.58 billion, for the first time surpassed 50 percent of its total trade volume. In 2015, this number significantly increased to about $5.7 billion, equivalent to 91.34 percent of the nation's total trade

(KOTRA 2016, 15). This statistical data excluded inter-Korean trade, as ROK institutions regard the trade between the two Koreas as internal exchanges. In 2005, the size of inter-Korean trade was approximately $1 billion, and this increased to $2.7 billion in 2015, as seen in Figure 10.4. However, inter-Korean trade dramatically shrank due to the shutdown of the Kaesong Industrial Complex in *January* 2016 after North Korea's *fourth* nuclear test. After then, North Korea more heavily depends on its economic relationship with China. It appears, however, that Chinese aid itself is not sufficient for the revitalization of North Korea's stagnant economy.

Thanks to these limitations, North Korea has had trouble in achieving economic growth, but it is noteworthy that the DPRK economy has undergone significant changes in many respects. North Korea has about 404 government-approved markets, and their sizes continue to grow based on satellite images. Approximately 1.1 million people, equivalent to 4.6–4.8 percent of the nation's total population of 25 million, are now working as retailers or managers in those markets (Hong 2017). Unofficial market activities are also widespread, including the production and sales of shoes, clothing, sweets, and bread from people's homes, as well as the smuggling of black market products like Hollywood movies and ROK television dramas. Other popular businesses encompass the sale of liquid petroleum gas and solar panels, which can resolve the chronic lack of electricity in individual households, and the management of car washes, gas stations, and even real estate businesses (Yang 2016). According to the director of ROK's intelligence service, more than 40 percent of North Koreans currently participate in some form of private enterprise (Choe 2017).

As marketization has progressed, they have become a central part of North Korean people's lives, and the symbiotic relationship between state officials and private entrepreneurs is now salient. While the state provides resources like buildings, electricity, transport, and security for the market, the market provides tax revenues to the state, and goods and services to the people (Yang 2015). The DPRK government is estimated to annually collect at least $81 million in taxes from the general markets, and the authorities have tried to amass more by ordering home-based businesses to move into formal marketplaces, according to Cha Moon-seok, a researcher at the Institute for Unification Education of South Korea (Choe 2017).

Furthermore, the newly emerging class of rich private entrepreneurs, referred to as *donju*, actively conduct business under the protection of party officials. For instance, *donju* rent resource-strapped state enterprises and produce goods, such as shoes and garments, using state buildings. In return for paying rent, *donju* share their profits with factory managers and state officials. Such red capitalists also import busses and trucks to run transportation services using license plates obtained from state companies. Some *donju* even open private pharmacies and rent farmland and mines, working with their own employees and equipment. In state-led large construction projects, *donju* are also expected to make "loyalty donations," which can include foreign currency, and to give building materials, oil or food for workers. In return for these donations, the DPRK government frequently confers medals and certificates on the *donju*, and they utilize these awards as signs of governmental protection of their business activities, even though they are officially illegal (Yang 2016; Choe 2017).

Therefore, the privatization of the means of production is gradually taking place in a practical manner, though such means still officially belong to the DPRK state. Nevertheless, it is necessary to note that these changes do not signify that the North Korean economy is actually growing. The current North Korean economy is in an abnormal condition, as the DPRK leader, Kim Jong-un, seeks to maintain his regime by distributing to elite groups a variety of privileges in order to exploit profits from the legal and illegal market sectors (Jung 2016).

A comparison with the Vietnamese economy

To further promote understanding of the North Korean economy, it would be useful to briefly examine how another Asian communist nation, Vietnam, achieved rapid economic development over the last three decades. Although China, another communist country, has attained much more dramatic economic growth than Vietnam, this section pays more attention to Vietnam, as China is an extreme outlier in terms of its economic, population, and territorial size. China has the world's largest population (about 1.35 billion) and third-largest territory (3.75 million square miles). It became the world's second-largest economy in 2010, and its GDP of $5.88 trillion trails only behind the United States' $14.66 trillion. Thus, it seems more reasonable to compare North Korea's economy with Vietnam's.

Vietnam, one of the world's poorest countries in the 1980s, successfully escaped poverty and became a lower middle-income country in the early 2010s. As shown in Figure 7.3, Vietnam's GDP, which was just $4.8 billion in 1985, increased to $31.2 billion in 2000, eventually reaching $193.2 billion in 2015. By contrast, North Korea's GDP of $12.1 billion in 1985 was much larger than Vietnam's, but the DPRK failed to grow much, only remaining around $16.3 billion in 2015. Figure 7.4 depicts that since 1990, Vietnam's annual GDP growth rate has been over 5 percent for every year except one. As illustrated in Figure 7.5, Vietnam's per capita GDP at current US dollars was only $79 in 1985, but it drastically increased to $2,015 in 2014. This high economic growth contributed to the reduction of Vietnam's poverty rate (below $1.9 a day), which changed from 49.21 percent in 1992 to 34.79 percent in 1998 and only 3.23 percent in 2012 (World Bank 2015). In 1989, Vietnam exported 1.4 million tons of rice for the first time, and by 2008 it exported 4.7 million tons (Tuan 2009, 38). By 2008, Vietnam had switched from being a country with chronic food shortages to the world's second-largest rice exporter after Thailand.

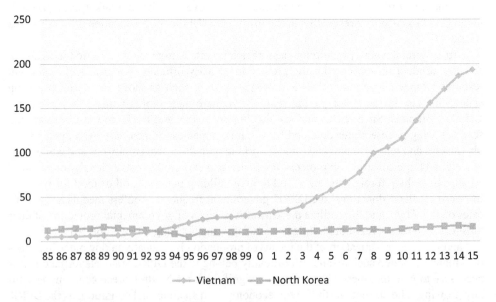

Figure 7.3 North Korea's GDP in comparison with Vietnam, 1985–2015 (unit: US$ billion)

Source: United Nations. Available at http://unstats.un.org/unsd/snaama/dnllist.asp.

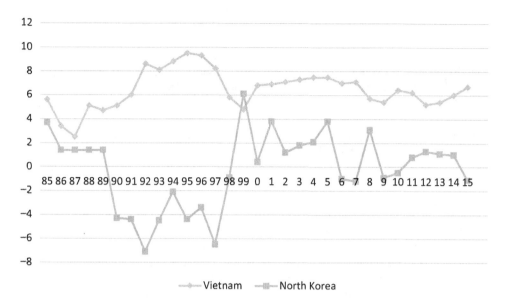

Figure 7.4 Vietnamese and North Korean GDP growth rate, 1985–2015 (unit: percent)

Source: United Nations. Available at http://unstats.un.org/unsd/snaama/dnllist.asp.

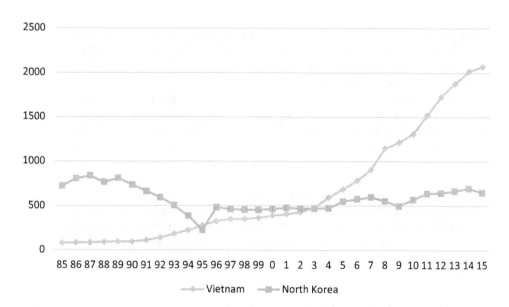

Figure 7.5 North Korea's GDP per capita in comparison with Vietnam, 1985–2015 (unit: US$)

Source: United Nations. Available at http://unstats.un.org/unsd/snaama/dnllist.asp.

Up until the mid-1980s, the Vietnamese economy was in a dire condition. Following the end of the Vietnam War in 1975, South and North Vietnam were reunited under the Socialist Republic of Vietnam. The northern model of the agrarian collectivization, industrial nationalization, and Soviet-style centralized planning was imposed on the South. As a result of its centrally planned economy, Vietnam indeed suffered serious economic problems, including chronic food shortages, low productivity, and large budget deficits (Stradiotto and Guo 2007, 198). To address these issues, the Vietnamese government adopted a hybrid, mixed-ownership economy involving the state and private enterprises in 1979, and it created a two-tiered agricultural production system in 1981. These liberalization measures allowed production groups on cooperative land to sell surplus products on the free market. These reform measures, however, failed to resolve the economic crisis in Vietnam due primarily to the increase in fiscal deficits and high inflation. In addition, China's aid to Vietnam ceased in 1978 due to the deteriorated relationship between the two nations caused by Vietnam's invasion of Cambodia. The amount of aid from the Soviet Union also decreased significantly, because Soviet leaders perceived that 2$ billion in Soviet aid in 1980 had been wasted (Lee 2011, 45). Subsidizing unprofitable state-owned enterprises worsened large budget deficits, and agricultural production declined significantly by the mid-1980s. Furthermore, the Vietnamese economy suffered an inflation rate of 700 percent (Lee 2011, 59–60).

Facing grim conditions, different factions of Communist Party leaders debated over how to resolve the economic crisis. According to Balazs Szalontai, "at the 6th Congress of the Communist Party of Vietnam (December 15–19, 1986), the leaders declared that the previous policy of heavy industrialization, combined with the neglect of agricultural and consumer goods production, had yielded disastrous results" (Szalontai 2008, 210). Based on this recognition, the Vietnamese government commenced the *Doi Moi* (renovation) policy in 1986 and adopted far more radical, comprehensive reform measures in 1989. They included the abolishment of price controls, the legalization of private ownership, the liberalization of the private sector, the withdrawal of subsidies from unprofitable state enterprises, the promotion of foreign investment, the introduction of a modern legal framework, and agricultural reforms, such as the provision of private land-use rights and freedom of households to make all decisions on production and investment (European Institute for Asian Studies 2011; Stradiotto and Guo 2007, 199). These highly intensive reform measures continued into the 1990s and 2000s without serious disruption (Lee 2011, 63–4).

When top leaders in Vietnam sought to adopt economic reforms, they also had favorable domestic conditions, such as traditionally decentralized collective leadership and pragmatic ideology. Unlike North Korea, Vietnam does not have a paramount leader. Instead, the party General Secretary, President, and the Prime Minister share power and thus form collective leadership. Particularly, the Politburo of the Communist Party of Vietnam, which consists of 19 members, directs the general orientation of the government and decides policies. This system of collective leadership is more flexible and effective in managing economic reform and development than one ruled by a single superior leader, because it can be easier for top leaders to detect problems through mutual discussions and to change policy courses. Furthermore, Vietnamese leaders were not seriously constrained by Marxism-Leninism or "Ho Chi Min Thought," which had been formal ideologies in the country. Instead, the leaders desired to adopt drastic economic reform measures based on pragmatism (Govindasamy, Park and Tan 2014, 96).

In addition, Vietnam's geographic location is extremely favorable for agriculture, which has been a key to its economic development. The annual average temperature ranges from 22 to 27 Celsius year-round except in the northern parts of Vietnam. The country's climate, characterized by a considerable amount of sun and a high rate of rainfall, has notably helped cultivate crops such as rice (Weather Online 2017). Furthermore, Vietnam improved its interactions with foreign countries starting in the early 1990s. Up until the late 1980s, Vietnam suffered from economic sanctions by Western countries due to the Vietnam War and its invasion of Cambodia. As a result, the country could not receive Official Development Assistance from international organizations, including the International Monetary Fund, the World Bank, and the Asian Development Bank. However, in the wake of its withdrawal from Cambodia in 1989, Vietnam gradually and increasingly became integrated into the international community. The nation normalized its relations with Japan and the United States in 1991 and signed an agreement on textile trade with the European Community in 1992. After joining the Association of Southeast Asian Nations in 1995, Vietnam also became a member of the Asia-Pacific Economic Cooperation in 1998. In the wake of these events, Vietnam signed the Bilateral Trade Agreement with the United States and developed permanent trade relations with Washington in 2007. In that same year, Vietnam became a member of the World Trade Organization (Govindasamy, Park and Tan 2014, 87–8). The rapidly changing amount of foreign direct investment in Vietnam reflects these improved relationships. FDI net inflows to Vietnam in current US dollars increased from $690,000 in 1984 to $180 million in 1990 and $9.2 billion in 2014 (World Bank 2015). As such, Vietnam has fostered highly constructive relationships with major countries, such as the United States, European Union members, and Japan, all of which have a capacity to help its economic development.

Therefore, Vietnam was able to accomplish economic development based on its leaders' clear vision for economic reform, favorable domestic factors such as collective leadership and pragmatist ideology, and good geographical location and improved relationships with economically affluent countries, particularly the United States and Japan. Compared to Vietnam, however, North Korea has unfavorable internal and external conditions for its economic reform and development. Internally, North Korea has difficulty in adopting full-fledged economic reforms due to the fear of regime collapse. Its inflexible political system dominated by a paramount leader, hereditary power transition system, and strict political ideology based on *Juche* have been also harmful to economic development. Externally, the longstanding nuclear/missile standoff with the international community has seriously restrained the inflow of international aid and investments, thereby hindering the nation's successful economic development.

Conclusion

This chapter explained why North Korea has long suffered economic stagnation and reviewed the long-term variations in the North Korean economy over the last seven decades. In the 1950s after the Korean War, the DPRK saw a quick economic recovery by adopting a strategy of mass mobilization of labor under a Soviet-style command economy. However, the North Korean economy continued to decline from the 1960s because of the inherent ineffectiveness of the centrally planned economy, great emphasis on heavy industry and militarization, ineffective/expensive construction projects, the decline of Soviet aid, and economic autarky based on the ideology of self-reliance.

In the 1990s, the North Korean economy, which had already been seriously weakened by such factors, plunged into an unprecedented economic crisis and massive famine. This humanitarian catastrophe resulted from the collapse of the Soviet Union, natural disasters such as drought and flooding, and the DPRK regime's mismanagement. After this famine, top leader Kim Jong-il adopted some economic reforms, such as the July 1st Measures and the establishment of general markets, but he then reverted to anti-market policies, such as the 2009 currency reform, to regain his regime's grip on power. Although North Korea recovered from the desperate economic crisis under the rule of Kim Jong-il, but economic stagnation continued.

Unlike his father, Kim Jong-un has quite persistently pursued economic reform measures without reverting to anti-market measures. However, North Korea's economy has not notably improved based on macroeconomic indicators such as GDP and per capita GDP. Nevertheless, North Korea is currently experiencing significant changes, such as the deepening of marketization, the rise of private entrepreneurs, and an expanded symbiotic relationship between the state and markets. Considering Vietnam's successful economic reforms and development, the DPRK state should take drastic steps, including the adoption of institutionalized market-oriented policies and the improvement of relationships with the United States, South Korea, and Japan, to revitalize the nation's economic condition. It is indispensable for North Korea to conduct significant reforms and open its doors to the outside world as Vietnam has done, but it appears that the DPRK regime could not easily take such steps because of the fear of regime collapse.

References

Abrahamian, Andray, and Curtis Melvin. 2015. "North Korea's Special Economic Zones: Plans vs. Progress." *38 North*, November 23. Available at: http://38north.org/wp-content/uploads/2015/11/38-North-SEZ-Plans-v-Progress-112315.pdf.

Cha, Victor. 2012. *The Impossible State: North Korea, Past and Future*. New York: HarperCollins Publishers.

Choe, Sang-hun. 2017. "As Economy Grows, North Korea's Grip on Society Is Tested." *The New York Times*, April 30. Available at: www.nytimes.com/2017/04/30/world/asia/north-korea-economy-marketplace.html?_r=0.

Choi, Yong-hwan. 2016. *Marketization of North Korea and the Birth of a Kleptocratic State*. Suwon: Gyeonggi Research Institute.

Daily NK. 2015. "Reform Certain, But to What Degree?" March 6.

Eberstadt, Nicholas. 2007. *The North Korean Economy: Between Crisis and Catastrophe*. London: Transaction Publishers.

Eberstadt, Nicholas. 2010. *Policy and Economic Performance in Divided Korea During the Cold War Era: 1945–1991*. Washington, DC: AEI Press.

European Institute for Asian Studies. 2011. "Report-EIAS Briefing Seminar: 25 Years of Economic Reform in Vietnam." October.

French, Howard W. 2005. "North Korean Experiments, with China as Its Model." *The New York Times*, March 28. Available at: www.nytimes.com/2005/03/28/world/asia/north-korea-experiments-with-china-as-its-model.html?_r=0.

Goto, Fujio. 1982. "Indexes of North Korean Industrial Output 1944–1975." *KSU Economic and Business Review* 9: 145–85.

Govindasamy, Geetha, Ching Kyoo Park, and Er-Win Tan. 2014. "Designing Economic Reforms: The Cases of North Korea and Vietnam." *International Journal of Korean Unification Studies* 23 (1): 73–101.

Haggard, Stephen, and Marcus Noland. 2007. *Famine in North Korea: Markets, Aid and Reform*. New York: Columbia University Press.

Haggard, Stephen, and Marcus Noland. 2009. "Famine in North Korea Redux?" *Journal of Asian Economics* 20 (4): 384–95.

Hong, Min. 2017. "Regional Distribution of North Korea's General Markets and Their Management Conditions." *KDI North Korean Economic Review* March: 3–21.

Ireson, Randall. 2015. "DPRK Agricultural Policy: Chinese-Style Reform or Muddling Towards Autonomy?" *38 North*, January 27. Available at: http://38north.org/2015/01/rireson012715/.

Jeong, Sei-jin. 2000. *From Planning to Market: The Political Economy of Transition in the North Korean System*. Seoul: Hanul. (in Korean)

Jung, Hyung-gon. 2016. "North Korea's Economic Changes and Research on North Korea." *KDI North Korean Review* (December): 25–9. (in Korean)

Kim, Sung Chull. 2006. *North Korea Under Kim Jong Il: From Consolidation to Systemic Dissonance*. Albany: State University of New York Press.

Kim, Yeon-cheol. 1997. *Crisis in North Korea's Ration System and Prospects for Market Reform*. Seoul: Samsung Economic Institute. (in Korean)

Koh, B. C. 1993. "The War's Impact on the Korean Peninsula." *The Journal of American-East Asian Relations* 2 (1): 57–76.

Kotlin, Stephen, and Charles K. Armstrong. 2006. "A Socialist Regional Order in Northeast Asia After World War II." In *Korea at the Center: Dynamics of Regionalism in Northeast Asia*, edited by Charles K. Armstrong, K. Gilbert Rozman, Samuel S. Kim, and Stephen Kotlin. Armonk, NY: M.E. Sharpe.

KOTRA. 2016. *2015 North Korean Trade*. Seoul: KOTRA. (in Korean)

Ku, Yangmo. 2013. "The Emergence of Deng Xiaoping in North Korea? Determining the Prospects for North Korean Economic Reform." *Yale Journal of International Affairs* 8 (2): 76–86.

Kwon, K. J., and Ben Westcott. 2016. "Kim Jong Un Has Executed Over 300 People Since Coming to Power." *CNN*, December 29. Available at: www.cnn.com/2016/12/29/asia/kim- jong-un-executions/.

Lankov, Andrei. 2015. *The Real North Korea: Life and Politics in the Failed Stalinist Utopia*. Oxford: Oxford University Press.

Lankov, Andrei. 2016. "A Dynastic Polity in Economic Stagnation and Decline." In *Routledge Handbook of Modern Korean History*, edited by Michael J. Seth. London: Routledge.

Lee, Hanwoo. 2011. *Political Economy of Vietnamese Economic Reform*. Seoul: Sogang University Press. (in Korean)

Lee, Hy-Sang. 2001. *North Korea: A Strange Socialist Fortress*. Westport, CT: Praeger.

Lee, Suk. 2014. *Review of Economic Studies on North Korea and Its Policy Implications*. Sejong: Korea Development Institute. (in Korean)

Ministry of Unification. 2017. "North Korea's Economic Policy Changes and Prospects for Economic Reform and Opening." Available at: http://nkinfo.unikorea.go.kr/nkp/overview/nkOverview.do?sumryMenuId=EC204. (in Korean)

Myre, Greg. 2017. "Giving Up Nuclear Weapons: It's Rare, But It's Happened." *NPR News*, May 8. Available at: www.npr.org/sections/parallels/2017/05/08/526078459/giving-up-nuclear-weapons-its-rare-but-its-happened.

Natsios, Andrew S. 2001. *The Great North Korean Famine*. Washington, DC: United States Institute of Peace Press.

Noland, Marcus. 2016. "The North Korean Famine." In *Routledge Handbook of Modern Korean History*, edited by Michael Seth. New York: Routledge.

Park, Han S. 2002. *North Korea: The Politics of Unconventional Wisdom*. Boulder, CO: Lynne Rienner.

Park, Hyung-joong. 2013. "North Korea's 'New Economic Management System': Main Features and Problems." *Korea Focus*, October. Available at: www.koreafocus.or.kr/design2/layout/content_print.asp?group_id=105092.

Park, Yong-Soo. 2009. "The Political Economy of Economic Reform in North Korea." *Australian Journal of International Affairs* 63 (4): 529–49.

Radio Free Asia. 2013. "Income Inequality Is Widening Between Pyongyang and Local Areas." August 20. Available at: www.rfa.org/korean/weekly_program/bd81d55c- c774ac8c-bb38c81c-c9c0c694/fe-cp-08202013135934.html. (in Korean)

Seth, Michael J. 2010. *A Concise History of Modern Korea: From the Late Nineteenth Century to the Present*. Lanham, MD: Rowman & Littlefield Publishers.

Shin, Hyon-hee. 2013. "Technocrat's Return a Sign of Reform?" *The Korea Herald*, April 2. Available at: www.koreaherald.com/view.php?ud=20130402000897&mod=skb.

Snyder, Scott. 2013. "Kim Jong Un's Reign of Fear: What's Next?" *Los Angeles Times*, December 16. Available at: http://articles.latimes.com/2013/dec/16/opinion/la-oe-snyder-north- korea-jang-20131216.

Stradiotto, Gary, and Sujian Guo. 2007. "Market Socialism in North Korea: A Comparative Perspective." *Journal of the Asia Pacific Economy* 12 (2): 188–214.

Suh, Sang-chul. 1978. *Growth and Structural Changes in the Korean Economy, 1910–1940*. Cambridge, MA: Harvard University Press.

Szalontai, Balazs. 2008. "The Diplomacy of Economic Reform in Vietnam: The Genesis of Doi Moi, 1986–1989." *The Asiatic Studies* 51 (2): 199–252.

Szalontai, Balazs, and Changyong Choi. 2012. "The Prospects of Economic Reform in North Korea: Comparisons with China, Vietnam, and Yugoslavia." *Europe-Asia Studies* 64 (2): 227–46.

Tuan, Hoang Anh. 2009. "Doi Moi and the Remaking of Vietnam." *Global Asia* 4 (3): 37–41.

United Nations. 2015. "National Accounts Main Aggregates Database." Available at: https://unstats.un.org/unsd/snaama/dnllist.asp.

Weather Online. 2017. "Vietnam's Climate." Available at: www.weatheronline.co.uk/reports/climate/Vietnam.htm.

World Bank. 2015. "Databank." Available at: http://data.worldbank.org/country/vietnam.

Yang, Mun-su. 2015. *North Korea's Planned Economy and Marketization*. Seoul: Institute for Unification Education.

Yang, Mun-su. 2016. "North Korea's Marketization in 2015 and its Future Prospects." *KDI North Korean Economic Review* January: 13–34. (in Korean)

8 North Korean nuclear crises

Inyeop Lee

The North Korean nuclear crisis that started in 1994 has been the source of threat and instability at a regional and global level. The Democratic People's Republic of Korea (DPRK) is no longer a party to the Treaty on the Non-Proliferation of Nuclear Weapons since 2003. The country has tested long-range missiles several times and conducted six nuclear tests on October 2006, May 2009, February 2013, January 2016, September 2016, and September 2017. North Korea's capability to deliver nuclear weapons on target is still limited by its missile and nuclear technology. It can currently reach South Korea, and parts of Japan, Russia and China. But Pyongyang has stockpiled nuclear weapons materials and improved its technology to extending its missile range and to mount its warheads to a missile. The United States has attempted diplomatic efforts since 1993 to dismantle North Korea's nuclear program. There were promising initiatives and negotiations in which both Washington and Pyongyang involved, such as the 1994 Geneva Agreed Framework, the 2000 DPRK–US Joint Communiqué, the Joint Statement of the Six Parties on September 19, 2005, the Six-Party agreement on "Initial Actions for the Implementation of the Joint Statement" on February 13, 2007, and the agreement on "Second-Phase Actions for the Implementation of the Joint Statement" October 3, 2007. In spite of all those efforts, the United States and neighboring countries could not achieve the goal of the denuclearization of North Korea. This chapter explains the historical background and fundamental motives of North Korea's nuclear development. It traces the process of negotiations with the 1994 Geneva Agreement and the 2000 DPRK–US Joint Communiqué, both under the Bill Clinton administration, and the process of Six-Party Talks under the George Bush administration, and analyzes the Barack Obama administration's policy of "strategic patience." Finally, it will discuss what were the major obstacles in resolving North Korean nuclear issue.

Historical background of the North Korean nuclear crisis

The roots of nuclear crisis can be traced back to the division of the Korean Peninsula and the Korean War. The horrifying memories of the Korean War left strong foreign threat perceptions to both Koreas and contributed to intense military confrontation throughout the Cold War period, as described in Chapter 1. North Korea invaded South Korea on June 25, 1950, and the United Nations decided to intervene. Throughout the war, the American Air Force heavily bombed North Korea and wiped North Korea's capital city, Pyongyang, off the map, and destroyed 50 percent of North Korean cities and 80 percent of infrastructure. Therefore, the estimated number of casualties in the North, 1,316,579, was more than double than that in South Korea (595,000), (Cumings 2004a, 16). The United States already used atomic bombs against Hiroshima and Nagasaki at the end of the Pacific War, and North Korea correctly believed that the United States considered the use of nuclear weapons. Gen. Douglas Mac-Arthur requested the use of atomic bombs on July 9th, 1950, just two weeks after the war's start. When the Chinese forces intervened and the war became a stalemate, Gen. Douglas MacArthur considered using atomic bombs more seriously. In a 1954 interview, he discussed his plan to use atomic bombs to win the war in ten days: "I would have dropped between 30 and 50 atomic bombs . . . strung across the neck of Manchuria," and "spread behind us – from the Sea of Japan to the Yellow Sea – a belt of radioactive cobalt . . . it has an active life of between 60 and 120 years. For at least 60 years there could have been no land invasion of Korea from the North" (Cumings 2004a, 21–2). On November 30, 1950, President Harry Truman asserted, "the United States might use any weapon in its arsenal," implying the possibility of the use of the atomic bombs (Cumings 2004b). Gen. MacArthur also submitted "a list of retardation targets" to be neutralized by 26 atomic bombs on December 24, 1950. The US military held a nuclear bombing simulation, named "Operation Hudson Harbor," by flying B-29 fighters over North Korea in September and October 1951. On May 20, 1953, President Dwight Eisenhower and the National Security Council tried to pressure North Koreans into accepting a ceasefire by approving the use of atomic bombs if the Chinese and North Koreans refused to sign the Armistice Agreement. Thus, Eisenhower and Secretary of State John Foster Dulles later claimed that the threat of nuclear weapons was effective in ending the War.

The threat of nuclear weapons was realistic during subsequent Cold War confrontations with North Korea. The United States introduced nuclear weapons into South Korea in January 1958, only few years after the Korean War, including 280-mm atomic cannons and Honest John nuclear-capable missiles. The US Air Force also stationed a squadron of nuclear-tipped Matador cruise missiles in Korea in 1959 (Pincus 2006). The Lyndon Johnson administration considered the use of nuclear weapons during the *Pueblo* incident in 1968. The United States also flew the nuclear-capable B-52 bombers after the shooting down of a US EC-121 spy plane by the North in 1969. As a response to the Ax Murder incident, the killing of two US Army officers by North Korean soldiers in the Joint Security Area (JSA) in 1976, the United States deployed B-52 bombers again. When the United States developed a strategy to use nuclear weapons in earlier stages of wars in the mid-1960s and a strategy to deep strike underground facilities in the mid-1970s, North Korea redeployed 80 percent of solders along the Demilitarized Zone (DMZ) so that they could invade the South quickly and survive any nuclear attacks (Cumings 2004a, 54–5). Therefore, Kim Il-sung remarked that North Korea "does not intend to attack, nor could it. More than 1,000 US nuclear warheads are stored in South Korea, ostensibly for defense, and it would take only two of them to destroy [the North]" (quoted in Litwak 2007, 284) in a conversation with East German leader Erich Honecker in October 1986.

Therefore, North Korea began its nuclear program as early as the late 1950s by signing nuclear cooperation agreements with China and the Soviet Union. North Korea sent 30 students to the Soviet Union to study nuclear physics. North Korea established the Yongbyon nuclear facility in 1964, and expanded it with a small research reactor provided from the Soviet Union a year later. The need to deter a US invasion was the major motivation in its continued development. Secondary reasons included the need for energy sources and a fear of abandonment following the Soviet decision to withdraw missiles from Cuba in 1962. South Korean President Park Jung-hee also explored a nuclear weapons program due to fear of abandonment by the United States. The United States reaffirmed its use of nuclear weapons to defend South Korea and pressured South Korea to ratify the Nuclear Non-proliferation

Treaty (NPT) in 1975. North Korea constructed a 5-megawatt (MW) gas-graphite nuclear reactor in Yongbyon in the early 1980s and started its operation in 1986. In December 1985, Pyongyang signed the NPT under pressure from Moscow and its promise of four light-water nuclear power reactors, but it delayed completion of a safeguards agreement with International Atomic Energy Agency (IAEA).

The development of nuclear weapons was also driven by the shifting balance of power against the North from the 1980s and the collapse of the Cold War, which ushered in an era of diplomatic isolation. North Korea achieved much faster economic development in 1960s compared to South Korea, but the South began to catch up in 1970s. South Korea's economy grew exponentially in the 1980s, while North Korea experienced almost none or even negative economic growth in the 1980s and 1990s. North Koreans experienced food shortages and extreme economic deprivation in the 1990s (Kang 2003, 349), caused by its own systemic problems, the end of Soviet aid, and a lack of trading partners when the Communist Bloc collapsed. When the South normalized relations with the USSR in 1990 and China in 1992, the North never came to terms with the United States or Japan for cross-recognition. The United States expected that North Korea might collapse as had other communist countries. When the Soviet Union, under Mikhail Gorbachev, normalized relations with Seoul in September 1990, North Korea released a memorandum warning that Moscow–Seoul normalization would mean an end to the DPRK–USSR alliance, and that Pyongyang would have "no other choice but to take measures to provide for ourselves some weapons for which we have so far relied on the alliance," referring to nuclear weapons (Korean Central News Agency [KCNA], September 18, 1990, quoted in Mack 1993). North Korea was paranoid about its own survival with the crumbling of the Berlin wall in 1989, German reunification by the West's absorption of the East in 1990, and the disintegration of the Soviet Union 1991.

The memories of the Korean War, the continued possibility of military confrontation on the Peninsula, the fear of nuclear war throughout the Cold War, and the shifting balance of power against the North and its desire for survival and negotiation with the United States all contributed to North Korea's desire for nuclear weapons. Therefore, the problem cannot be resolved without addressing such security issue for North Korea (Harrison 2002, 257–8). North Korea's nuclear program has multiple purposes. It has generated electricity in a country with no oil but rich natural uranium. It can bridge the gap in conventional weapons capability for a small country (Sagan and Waltz 2002, 239). It has served as a bargaining chip in negotiations with the United States, and it could guarantee its survival if negotiations failed.

The first North Korean nuclear crisis and the Clinton administration

The first opportunity to resolve the North Korean nuclear issue occurred once the Cold War structure in Asia had started to crumble. President George H.W. Bush announced in 1991 the worldwide withdrawal of tactical nuclear weapons from abroad, including from South Korea. Intercontinental ballistic missiles (ICBMs) could and did still provide a nuclear umbrella for South Korea without the deployment of nuclear weapons on South Korean soil. The United States also wanted to pressure North Korea for denuclearization by withdrawing its own nuclear weapons from the South in 1991, since the United States had acquired intelligence in 1989 that the Yongbyon facility could extract weapons-grade plutonium from spent nuclear reactor fuel. The two Koreas became members of the UN together in 1991 and the Roh Tae-woo administration in South started conversations with the North for peace and reconciliation. They signed "the Agreement on Reconciliation, Non-Aggression and Exchanges and Cooperation between the South and the North" on December 13, 1991, and signed a "Joint

Declaration on the Denuclearization of the Korean Peninsula" on December 31, 1991. The two nations pledged to use nuclear energy for peaceful purposes only and not obtain nuclear weapons nor any nuclear processing and uranium enrichment facilities. The United States decided to cancel Team Spirit joint military exercises in 1992 to promote North Korean cooperation on nuclear inspections. North Korea signed a comprehensive safeguards agreement with the IAEA in the same year. The IAEA conducted inspections to verify the inventory of nuclear materials submitted by the North in 1992 and 1993. The IAEA, however, experienced tensions with the North when requesting "special inspections" for declared and undeclared sites. The United States and South Korea also held conversations with the North on the nuclear issue, but they ended without tangible results. The North Korean delegation wanted to continue bilateral talks for diplomatic normalization, surprisingly suggesting it would not object to United States troops stationed in the Peninsula after national unification. This statement radically diverged from its traditional position of asking for the withdrawal of all US forces. The US delegation, though, omitted tangible incentives or the possibility of diplomatic normalization. There was lack of consensus between hawks and doves in the United States on policy toward the North, and the hawks may have believed that North Korea would collapse as had its Eastern European allies. The Roh government was also critical of direct US–DPRK negotiations on the nuclear issue without South Korea as a primary negotiator (Wit, Poneman and Gallucci 2004, 12). Finally, the United States and South Korea announced plans to resume the Team Sprit joint military exercise in early 1993, and North Korea withdrew from high-level talks with Seoul and rejected the IAEA's request for special inspections.

The negotiations ended without any tangible outcome, while political leaders changed in the United States and South Korea. Bill Clinton came to office on January 20, 1993, and Kim Young-sam took office in South Korea on February 25, 1993. North Korea announced its intention to withdraw from the NPT in the middle of the Team Spirit military exercise in March 1993. After working-level talks with the US representatives in New York, North Korea suspended its withdrawal from the NPT in June 1993. The United States and North Korea conducted high-level talks in Geneva in September. When the United States agreed to suspend the 1994 Team Spirit exercises, North Korea agreed to accept IAEA inspections in December 1993. But the IAEA then announced that it could not draw conclusions on the possible diversion of nuclear material for weapons program after previous inspections. The Republican Party in the United States criticized negotiations and compromises toward North Korea. President Kim Young-sam in the South also made critical comments toward the North and tried to add preconditions to the negotiations to show South Korea's influence and to appeal to conservative citizens and media in the South.

Negotiations stalled in early 1994, and tensions escalated. Washington announced its plan to send Patriot missiles to South Korea and resumed Team Spirit in January 1994. The North Korean delegation chief, in an inter-Korean meeting on March 19, 1994, warned that Seoul, just 50 km south of the border, may turn into a "sea of flames" if war broke out. Kim Young-sam, on June 6, 1994, warned the North that any reckless action would lead to self-destruction. North Korea finally withdrew from the IAEA on June 13, and the United States called for sanctions in the UN Security Council. The Clinton administration discussed a plan to strengthen the US military presence on the peninsula and the possibility of preemptive strikes on the Yongbyon facility in June 16, 1994. Pyongyang responded that any strike against the North would be considered all-out war. The simulation of full-scale warfare in Korea showed Washington that it would result in one million causalities in the South, including tens of thousands of American troops.

In the middle of heightened tensions, former President Jimmy Carter visited North Korea on June 15–18, 1994. He reached a tentative agreement with Kim Il-sung that would freeze and eventually dismantle North Korea's nuclear activities in exchange for a US pledge to resume high-level talks for a package deal (Sigal 1998, 132). The United States and North Korea restarted negotiations and signed the Agreed Framework, or Geneva Agreement, on October 21, 1994. North Korea agreed to freeze and replace the graphite-moderated 5-MW nuclear reactor with the more nuclear proliferation-resistant 'light-water reactors' and to stop the construction of 50-MW and 200-MW graphite-moderated reactors. The United States promised to construct a 2000-MW light-water reactor power plants by 2003 and to provide heavy fuel oil to the North until the completion of the new plants. North Korea also agreed to allow inspection of old waste sites when construction began on the new plants. Both sides agreed to pursue step-by-step diplomatic normalization, and Pyongyang decided to remain a party to the NPT.[1]

There was, however, an important gap between the two sides. While Pyongyang considered the agreement as a legally binding treaty and a guarantee of diplomatic normalization, Washington did not consider the implementation of the Agreement as a legal obligation, including the construction of light-water reactors by 2003. It became more difficult for the Clinton administration to implement the Agreement when the Republican Party had a landslide victory in the mid-term congressional elections on November 7, 1994, only 17 days after signing the Geneva Agreement. The new Congress diminished the Clinton administration's financial and political resources to implement the Geneva Agreement. The Republican Party was skeptical about negotiations with Pyongyang and still believed in an impending collapse of North Korea. They obstructed the implementation of the Agreement, the construction of the light-water reactors was delayed, and negotiations for diplomatic normalization with Pyongyang did not even start. North Korea, losing patience, responded by testing long-range missiles that flew over Japan in August 1998. The United States also acquired some intelligence on a new suspected nuclear site at Kumchang-ri and demanded an inspection. The United States provided 600,000 tons of food to the North and sent inspectors to the site on May 18–24, 1999, but they only found empty tunnels not suitable for installing nuclear facilities (Gertz 1991).

New momentum for diplomatic efforts came with the election of Kim Dae-jung as the new president of South Korea and the origins of the Perry Process in 1998. Kim Dae-jung's "Sunshine Policy" toward North Korea found common interest in the Clinton administration's effort with the Perry Process to improve its North Korean relationship "in a step-by-step and reciprocal fashion." William Perry, a former Defense Secretary and special envoy on the North Korea issue, visited Pyongyang from May 25 through 28, 1999. He concurrently maintained close cooperation with Kim Dae-jung in producing 'The Perry Report.' The report suggested an engagement policy with Pyongyang to prioritize the denuclearization of North Korea, rejecting the possibility of an impending collapse of the North (Wit, Poneman and Gallucci 2004, 375). Clinton announced the lifting of limited number of sanctions imposed upon North Korea under the Trading with the Enemy Act, the Defense Production Act, and the Commerce Department's Export Administration Regulations in September 1999. In response, North Korea halted missile tests during the ongoing talks. South Korean President Kim Dae-Jung and North Korean leader Kim Jong-il held a historic summit meeting in Pyongyang on June 15, 2000. Both leaders embraced the ideals of peace and reconciliation and started economic cooperation and cultural exchanges. Kim Jong-il's close adviser, Vice Marshal Jo Myong-rok, visited Washington as a special envoy from October 9 to 12, 2000. In a quasi-summit meeting, he met President Clinton and other high-level officials and issued a US–DPRK Joint Communiqué. The United States and the DPRK decided to cease hostile intentions toward the other, to build a new relationship, to reduce tensions on the Korean Peninsula, and to resolve the missile issue.[2] As a response, Secretary of State Madeleine Albright and Ambassador Wendy Sherman visited Kim Jong-il in Pyongyang on October 24, 2000. Kim was very satisfied with the meeting, and he even pledged that North Korea would conduct no further tests of long-range missiles and "refocus his country's resources on economic development" as China had under Deng Xiaoping (Pritchard 2003). Albright later said that her visit was intended to pave the way for a visit to North Korea by President Clinton that could have generated a momentum for a final deal on the missile program and denuclearize North Korea (Albright and Woodward 2003, 459).[3] The Clinton administration, though, did not have enough time for the summit meeting with Kim Jong-il. The presidential election dispute at the end of 2000 prevented any bold move regarding Pyongyang. President-elect George W. Bush's team also warned the White House not to make any major movies that would bind the incoming administration. Clinton mentioned "insufficient time to complete the work at hand" and decided not to visit Pyongyang. The momentum for a diplomatic solution at the end of 2000 subsided, and the Republicans who had criticized Clinton's approach now controlled the executive and legislative branches. (Wit, Poneman and Gallucci 2004, 376–7; Kim 2010, 64).

The second North Korean nuclear crisis and the Bush administration

Positive momentum on North Korea's nuclear program was building on the Korean Peninsula when President Bush took office in January 2001. South Korean President Kim Dae-jung's Sunshine Policy had led to a historic summit meeting with Kim Jong-il on June 15, 2000. The meeting led to inter-Korean economic cooperation, cultural exchanges, and the reunion of separated families. Secretary of State Albright visited Pyongyang in October 2000, and Kim Jong-il promised to stop missile tests and start economic reforms. Kim Jong-il announced the establishment of the Sinuiju Special Administrative Region in September 2002 (Petrov 2012). When Japanese Prime Minister Junichiro Koizumi visited Pyongyang and met Kim in September 2002, the latter apologized for kidnapping Japanese citizens in the 1970s and 1980s. The Bush administration, though, criticized Clinton's approach toward Pyongyang as 'a reward for bad behavior' and expressed strong skepticism over North Korean regime. The 9/11 terrorist attacks were a crucial moment for the emergence of the Bush Doctrine of preemption. In his State of the Union address on January 29, 2002, President Bush included North Korea, Iran, and Iraq as an "Axis of Evil."[4] The administration also identified North Korea, China, and other 'rogue states' as potential targets of nuclear weapons in the 2001 Nuclear Posture Review that leaked to the media (Bleek 2012). North Korea criticized the disclosure as a blatant violation of the Geneva Agreement, in which the United States pledged not to threat or attack North Korea with nuclear weapons. President Bush also outlined a shift in US internationalism away from the Cold War policies of containment and deterrence to an open advocacy of preemptive, or even preventive, military action to prevent terrorists, and regimes that sponsor terror, from threatening the United States with weapons of mass destruction in his speech at West Point.[5] According to Pritchard (2007; 11–15), however, Pyongyang did not clearly understand the change in US administrations and wanted the Bush administration "to pick up where the Clinton administration had left off" right up until the second nuclear crisis emerged.

The Second North Korean nuclear crisis started when James Kelly, Assistant Secretary of State for Asia and the Pacific, visited Pyongyang on October 3–5, 2002, for the first high-level talks under the Bush administration. Kelly accused Pyongyang for violating the Geneva Agreement by having a secret highly enriched uranium (HEU) program. The Central Intelligence Agency (CIA) claimed that North Korea had purchased large quantities of materials to build a centrifuge facility to enrich uranium. After this visit, the Bush administration announced that North Korea admitted a secret HEU program that violated the Agreed Framework. North Korea, however, denied the claim by stating that Kang Sok-ju only told Kelly that North Korea was "entitled" to have such a program or "an even more powerful one" to deter a preemptive US attack (Harrison 2005). Evidence on the scope of North Korean HEU program is unclear. Donald Gregg, former US ambassador to South Korea from 1989–1993 who visited Pyongyang with Don Oberdorfer one month after Kelly's visit, claimed that Pyongyang actually stated it was entitled to have nuclear weapons, but would prefer an extensive new peace treaty. He accused Kelly of interpreting or distorting the statement as "an admission of an illegal uranium program" (*PBS* 2003). Testimony from Abdul Qadeer Khan, who ran a black market nuclear supply ring from Pakistan, demonstrated that North Korea had obtained centrifuge prototypes and blueprints as well as a shipment of high-strength aluminum tubes to North Korea by a German firm (Pritchard 2007, 28–9). David Albright, from the Institute for Science and International Security, said that "firm evidence to support the existence or schedule of the construction of a large-scale centrifuge has not emerged and evidence of large-scale procurements of sensitive centrifuge items remains missing" (Albright 2007). Diplomat Christopher Hill, in his speech at the Brookings Institute on February 22, 2007, said that North Korea had imported equipment that could be used for uranium enrichment, but "it would require a lot more equipment than we know that they have actually purchased" to make the thousands of centrifuge cascades needed for a weapons-grade uranium enrichment facility (Harrison 2008).

The Bush administration declared that the North had violated the Geneva Agreement and announced the suspension of all future shipments of heavy fuel oil to North Korea in mid-November (Dao 2002). The shipment of heavy fuel oil was the only part of the Geneva Agreement that North Korea believed the United States had implemented, as construction of light-water reactors was never completed and the Bush administration had included North Korea as one of the targets of a preemptive nuclear strike. North Korea declared that it was Washington that had dismantled the Agreement and restarted its confrontational policies (*Joongang Ilbo* 2002). The North announced the unfreezing of its nuclear program and the restarting of the three-reactor complex at Yongbyon (Struck 2002). North Korea started to remove seals and surveillance cameras at Yongbyon and expelled the IAEA monitors on December 21, announcing that it would finally withdraw from the NPT (Goodman 2002). Some scholars have criticized the Bush administration for letting the Agreed Framework collapse, letting North Korea reprocess its fuel rods and extract plutonium to increase its nuclear stockpile in the name of punishing a HEU program that may not even have existed or in an experimental stage (Harrison 2005; Harrison 2008; Albright 2007; Cumings 2007). North Korea then unsealed its plutonium program, which has been frozen since 1994 (Pritchard 2007, 44; Hecker 2010).

While North Korea revived its nuclear weapons program, neighboring countries urged the United States to restart a dialogue with North Korea (Hutzler and Solomon 2003). Pyongyang demanded bilateral talks, though, and Washington insisted that any negotiations should be in a multilateral framework. Bush administration believed that bilateral talks with North Korea itself would somehow reward Pyongyang (Pritchard 2007, 55). It also believed that Pyongyang has been deceptive in bilateral negotiations, and so, it wanted to pressure North Korea in a multilateral negotiation with other participants. As a compromise, the United

States and North Korea had a trilateral meeting with China in Beijing on April 23–25, 2003 that repeated the same demands without any progress. The new Roh Moo-hyun administration in South Korea continued Kim Dae-jung's Sunshine Policy with his "Peace and Prosperity Policy." He expanded economic cooperation, cultural exchanges, and humanitarian assistance to the North in spite of the nuclear crisis. The Roh administration also mediated between Washington and Pyongyang. With diplomatic effort from South Korea and China, Pyongyang finally accepted a new round of Six-Party Talks and Washington agreed to have "informal" bilateral talks within the multilateral talks (Kynge and Ward 2003). The Six-Party Talks are hosted in Beijing and chaired by China and attended by China, Japan, North Korea, Russia, South Korea, and the United States to dismantle North Korea's nuclear program. The first three rounds of the Six-Party Talks were held in August 2003 and February 2004, but they did not make meaningful progress. North Korea suggested a "package solution" similar to the Agreed Framework in a "word for word and action for action" process whereby North Korea would dismantle its nuclear program, while the United States signed a legally binding non-aggression treaty.[6] The Bush administration insisted that Pyongyang should give up its nuclear program first with "complete, verifiable, irreversible disarmament" (CVID) as a precondition to any United States concession. Secretary of State Condoleezza Rice, in her remarks before the Senate Foreign Relations Committee on January 18, 2005, referred to North Korea as one of the six 'outposts of tyranny' (*BBC* 2005). North Korea reacted with harsh criticism, and it took 13 months for Pyongyang to come back to the Six-Party Talks after mediation by China and South Korea. The six parties reached an agreement on September 19, 2005. According to the Joint statement of the Six-Party Talks on September 19, 2005, North Korea agreed to "abandon all nuclear weapons and nuclear programs and return to the NPT as soon as possible." The other parties respected "North Korea's right to peaceful use of nuclear energy" and promised to discuss "the light-water reactors" issue "at an appropriate time." The United States "affirmed it has no intention to attack or invade North Korea and will provide a security guarantee to this effect." The United States and North Korea agreed to "work to normalize their relations," and "to respect each other's sovereignty, exist peacefully together."[7] Such an achievement was possible only after the Bush administration withdrew from its original position of CVID.

On the very next day, though, this agreement met an obstacle when the United States Treasury froze North Korean bank accounts containing about $25 million after at Banco Delta Asia (BDA) next day after accusing North Korea of various illegal activities, including money laundering and counterfeiting US dollars. This move demonstrated the bureaucratic complexity behind US policy, where multiple organizations within a government compete with each other as Graham Allison (Allison and Zelikow 1999) has explained. North Korea resorted to brinkmanship by withdrawing from the Six-Party Talks, launching a long-range Taepodong-2 and several medium-range rockets on July 4, 2006 (Feffer 2006; Sigal 2006), and conducting its first nuclear test on October 9, 2006. It is important to note that the nuclear bomb was made from a plutonium-based program unfrozen after the end of the Geneva Agreement and not of the highly enriched uranium program that the Bush administration had accused Pyongyang of having in October 2002.

The Bush administration was already under domestic criticism for its aggressive Iraq policy, and the North Korean nuclear test was depicted another diplomatic failure. The Republican Party experienced crushing defeats in the November 2006 mid-term elections, and the hardline neoconservatives in the administration lost influence. South Korea and China with their mediation diplomacy also contributed to a diplomatic breakthrough with the Six-Party

Talks as well as domestic political changes in the United States. Washington started bilateral negotiations with Pyongyang in November 2006 in an attempt to bring North Korea back to the Six-Party Talks by resolving the BDA issue. On February 13, 2007, the six parties agreed on the Initial Action for the Implementation of the 2005 Joint Statement.[8] In the statement, North Korea agreed to "shut down and seal the Yongbyon nuclear facility, including the reprocessing facility and invite back IAEA personnel to conduct all necessary monitoring and verifications." In return, the other five parties pledged to "provide emergency energy assistance to North Korea in the initial phase of 50,000 tons of heavy fuel oil, to commence within 60 days." All six parties agreed to take positive steps for 'peace and stability in Northeast Asia' and to "negotiate permanent peace regime on the Korean Peninsula" (Arms Control Association 2017).

The participants also agreed on Second-Phase Actions for the Implementation of the Joint Statement at the end of the sixth round of the Six-Party Talks on October 3, 2007. In the statement, the

> DPRK agreed to disable all nuclear facilities subject to September 2005 Joint Statement and February 13 Agreement, including the disablement of three facilities at Yongbyon by 31 December 2007: the 5 MW Experimental Reactor, the Reprocessing Plant, and the Nuclear Fuel Rod Fabrication Facility, [and to provide] a complete and correct declaration of all its nuclear programs in accordance with the February 13 agreement by 31 December 2007.

The United States pledged to remove the DPRK from its list of state sponsors of terrorism, terminate the application of the Trading with the Enemy Act to the DPRK, and provide one million tons of heavy fuel oil to North Korea.[9] North Korea provided the United States with documents on its plutonium program on May 8 and also with the details of its nuclear program on June 26, 2008. North Korea televised the destruction of the cooling tower at the Yongbyon nuclear reactor on June 27, 2008. The United States removed North Korea from the list of state sponsors of terrorism and lifted some sanctions under the Trading with the Enemy Act (Choe 2008). The domestic politics of the United States, pressure from other participants in the Six-Party Talks, and North Korea's brinkmanship with missile and nuclear tests pushed the Bush administration to adopt more realistic measures instead of CVID.

This momentum, however, met obstacles when the Bush administration requested a far-reaching verification plan and demanded "full access to any site, facility or location deemed relevant to the nuclear program, including military facilities," allowing US inspectors to "take photographs and make videos, remain on site as long as necessary, make repeated visits and collect and remove samples." China, South Korea, and Russia warned this would stall the progress of the talks, and Assistant Secretary of State Hill and his aides also opposed the request. North Korea criticized the US demands as a betrayal of the agreement (Kessler 2008). The diplomatic efforts subsided when the Bush administration was in a lame duck status, and it coincided with Kim Jong-il's stroke in mid-August that started a succession process that diverted Pyongyang's attention. Both sides lacked the trust or time to move further. New conservative South Korean President Lee Myung-bak (2008–2013) also reversed Kim Dae-jung and Roh Moo-hyun's approach with more hawkish policies toward Pyongyang. There has been no other meeting when the Six-Party Talk in December 8, 2008, ended without any meaningful outcome.

The Obama administration's North Korea policy

President Barack Obama, due to a willingness to engage "rogue" states as announced in his presidential campaign and inaugural address, was expected to start diplomatic efforts toward Pyongyang. In his remarks on Iraq in Fayetteville, NC, on March 19, 2008, he stated,

> we cannot seize opportunities to resolve our problems unless we create them. That is what Kennedy did with Khrushchev; that's what Nixon did with Mao; what Reagan did with Gorbachev. And that is what I will do as president of the United States.

In a May 16, 2008 press conference in Watertown, SD, he stated,

> What I have said is that I will meet with not just our allies and our friends but I will initiate tough diplomacy with our enemies. That includes Syria, Iran, North Korea and Venezuela. I would meet with them and I would meet with them without preconditions although with preparation.
>
> (Farley 2008)

In his first presidential debate with John McCain, he pointed out that the US efforts at isolating Iran and other rogue states had actually "accelerated their efforts to get nuclear weapons." He also acknowledged that the United States has "at least made some progress" in North Korean issue when "the Bush administration reversed course" and "re-engaged North Korea." In his inaugural address, President Obama promised that he would offer an "outstretched hand to those who will unclench their fists."[10] Secretary Hillary Clinton, in her speech to the Asia Society in New York on February 13, 2009, right before her first overseas diplomatic trip to East Asia, also suggested the possibility of a grand bargain with Pyongyang by saying,

> If North Korea is genuinely prepared to completely and verifiably eliminate their nuclear weapons program, the Obama Administration will be willing to normalize bilateral relations, replace the peninsula's long standing armistice agreements with a permanent peace treaty, and assist in meeting the energy and other economic needs for the North Korea people.

She also commented on February 15 that North Korea's nuclear program is "the most acute challenge to stability in northeast Asia" and

> the Obama administration is prepared to seek a permanent, stable peace with Pyongyang as long as its regime pursues disarmament and does not engage in aggression against neighboring South Korea. The United States has a great openness and willingness to working with them.

President Obama also emphasized, in a statement from Prague, Czech Republic on April 5, 2009, the importance of the Six-Party Talks by saying that

> the United States is fully committed to maintaining security and stability in northeast Asia and we will continue working for the verifiable denuclearization of the Korean Peninsula through the Six-Party Talks. The Six-Party Talks provide the forum for achieving

denuclearization, reducing tensions, and for resolving other issues of concern between North Korea, its four neighbors, and the United States.[11]

North Korea, however, conducted a failed multi-stage Teapodong-2 rocket test in the name of a satellite launch in April and a second nuclear test in May 2009. Both actions prevented the resumption of negotiations between Washington and Pyongyang and the restarting of the Six-Party Talks. Such provocative actions from North Korea could have been the result of the need to consolidate a regime in the middle of succession process and to pressure the new Obama administration by negotiating from a position of strength. As a consequence, the United States coordinated UN Security Council Resolution 1874 in June 2009 that condemned North Korea's missile and nuclear tests and imposed economic and commercial sanctions on North Korea. Such actions in the early period of the Obama administration made it more difficult for Obama to initiate diplomacy with Pyongyang, while seriously limiting his political capital and Congressional support. Congress rejected the Obama administration's request for financial support for diplomatic negotiations with Pyongyang, including US food aid. In May 2009, President Obama declared that his administration would "not fall into the same pattern with North Korea," and Defense Secretary Robert M. Gates stated that the Obama administration "will not buy this horse for a third time." In June 2009 in France, President Obama mentioned that "North Korea's actions over the last several months have been extraordinarily provocative," and he is "not intending to continue a policy of rewarding provocation." Secretary Clinton, in a speech in October 2009, reaffirmed that

> North Korea's return to the negotiating table is not enough. Current sanctions will not be relaxed until Pyongyang takes verifiable, irreversible steps toward complete denuclearization. Its leaders should be under no illusion that the United States will ever have normal, sanctions-free relations with a nuclear armed North Korea.[12]

The alleged sinking of South Korean Warship *Cheonan* in March and the shelling of Yeonpyeong Island by North Korea in November 2010 posed another serious challenge to negotiations. A multinational investigation team led by South Korea claimed that a North Korean submarine sank the *Cheonan* by a torpedo, taking 46 sailors' lives. After eight months of the *Cheonan* sinking, North Korea made a warning over South Korean military exercises around the disputed maritime border between the two sides, and then fired over 170 artillery rounds toward Yeonpyeong Island in the Yellow Sea that killed two South Korean marines and two civilians. It should be also noted that conservative President Lee Myong-bak was skeptical about his two predecessors' policy of engaging North Korea. Under the President Lee, South Korea did not play the role of mediator between the United States and North Korea. Seoul also lost its diplomatic channels and leverage over Pyongyang. In response to North Korea's provocations, the Obama administration bolstered trilateral coordination among Washington, Seoul, and Tokyo and conducted a series of military exercises in cooperation with the South Korean military, including the deployment of the *USS George Washington* aircraft carrier to the Yellow Sea.

In November 2010, North Korea invited a group of US nuclear experts, including Stanford University scientist Siegfried Hecker, to its uranium enrichment facility in Yongbyon to show off its experimental light-water reactor and a more sophisticated gas centrifuge uranium enrichment facility. At this moment, there is no question that North Korea runs both plutonium and uranium enrichment program capable of producing fissile material. The Obama administration resumed three rounds of direct and bilateral talks with Pyongyang from July 2011. Even though the talks stalled shortly after Kim Jong-il's death, they resumed. The two sides reached the so-called Leap Day Agreement on February 12, 2012, under which the Obama administration declared it had "no hostile intent" toward North Korea, promised to provide 240,000 metric tons of food and nutritional aid for young children, pregnant mothers, and the elderly, and to increase cultural exchanges in return for Pyongyang's moratorium on nuclear tests, long-range missile launches, and uranium enrichment activities at the Yongbyon nuclear facility. North Korea also agreed to readmit IAEA inspectors. The agreement, however, quickly fell apart with North Korea's failed launching of long-range rocket (called Unha-3 by North Korea) on April 13, 2012, soon after Kim Jong-un had assumed office. North Korea insisted that satellite launches were not part of an agreement prohibition and the launch was to honor the 100th anniversary of the birth of its founder Kim Il-sung. The Obama administration, though, declared the agreement nullified and ended its denuclearization dialogue with Pyongyang.

In a November 2012 speech at the University of Yangon in Myanmar, President Obama had mentioned his "outstretched hand" to Pyongyang if North Korea pursues the path of denuclearization and reform, signaling some possibility of negotiations (Snyder 2012). But a successful launch of multi-stage rocket (called Unha-3 by North Korea) put a Kwangmyŏngsŏng-3 satellite into orbit. The third and most successful underground nuclear test based on "miniaturized lighter nuclear device with greater explosive force," according to North Korea in February 2013, forestalled further negotiations. The Obama administration, in concert with the governments of South Korea and Japan, pressured the North with more sanctions, isolation, and military exercises. The UN Security Council passed a resolution condemning North Korea and imposing new round of harsher sanctions under Resolutions 2087 and 2094, which were even approved by China, whose relations with Pyongyang had become relatively strained. The United States and South Korea conducted joint military exercises with the US deployment of B-2 stealth bombers and B-52 bombers capable of nuclear strikes, F-22 fighters over South Korea, and a new Terminal High Altitude Area Defense (THAAD) missile defense system deployed to nearby Guam. North Korea unleashed unusually hostile remarks against the United States, South Korea, and Japan, including the threat to use its nuclear weapons against targets in the United States.

"Strategic Patience" represents the Obama administration's North Korea policy, especially after "Leap Day Agreement" fell apart (*Voice of America* 2009). Washington made it clear that North Korea will not receive any benefits until it demonstrates a serious commitment to denuclearization as promised in the 2005 Six-Party Talks. Washington has placed more sanctions and pressure on the North to force it back to the negotiating table, and it has strengthened cooperation with Seoul and Tokyo to demonstrate its strong military commitment in the region. For example, President Obama, in a press conference at the Nuclear Security Summit in April 2010, stated,

> I think it's fair to say that North Korea has chosen a path of severe isolation that has been extraordinarily damaging to its people, and that it is our hope that as pressure builds for North Korea to improve its economic performance, for example, to break out of that isolation that we'll see a return to the Six-Party talks and that we will see a change in behavior.

He also added "the approach that we've taken with respect to North Korea makes it more likely for them to alter their behavior than had there been no consequences whatsoever to them testing a nuclear weapon." He repeated the same logic of "Strategic Patience" several times. He explained, at a Joint Press Conference with Prime Minister Noda of Japan in April 2012, that "what I've tried to do since I came into office is to make sure that North Koreans understand that the old pattern of provocation that then gets attention and somehow insists on the world purchasing good behavior from them, that that pattern is broken." In his interview with ABC News in March 2013, he said engagement could only come after evidence of "responsible behavior" from the North Koreans. "One thing we've tried to do is to make sure that we're not gonna to reward bad behavior," he added as a response to N.B.A. star Dennis Rodman's visit to North Korea and the message that Kim Jong-un wanted a direct call from Mr. Obama. In NBC's *Today* Show in April 2013, he also pointed out "the same kind of pattern that we saw his father engage in, and his grandfather before that" and added, "You don't get to bang your spoon on the table and somehow you get your way" (Halper 2013).

North Korea announced that it had successfully tested its fourth nuclear weapon, an "experimental hydrogen bomb," on January 6, 2016, which was its fourth nuclear test. On September 9, 2016, North Korea conducted its fifth nuclear test and announced the successful test of a warhead that can be mounted onto a rocket.

Obama administration actually tried some serious diplomacy in its earlier period, but many factors have prevented meaningful diplomatic success between Washington and Pyongyang. First of all, North Korea has conducted unusually provocative actions, including nuclear tests and launching of rockets (or satellites, as North Korea insists). Some analysts explain that Kim Jong-un needed to strengthen his legitimacy during the succession process. For example, the launching of a Taepodong-2 missile in 2012 was related to the 100th anniversary of the birth of their founder Kim Il-sung that year. Kim Jong-il had also declared that North Korea would be a powerful and prosperous nation by 2012. The tests could have targeted domestic goals rather than trying to threaten the United States. Domestic political changes in South Korea also played an important role. As President Bush did not want to continue Clinton's engagement policy toward Pyongyang, President Lee, who came to office in 2008, generally neglected the policies and achievements of the two previous presidents. These included agreements made during the summit meeting in 2000 between Kim Dae-jung and Kim Jong-il, and in 2006 between Ro Moo-hyun and Kim Jong-il to expand economic cooperation and start a Special Zone in the disputed maritime border in the West Sea. North Korea also exacerbated inter-Korean relations by conducting attacks on South Korea. President Lee imposed sanctions against North Korea and suspended inter-Korean trade, except at the Kaesong Industrial Complex. President Park Geun-hye (2013–2017) also continued President Lee's conservative policies, expecting North Korea's collapse and absorption of the North by the South. The Park administration's decision to deploy the American THAAD missile defense system infuriated Beijing and ended its cooperation in approaching North Korean problem. She also made a decision to completely shut down the Kaesong Industrial Complex in 2016, which was the symbol of inter-Korean economic cooperation, in the name of pressuring North Korea after its missile and nuclear tests. While the Bush administration's policy turned from a hawkish approach to diplomatic negotiations, the Obama administration moved in the opposite direction from diplomatic engagement to strategic patience. It did not reward North Korea, but the policy was ineffective in preventing North Korea from testing its nuclear weapons and increasing its stockpiles of nuclear weapons.

The source of failure

Why has it proven so difficult to resolve the North Korean nuclear crisis? This part will discuss the three major reasons that have obstructed resolution of the North Korean nuclear crisis: an intense security dilemma and lack of trust, domestic political changes in the involved countries and their impact in negotiations, and the clashing national interests and foreign policy goals of the involved countries.

As discussed in the historical background, the basic motivation behind North Korea's nuclear gamble is a powerful and fundamental desire for national survival and security. North Korea has been paranoid, isolated, and still haunted by the memories of the Korean War and Cold War confrontations. Contrary to the common belief that North Korea has always been the source of nuclear threats on the Korean Peninsula, nuclear weapons existed in the South throughout the Cold War period. The United States introduced nuclear weapons in 1958, right after the end of the Korean War, and those weapons were operational until the withdrawal of all nuclear weapons in 1991. Saddam Hussein and Muammar Gaddafi's miscalculations and failure to guarantee their survival could also have made North Korean leaders even more cautious in trusting the United States and in making any bold moves in diplomatic solutions. There has been a vicious cycle of mutual security dilemmas in the Korean Peninsula, ranging from the separation of the country into two contrasting regimes, the North Korean invasion and the Korean War, the Cold War confrontation for 60 years, and finally the isolation of North Korea at the end of the Cold War and North Korea's attempt to develop a nuclear program. There is no doubt that North Korea is an extremely centralized autocratic country with a third-generation family succession that commits human rights abuses and even starves its own people. But survival of the nation is the most basic need of any countries, regardless of the regime type or moral standard. North Korea will never trade or surrender its only deterrence and diplomatic leverage unless they acquire an alternative measure to guarantee their national security. It is futile trying to convince Pyongyang to give up nuclear weapons only with economic incentives, economic sanctions, or the promise of negotiations without including a peace treaty or non-aggression pact to end the Korean War and achieve diplomatic normalization between Washington and Pyongyang.

Domestic political changes in the involved countries caused major shifts in their foreign policy approaching North Korean nuclear issue and made it difficult to continue a consistent policy. For example, the Republican victory in the mid-term elections in November 1994 gave the Republican Party enough power to constrain Clinton's capability to implement the Geneva Agreement. The election of Kim Dae-jung in the South Korean presidential election generated a new momentum with his Sunshine policy, and Clinton and could renew his diplomatic efforts in close coordination with Seoul. Pyongyang also responded with diplomacy and limited reforms, and Washington and Pyongyang conducted high-level visits to finally agree upon the US–DPRK Joint Communiqué of October 12, 2000. The momentum, however, ended when President Bush took office in 2001. The Bush administration neglected the diplomatic momentum generated at the end of Clinton administration and started a hawkish confrontation policy toward North Korea. The intelligence on the HEU program and the second nuclear crisis finally abolished the Geneva Agreement. The domestic political change around November 2006 with the landslide victory of Democratic Party and domestic criticism over Bush foreign policy of unilateralism and Iraqi turmoil finally changed his North Korea policy from confrontation to engagement. The Bush administration applied serious diplomacy via the Six-Party Talks and achieved the outcomes, but the negotiation stopped when the United States requested a far-reaching verification plan. Therefore, some scholars pointed out that "North Korea's nuclear strategy is being shaped and reshaped as much in Washington's domestic politics, if not more so, than in Pyongyang's Black Box" (Kim 2010, 80), and Washington, as well as Pyongyang, bears responsibility for the failure of negotiation because of "its unwillingness to make promises and keep them" (Sigal 2003). South Korea also experienced political change from a liberal to a conservative president when Lee Myong-bak came to office in 2008 and Seoul pursued a more confrontational policy with Pyongyang instead of playing the role of mediator and facilitator in the negotiation. Kim Jong-il's stroke that started a succession process in the North also diverted Pyongyang's attention to domestic issues and away from meetings with Washington. The Obama administration's attempted negotiation with Pyongyang achieved some limited success such as the Leap Day agreement in early 2012. But series of North Korean provocations toward South Korea and nuclear and missile tests pushed the Obama administration into the policy of "strategic patience." The succession process and Kim Jong-un's domestic need to consolidate his political power could drive such provocations. The tragedy of the North Korean nuclear issue is that frequent domestic political changes in the involved states can include 'veto players' into negotiation that can easily block progress.

The experiences of failed negotiation also caused strong mutual distrust, and both Washington and Pyongyang have criticized each other for the lack of implementation of each other's promises. From Washington's perspective, North Korea broke the Geneva Agreement with its secret uranium enrichment program in 2002, and Pyongyang continuously developed its nuclear capability while buying more time by engaging negotiation and seeking more and more rewards from the United States. In the process of the Six-Party Talks, the United States removed North Korea from the "list of state sponsors of terrorism" and lifted some sanctions under the Trading with the Enemy Act, but Pyongyang rejected the US demand for a verification plan and finally dismantled the Six-Party Talks. From Pyongyang's point of view, the United States nullified the Geneva Agreement by never completing light-water reactors or seriously pursue diplomatic normalization with Pyongyang and finally stopped the shipment of heavy oil. In the Six-Party talks, Pyongyang provided the United States with documents of its nuclear program and destroyed the cooling tower at the Yongbyon, but Washington demanded a far-reaching verification plan and demanded full access to any site, facility or location, which is unreasonable request for any sovereign state. Throughout the process of negotiation, Washington and Pyongyang basically argue that their counterpart should move first and prove their commitment for negotiation. In other words, Pyongyang would consider denuclearization only if the US guarantee its survival by peace treaty and diplomatic normalization first. Washington, however, want Pyongyang to first demonstrate denuclearization commitment before talks and then it would consider diplomatic normalization and a peace treaty (*Yonhap News* 2016). Lack of trust between the two sides made it impossible to turn this vicious cycle of negotiation failure into virtuous cycle of exchanging commitment and implementation. At this moment, it is questionable whether Pyongyang would give up its nuclear program even if Washington did provide a security guarantee and a peace treaty first. Kim Jong-un is still going through a process of political consolidation, and he might be afraid of making any concession to Washington that would make him a weak leader. North Korea already acquired nuclear and missile technology as a strong deterrence for their survival. It would be very difficult to give up such tangible guarantee in exchange for uncertain diplomatic commitment from Washington, even if Washington makes such promises. Pyongyang will be defenseless if it denuclearizes first, and it will lose its only leverage in the negotiation with Washington. For example, North Korea proclaimed itself a "nuclear state" by a revision of its constitution in 2012 (Kwon 2012). In the 7th Party Congress in North Korea in 2016, Kim Jong-un reaffirmed its status as a nuclear power (Frank 2016). Therefore, the security guarantee should be a legally binding one that would be guaranteed by including all members of the Six-Party Talks in an established multilateral framework.

Another challenge for North Korean nuclear issue was the regional competition and the global strategy of the involved states. The issue is not isolated and independent one but combined with the regional and global issues such as the war against terrorism and the rivalry between the United States and China. For example, the Bush administration was heavily influenced by 9/11 terrorist attacks, and its North Korea policy was conducted as a part of his war against terrorism and Bush doctrine. The Bush administration did not have an expert on North Korean issues, and so, Pritchard (2007, 45) who worked under the first Bush administration stated that "the number of people in positions of responsibility who had even a modicum of experience regarding North Korea was extremely limited." Instead of understanding North Korea's unique situation, it was viewed as a part of axis of evil or one of the rogue states. The Obama administration's pivot to Asia is mainly concerned about China rather than North Korea, and the rise of China and Sino–US strategic competition have made the North Korean issue more complex. The United States could be tempted to manage the North Korean threat to justify its intervention in Asia and strengthen its presence in the name of North Korean threat. North Korea has also exploited this Sino–US rivalry for its regime survival. China wants North Korea to give up its nuclear weapons program and pursue Chinese-style economic reforms, but it does not want North Korea to collapse and be absorbed by South Korea. Also, US forces could extend into the Chinese border. Therefore, China has been providing critical resources for North Korea's survival and protecting it from international pressure.

Conclusion

The clear lesson from the history of negotiations is that the nuclear crisis in North Korea will not automatically disappear unless its root cause is addressed (Harrison 2002, 257–8). Neglecting North Korea or waiting for its collapse will not resolve the problem and will only cause Pyongyang to increase its stockpiles and technology of nuclear weapons and missiles. Time is not necessarily on Washington's side. It has become clear that American policymakers seriously underestimated the durability of North Korea. It will not collapse in the near future, and one North Korean expert expects that Pyongyang might obtain as many as one hundred nuclear weapons by 2020 (Joel Witt in his interview). The United States and neighboring states should acknowledge the root cause of the problem that is the security dilemma in the Korean Peninsula stemming from the division of Korea, the Korean War, and 60 years of intense military confrontation. North Korea's nuclear and missile programs are unacceptable, but Pyongyang would not give up those programs unless they found some alternative to address their security concerns. The goal should be eventually exchanging North Korea's nuclear and missile programs with a peace treaty and diplomatic normalization. To achieve such goal, the United States and neighboring countries should start a long-term process to build trust and conduct step by step implementation process between Pyongyang and Washington by monitoring Pyongyang's denuclearization process and also by guaranteeing North Korea's security in a multilateral framework. The process should not be interrupted or obstructed by short-term domestic changes or by the temptation to use this issue for other domestic political goals or global strategic purposes.

Notes

1 "Press Briefing by Ambassador Gallucci on Korea." *White House Press Briefing*, October 18, 1994. Available at http://web.archive.org/web/20061028174123/www.clintonfoundation.org/legacy/101894-press-briefing-by-ambassador-gallucci-on-korea.htm.
2 U.S.-DPRK Joint Communiqué, Washington, DC, October 12, 2000. Available at http://1997-2001.state.gov/www/regions/eap/001012_usdprk_jointcom.html.
3 *State Department Paper*, Talking Point for S/Ivanov Telephone Call, October 29, 2000. Available at http://www2.gwu.edu/~nsarchiv/NSAEBB/NSAEBB164/EBB%20Doc%2020.pdf.
4 "Text of President Bush's 2002 State of the Union Address." *The Washington Post*, January 29, 2002. Available at www.washingtonpost.com/wp-srv/onpolitics/transcripts/sou012902.htm.
5 "The National Security Strategy of the United States of America." September 2002. Available at www.whitehouse.gov/nsc/nss.pdf; "Remarks by the President at the 2002 Graduation Exercise at West Point." June 1, 2002.
6 See "Keynote Speeches Made at Six-Way Talks." *Korean Central News Agency*, August 29, 2003. Available at www.kcna.co.jp/item/2003/200308/news08/30.htm.
7 "Joint Statement of the Fourth Round of the Six-Party Talks Beijing." September 19, 2005. Available at www.state.gov/p/eap/regional/c15455.htm.
8 "Initial Actions to Implement Six-Party Joint Statement." February 13, 2007. Available at http://2001-2009.state.gov/r/pa/prs/ps/2007/february/80508.htm.
9 "Second-Phase Actions for the Implementation of the September 2005 Joint Statement." October 3, 2007. Available at http://2001-2009.state.gov/r/pa/prs/ps/2007/oct/93217.htm.
10 "President Barack Obama's Inaugural Address." *The White House Blog*, January 21, 2009. Available at www.whitehouse.gov/blog/ inaugural-address.
11 Statement by the President from Prague, Czech Republic, April 5, 2009. Available at www.whitehouse.gov/the_press_office/Statement-by-the-President-North-Korea-launch/.
12 Secretary Hillary Clinton's Speech at the United States Institute of Peace, October 21, 2009, Department of State No. 2009/1049.

References

Albright, David. 2007. "North Korea's Alleged Large-Scale Enrichment Plant: Yet Another Questionable Extrapolation Based on Aluminum Tubes." *The Institute for Science and International Security (ISIS)*, February 23. Available at: www.isis-online.org/publications/dprk/DPRKenrichment22Feb.pdf.

Albright, Madeleine, and Bill Woodward. 2003. *Madam Secretary: A Biography of Madeleine Albright*. New York, NY: Hyperion.

Allison, Graham T., and Philip Zelikow. 1999. *Essence of Decision: Explaining the Cuban Missile Crisis*, Second edition. New York: Longman.

Arms Control Association. 2017. "Chronology of U.S.-North Korean Nuclear and Missile Diplomacy." *Arms Control Association*, April. Available at: www.armscontrol.org/factsheets/dprkchron.

BBC News. 2005. "Rice Names 'Outposts of Tyranny.'" January 19. Available at: http://news.bbc.co.uk/2/hi/americas/4186241.stm.

Bleek, Philip C. 2012. "Nuclear Posture Review Leaks; Outlines Targets, Contingencies." *Arms Control Today* 32 (April 2002); U.S. Nuclear Posture Review, January 8, 2002. Available at: www.globalsecurity.org/wmd/library/policy/dod/npr.htm.

Choe, Sang-Hun. 2008. "North Korea Destroys Cooling Tower at Nuclear Plant." *The New York Times*, June 27. Available at: www.nytimes.com/2008/06/27/world/asia/27iht-korea.1.14044540.html?_r=0.

Cumings, Bruce. 2004a. *North Korea, Another Country*. New York: The New Press.

Cumings, Bruce. 2004b. "Korea: Forgotten Nuclear Threats." *Le Monde diplomatique*, December. Available at: http://mondediplo.com/2004/12/08korea.

Cumings, Bruce. 2007. "Kim Jong Il Confronts Bush – and Wins: A New Page in North-South Korean Relations." *Policy Forum Online 07–079A*, October 19.

Dao, James. 2002. "Bush Administration Halts Payments to Send Oil to North Korea." *The New York Times*, November 14.

Farley, Robert. 2008. "He Has Said It Again and Again." *Politifact*, May 21. Available at: www.politifact.com/truth-o-meter/statements/2008/may/21/john-mccain/he-has-said-it-again-and-again/.

Feffer, J. 2006. "North Korean Fireworks?" *Policy Forum Online 06–52*, The Nautilus Institution.

Frank, Rüdiger. 2016. "The 7th Party Congress in North Korea: An Analysis of Kim Jong Un's Report." *The Asia-Pacific Journal* 14 (14). Available at: http://apjjf.org/2016/14/Frank.html.

Gertz, Bill. 1991. "North Korean Site Yields Only a System of Empty Tunnels." *The Washington Times*, May 28.

Goodman, Peter S. 2002. "N. Korea Moves to Activate Complex." *The Washington Post*, December 27. Available at: www.washingtonpost.com/archive/politics/2002/12/27/n-korea-moves-to-activate-complex/a9c1f03e-4f9c-4fe8-b34c-fe0b388dd396/?utm_term=.39d83954597e.

Halper, Daniel. 2013. "Obama: I 'Anticipate That North Korea Will Probably Make More Provocative Moves.'" *Weekly Standard*, April 16. Available at: www.weeklystandard.com/obama-i-anticipate-that-north-korea-will-probably-make-more-provocative-moves/article/717923.

Harrison, Selig S. 2002. *Korean Endgame: A Strategy for Reunification and U.S. Disengagement*. Princeton, NJ: Princeton University Press.

Harrison, Selig S. 2005. "Did North Korea Cheat?" *Foreign Affairs* 84 (1): 99–110.

Harrison, Selig S. 2008. "What A.Q. Khan Knows." *The Washington Post*, January 31. Available at: www.washingtonpost.com/wp-dyn/content/article/2008/01/30/AR2008013003214.html.

Hecker, Siegfried S. 2010. "Lessons Learned from the North Korean Nuclear Crises." *NAPSNet Policy Forum Online*, January 20. Available at: www.nautilus.org/fora/security/10006Hecker.pdf.

Hutzler, Charles, and Jay Solomon. 2003. "Allies Press U.S. to Ease Position on North Korea." *The Wall Street Journal*, January 6.

Joongang Ilbo. 2002. "Statement Released to Blame U.S. for Rupture of 1994 Pact." November 21.

Kang, David C. 2003. "Acute Conflicts in Asia After the Cold War: Kashmir, Taiwan, and Korea." In *Asian Security Order*, edited by Muthiah Alagappa, 349–79. Stanford, CA: Stanford University Press.

Kim, Samuel. 2010. "North Korea's nuclear strategy and the interface between international and domestic politics." *Asian Perspective*, 34 (1): 49–85.

Kessler, Glenn. 2008. "Far-Reaching U.S. Plan Impaired N. Korea Deal." *The Washington Post*, September 26. Available at: www.washingtonpost.com/wp-dyn/content/article/2008/09/25/AR2008092504380.html?sid=ST2008092600020.

Kwon, K. J. 2012. "North Korea Proclaims Itself a Nuclear State in New Constitution." *CNN*, May 31. Available at: www.cnn.com/2012/05/31/world/asia/north-korea-nuclear-constitution/index.html.

Kynge, James, and Andrew Ward. 2003. "U.S. Set for 'Bilateral' Talks with N. Korea." *Financial Times*, August 27.

Litwak, Robert. 2007. *Regime Change: U.S. Strategy Through the Prism of 9/11*. Baltimore, MD: The Johns Hopkins University Press.

Mack, Andrew. 1993. "The Nuclear Crisis on the Korean Peninsula." *Asian Survey* 33 (4): 339–59.

PBS. 2003. "PBS Interview with Ambassador Donald Gregg." February 20. Available at: www.pbs.org/wgbh/pages/frontline/shows/kim/interviews/gregg.html.

Petrov, Leonid. 2012. "North Korea's New Special Economic Zone Going Nowhere." *East Asia Forum*, July 4. Available at: www.eastasiaforum.org/2012/07/04/north-korea-s-new-special-economic-zone-going-nowhere/.

Pincus, Walter. 2006. "N. Korean Nuclear Conflict Has Deep Roots." *Washington Post*, October 15. Available at: www.washingtonpost.com/wp-dyn/content/article/2006/10/14/AR2006101401068.html.

Pritchard, Charles. 2003. "A Guarantee to Bring Kim into Line." *Financial Times*, October 10.

Pritchard, Charles. 2007. *Failed Diplomacy: The Tragic Story of How North Korea Got the Bomb*. Washington, DC: Brookings Institution Press.

Sagan, Scott, and Kenneth Waltz. 2002. *The Spread of Nuclear Weapons: A Debate Renewed*. New York. W.W. Norton.

Sigal, Leon V. 1998. *Disarming Strangers: Nuclear Diplomacy with North Korea.* Princeton, NJ: Princeton University Press.

Sigal, Leon V. 2003. "Did the United States Break the Agreed Framework?" *History News Network,* March 31, 2003. Available at http://hnn.us/articles/1353.html.

Sigal, Leon V. 2006. "What North Korea's Missile Test Means." *Policy Forum Online,* The Nautilus Institution.

Snyder, Scott. 2012. "What Message Will Kim Jong-un Take from the Obama Visit to Myanmar." *Asia Unbound, Council on Foreign Relations,* November 19. Available at: www.cfr.org/blog/what-message-will-kim-jong-un-take-obama-visit-myanmar.

Struck, Doug. 2002. "North Korea Says It Will Renew Work at Reactors." *The Washington Post,* December 13, p. A1.

Voice of America. 2009. "Clinton Calls 'Exploratory' Meeting with North Korea 'Quite Positive." *Voice of America,* December 10.

Wit, Joel S., Daniel B. Poneman, and Robert L. Gallucci. 2004. *Going Critical: The First North Korean Nuclear Crisis.* Washington, DC: Brookings Institution Press.

Yonhap News. 2016. "U.S. Says N. Korea Should First Demonstrate Denuclearization Commitment Before Talks." *Yonhap,* May 19. Available at: http://english.yonhapnews.co.kr/northkorea/2016/05/19/0401000000AEN20160519000500315.html.

9 North Korean human rights

Inyeop Lee

In the 1990s, serious famine and food shortage took place in North Korea. Many North Koreans left the country and began to testify about the isolated country's political and economic conditions. Most countries and multilateral organizations have expressed serious concerns and criticisms regarding North Korea's human rights conditions. To evaluate human rights conditions in North Korea, this chapter will discuss existing theories and perspectives on human rights, and review North Korea's own positions on this issue which were expressed in its constitution and reports submitted to international organizations. Then the chapter will explore specific human rights violations in North Korea such as the famine and food shortage of the 1990s, refugee issues, and civil and political rights in North Korea. It will also overview international criticism from major international organizations and the positions of neighboring countries such as the United States, China, Japan, and South Korea. Finally, the chapter will introduce international debates on this issue and evaluate existing solutions to improve North Korea's human rights condition. It will conclude by showing how North Korea's human right conditions are interconnected with its unique domestic and international conditions, and explain why it is important to position the goal of improving human rights in the broader context of a holistic and long-term approach that can solve North Korea's security, economic, and human rights conditions in a step-by-step process involving all relevant actors in the region.

Theories and perspectives on human rights

The concept of human rights involves engaging in various theoretical debates. Universalists and cultural relativists, those in the First World and the Third World, and capitalists and communists during the Cold War have argued over its definitions and scope and the measures needed to improve human rights. Universalists argue that human rights are inalienable and inherent to all human beings, and basic human rights must be applied universally regardless of "nationality, place of residence, sex, national or ethnic origin, colour, religion, language, or any other status (1948)."[1] They explain that there are comprehensive, authoritative human rights norms widely accepted as binding on all states. For example, The Universal Declaration of Human Rights (1948), adopted in Paris by the United Nations (UN) General Assembly, is widely accepted as a globally applicable definition of human rights. The universality of human rights was reaffirmed in the Teheran (1968) and Vienna World Conferences (1993), which declared that it is a state's duty to protect and promote all human rights and fundamental freedoms. It is also elaborated in two major treaties, the International Covenant on Economic, Social and Cultural Rights and the International Covenant on Civil and Political Rights that both came into force in 1976 (Donnelly and Howard 1987, 79–106).

Cultural relativists, on the other hand, claim that "human rights are a Western construct with limited applicability" (Pollis and Schwab 1979, 1–18). They argue that each culture has different social norms and values, and so alien Western values cannot be imposed upon non-Western societies (American Anthropological Association 1947). For example, some Asian leaders, such as Mahathir Mohamad from Malaysia and Lee Kuan Yew from Singapore, presented the concept of 'Asian Value' during the 1997 Asian financial crisis. They stressed that Asian societies have unique principles of collectivism and communitarian culture that prioritize group rights over individual rights (Zakaria 1994; Kim 1994). Some cultural relativists even argue that the universal application of human rights amounts to Western, neo-colonial intervention. Some critics from the Third World also claim that developing countries cannot afford to meet Western standards of human rights when they prioritize economic development to escape poverty over human rights. Universalists also criticize cultural relativists. They believe basic concepts of human rights can be found in every society regardless of cultural diversity, and that even Third World countries joined in the drafting of the Universal Declaration and other basic human rights documents. They also point out that authoritarian leaders have adopted cultural relativism to justify human rights abuses and to protect the interests of those in power that benefit by specific, though harmful, cultural practices. Authoritarianism is not an essential condition for development, and some cultural practices that violate basic human rights cannot be justified in the name of cultural diversity (Donnelly and Howard 1987, 79–106).

While the First World tends to define human rights as an individual's right to freedom and civil and political rights, the Third World emphasizes collectivist and holistic rights, including economic, social, and cultural rights. Especially during the Cold War period, Western developed countries highlighted rights to freedom, and the Socialist and underdeveloped countries emphasized social rights. In Teheran (1968) and Vienna (1993), the participants tried to compromise between the right to freedom and social rights by saying "the international community must treat human rights globally in a fair and equal manner, on the same footing, and with the same emphasis" (1993).[2] Even within the First World, the scope of basic human rights is disputed. For example, American Republican President Ronald Reagan claimed that economic and social rights were not really true human rights, while the Jimmy Carter administration from the Democratic Party paid more attention to economic and social rights (Donnelly and Howard 1987, 79–106).

The right to peace and the right to development are also discussed in the UN as well as right to freedom and social rights. The 'Proclamation of Teheran (1968)' specified that member nations recognized "that peace is the universal aspiration of mankind and that peace and justice are indispensable to the full realization of human rights and fundamental freedoms."[3] The UN General Assembly also adopted a "Declaration on Right of Peoples to Peace" in 1984, which asserted that

> the right of peoples to peace demands that the policies of States be directed towards the elimination of the threat of war, particularly nuclear war, the renunciation of the use of force in international relations and the settlement of international disputes by peaceful means.[4]

Developing countries also raised awareness of the right to development. The UN General Assembly adopted the "Declaration on the Right to Development" in 1986, saying that "the right to development is an inalienable human right" and that "all peoples are entitled to participate in, contribute to, and enjoy economic, social, cultural and political development."[5]

The Vienna Declaration reaffirmed that the Right to Development is "a universal and inalienable right and an integral part of fundamental human rights."[6] Those rights to peace and development raise a fundamental dilemma in the implementation of human rights. Measures taken to improve human rights, such as humanitarian interventions or economic sanctions, could compromise the rights to peace or to development in a target country. This issue will be discussed in the later part of this chapter.

North Korean view of human rights

North Korea is a signatory to four international conventions on human rights: the Covenant on Civil and Political Rights (ICCPR), the Convention on the Rights of the Child (CRC), the Convention on the Elimination of All Forms of Discrimination against Women (CEDAW), and the International Convention on Economic, Social and Cultural Rights (ECOSOC). North Korea notified the Secretary-General of the United Nations of its withdrawal from the ICCPR on 25 August, 1997. The Secretary-General, however, objected, and stated that such a withdrawal is not possible without the consent of all other signatory states. North Korea continues to submit reports to the UN regarding those conventions, and its government claims that it guarantees basic human rights to its citizens, including the rights of women and children as well as civil, political, economic, social, and cultural rights.[7]

North Korea includes several articles related to human rights in its Constitution. For example, Article 67 says, "Citizens are guaranteed freedom of speech, the press, assembly, demonstration and association. The State shall guarantee the conditions for the free activities of democratic political parties and social organizations." Article 66 asserts that

> All citizens who have reached the age of 17 have the right to elect and to be elected, irrespective of sex, race, occupation, length of residence, property status, education, party affiliation, political views or religious belief. Citizens serving in the armed forces also have the right to elect and to be elected.[8]

Article 69 says, "Citizens are entitled to submit complaints and petitions. The State shall investigate and deal with complaints and petitions impartially as stipulated by law." Article 68 guarantees religious freedom, as

> Citizens have freedom of religious belief. This right is granted through the approval of the construction of religious buildings and the holding of religious ceremonies. Religion must not be used as a pretext for drawing in foreign forces or for harming the State or social order.

Article 15 summarizes a commitment to participatory government even by expatriates by arguing that, also states, "The Democratic People's Republic of Korea shall champion the democratic national rights of Koreans overseas and their rights recognized by international law as well as their interests." Therefore, the North Korea government has accepted responsibility for the protection of human rights for its citizens and overseas Koreans according to its own claims, domestic law, and international treaties.

The country, however, tends to interpret human rights in only certain directions consistent to its own political ideology and policies. Article 3 and other parts of the constitution stress the '*Juche* ideology,' which means self-reliance and independence by proclaiming "The Democratic People's Republic of Korea is guided in its activities by the Juche idea and the Songun idea, a world outlook centred on people, a revolutionary ideology for achieving the independence of the masses of the people." Article 12 also explains, "The State shall adhere to the class line and strengthen the dictatorship of the people's democracy so as to firmly defend the people's power and socialist system against all subversive acts of hostile elements at home and abroad." Article 64 states,

> The State shall effectively guarantee the genuine democratic rights and freedoms as well as the material and cultural well-being of all its citizens. In the Democratic People's Republic of Korea the rights and freedoms of citizens shall be amplified with the consolidation and development of the socialist system.

Article 17 also summarizes its foreign policy principles of independence, equality, mutual respect, and non-interference by explaining,

> Independence, peace and friendship are the basic ideals of the foreign policy and the principles of the external activities of the Democratic People's Republic of Korea. The State shall establish diplomatic as well as political, economic and cultural relations with all friendly countries, on the principles of complete equality, independence, mutual respect, non-interference in each other's affairs and mutual benefit. The State shall promote unity with people all over the world who defend their independence, and resolutely support and encourage the struggles of all people who oppose all forms of aggression and interference and fight for their countries' independence and national and class emancipation.[9]

The articles in North Korea's constitution clearly show that North Korea views human rights within a framework of 'collectivism and class struggle.' Individual rights are conditional rather than universal and can be limited when necessary. For example, Kim Il-sung once stated that the concept of democracy cannot "provide freedom and rights to hostile elements who oppose socialism or impure elements who act against the interests of the People" (Song 2011, 104). Those individual rights are subordinate to collective rights and to national goals of self-reliance, independence, and development of its nation. North Korea tends to emphasize social rights for development and welfare over rights to individual freedom, namely civil and political rights. Under this system of beliefs, people's social rights can only be fulfilled through establishment of socialist system guided by the Communist Party. The North Korean government has proudly emphasized an 11-year compulsory education system, gender-equality legislation, and a maximum eight hour-workday. Having been influenced by Japanese colonialism and the Korean War, Pyongyang also underscores national sovereignty and self-reliance as core elements of human rights. The country will defend its national sovereignty and resist any foreign interventions even if an outsider tries to justify such moves on human rights or democratization grounds. In 2014, North Korea's Association for Human Rights Studies released a report on its own human rights situation as a reaction to a recent critical evaluation by the UN. The report explained that state sovereignty is a form of human rights, since the life under Japanese colonial rule had been like living a "miserable life worse than a dog of a family having funeral" (Taylor 2014).

Human rights conditions in North Korea

The famine and food shortage in the 1990s

North Korean human rights issues received global attention at the end of 1990s. The collapse of the Soviet Union in 1991 stopped economic aid to North Korea, including cheap oil. The North lost many of its other trading partners when other communist allies in Eastern Europe collapsed. Food production and imports fell sharply. Floods and draughts exacerbated this situation by destroying infrastructure and spreading infectious diseases. The country could not respond to these shocks with its rigid political and economic system. Having only 20 percent of its mountainous terrain as arable land, the country had never experienced food self-sufficiency. North Korea began to suffer from severe famine and food shortages. The North Korean regime and media used the term "Arduous March" for its propaganda campaign in 1993 to encourage the North Korean people to endure hardship and stay loyal to the regime, using the historical example of Kim Il-sung's painful struggle as an anti-Japanese guerrilla fighter. But local industries had collapsed, and the public distribution system for food supplies stopped functioning. The remote regions far from the capital city suffered the most severe damage. Hundred thousand of North Koreans starved to death, and another hundred thousand left the country for food and survival. Out of North Korea's approximately 22 million population, between 240,000 and 3,500,000 people died from starvation or hunger-related illnesses at the end of 1990s (Haggard and Noland 2007).

The situation has improved since the worst famine and food shortages in 1990s, especially with some limited reforms around 2008, but the catastrophe had lasting impacts on the North Korean population, especially on children (Shim 2016). During a visit to North Korea in 2011, former US President Jimmy Carter reported, "a third of the children there are malnourished and stunted in their growth because of a deprivation of adequate food supplies" (Bristow 2011). The World Food Programme reported, "one in every three children remains chronically malnourished or 'stunted', meaning they are too short for their age." Recent research shows that there are height gaps between North Korean and South Korean men: 1.2–3.1 inches for adult males and 1.6 inches for pre-school boys (Knight 2012). According to a nutrition assessment of 6,000 children in seven provinces and three cities of North Korea conducted by North Korean government with the United Nations Children's Fund (UNICEF) and the World Food Programme in 2002, the prevalence of underweight children is 20.15 percent, children stunted is 39.22 percent, and of children wasted is 8.12 percent (UNICEF 2002).

North Korean refugees

With the famine and food shortage, many North Koreans left the country by crossing North Korea's border to China's Northeastern region for their survival. Some defectors then fled to a third country, mostly to South Korea as a final destination, while others stayed in China. According to 2012 report, approximately 100,000 to 200,000 North Korean refugees are living in China. China refuses to grant North Korean defectors refugee status since it is North Korea's close ally, and it considers defectors to be illegal economic migrants rather than political refugees. The Chinese government also worries that such recognition would invite massive outflows of refugees that would destabilize North Korea and China's Northeast region (Margesson, Chanlett-Avery and Bruno 2007). The defectors in China have neither legal protection nor access to social welfare. They live under the constant threat of arrest and deportation by Chinese Public Security Police (Kumar 2012).[10] China has been repatriating the refugees back to the North, and they face harsh interrogations and punishment in reeducation camps or political prison camps, since the regime treats their defection as treason and a betrayal of their country. The punishments over those who had contacted South Korean Christian missionaries or NGO activists tend to be harsher. The UN General Assembly expressed concern regarding

> the situation of refugees and asylum-seekers expelled or returned to the Democratic People's Republic of Korea and sanctions imposed on citizens of the Democratic People's Republic of Korea who have been repatriated from abroad, leading to punishments of internment, torture, cruel, inhuman or degrading treatment or the death penalty, and in this regard urges all States to respect the fundamental principle of non-refoulement, to treat those who seek refuge humanely and to ensure unhindered access to the United Nations High Commissioner for Refugees and his Office, with a view to improving the situation of those who seek refuge.[11]

A large number of females experience human trafficking, prostitution, and forced marriage as refugees. Many females become married to Chinese men who cannot find a bride due to serious gender imbalances in China. Their children have neither Chinese nationality nor access to basic education and medical services.

North Korean defectors who seek passage to South Korea go through a risky journey through China and other countries. They must sneak past Chinese police and enter one of the foreign embassies or foreign schools not directly under Chinese legal jurisdiction. They then seek asylum and ask to be sent to South Korea (*ABC* News 2002). Or they follow the long route to Mongolia or Southeast Asian countries such as Thailand, Laos, or Vietnam. In the process, they often receive help from South Korean Christian missionaries or human rights activists, or they hire escape brokers to guide them. Refugees who arrive in South Korea will go through a screening process by the National Intelligence Service to ensure they are not spies. Then they spend 12 weeks in Hana Center (Hanawon), where they are educated for their transition to South Korean society. The South Korean government then supports them with financial aid and housing for resettlement (MacLeod 2011; Kirk 2004). As of 2017, the total number of North Korean defectors who entered South Korea after the Korean War (1950–1953) is about 30,490 (see Table 9.1). Only 641 successfully made it to South Korea between 1950 and 1993, and the number began sharply increasing after 1994 with the degraded economic situation in the North.[12] Many defectors experience hardships and challenges in the South even though they are free from food shortages and the dangers of arrest and deportation. They find it very difficult to survive in a capitalist society with intense competition. They also suffer from loneliness and discrimination based on biases and stereotypes that South Koreans have toward North Korean refugees. Defectors also suffer from post-traumatic stress disorder due to the extreme conditions they experienced while living in the north and in the process of their escapes. They also experience guilt from leaving family members and relatives behind. They feel anxiety due to poverty and relative deprivation in South Korean society, and they face an uncertain future with a lack of hope and belongingness. Some of them are in debt due to the payment to brokers for their escape or for that of their family members. The payment required by brokers is sometimes greater than the financial aid given from the South Korean government for their resettlement. Recent research shows that 20.5 percent of defectors had suicidal thoughts, which is three times higher than South Korea's already high average of 6.8 percent (*Chosun Daily* 2015a, 2015b; Go 2014).

Table 9.1 Status of North Korean defectors entering South Korea (March 2017)

Criteria/Year	~1998	~2001	2002	2003	2004	2005	2006	2007	2008	2009	2010	2011	2012	2013	2014	2015	2016	2017.3 Estimated	Total
Male	831	565	510	474	626	424	515	573	608	662	591	795	404	369	305	251	299	46	8,848
Female	116	478	632	811	1,272	960	1,513	1,981	2,195	2,252	1,811	1,911	1,098	1,145	1,092	1,025	1,119	232	21,642
Total	947	1,043	1,142	1,285	1,898	1,384	2,028	2,554	2,803	2,914	2,402	2,706	1,502	1,514	1,396	1,276	1,418	278	30,490
Female Percentage	12%	46%	55%	63%	67%	69%	75%	78%	78%	77%	75%	70%	72%	76%	78%	83%	79%	83%	71%

Source: Status of North Korean Defectors ("Bukhanitaljumin Hyunhwang"). Ministry of Unification. Resettlement Support Division. Available at www.unikorea.go.kr/content.do?cmsid=1440.

Civil and political rights in North Korea

The famine and the growing number of defectors in the 1990s raised international awareness of the human rights conditions in North Korea. The testimonies of defectors became the major source of information on the most isolated and secretive country in the world. Most scholars and multilateral organizations have claimed human rights are severely limited in North Korea, especially in terms of civil and political rights. For example, the Commission of Inquiry on Human Rights in the Democratic People's Republic of Korea in its February 2014 report submitted to the UN General Assembly concluded, "systematic, widespread and gross violations of human rights" which may "constitute crimes against humanity." It listed six categories of major human rights violations in North Korea: violations of the freedoms of thought, expression and religion; discrimination on the basis of State-assigned social class (*songbun*), gender, and disability; violations of the freedoms of movement and residence, including the freedom to leave one's own country and the prohibition of refoulment; violations of the right to food and related aspects of the right to life; arbitrary detention, torture, executions, enforced disappearance and imprisonment in political prison camps; and enforced disappearances of persons from other countries, including through abduction.[13]

There is an extensive domestic monitoring system of informants, and the North Korean government categorizes its citizens according to a system of ascribed status (*Songbun*) based on family background and loyalty to the regime. The three main classifications, the core class, the wavering class, and the hostile class, and about 50 sub-classifications, will affect access to education, employment, and party membership (Collins 2012). Starting his career as a guerrilla fighter against Imperial Japan, establishing a communist regime against the capitalist South, and waging the Korean War and the Cold War, North Korea's founder Kim Il-sung denied civil rights for people who opposed the communist regime. He stated that the concept of democracy cannot "provide freedom and rights to hostile elements who oppose socialism or impure elements who act against the interests of the People" (Song 2011, 104). Kim Il-sung purged and executed most of his political competitors and even many faithful communists in addition to those openly hostile to the communist regime (Person 2013). In 2013, Jang Sung-taek, the uncle of North Korean leader Kim Jon-un, was disappeared and expelled from his public position. The state media announced that he was executed (Fisher 2013). Political prisoners experience torture and harsh interrogations, imprisonment, forced labor, and public executions. In spite of the guarantee of an independent judiciary in the constitution, a number of defectors testified that courts are not independent from the executive, and defense lawyers are not always assigned. Even if they are assigned, they have to support governmental policy rather than protect their clients. A number of defectors also testified that many inmates in prison camps did not have a trial and were not informed about their charges or had legal counsel. The death penalty is often administered for political and common crimes without fair trials. Public executions were also conducted for high crimes by firing squad. The conditions of North Korean prisons are harsh and life-threatening due to starvation, illness, slave labor, torture, and secret executions (Hawk 2012; Do et al. 2015). The UN General Assembly expressed its concern about the use of

> torture and other cruel, inhuman or degrading treatment or punishment, public executions, extrajudicial and arbitrary detention, the absence of due process and the rule of law, imposition of the death penalty for political reasons, the existence of a large number of prison camps and the extensive use of forced labour.[14]

In spite of written guarantees in the constitution, the freedoms of thought, conscience, religion, opinion and expression, peaceful assembly and association, and access to information are severely restricted. The government controls and operates all media including radio, television, and news providers. Most of the media and cultural activities focus on praising the cult of personality of the leader and communist propaganda. Religious freedom is severely restricted, and all religious activity is under tight governmental supervision. Defectors who contact Christian missionaries are subject to harsher punishment, and several foreigners have been imprisoned for their religious activities. The UN General Assembly has expressed concern on the

> all-pervasive and severe restrictions on the freedoms of thought, conscience, religion, opinion and expression, peaceful assembly and association, and on equal access to information, by such means as the persecution of individuals exercising their freedom of opinion and expression, and their families.[15]

Ironically, North Korea, a self-declared worker's heaven, does not allow workers to form labor union, bargain, or strike. It is one of the few countries that is not a member of the International Labour Organization (ILO). The only existing trade union is under the tight control of the government. Therefore, the UN General Assembly expressed its concern on "Violations of workers' rights, including the right to freedom of association and collective bargaining, the right to strike as defined by the obligations of the Democratic People's Republic of Korea under the International Covenant on Economic, Social and Cultural Rights, and the prohibition of the economic exploitation of children and of any harmful or hazardous work of children as defined by the obligations of the Democratic People's Republic of Korea under the Convention on the Rights of the Child."[16]

Freedoms of movement and residence are also severely restricted. The government strictly controls domestic and foreign travel by requiring governmental approval. The government controls immigration and emigration. The government also decides where all citizens reside. Only the political elite and the core class members are allowed to live in the capital city of Pyongyang, which has a much better environment. The government can relocate its citizens as a form of punishment. Political punishment and purging commonly involve enforced disappearance into political prison camps. Since its citizens cannot freely travel or leave the country, defectors are considered as criminals who have betrayed the state. The UN General Assembly has expressed concern about "limitations imposed on every person who wishes to move freely within the country and travel abroad, including the punishment of those who leave or try to leave the country without permission, or their families, as well as punishment of persons who are returned by other countries."[17]

The human rights of minorities, including women and the disabled, are also restricted. The White Paper on Human Rights in North Korea 2015, published by the South Korean-based Korea Institute for National Unification, stated that an understanding of sexual offenses appears to be very poor in the North (Do et al. 2015). The report explains, "Most residents don't think critically of sex crimes, and women cannot help but acquiesce to sex crimes due to the social atmosphere of downplaying women." For example, 62.5 percent of respondents in the survey of defectors said sex crimes are not punished by criminal law. It is not easy for women to file for divorce either, as it requires paying bribes. A number of defectors testified that repatriated female defectors who are suspected of being impregnated by Chinese men are routinely forced to have abortions (Brooke 2002). Some defectors also testified that the physically or mentally disabled are sent to special camps, and babies born with birth defects are put to death (Disabled Peoples' International 2012). The UN General Assembly has expressed its concern about "continuing violation of the human rights and fundamental freedoms of women, in particular the trafficking of women for the purpose of prostitution or forced marriage and the subjection of women to human smuggling, forced abortions, gender-based discrimination and violence," and on

> continuing reports of violations of the human rights and fundamental freedoms of persons with disabilities, especially on the use of collective camps and of coercive measures that target the rights of persons with disabilities to decide freely and responsibly on the number and spacing of their children.[18]

International criticism

Most countries and multilateral organizations have expressed concerns and criticisms regarding North Korea's human rights conditions. International organizations, such as the UN, the United States and its allies, and the European Union, and some non-governmental organizations (NGOs) such as Amnesty International, Human Rights Watch and Freedom House, have condemned North Korea for its violations of basic human rights and freedoms (Amnesty International 2016; Human Rights Watch 2017; Freedom House 2016). For example, Freedom House has marked North Korea as one of the most repressive societies since the survey was launched in 1973. As of 2016, North Korea has received the worst grade of 7 in all categories of civil liberties and political rights. It received an overall 'Not Free' status.

The UN Human Rights Council and General Assembly have adopted resolutions condemning North Korea on human rights grounds. The first resolution was initiated by the European Union and adopted in April 2003 by the Human Rights Council. It requested access by international humanitarian NGOs for transparent food distribution, mandated no punishment for defectors and a resolution of the abduction issue, and expressed concerns over labor standards, torture and discrimination, a lack of basic freedoms and denials of women's and children's rights. The second resolution adopted by the council in April 2004 requested that North Korea cooperate with the UN and international society to verify claims made on its systematic and widespread human rights violations. It also appointed Vitit Muntarbhorn, an international law professor from Thailand, as the Special Rapporteur on the Situation of Human Rights in the Democratic People's Republic of Korea. After a 3rd resolution adopted by the council in April 2005, the UN General Assembly adopted a resolution in November 2005 and every year since that condemns North Korea's human rights violations. The General Assembly resolution in 2011 stated the existence of "systematic, widespread and grave violations of human rights," including public executions and arbitrary detentions. Pyongyang rejected the resolution by saying it was "politically motivated and based upon untrue fabrications" (Security Council Report 2012). In 2013, The United Nations Commission of Inquiry on Human Rights in the DPRK had public hearings in Seoul that heard testimony from defectors. Hearings in Japan also gathered information from relatives of Japanese citizens abducted by North Korea in the 1970s and 1980s. Pyongyang denounced the inquiry as "a political plot." In February 2014, a UN special commission published a detailed 400-page report based on testimonies of refugees documenting "unspeakable atrocities" and concluding the country had violated human rights "without any parallel in the contemporary world."[19] Pyongyang dismissed the findings as a "political plot" and "a product of politicization of human rights on the part of the EU and Japan, in alliance with the US hostile policy" (Asia Bulletin 2014). It also argued that "The US is a living hell" by publishing its own investigation of human rights violations in the United States. North Korea's Association for Human Rights Studies published a lengthy report on its own human rights situation later that year. The 53,558 worded document claims that North Koreans enjoy "genuine human rights," and "feel proud of the world's most advantageous human rights system" (Taylor 2014). North Korea, on the other hand, announced that it would accept 113 of the 268 recommendations for human rights improvements issued by the UN's Human Rights Council's Universal Periodic review as a gesture to improve its international image (Byul 2014). On November 18, 2014, the UN General Assembly voted in favor of a resolution that referring North Korea's leaders to the International Criminal Court (ICC) for crimes against humanity and approved of "targeted sanctions" for its human rights abuses. Since the UN Security Council, rather than the General Assembly, has the authority to refer a country to the ICC, and China and Russia would veto such measure, the resolution was merely a recommendation (Sanchez 2014).

The United States has played a leading role in condemning North Korea's human rights conditions. The American focus on North Korea's human rights record came to the forefront with the inauguration of President George W. Bush. Influenced by a moralistic and evangelical Christian perspective, Bush expressed his distrust of Kim Jong-il and North Korean regime several times. In an interview with reporter Bob Woodward (2002, 340), Bush said, "I loathe Kim Jong Il" and "I've got a visceral reaction to this guy because he is starving his people. And I have seen intelligence of these prison camps – they're huge – that he uses to break up families, and to torture people." He also included North Korea as one part of the "axis of evil" in his State of the Union address in 2002.[20] North Korea, he stated, was an evil that should be defeated or should be allowed to collapse by external pressure rather than become a negotiating partner. While President Bill Clinton prioritized the elimination of nuclear weapons and missile programs in North Korea by diplomatic negotiations, Bush expanded the range of objectionable issues to also include North Korea's role in terrorism, drug trafficking, counterfeiting, and human rights violations (Lee and Miles 2006, 160). US envoy and former UN Ambassador Jeane Kirkpatrick, in a speech to the UN Human Rights Commission on April 2, 2003, said, "the commission must confront North Korea on its abominable humans rights record and demand accountability by its leaders," and "it is hard to imagine the possibility of a country whose citizens endure a worse or more pervasive abuse of every human right." She added that this situation, combined with famine conditions, "makes (North Korea) truly a hell on Earth" (*The Washington Times* 2003). The US Committee for Human Rights in North Korea (HRNK) was established in October 2002 and the North Korea Freedom Coalition (NKFC) formed in June 2003. Those groups promoted North Korea's human rights agenda in Congress with briefings, conferences, and testimonies at congressional hearings. They also supported the attempt to pass the North Korean Freedom Act of 2003 on November 11 of that year.[21] The revised version of the original bill, the North Korean Freedom Act of 2004,[22] was signed into law on October 18, 2004, and reauthorized as "The North Korean Human Rights Reauthorization Act" signed into effect on October 7, 2008, under President Bush.[23]

Japan has also been very vocal in criticizing North Korea's human rights record. Japan's criticism is focused on the abduction issue. Prime Minister Koizumi Junichiro became the first Japanese leader to visit Pyongyang in September 2002. He discussed diplomatic normalization between the two countries, and Kim Jong-il admitted the involvement of North Korea's "special institutions" in the kidnapping of Japanese nationals in the late 1970s and early 1980s. Five survivors were allowed to visit Japan, and they decided not to return to the North. North Korea said that the other abductees had died due to illness or in natural disasters. Megumi Yokota was one of the abductees who was forced to teach North Korean spies how to speak Japanese, and the North returned her cremated remains and claimed she had committed suicide. The Japanese government and her family doubted the authenticity of the remains after a DNA test. Conservative politicians, such as Abe Shinzo, played a leading role in raising criticism over the overall abduction issue.

China has supported North Korea economically and diplomatically. China also maintains a cultural relativist view on human rights and prioritizes national sovereignty over universal human rights. North Korea is one of the few remaining communist allies of China. Both sides fought together against Imperial Japan in World War II and against the United States during the Korean War. The relationship is often described as 'lips and teeth,' in the words of former People's Liberation Army Marshall Zhu De. China does not want North Korea to collapse either by a massive outflow of refugees or by excessive external pressures and sanctions. The South might then absorb the North, and China would face US forces stationed in a unified Korea along China's border (Moore 2008). Therefore, China has provided foods, fuels, and economic aid. It has also blocked international criticism and vetoed strong sanctions or pressures against Pyongyang in the UN and other forums. For example, China has expressed strong regret over UN resolutions criticizing North Korea's human rights conditions by denouncing them as a politicization of human rights and explaining that North Korea has made progress.[24] Beijing also made it clear that it would veto any attempt in the UN Security Council to bring North Korean leaders before the International Criminal Court. It has repatriated North Korean defectors back to North Korea and refuses to give refugee status to the defectors on the grounds that doing so would trigger a massive outflow of refugees (Margesson, Chanlett-Avery and Bruno 2007). China does not want the nuclear crisis in North Korea to destabilize the region, endanger its economic development, and spread nuclear weapons to Japan, South Korea, and Taiwan either. Therefore, it has emphasized diplomatic solutions, such as the Six-Party Talks, while supporting minimum resources for North Korea's survival and encouraging Pyongyang to follow China's path of economic reforms. Some critics of North Korea claim that China is an enabler and complicit in North Korean human rights abuses (Kirkpatrick and Cha 2014; Richardson 2016).

South Korea's position on North Korean human rights issues has depended on its domestic political landscape. Two liberal presidents, Kim Dae-jung (1998–2003) and President Roh Moo-hyun (2003–2008), adopted an engagement policy, known as the Sunshine Policy, toward North Korea by promoting dialogue and economic cooperation. The Sunshine Policy was modeled after the famous 'Ostpolitik' by Willy Brandt from West Germany that engaged East Germany to achieve "change through rapprochement." It followed 'neofunctionalism' as a theory of international relations that emphasized a 'spillover' effect of cooperation from economic to military and security issues. For example, South Korean Unification Minister Chung Dong-young (2004–2006) under President Roh Moo-hyun, said, "Human rights problems in communist countries have never been solved by way of applying pressure." He also claimed, "it was detente and peaceful engagement that resolved human rights problems in the Soviet bloc and China" along this line (Lee 2004). Two Koreas started cultural exchanges and reunions of separated families, and Seoul began to provide humanitarian aid to the North. Both Koreas agreed to establish the Kaesong Industrial Complex for inter-Korean economic cooperation to merge South Korean capital and technology with North Korea's cheap and well-trained labor force. The liberal South Korean presidents wanted to solve the North Korean nuclear crisis via peaceful diplomatic negotiations, such as in the Six-Party Talks (2003–2007) by persuading both Washington and Pyongyang to negotiate. Two liberal presidents did not want to provoke North Korea by criticizing its human rights situation and thereby place more obstacles in the way of already tricky process of nuclear negotiations. Those two administrations refrained from directly condemning North Korea and abstained from voting for UN resolutions regarding North Korea's human rights conditions. A large number of North Korean refugees have been accepted into South Korea under these two presidents, but they wanted to maintain a low profile on refugee issues so as not to provoke North Korea and undermine inter-Korean cooperation (Margesson, Chanlett-Avery and Bruno 2007). South Korea's liberal governments' position on the North Korean human rights situation has been a source of political controversy. When the US Congress passed the North Korean Human Rights Act of 2004, South Korean politicians were divided on it between conservatives and liberals (*Chosun Daily* 2004).[25] Conservative party members criticized the Roh Moo-hyun government's North Korea policy and attempted to pass the North Korea Human Rights Act in the South Korean National Assembly. While liberals favored continued cooperation with the North using quiet diplomacy, conservatives wanted to join the Bush administration in condemning North Korea's poor human rights conditions.

The two conservative presidents, Lee Myung-bak (2008–2013) and Park Geun-hye (2013–2017), directly condemned North Korea's nuclear policy and human rights conditions. They also voted for the UN's annual resolutions on North Korea's poor human rights record. Inter-Korean relations and economic cooperation deteriorated under these conservative presidents. The Six-Party Talk never resumed after 2007. After the 2010 sinking of the South Korean naval ship Cheonan, President Lee imposed sanctions against North Korea (the May 24 measures) by suspending inter-Korean trade except at the Kaesong Industrial Complex and by banning most cultural exchanges and North Korean ships from South Korean territorial waters. President Lee also said, "Reunification will definitely come. . . . I believe that the time has come to start discussing realistic policies to prepare for that day, such as a reunification tax" in a speech on the 65th anniversary of Korean liberation from Japan. Critics argue that North Korea, at the lowest point of inter-Korea relations, could take his comment on a unification tax as South Korean preparation for a sudden collapse of the North Korean government (Choe 2010). In 2014, in her first presidential press conference, President Park Geun-hye mentioned, "I believe reunification would be a chance for the economy to make a huge leap." She described, "Reunification is '*daebak*" [a jackpot] when a reporter asked for further details on preparatory measures for reunification (*Joongang Ilbo* 2015). She also allegedly said that "Unification could happen tomorrow, so you need to be making preparations" at a closed-door intensive round table session with the Presidential Committee for Unification Preparation (PCUP) in 2015 (*The Hankyoreh* 2015). Some critics interpreted her comment as an unrealistic expectation of North Korea's impending collapse and the absorption of the North by the South. After North Korea's fourth nuclear test in January 2016 and rocket launch a month later, President Park also ordered the Kaesong Industrial Complex completely shut down. The North Korean Human Rights Act (NKHRA) passed the National Assembly on March 3, 2016. It intended to provide humanitarian assistance to afflicted individuals in North Korea and defectors, and to provide financial assistance to South Korean NGOs working on North Korean human rights issues.

Debates on North Korea's human rights issue

North Korea has strongly rejected most of charges of human rights violations and even accused the criticism by outside critics and defectors as "a pretext for overthrowing its *Juche*-based socialist system" (*KCNA* 2005). North Korea tends to justify its human rights conditions in the name of defending national sovereignty and socialist political and economic system. North Korean leaders believe it is necessary to maintain social control and limit certain freedoms and rights since the country has been under more than 60 years of military confrontation with the most powerful country in the world. Therefore, Pyongyang has blamed American hostile policy toward Pyongyang and the imposition of economic sanctions, while asking the international community to provide more economic and food aid. According to the discussion of human rights theories in the first part of this chapter, the North Korean view of human rights can be categorized as an extreme version of cultural relativism and a Third World communist view of human rights. Marxism, Confucian culture, and the *Juche* ideology have also heavily influenced the unique perspective of human rights in North Korea (Park 2002; Song and Weatherley 2008). Even recognizing North Korea's unique situation, however, there is no question that North Korea's political persecution and extremely limited individual freedoms cannot be justified according to most of existing human rights standards.

One of the major challenges in assessing North Korea's human rights condition is the lack of access to information due to its isolation and tight domestic control. Therefore, the testimonies of refugees and defectors have been the main source of information. Since refugees and defectors went through harsh suffering in the North and during the process of defection, they tend to describe the country in very negative ways. Many of the defectors are associated with conservative political forces and NGOs in South Korea and the United States. They usually prefer more hostile approaches toward North Korea and tend to dramatize and even exaggerate their experiences to generate global attention and put pressure on North Korea so that the regime might collapse or be replaced. For example, Lee Soon-ok, who defected from North Korea in 1994, claimed that she was in a prison camp for political prisoners. She testified before the US Senate on her experiences and published her story. She witnessed severe beatings, torture, and chemical and biological warfare experiments on inmates in the prison (*NBC* News 2003).[26] She even said she saw security officers in a metal factory inside of a prison camp killing Christians "by pouring molten iron" on elderly Christians who refused to deny their Christian beliefs and accept the *Juche* ideology of the State.[27] Later, some defectors claimed that many of her testimonies were exaggerated or fabricated, and that she had been in prison for economic and social offenses rather than political offenses. Shin Dong-hyuk is another defector who claimed to be imprisoned to the notorious Camp 14, a total control zone for political prisoners, at the age of 13 because of political charges against his family. He said he was forced to watch his mother and brother executed for trying to escape the camp. His story was published by a former *Washington Post* reporter with the title of "Escape from Camp 14" in 2012 and translated into 27 languages. He became a star witness in the UN's investigation of North Korean human rights violations, and he met with the UN human rights chief in Geneva and John Kerry, who urged international attention on North Korea's human rights abuses. Later, many experts and defectors raised questions about his testimony. Shin retracted central parts of his 2012 book. He actually spent most of time in the less brutal Camp 18 for economic and social offense rather than Camp 14. He went to prison at the age of 20 rather than 13, and his mother and brother might have been executed for other reasons rather than trying to escape the prison (Choe Sang-Hun 2015).

Conservatives in the United States and South Korea tend to welcome any testimonies by defectors without asking for authentication as long as they paint the North in a brutal light. Strong nations can also use humanitarian concerns to mask geopolitical interest (Lobel & Ratner 1999), and some critics believe that the United States has politicized North Korea's human rights record to use as a foreign policy tool to exercise leverage over North Korea. Others have pointed out the existence of "orientalism" (Said 1978) in the Western perception of the North, depicting it as uncivilized and barbaric "others" in stereotypical fashion (Abrahamian 2011; Barkawi 2013; Xiao 2015).

Another major problem is that external actors have very limited options in approaching North Korea's domestic situation, and scholars have debated the effectiveness of existing options. Some NGOs and the UN human rights investigators have suggested that North Korean leaders should be prosecuted for crimes against humanity either at the International Criminal Court (ICC) or in a third country (*VICE News and Reuters* 2016). Referring North Korean leaders to the ICC for crimes against humanity is impossible since China and Russia would veto such proposal in the Security Council (Sanchez 2014). Economic sanctions are one of the most common methods used toward Pyongyang as leverage to transform Pyongyang's behavior on nuclear issues and human rights violations. Conservatives in the United States and South Korea have been predicting an imminent collapse of North Korea since the mid-1990s (Foster-Carter 2015). They even argue that the United States and South Korea could make North Korea surrender to external pressure or implode by adding more economic sanctions, supporting defectors, and encouraging defections from the already unstable country. North Korea, however, shows no sign of collapse so far. The United States has imposed and maintained numerous economic sanctions over North Korea since the Korean War to retaliate against North Korean threats to the South, to protest human rights abuses, to impair its military capability, and to enhance the potential for regime change. The Clinton administration relaxed some sanctions after the 1994 Geneva agreement, but the Bush administration, after the second nuclear crisis in 2002, tightened sanctions in the name of denuclearization. Even after deleting North Korea from its list of state sponsors of terrorism in October 2008 as a consequence of some progress after the Six-Party Talks, North Korea is still under 19 different economic sanctions. Such sanctions preclude any meaningful foreign investment or global trade in North Korea. North Korea already lost most of its trading partners after the collapse of the communist allies and under sanctions imposed by the UN and other nations. China has been its main trading partner and provider of critical resources for its survival (Oh and Ryu 2011). The problem with sanctions over North Korea is that they isolate and contain North Korea, but have not pushed it to make economic or political changes other than increasing dependence on China. As Secretary of Defense Donald Rumsfeld proposed in a secret memorandum leaked to the *New York Times* in 2003, the United States had a wishful thinking of persuading China to join its efforts to pressure North Korea so that the North would either change its actions or implode (Watts 2003). Beijing has made it very clear that it does not want North Korea to collapse and that it will continue to aid and trade with the North. China lost massive numbers of soldiers in the Korean War to defend North Korea. It wants North Korea to exist as a buffer zone between its military and US forces stationed in the South. The critics also claim that sanctions mostly punish ordinary people while strengthening the regime that controls the distribution of limited resources (Addis 2003). Sanctions may further generate a 'rally 'round the flag' effect, solidify North Korean society, (Galtung 1967) and let the Pyongyang regime divert people's anger toward external actors such as the United States rather than against their own leaders' mismanagement of the economy. Some scholars report a significant economic recovery in North Korea recently with limited reform measures made under the Kim Jong-un regime (Feron 2014) to expand informal markets (Smith 2015). North Korea has neither adopted full-scale Chinese-style economic reforms nor collapsed like other socialist states. It maintains sovereignty and social stability with nuclear weapons development and tight social control. Pyongyang fears that serious Chinese-style economic reforms might destabilize their socialist political and economic system and endanger their national security since the country still faces military confrontation with the United States under a siege mindset (Buzo 1999; Kong 2014; Oh and Hassig 1999). Therefore North Korea's economic problems and human rights conditions are not separable from its security issues (Carlin and Wit 2006; Kim 2006). In the end, there must be some breakthrough in diplomatic negotiations to solve the nuclear and missile problems. A resulting peace treaty and diplomatic normalization would likely then improve North Korea's economic and human rights conditions.

An extreme option to solve the human rights and nuclear problems would be foreign military intervention against North Korea, such as with a surgical strike or full-scale war. Some universal human rights advocates support foreign intervention to stop human rights violations when they are intentional and massive in scale (Heinze 2004). Michael Walzer (1977, 90) argues that outside intervention must be permitted in the cases of "gross, persistent and systemic violations of basic human rights." But foreign interventions are at odds with the principle of national sovereignty, and their implementation is challenging. Even more human rights abuses, regional conflicts, and instability can emerge in the process of stopping abuses and attempting to transition a nation to democracy (Fein 1987). Donnelly and Howard (1987, 79–106) point out that the Universal Declaration contains no enforcement mechanisms, and so its implementation and enforcement are generally left to individual states. Former UN Secretary-General, Kofi Anan (1999) discussed the basic dilemma of human rights intervention. He says that the Charter of UN "gave great responsibilities to great powers" but "also safeguard against abuse of those powers." For example, Article 2.7 protects "national Sovereignty from foreign intervention" and Chapter VI underscores the "peaceful settlement of disputes." On the other hand, Chapter VII mentions "the action the UN must take when peace comes under threat or broken, or is actually broken." Overall, Kofi Anan sides with universalism and humanitarian intervention by saying that "national sovereignty can be set aside for the Security Council's overriding duty to preserve international peace and security." He adds, "sovereignty was never meant as a license for governments to trample on human rights and dignity." The definitions of "international peace and security" and "severe violations of basic human rights," however, are not always clear. The measures outside actors choose can be controversial.

An unlimited level of destruction expected from a future war on the Korean Peninsula also makes a military option against the North virtually impossible. With conventional weapons in 1950s, the Korean War killed almost 10 percent of the entire population on the Korean Peninsula. When President Bill Clinton contemplated a preemptive strike on North Korea's Yongbyon nuclear reactor in the middle of 1994 nuclear crisis, the Pentagon reported that such military action would claim a million lives during the first 24 hours, including massive US troop casualties, and that was before North Korea even possessed nuclear weapons (Powell 2017). With North Korea having nuclear weapons and heavy stockpiles of biological, chemical, and conventional weapons, another war in the peninsula might turn out to be a disaster never seen before. It does not require an expert to conclude that a military intervention in the name of human rights would generate a more extreme human rights crisis than North Korea's current one. The outbreak of a war might also invite China to intervene, and thereby plunge the world into a global conflict.

It is important to discuss how to approach North Korea's human rights issues. Conservatives in the United States and South Korea tend to emphasize human rights abuses in the North and the oppressive nature of the regime itself, as well as the threat from its nuclear and missile programs. Liberals pay attention to human rights issues, but prioritize and focus on imminent security issues. For example, President Bill Clinton's priority was exchanging Pyongyang's nuclear and missile program with diplomatic normalization and other incentives, while President George W. Bush was fundamentally skeptical of the Pyongyang regime in terms of its oppressive nature and human rights abuses. Bush was critical of Clinton's approach and did not utilize the positive momentum generated at the end of the latter's administration. He refused direct talks with Pyongyang early in his first term. President Bush raised the bar even higher by expanding the focus to include not just nuclear and missile programs, but also internal policies and human rights conditions. Therefore, criticism of North Korean human rights violations in real world diplomacy could place more preconditions and obstacles in negotiations, even though there are clear human rights violations in the North and clear justifications to pay attention to them.

Conservatives do not want to address Pyongyang's security issues and normalize relations with the Pyongyang regime because North Korea is led by a dictatorship that abuses human rights and does not seek economic reform. But Pyongyang might not try serious reform and social changes until it sees serious improvements in its security condition. The uncomfortable truth about North Korea's human rights issue is that most existing measures and attempts by the United States, other nations, and international institutions have rarely worked to actually improve North Korea's human rights conditions. Most sanctions were only successful in isolating the country and undermining its economic and military capabilities rather than seriously changing North Korean people's lives. North Korea's economic and human rights conditions cannot easily be separated from its unique security conditions. Therefore, the critics of conservative approaches will argue that the improvement of human rights in North Korea should be positioned as a long-term goal. It should be addressed only after participants in negotiations reach some critical level of success on issues such as nuclear weapons programs and diplomatic normalization, this transforming a vicious cycle into a virtuous cycle of negotiation.

Conclusion

This chapter examined the North Korean human rights issues that began to receive more attention during the 1990s. With its inefficient economic system, natural disasters, international isolation, and loss of trading partners after the collapse of the Cold War, North Korea has experienced serious economic depression and food shortages. Many refugees escaped the country and spread information on human rights abuses within the secluded country. Under the Kim family's three generational successions and centralized political and economic system, North Korea has violated the basic rights of its own people, such as the rights to food, freedom of thought, conscience, and religion. North Koreans suffer from arbitrary detention, torture, and executions in prison camps. South Koreans and the global publics have debated how to improve the human rights situation in North Korea. Conservatives in the US and South Korea, who believe that the collapse of the regime is imminent, blame the North Korean regime and demand more political pressures and economic sanctions. Liberals are more focused on humanitarian aid for the North Korean people and seeking diplomatic negotiation and economic reform. There were different options, such as imposing more economic sanctions, prosecuting North Korean leader in the ICC, and planning humanitarian military interventions. Considering North Korea's unique domestic and international conditions, most of those measures have not been successful in improving North Korea's human rights conditions. Therefore, it is necessary to position the goal of improving human rights in the broader context of a holistic and long-term approach that can solve North Korea's security, economic, and human rights conditions in a step-by-step process involving all relevant actors in the region.

Notes

1　The United Nations Office of the High Commissioner of Human Rights, "What Are Human Rights?" 1948. Available at www.ohchr.org/en/issues/pages/whatarehumanrights.aspx.

2　The United Nations Office of the High Commissioner of Human Rights, "Vienna Declaration and Programme of Action," 1993. Available at www.ohchr.org/EN/ProfessionalInterest/Pages/Vienna. aspx.

3　*Proclamation of Teheran, Final Act of the International Conference on Human Rights*, Teheran, April 22 to May 13, 1968. U.N. Doc. A/CONF. 32/41 at 3 (1968).

4　*Declaration on the Right of Peoples to Peace*, Approved by General Assembly resolution 39/11 of November 12, 1984. Available at www.ohchr.org/EN/ProfessionalInterest/Pages/ RightOfPeoplesToPeace.aspx.

5　*Declaration on the Right to Development*, Approved by General Assembly resolution 41/128 of December 4, 1986. Available at www.un.org/documents/ga/res/41/a41r128.htm.

6　The United Nations Office of the High Commissioner of Human Rights, "Vienna Declaration and Programme of Action." Available at www.ohchr.org/EN/ProfessionalInterest/Pages/ Vienna.aspx.

7　Second periodic report of the Democratic People's Republic of Korea on its implementation of the International Covenant on Civil and Political Rights CCPR/C/PRK/2000/2 4 May, 2002; Second periodic reports of the Democratic People's Republic of Korea on its implementation of the International Covenant on Economic, Social and Cultural Rights, E/1990/6/Add.35 May 15, 2002; Second periodic reports of States parties to the Convention on the Rights of the Child CRC/C/65/ Add.24 November 5, 2003; Consideration of report submitted by States Parties under article 18 of the Convention on the Elimination of All Forms of Discrimination against Women CEDAW/C/ PRK/1, September 11, 2002.

8　It, however, adds, "A person who has been disenfranchised by a Court decision and a person legally certified insane do not have the right to elect or to be elected" and mentions the possibility of limiting this right by a court decision.

9　North Korea, *Socialist Constitution of the Democratic People's Republic of Korea*. Pyongyang, North Korea. 2014.

10　Congressional-Executive Commission on China, *Annual Report*, October 10, 2012. Available at www.cecc.gov/publications/annual-reports/2012-annual-report.

11　UN General Assembly. "Sixty-Third Session Third Committee, Promotion and Protection of Human Rights: Human Rights Situations and Reports of Special Rapporteurs and Representatives." October 30, 2008. Available at www.securitycouncilreport.org/atf/cf/%7B65BFCF9B-6D27-4E9C-8CD3-CF6E4FF96FF9%7D/NKorea%20AC363L26.pdf.

12　Resettlement Support Division, Republic of Korea, Ministry of Unification. "Status of North Korean Defectors entering South Korea, Resettlement Support Division." 2017. Available at www. unikorea.go.kr/content.do?cmsid=1440.

13　The Commission of inquiry on human rights in the Democratic People's Republic of Korea. "Report of the detailed findings of the commission of inquiry on human rights in the Democratic People's Republic of Korea." February 7, 2014. Available at www.un.org/ga/search/view_doc. asp?symbol=A/HRC/25/CRP.1.

14　UN General Assembly document on Agenda item 64 (c): Sixty-third session Third Committee. "Promotion and Protection of Human Rights: Human Rights Situations and Reports of Special Rapporteurs and Representatives." October 30, 2008. Available at www.securitycouncilreport.org/ atf/cf/%7B65BFCF9B-6D27-4E9C-8CD3-CF6E4FF96FF9%7D/NKorea%20AC363L26.pdf.

15　Ibid.

16　Ibid.

17　Ibid.

18　Ibid.

19　United Nations Office of the High Commissioner. "Report of the Commission of Inquiry on Human Rights in the Democratic People's Republic of Korea". United Nations Office of the High Commissioner for Human Rights. February 17, 2014. Available at www.ohchr.org/EN/HRBodies/ HRC/CoIDPRK/Pages/ReportoftheCommissionofInquiryDPRK.aspx.

20　President George W. Bush. 2001. "State of the Union address, 2001." Available at www.washingtonpost.com/wp-srv/nation/specials/attacked/transcripts/bushaddress_092001.html.

21 S.1903 (108th), "The North Korea Freedom Act of 2003," introduced by Sen. Sam Brownback, November 11, 2003. Available at www.govtrack.us/congress/bills/108/s1903/text.
22 H.R. 4011 (108th): North Korean Human Rights Act of 2004. Available at www.govtrack.us/congress/bills/108/hr4011/text.
23 H.R. 5834 (110th): North Korean Human Rights Reauthorization Act of 2008. Available at www.govtrack.us/congress/bills/110/hr5834/text.
24 "Palestinian Self-Determination, Human Rights in Democratic People's Republic of Korea Addressed In Texts Approved By Third Committee." United Nations. November 17, 2005. Available at www.un.org/press/en/2005/gashc3840.doc.htm (Retrieved DEC 15, 2016).
25 H.R. 4011 (108th): North Korean Human Rights Act of 2004. Available at www.govtrack.us/congress/bills/108/hr4011/text.
26 Bureau of Democracy, Human Rights, and Labor (US State Department), *2004 Country Reports on Human Rights Practices: Korea, Democratic People's Republic of* February 28, 2005.
27 *Testimony of Ms. Soon Ok Lee*, the US Senate, June 21, 2002.

References

ABC News. 2002. "N. Korean Refugees Storm China's Embassies." July 6. Available at: http://abcnews.go.com/Nightline/story?id=128566&page=1.

Abrahamian, Andray. 2011. "Documentary Film and North Korea." *38 North*, May 20. Available at: www.38north.org/2011/05/abrahamian052011/.

Addis, Adeno. 2003. "Economic Sanctions and the Problem of Evil." *Human Rights Quarterly* 25 (3): 573–623.

American Anthropological Association. 1947. "Statement on Human Rights." *American Anthropologist* 49 (4): 539–43.

Amnesty International. 2016. *The Amnesty International Report 2015/16: North Korea 2015/2016*. Available at: www.amnesty.org/en/countries/asia-and-the-pacific/north-korea/report-korea-democratic-peoples-republic-of/.

Anan, Kofi. 1999. *The Question of Intervention: Statements by the Secretary-General*. New York: United Nations.

Asia Bulletin. 2014. "UN Panel on North Korea Details Horrific Torture, Appeals to World to Act." *Asia Bulletin*, February 18. Available at: www.asiabulletin.com/index.php/sid/220121420.

Barkawi, Tarak. 2013. "Nuclear Orientalism." *Aljazeera*, April 17. Available at: www.aljazeera.com/indepth/opinion/2013/04/201341695253805841.html.

Bristow, Michael. 2011. "Ex-Leaders Head for North Korea." *BBC News Asia-Pacific*, April 25. Available at: www.bbc.com/news/world-asia-pacific-13185053.

Brooke, James. 2002. "N. Koreans Talk of Baby Killings." *The New York Times*, June 10. Available at: www.nytimes.com/2002/06/10/world/n-koreans-talk-of-baby-killings.html.

Buzo, Adrian. 1999. *The Guerilla Dynasty: Politics and Leadership in North Korea*. London: I B Tauris.

Byul, Ryan-im. 2014. "Yongusil 50: A Cause for Optimism – Michael Kirby in Hong Kong." *Sino-NK*, October 26. Available at: http://sinonk.com/2014/10/26/kirby-in-hong-kong/.

Carlin, Robert L., and Joel Wit S. 2006. "The Debate in Bloom." *The Adelphi Papers* 46 (382): 35–52.

Choe, Sang-Hun. 2010. "South Korean Leader Proposes a Tax to Finance Reunification." *The New York Times*, August 15. Available at: www.nytimes.com/2010/08/16/world/asia/16korea.html.

Choe Sang-Hun. 2015. "Prominent North Korean Defector Recants Parts of His Story of Captivity." *The New York Times*, January 18. Available at: www.nytimes.com/2015/01/19/world/asia/prominent-north-korean-defector-shin-dong-hyuk-recants-parts-of-his-story.html.

Chosun Daily. 2004. "U.S. Senators Scramble to 'Hot-Line' North Korean Human Rights Act." September 10. Available at: http://english.chosun.com/site/data/html_dir/2004/09/10/2004091061033.html.

Chosun Daily. 2015a. "Most Defectors Suffer from Depression." March 12. Available at: http://english.chosun.com/site/data/html_dir/2015/03/12/2015031200809.html.

Chosun Daily. 2015b. "People Smugglers Tie N. Korean Defectors into Crippling Debt." March 14. Available at: http://english.chosun.com/site/data/html_dir/2015/03/14/2015031400471.html.

Collins, Robert. 2012. *Marked for Life: Songbun, North Korea's Social Classification System*. Washington, DC: Committee for Human Rights in North Korea.

Disabled Peoples' International. 2012. "U.N.: N. Korea Puts Disabled in Camps." *Disabled Peoples' International*, March 23. Available at: https://web.archive.org/web/20120323130109/www.dpi.org/lang-en/resources/details.php?page=753.

Do Kyung-ok, Kim Soo-Am, Han Dong-ho, Lee Keum-Soon, and Hong Min. 2015. *White Paper on Human Rights in North Korea 2015*. Seoul, Korea: Korea Institute for National Unification.

Donnelly, Jack, and Rhoda E. Howard. 1987. *International Handbook of Human Rights*. New York: Greenwood Press.

Fein, Helen. 1987. "More in the Middle: Life-Integrity Violations and Democracy in the World." *Human Rights Quarterly* 17 (1): 170–91.

Feron, Helen. 2014. "Doom and Gloom or Economic Boom? The Myth of the 'North Korean Collapse.'" *Japan Focus* 18 (3): 1–23.

Fisher, Max. 2013. "Even by North Korean Standards, This Announcement of Jang Song Thaek's Execution Is Intense." *Washington Post*, December 12. Available at: www.washingtonpost.com/news/worldviews/wp/2013/12/12/even-by-north-korean-standards-this-announcement-of-jang-song-thaeks-execution-is-intense/?utm_term=.ea2a754da0c4.

Foster-Carter, Aidan. 2015. "Obama Comes Out as a North Korea Collapsist." *The Diplomat*, January 30. Available at: http://thediplomat.com/2015/01/obama-comes-out-as-a-north-korea-collapsist/.

Freedom House. 2016. *Freedom in the World 2016: North Korea, Freedom House*. Available at: https://freedomhouse.org/report/freedom-world/2016/north-korea.

Galtung, Johan. 1967. "On the Effects of International Economic Sanctions, with Examples from the Case of Rhodesia." *World Politics* 19 (3): 378–416.

Go, Myong-Hyun. 2014. "Resettling in South Korea: Challenges for Young North Korean Refugees." *Issue Briefs*, The Asian Institute for Policy Studies, August 8. Available at: http://en.asaninst.org/contents/resettling-in-south-korea-challenges-for-young-north-korean-refugees/.

Haggard, Stephan, and Marcus Noland. 2007. *Famine in North Korea: Markets, Aid and Reform*. New York: Columbia University Press.

The Hankyoreh. 2015. "Pres. Park Reportedly Says Reunification 'Could Come Tomorrow.'" August 18. Available at: http://english.hani.co.kr/arti/english_edition/e_northkorea/704897.html.

Joongang Ilbo. 2015. "Opening Path to Unification." September 24. Available at: http://mengnews.joins.com/view.aspx?aId=3009597.

Hawk, David. 2012. *The Hidden Gulag*, Second edition. Washington, DC: Committee for Human Rights in North Korea.

Heinze, Eric A. 2004. "Humanitarian Intervention: Morality and International Law on Intolerable Violations of Human Rights." *International Journal of Human Rights* 8 (4): 471–90.

Human Rights Watch. 2017. "World Report 2017: North Korea, Events of 2016." Available at: www.hrw.org/world-report/2017/country-chapters/north-korea.

KCNA (Korea Central News Agency). 2005. "KCNA Refutes U.S. Anti-DPRK Human Rights Campaign." *KCNA*, November 8. Available at: www.kcna.co.jp/item/2005/200511/news11/09.htm.

Kim, Dae Jung. 1994. "Is Culture Destiny? The Myth of Asia's Anti-Democratic Values." *Foreign Affairs*, November/December.

Kim, Sung Chull. 2006. *North Korea Under Kim Jong Il: From Consolidation to Systemic Dissonance*. New York: SUNY Press.

Kirk, Don. 2004. "N. Korean Defectors Face New Challenges on Journey South." *Christian Science Monitor*, December 29. Available at: www.csmonitor.com/2004/1229/p07s01-woap.html.

Kirkpatrick, Melanie, and Victor Cha. 2014. "China Is Complicit in North Korea's Human Rights Abuses." *Foreign Policy*, July 21. Available at: http://foreignpolicy.com/2014/07/31/china-is-complicit-in-north-koreas-human-rights-abuses/.

Knight, Richard. 2012. "Are North Koreans Really Three Inches Shorter than South Koreans?" *BBC News*, April 23. Available at: www.bbc.com/news/magazine-17774210.

Kong, Tat Yan. 2014. "The Political Obstacles to Economic Reform in North Korea: The Ultra Cautious Strategy in Comparative Perspective." *The Pacific Review* 27 (1): 73–96.

Kumar, T. 2012. "China's Repatriation of North Korean Refugees." *Amnesty International USA*, March 5. Available at: www.amnestyusa.org/news/news-item/china-s-repatriation-of-north-korean-refugees.

Lee, Jong-Heon. 2004. "Seoul Concerned About Human Rights Fallout." *UPI*, October 19. Available at: www.upi.com/Business_News/Security-Industry/2004/10/19/Seoul-concerned-about-human-rights-fallout/UPI-55931098197565/#ixzz359wmKC9D.

Lee, Karin, and Adam Miles. 2006. "North Korea on Capitol Hill." In *The Future of US-Korean Relations: The Imbalance of Power* (chapter 8), edited by J. Feffer. New York: Routledge.

Lobel, Jules, and Michael Ratner. 1999. "Bypassing the Security Council: Ambiguous Authorizations to Use Force, Cease-Fires and the Iraqi Inspection Regime." *American Journal of International Law* 93 (1): 124–54.

MacLeod, Calum. 2011. "North Korean Defectors Learn to Adapt in South." *USA Today*, December 20. Available at: http://usatoday30.usatoday.com/news/world/story/2011-12-20/north-korean-defectors/52131816/1.

Margesson, Rhoda, Emma Chanlett-Avery, and Andorra Bruno. 2007. "North Korean Refugees in China and Human Rights Issues: International Response and U.S. Policy Options." *CRS Report for Congress*, September 26.

Moore, G. J. 2008. "How North Korea threatens China's Interests: Understanding Chinese 'duplicity' on the North Korean nuclear issue." *International Relations of the Asia-Pacific* 8 (1): 1–29.

NBC News. 2003. "A Survivor: Soon Ok Lee, 7 Years of Torture in N. Korean Prison Camp." January 15. Available at: www.nbcnews.com/id/3071464/ns/us_news-only/t/survivor-soon-ok-lee/#.WULpSPryu34.

Oh, Jin Hwan, and Ji Yong Ryu. 2011. "The Effectiveness of Economic Sanctions on North Korea: China's Vital Role." *The Korean Journal of Defense Analysis* 23 (1): 117–31.

Oh, Kongdan, and Ralph C. Hassig. 1999. "North Korea Between Collapse and Reform." *Asian Survey* 39 (2): 287–309.

Park, Han S. 2002. *North Korea: The Politics of Unconventional Wisdom*. Boulder, CO: Lynne Rienner Publishers.

Person, James. 2013. "Commentary: North Korea's Purges Past." *The National Interest*, December 30.

Pollis, Adamantia, and Peter Schwab. 1979. "Human Rights: A Western Concept with Limited Applicability." In *Human Rights: Cultural and Ideological Perspectives,* edited by Adamantia Pollis and Peter Schwab. New York: Praeger.

Powell, Bill. 2017. "What War with North Korea Looks Like." *Newsweek*, April 25. Available at: www.newsweek.com/2017/05/05/what-war-north-korea-looks-588861.html.

Richardson, Sophie. 2016. "Dispatches: China's Tired Line on Human Rights in North Korea." *Human Rights Watch*, March 15. Available at: www.hrw.org/news/2016/03/15/dispatches-chinas-tired-line-human-rights-north-korea.

Said, Edward W. 1978. *Orientalism*. London: Penguin Group.

Sanchez, Ray. 2014. "UN Votes Against North Korea on Human Rights." *CNN*, November 19. Available at: http://edition.cnn.com/2014/11/18/world/asia/un-north-korea-vote/index.html.

Security Council Report. 2012. "Monthly Forecast: ASIA, DPRK (North Korea) February 2012." *Security Council Report*. Available at: www.securitycouncilreport.org/monthly-forecast/2012-02/lookup_c_glKWLeMTIsG_b_7966259.php.

Shim, Elizabeth. 2016. "North Korea Mortality Rates Are Declining, UN Group Says." *UPI*, June 1. Available at: www.upi.com/Top_News/World-News/2016/06/01/North-Korea-mortality-rates-are-declining-UN-group-says/6591464832413/.

Smith, Hazel. 2015. *North Korea: Markets and Military Rule*. Cambridge: Cambridge University Press.

Song, Jiyoung. 2011. *Human Rights Discourse in North Korea: Post-Colonial, Marxist, and Confucian Perspectives*. New York, NY: Taylor & Francis.

Song, Jiyoung, and Robert Weatherley. 2008. "The Evolution of Human Rights Thinking in North Korea." *Journal of Communist Studies and Transitional Politics* 24 (2): 272–296.

Taylor, Adam. 2014. "North Korea Wrote a 53,558-Word Report on Its Human Rights Record. The Conclusion? It's Pretty Good." *Washington Post*, September 17. Available at: www.washington-post.com/news/worldviews/wp/2014/09/17/north-korea-wrote-a-53558-word-report-on-its-human-rights-record-the-conclusion-its-pretty-good/?utm_term=.af0428e36e1d.

UNICEF. 2002. "Nutrition Assessment 2002 D.P.R. Korea." Available at: www.unicef.org/dprk/nutrition_assessment.pdf.

VICE News and Reuters. 2016. "UN Calls for Kim Jong-un to Be Prosecuted for Crimes Against Humanity." March 14. Available at: https://news.vice.com/article/un-calls-for-kim-jong-un-to-be-prosecuted-for-crimes-against-humanity.

Walzer, Michael. 1977. *Just and Unjust Wars*. New York: Basic Books.

The Washington Times. 2003. "N. Korea Rights Abuses Under U.N. Scrutiny." April 2. Available at: www.washingtontimes.com/news/2003/apr/2/20030402-090522-6215r/.

Watts, Jonathan. 2003. "US to Hold Talks with Pyongyang on Nuclear Arms." *The Guardian*, April 22. Available at: www.theguardian.com/world/2003/apr/22/usa.northkorea.

Woodward, Bob. 2002. *Bush at War*. New York: Simon and Schuster.

Xiao, Madelyne. 2015. "'The Interview' and Persistent Orientalism in Film." *The Stanford Daily*, February 13. Available at: www.stanforddaily.com/2015/02/13/the-interview-and-persistent-orientalism-in-film/.

Zakaria, Fareed. 1994. "A Conversation with Lee Kuan Yew." *Foreign Affairs* 73 (2): 109–26.

10 Inter-Korean relations and reunification

Yangmo Ku

The Cold War at the global level ended two and a half decades ago, but the Korean Peninsula is still not free from Cold War-like confrontations. North and South Korea, which share same historical, cultural, and ethnic heritages, hold sharply divergent ideologies and political/economic systems. North Korea, which has maintained a dictatorial communist system based on the *Juche* ideology, runs counter to South Korea that has developed a liberal democracy and a capitalist economy. With these discrepancies, the two Koreas have continued military enmity and rivalry as well. This situation begs important questions: How and to what extent has the relationship between North and South Korea varied since 1948 when the two Koreas were established? What factors have most influenced inter-Korean relations? Is there a high possibility of achieving Korean reunification in the foreseeable future?

Addressing these questions, this chapter suggests that top political leaders in both Koreas played a pivotal role in altering inter-Korean relations. In other words, inter-Korean relations have fluctuated depending on the thoughts and strategies top leaders in both nations have vis-à-vis the other. The role of these agents was also constrained by domestic conditions and international political structures. Although they acted as indirect influences, domestic conditions and external structures worked as either permissive/inductive or restrictive conditions for the development of inter-Korean relations. This chapter first examines the evolution and fluctuations of inter-Korean relations while examining the roles of top leaders, domestic conditions, and international structures in shaping inter-Korean relations. And it then addresses the issue of Korean reunification in terms of the necessity of unification, the methods of unification, and the challenges on the way to unification. Finally, this chapter ends with a summary and several policy implications.

Existential antagonism (1948–1970)

Korean liberation in 1945 from the Japanese colonial rule did not lead to the formation of a unified Korean state. Rather, internal strife between leftists and rightists within Korea set the stage for the division of the nation, while the Cold War rivalry between the United States and the Soviet Union structured the actual partition. These two WWII allies agreed to divide Korea into two occupation zones along the 38th parallel – with Moscow controlling the northern region and Washington the southern – until the establishment of a unified Korean state. This temporary solution for the Korean power vacuum occasioned by Japan's surrender continued as the Cold War gained traction. Given starkly different ideologies, interests, and political systems, the United States and the Soviet Union failed to agree on the creation of a unified national government on the Korean Peninsula. This impasse culminated into the creation of separate states – the Republic of Korea (ROK or South Korea) and the Democratic People's Republic of Korea (DPRK or North Korea) in 1948.

During this initial period of state formation between 1948 and 1970, the relationship between the two Koreas was intensely antagonistic. As historian Charles Armstrong posits, inter-Korean relations during this period can be characterized as "existential antagonism: each Korean state saw the very existence of its rival as a threat to its own existence, and held as its explicit goal the elimination of the other" (Armstrong 2005, 4). This antagonism peaked when North Korea, supported by the Soviet Union, invaded the South in June 1950. As a result of the Korean War (1950–1953), the two Koreas suffered three million human causalities, the wide-ranging destruction of industrial facilities and infrastructure, and deepening mutual hostility. After this destructive war, for which there was no clear victor, South Korea continued to view the North as an illegitimate and threatening regime that had to be defended against at all cost. On the other hand, recognizing the South as a weak and unstable regime that would fall apart due to its internal contradictions, North Korea prepared to militarily reunify the country when the opportunity permitted.

As key agents affecting inter-Korean relations, top leaders in both Koreas took extremely hostile stances. In the wake of the ceasefire agreement in 1953, South Korea's first president, Rhee Syngman (1948–1960), who held strong anti-communist sentiments, aspired to invade the North to achieve Korean unification, although observers viewed his rhetoric as largely theoretical. The ROK's next president, Park Jung-hee (1961–1979), who came to power by a military coup, also had a strong enmity toward North Korea. He took advantage of anti-communism to strengthen his weak political legitimacy. In the same vein, the founder of North Korea, Kim Il-sung (1948–1994), persistently sought to attain Korean unification through military force and/or political upheavals such as a communist revolution within South Korea. North Korea's military infiltrations in the South, which had begun after 1953, significantly increased in the 1960s as attempts to destabilize South Korean society and instigate an insurgency. In 1961, for instance, North Korean troops attacked a South Korean guard post, resulting in one South Korean soldier's death and four injuries. In 1963, two American soldiers were killed and three were injured by an ambush laid by North Korean soldiers inside the joint security area. Particularly between 1966 and 1969, North Korean forces infiltrated in the South more than 750 times; these actions are known as the "Second Korean War" (Heo and Roehrig 2014, 30). North Korea's aggressive acts reached a pinnacle in January 1968, when 31 commandos came near Blue House, the South Korean presidential palace, to assassinate President Park, though their attempt failed. In response to this infuriating incident, Park designed a covert operation to kill Kim Il-sung by creating a commando group. In 1971, however, Park cancelled the operation due to improving prospects for inter-Korean dialogue (Agov 2016, 372).

Under this cloud of enmity, the South and North Korean public had little impact on their leaders' approaches to inter-Korean relations, because they were under harsh authoritarian rule. In addition, the international structural setting was extremely unfavorable to inter-Korean relations. South and North Korea were deeply entrenched in their respective Cold War blocs, which reinforced inter-Korean confrontation and prohibited mutual peaceful contacts. This structurally restrictive condition continued up until the emergence of détente in US–Soviet relations and a rapprochement in US–China relations in the early 1970s.

Fluctuations between reconciliation and confrontation (1971–1997)

During the 1971–1997 period, the pendulum of inter-Korean relations swung between reconciliation and confrontation. Unlike the previous era of existential antagonism, this period sometimes saw the easing of military tension and the advent of some cooperative measures in inter-Korean relations, including the holding of bilateral talks, the reunion of separated families, humanitarian assistance, and the adoption of peace-promotion agreements. These changes were significant in that each Korea for the first time recognized the other as a co-existing political system, although not reaching the level of reconciliation as shown in the Sunshine era (1998–2007), which is addressed in a subsequent section. On the other hand, this period was also fraught with provocative actions, primarily taken by North Korea, that heightened tensions between the two Koreas. Among these aggressive acts were the infiltrations of North Korean forces into the South, attempts to assassinate ROK presidents Park Jung-hee and Chun Doo-hwan, the explosion of a South Korean passenger airplane, and the development of nuclear weapons. From the North Korean perspective, the deployment of US nuclear weapons in South Korea, which lasted from 1958 to 1991, and the annual large-scale US–ROK joint military exercise called Team Spirit, initiated in 1976, were continual threats to the DPRK regime (Lee 2009).

In the early 1970s, a substantial change in the international political structure worked as permissive or inductive conditions in which primary agents in both Koreas intended to improve inter-Korean relations for their own purposes. Acknowledging the failed war in Vietnam, US President Richard Nixon adopted the Guam Doctrine in July 1969, also known as the Nixon Doctrine. According to this doctrine, US allies in Asia had to take the primary responsibility for defending themselves from domestic turmoil and external invasions, although the United States would preserve security commitments made with its allies. In line with this doctrine, in March 1970, the United States withdrew 20,000 forces from South Korea. Under the relaxation of US–Soviet tensions, or détente, the United States also normalized relations with China, which it had fought against during the Korean War.

Facing these dramatic structural changes, top political leaders in the two Koreas for the first-time initiated bilateral dialogues in 1971. ROK President Park Jung-hee was seriously concerned about South Korea's national security due to the weakened American security commitment. Under this circumstance, the Park regime felt it necessary to dialogue with North Korea to protect South Korea's security. For his part, North Korean supreme leader Kim Il-sung perceived that peaceful unification could come true because the time of revolutionary change in South Korea was approaching. Given this rationale, Kim Il-sung accepted the dialogue suggestion made by President Park (Kim 2014, 102–15). As a result of these dialogues, the two Koreas signed the July 4 Joint Communiqué in 1972, which elucidated three principles of peaceful unification: (1) to achieve unification without foreign interference; (2) to seek peaceful unification; and (3) to consolidate unity despite different ideologies and political systems. As in the previous period, South and North Korea's authoritarian leaders were not bounded by public opinion in forging their foreign policies.

The 1972 Joint Communiqué was the first official agreement made between North and South Korea, but it revealed clear limits. The agreement was not implemented due to the two sides' starkly divergent views, although it enhanced the expectation of a peaceful reunification among Korean people. South Korea placed the priority on gradually building trust in non-military issues and only then dealing with politico-military issues. North Korea argued for the immediate reduction of military forces in both Koreas and the withdrawal of all foreign military forces from the Korean Peninsula. In addition, top leaders in both Koreas ironically strove to consolidate their dictatorial rule in the wake of the signing of the joint communiqué. In October 1972, DPRK supreme leader Kim Il-sung promulgated the Socialist Constitution, which instituted an undisputable one-man dictatorship. In December 1972, ROK President Park Jung-hee also declared the *Yushin* Constitution, which gave him dictatorial powers with no limits on reelection.

Meanwhile, North Korea's provocative acts soon soured temporarily improved inter-Korean relations. Antagonistic feelings among South Koreans significantly increased in August 1974, when a Japanese-born Korean, Moon Se-kwang, with North Korean support, attempted to assassinate ROK President Park Jung-hee during a speech commemorating Korean independence day. President Park survived, but his wife, Yook Young-soo, was shot to death. In August 1976, the "ax murder incident," in which two American soldiers were killed by North Koreans soldiers in the Joint Security Area of the Demilitarized Zone (DMZ), heightened military tensions on the Korean Peninsula. Furthermore, ROK President Chun Doo-hwan (1980–1988), barely survived a North Korean agents' attack on Rangoon, in Burma (presently Myanmar), when he visited with a cohort of high-ranking government officials in 1982. Many high-ranking South Korean government officials died, but President Chun survived, because he arrived to the event site slightly late.

In the mid-1980s, inter-Korean relations swung back to the reconciliation mode. For five months in 1983, the South Korean government launched a media event to search for families who went missing during the Korean War. This event significantly increased nationalistic feelings among many South Koreans, thereby exerting positive influence on inter-Korean relations. In 1984, the North Korean government provided a large amount of goods and materials to South Koreans who had suffered from severe flooding. Moreover, after a series of talks between the South and North Korean Red Cross committees, the two Koreas, for the first time in 1985, held reunions of separated families in both Seoul and Pyeongyang. They also exchanged musical performing artists (Kim 2014, 141–4). However, this conciliatory mood returned to strong enmity in November 1987, when North Korea exploded a bomb on Korean Air Flight 858 flying from Bagdad to Seoul, resulting in the death of all 115 people on board. By this terrorist attack, North Korea intended to destabilize South Korean society and intimidate other countries from taking part in the 1988 Seoul Olympics.

The end of the Cold War in the late 1980s and early 1990s provided top leaders in both Koreas with another permissive or inducive condition that spurred them to improve inter-Korean relations. Unlike former Soviet leaders, Mikhail Gorbachev launched a so-called New Thinking in the mid-1980s, which was composed of *Perestroika* (economic/bureaucratic reforms) and *Glasnost* (opening to political debate). This policy eventually brought about significant structural changes in international politics, such as the fall of the Berlin Wall, the collapse of Eastern European communist nations, and the demise of the Soviet Union. To cope with these dramatic changes, South Korean President Roh Tae-woo (1988–1993) launched a so-called *Nordpolitik* (northern diplomacy) that aimed at defusing tensions with communist countries and laying the foundation for peaceful unification. This *Nordpolitik* took after West German Chancellor Willy Brandt's *Ostpolitik* in the 1970s.

Given South Korea's rapid economic growth, the Roh administration utilized economic aid to improve relations with the Soviet Union/Russia, China, and North Korea. In September 1990, the Soviet Union, which had been struggling to transition to a market economy, normalized its relationship with South Korea. Placing great value on South Korea's economic importance, China also made formal ties with South Korea in August 1992. Applying this approach to North Korea, the Roh government took the initiative to promote inter-Korean trade and exchanges of visits in order to ease tensions on the Korean Peninsula. On the other hand, the Kim Il-sung regime was extremely upset with the betrayal of key allies, the Soviet Union and China. The increasingly uncertain international environment, however, influenced the DPRK regime to seek a more active dialogue with South Korea. As a result, the two Koreas simultaneously joined the United Nations in September 1991 and signed the Agreement on Reconciliation, Non-aggression, and Exchanges and Cooperation between the South and the North (also called Inter-Korean Basic Agreement) in December 1991. The two Koreas also made the Joint Declaration of South and North Korea on the Denuclearization of the Korean Peninsula in January 1992 (Agov 2016, 376–7). It is important to note that South Korea achieved a successful democratic transition in 1987, after which the South Korean public began to influence their government's policy toward North Korea. The South Korean public largely supported Roh's northern diplomacy.

The above-mentioned improved relationship between the two Koreas, prompted by the *Nordpolitik*, deteriorated due to the first North Korean nuclear crisis that began in 1993. Kim Il-sung, who remembered the possibility of American usage of nuclear weapons during the Korean War, continually sought to develop his own weapons during the Cold War. Using a nuclear research reactor provided by the Soviet Union in 1965, North Korea secretly pursued nuclear weapons. In return for the Soviet Union's promise to provide nuclear reactors, North Korea finally joined the Nuclear Non-proliferation Treaty (NPT) in 1985. Despite this signing, North Korea delayed its acceptance of inspections of its nuclear facilities by the International Atomic Energy Agency (IAEA). North Korea then declared its withdrawal from the NPT in 1993. These acts led to increased military tensions with the United States. In summer 1994, the Bill Clinton administration actually considered conducting surgical airstrikes on North Korea's nuclear facilities in Yongbyon. To defuse heightened tensions, former US President Jimmy Carter visited Pyongyang as a mediator to meet Kim Il-sung, and the conflict ended in bilateral negotiations between the United States and North Korea. Despite Kim Il-sung's sudden death, those negotiations eventually led to the making of the so-called Agreed Framework in October 1994. In return for freezing North Korea's nuclear development facilities, the United States promised to construct two light-water nuclear reactors to resolve the lack of electricity in North Korea. The United States also promised to annually provide 500,000 tons of heavy oils to North Korea until the two reactors were completely constructed.

Inter-Korean relations continually fluctuated during the Kim Young-sam presidency (1993–1998). ROK President Kim Young-sam originally had strong desire to improve inter-Korean relations. He was scheduled to meet Kim Il-sung in 1994 when the North Korean leader died two weeks beforehand. Kim Il-sung's death temporarily increased military tensions on the Korean Peninsula. Inter-Korean relations also soured because the Kim Young-sam administration prevented South Koreans from paying respect to the deceased North Korean leader. The intrusion of North Korean military spies into South Korea's east coast in 1996 dampened inter-Korean relations as well. The South Korean military continued to carry out annual military exercises with US forces. The Kim Young-sam administration at times provided humanitarian aids to North Korea, but this generosity did not lead to significant improvement in inter-Korean relations.

Sunshine and engagement era (1998–2007)

Compared to previous eras, the 1998–2007 period saw notable changes in inter-Korean relations. First of all, political relations improved significantly. ROK President Kim Dae-jung (1998–2003) and DPRK top leader Kim Jong-il (1997–2011) held a historic summit for the first time in Pyongyang in June 2000. After the summit, the two leaders issued the June 15 Joint Declaration that emphasized the following: (1) an independent resolution of Korean unification; (2) prompt resolution of humanitarian issues, such as exchange visits by separated family members; and (3) the consolidation of mutual trust by promoting economic cooperation and by stimulating exchanges in civic, cultural, sports, health, and other fields. The two sides also agreed to hold multiple dialogues to implement the above agreements.[1]

In October 2007, ROK President Roh Moo-hyun (2003–2008) and DPRK supreme leader Kim Jong-il had another summit in Pyongyang. Reaffirming the spirit of the June 15 Joint Declaration, the two leaders adopted a peace declaration calling for numerous action items, including: (1) resolving inter-Korean issues in the spirit of reconciliation, cooperation, and reunification, while not intervening in the internal affairs of the other; (2) proactively pursuing dialogue and contacts in various areas; (3) closely working together to end military hostilities, mitigate tensions, and guarantee peace on the Korean Peninsula; (4) replacing the current armistice regime with a permanent peace treaty; (5) promoting inter-Korean economic cooperation projects, such as the second-stage construction of the Kaesong Industrial Complex (KIC) and the creation of a special zone in the West Sea; (6) building infrastructure such as the Kaesong–Pyongyang expressway and shipbuilding complexes in Anbyeon and Nampo; and (7) fostering humanitarian cooperation and family reunions as well as collaboration in the realms of education, science and technology, culture, and sports.[2]

Given this political thaw, inter-Korean relations developed in diverse dimensions during the 1998–2007 period. In the wake of the first summit, South and North Korea held far more frequent dialogues on various issue areas up until 2007, as shown in Table 10.1. In particular, military and economic issues became important agenda items in inter-Korean dialogues starting in 2000. Until then, the two Koreas had not addressed such issues except for a few cases in 1984 and 1985. Moreover, cultural exchanges between the two Koreas considerably

Table 10.1 Inter-Korean dialogue, 1971–2015 (unit: frequency)

Subject\Year	71	72	73	74	75	76	77	79	80	84	85	86	87	88	89	90	91	92	93	94
Politics		4	7	6	2			3	10		2			8	7	15	12	80	4	10
Military																				
Economy										1	4									
Humanitarian Cooperation	18	32	4	12	8	6	5			2	6				8	2		8		
Sociocultural Exchanges								4		3	1	2	1		9	7	7			
Total	18	36	11	18	10	6	5	7	10	6	13	2	1	8	24	24	19	88	4	10

Subject\Year	95	97	98	99	00	01	02	03	04	05	06	07	08	09	10	11	12	13	14	15
Politics		7	4	8	18	2	4	5	2	10	5	13						1	2	3
Military					4	2	9	6	5	3	4	11	2		1	1			1	
Economy					3	3	14	17	13	11	8	22	3	4	3			22	3	1
Humanitarian Cooperation	3	4	1		2	1	3	7	2	4	3	3		2	3			1	1	1
Sociocultural Exchanges							2	1	1	6	3	6	1						1	
Total	3	11	5	8	27	8	32	36	23	34	23	55	6	6	7	1	0	24	8	5

Source: Ministry of Unification. Available at www.unikorea.go.kr/content.do?cmsid=3099.

increased during this period. Figure 10.1 demonstrates that, beginning in 2000, an increasing number of families separated by the Korean War were able to hold reunions every year. As illustrated in Figure 10.2, the number of South Korean visitors to North Korea sharply increased as well. These numbers amplify when Figure 10.2 includes South Koreans who regularly visited the Kaesong Industrial Complex and toured Mt. Geumgang. Between 2005 and 2015, an average of 100,000 South Koreans visited the KIC annually. Starting in 1998, approximately 2 million South Koreans visited Mt. Geumgang until July 2008, when the tour project suddenly ended due to the shooting death of a South Korean tourist by a North Korean soldier. In addition, more than 100,000 South Koreans toured the two most historical North Korean cities, Kaesong and Pyongyang in the mid-2000s (Ministry of Unification). As depicted in Figure 10.3, North Korean visitors to South Korea also notably increased, although the numbers are quite small.

Inter-Korean economic relations markedly improved as well. As illustrated in Figure 10.4, inter-Korean trade sharply grew during this time period. In 1998, the volume of inter-Korean trade was approximately $221 million, but this number expanded to $1.79 billion in 2007. This amount almost comprised one-third of North Korea's foreign trade in 2007, which was equivalent to the size of Soviet Union–North Korean trade that peaked in 1988 (Agov 2016, 382). As Figure 10.5 shows, moreover, both the South Korean government and private organizations provided North Korea with approximately $1.68 billion in aid between 1998 and 2007.

The creation of the Kaesong Industrial Complex was an unprecedented economic cooperation project between South and North Korea. After several years of negotiations, the two Koreas began to build the KIC in June 2003 and completed the first-phase of construction in October 2007 (Kim 2014, 263–4). This industrial park is located inside North Korea just

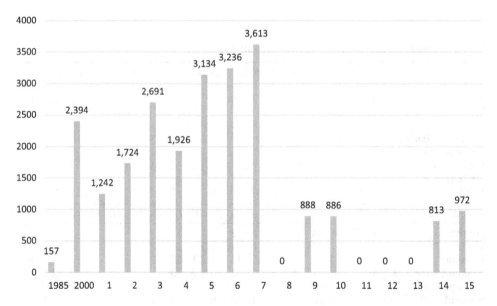

Figure 10.1 Government-led reunions of separated families, 1985–2015 (unit: person)

Source: Ministry of Unification. Available at www.unikorea.go.kr/content.do?cmsid=3099.

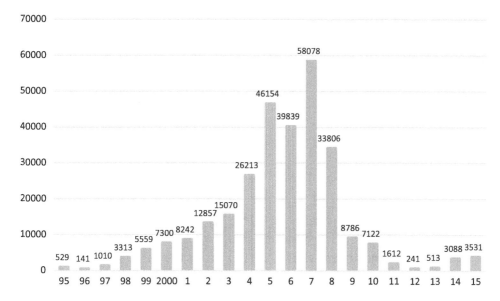

Figure 10.2 Number of South Korean visitors to North Korea, 1995–2015

Source: Ministry of Unification. Available at www.unikorea.go.kr/content.do?cmsid=3099.

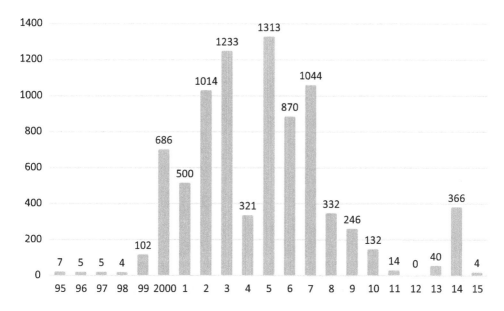

Figure 10.3 Number of North Korean visitors to South Korea, 1995–2015

Sources: Korea Tourism Organization. Available at http://kto.visitkorea.or.kr/kor/notice/data/statis/profit/board/view.
kto?id=423699&isNotice=true&instanceId=294&rnum=0; Ministry of Unification www.unikorea.go.kr/content.
do?cmsid=3099.

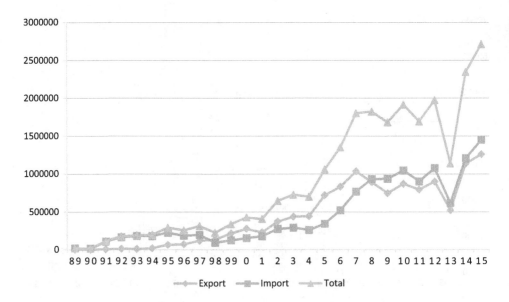

Figure 10.4 Inter-Korean trade volume, 1989–2015 (unit: US$ 1,000)

Source: Korea International Trade Association. Available at http://stat.kita.net/stat/nks/sum/SumTotalImpExpList. screen.

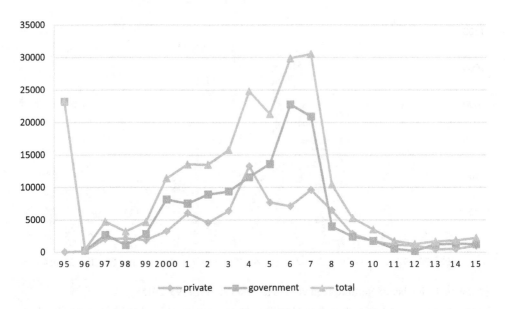

Figure 10.5 South Korea's aid to North Korea, 1995–2015 (unit: US$ 10,000)

Sources: Statistics Korea; Ministry of Unification. Available at www.unikorea.go.kr/content.do?cmsid=3099.

across the west end of the DMZ. This joint venture was based on the complementary advantages that the two Koreas had: the North's cheap labor and the South's capital and know-how for manufacturing consumer goods for export. North Korean workers employed in the KIC were paid $65 per month. South Korean companies, which had incentives, including political risk insurance from the ROK government, could manufacture products using North Korean cheap labor. Since all products manufactured in the industrial complex were exported to South Korea for sale, this project was the largest contributor to inter-Korean trade (*BBC News* 2016). As illuminated in Table 10.2, the number of North Korean workers continued to grow from 6,013 in 2005 to 54,988 in 2015. Its production also significantly increased from approximately $15 million in 2005 to $563 million in 2015.

In addition, South Korean perception of North Korea significantly improved during the 1998–2007 period, as depicted in Figure 10.6. In 1998, 24.8 percent of South Korean respondents perceived North Korea as a cooperative partner, and this number grew to 56.6 percent in 2007. On the other hand, 40.6 percent of South Koreans regarded North Korea as an object for alert in 1998, though this figure drastically decreased to 11.8 percent in 2007.

A key reason for the improved relationship between South and North Korea during the 1998–2007 period was the engagement policy adopted by two progressive South Korean presidents, Kim Dae-jung (1998–2003) and Roh Moo-hyun (2003–2008). Also important was Kim Jong-il's positive response to the engagement policy, although the DPRK regime had initially regarded the policy as a malevolent political tool for achieving Korean unification through South Korean absorption (Kim 2014, 213–14). President Kim Dae-jung, who had long been a political dissident under authoritarian rule, had a clear vision for inter-Korean reconciliation and peaceful unification through his so-called Sunshine Policy. The term 'Sunshine Policy' originated from Aesop's Fables involving the North Wind and the Sun. In that story, a passing traveler wrapped his cloak tighter to keep warm from a strong wind, but when he was exposed to sunshine, he naturally took his cloak off due to the heat. Based on this concept, the Kim Dae-jung administration adopted a warmer policy of reconciliation and cooperation toward North Korea, rather than keeping alive the bitter wind of Cold War confrontation. President Roh Moo-hyun also continued his predecessor's engagement policy, despite strong domestic opposition from conservatives in South Korea, by using a different term – the 'Peace and Prosperity' policy. The eruption of the second nuclear crisis in 2002–2003 prompted the Roh administration to exert pressure on North Korea via the Six-Party Talks to give up its nuclear program. The Roh government, however, paid more

Table 10.2 Kaesong Industrial Complex statistics, 2005–2015 (unit: US$ 10,000)

Year	2005	2006	2007	2008	2009	2010	2011	2012	2013	2014	2015
Company Number	18	30	65	93	117	121	123	123	123	125	125
DPRK Workers	6,013	11,160	22,538	38,931	42,561	46,284	49,866	53,448	52,329	53,947	54,988
ROK Workers	507	791	785	1,055	935	804	776	786	757	815	820
Amount of Production	1,491	7,373	18,478	25,142	25,648	32,332	40,185	46,950	22,378	46,997	56,330

Source: Ministry of Unification. Available at www.unikorea.go.kr/content.do?cmsid=3099.

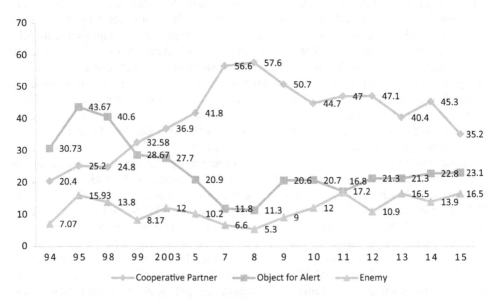

Figure 10.6 South Koreans' perception of North Korea, 1994–2015 (unit: percent)

Sources: Korea Institute for National Unification. Available at www.kinu.or.kr/www/jsp/prg/stats/PollList.jsp; Institute for Peace and Unification Studies. Available at http://tongil.snu.ac.kr.

attention to achieving inter-Korean reconciliation through improving ties and increasing interdependence (Heo and Roehrig 2014, 44).

The Sunshine Policy encompassed five central goals. The first goal was to prevent the outbreak of any war or military conflicts on the Korean Peninsula. As he had witnessed during the Korean War, President Kim Dae-jung firmly rejected war as destructive, and any attempt to unify Korea through violence would trigger another national division by planting the seeds of resentment. Second, the Kim Dae-jung government aimed at achieving de facto or quasi-unification as the first step toward the accomplishment of de jure or institutional unification. He assumed that legal unification could take a much longer time due to realistic restraints, such as sharply differing political systems of the two Koreas. The Kim administration aspired to create de facto unification "in which exchanges of personnel, goods, and services are fully activated and confidence-building and arms control can materialize." It was necessary for the two Koreas to first learn peaceful coexistence through exchanges and cooperation before attempting legal or institutional unification.

Third, rather than pushing for the North Korea's regime collapse, the Kim Dae-jung administration intended to foster incremental changes in North Korea via a policy of engagement and accommodation. It hoped that the increased exchanges and cooperation would promote changes in North Korea's institutions, behaviors, and public opinion, thus leading to reforms and ultimately peaceful coexistence and de facto unification. Fourth, South Korea aimed to be a central player in handling the Korean problem and the larger international security environment surrounding the Korean Peninsula. The Kim Dae-jung government clearly perceived that the four major powers in East Asia – the United States, China, Japan, and Russia – could not dictate a Korean solution, although he recognized their important roles in the region's affairs. Under this perception, the Kim government sought to dismantle Cold War structures by encouraging improved relations between former adversary states, such as the US–DPRK and Japan–DPRK. Thus, the Sunshine Policy posited that the realignment of the international environment could lead North Korea to become "a normal state, which is an essential prerequisite for improved inter-Korean relations and peace on the Korean Penin-sula." Finally, President Kim Dae-jung paid much attention to gaining a national domestic consensus and wide-ranging political support to implement the policy of reconciliation and cooperation. Kim believed that the "de-politicization of the North Korea issue, coupled with appropriate education and persuasion, may well mitigate domestic opposition, ultimately leading to national consensus and bipartisan political support" (Moon and Boo 2012, 130–6).

To achieve these ideals, the Kim Dae-jung government adopted "flexible dualism" as an important operating principle of the Sunshine Policy. This principle can be summarized as follows: "(1) Easy tasks first, and difficult tasks later; (2) Economy first, politics later; (3) Non-governmental organizations first, government later; and (4) Give first, and take later" (Moon and Boo 2012, 137). Out of these four components, the separation of politics and economics was the essence of flexible dualism. Due to the primacy of politics and its linkage to the economy, it was hard for former ROK governments to improve inter-Korean rela-tions in a consistent and meaningful manner. Although inter-Korean relations temporarily improved via socio-economic exchanges, these improvements did not continue long due to North Korea's intermittent military provocation or political tensions between the two Koreas. This interaction amplified the vicious cycle of distrust and enmity. To cut off this negative mechanism, the Kim administration continued to promote socio-economic exchanges and cooperation, even though North Korea took provocative military and political actions. Fol-lowing this principle, the Kim government maintained economic exchanges and cooperation despite the infiltration of North Korean submarines in the South, the resumption of a negative propaganda campaign by the North, and the naval skirmishes in the Yellow Sea.

Despite its evident merits, the Sunshine Policy had some shortcomings and limitations. First, a cash-for-summit scandal showed the corrupt side of the Sunshine Policy and seri-ously damaged President Kim Dae-jung's image and achievements. In June 2003, a special investigation revealed that the Kim government paid $500 million to Pyongyang before the June 2000 summit. $400 million was regarded as legitimate business investment in North Korea, but $100 million was sent by the South Korean government as an incentive for the Korean summit (*BBC News* 2003). It turned out that the historic summit, which had been viewed as a diplomatic breakthrough, was the outcome of a bribe. This scandal created a political storm in South Korean society. The head of Hyundai Asan, Jung Mong-heon, who had been charged with his involvement in the secret dealings with North Korea, committed suicide during the scandal (*Joongang Ilbo* 2003).

Second, some critics argue that the Sunshine Policy failed to transform North Korean society and its belligerent behavior during the 1998–2007 period. Although South Korea provided North Korea with a huge amount of aid, the North did not take reciprocal actions in response to the South's cooperative measures. Rather than opening its society, the DPRK regime still paid enormous attention to regime survival and continued to violate human rights (Hwang 2008, 102). In June 2002, two DPRK vessels crossed the Northern Limit Line, which had been considered an inter-Korean border in the Yellow Sea, and sparked a naval clash with South Korean vessels (Kirk 2002). In addition, the DPRK sought to develop weapons of mass destruction. Between the mid-1990s and the early 2000s North Korea provided mis-sile parts to Pakistan in return for gaining uranium-based nuclear technology (Sanger 2002). North Korea's clandestine uranium enrichment program in October 2002 triggered the sec-ond nuclear crisis, culminating in DPRK's withdrawal from the Nuclear Non-proliferation

Treaty in January 2003. North Korea also conducted its first underground nuclear test in October 2006 and a long-range Daepodong-2 missile test in July 2006 (Davenport 2016).

Moreover, unlike President Roh's *Nordpolitik*, President Kim Dae-jung's Sunshine Policy sparked a polarization of the South Korean public. Despite its initially high popularity, Kim's engagement policy continually faced harsh criticisms by ROK conservative politicians and citizens. Among the charges were that the Kim government, characterized as a pro-North Korea leftist regime, had damaged the ROK's national identity by unilaterally providing economic aid to the brutal North Korean dictatorship. South Korean aid only helped the dictatorial regime to survive and to develop weapons of mass destruction targeted at South Korea. These denunciations also applied to the Roh Moo-hyun administration, which had continued Kim's engagement policy toward North Korea. Facing this opposition, the two progressive governments pushed for their policies, as opposed to making every effort to persuade conservatives through open discussions. The lack of domestic consensus and support, therefore, significantly weakened the effectiveness of two governments' engagement policy toward North Korea (Shin 2013).

The United States also played a crucial role in influencing inter-Korean relations during this period in both positive and negative ways. Under a hawkish Republican-dominated Congress, US President Bill Clinton was not very supportive of the Sunshine Policy. In November 1998, he appointed former Secretary of Defense William Perry, who had in 1994 argued for surgical airstrikes on North Korea's nuclear facilities, as North Korea Policy Coordinator. Facing North Korea's launching of a Daepodong-1 ballistic missile in August 1998, President Clinton asked Perry to conduct a comprehensive review of US policy toward North Korea. Under these circumstances, it was natural to expect that the United States would take a more hardline approach to the DPRK. Thus ROK President Kim Dae-jung and his senior presidential secretary for foreign and security affairs, Im Dong-won, made great efforts to persuade Perry to shift away from his hawkish attitude toward North Korea (Im 2015, 305–29). As a result of this persuasion, in October 1999, Perry issued a report recommending a two-path strategy, under which if the DPRK removed its nuclear and missile threats, the United States would normalize relations with the DPRK and lift sanctions that had long constrained trade with the DPRK, among other positive steps. Otherwise, the United States and its allies would have to take negative actions to promote their security and contain the North Korean threat.[3] Under this so-called Perry Process, the two Koreas were able to hold their first inter-Korean summit in June 2000. The Clinton administration then invited DPRK Vice Marshall Cho Myung-rok to the White House in October 2000 to discuss improvements in US–DPRK relations. Two weeks later, US Secretary of State Madeleine Albright visited Pyongyang to meet with Kim Jong-il. Therefore, US support of Sunshine Policy contributed greatly to the improvement of inter-Korean relations.

On the other hand, the inauguration of President George W. Bush in February 2001 had a negative impact on inter-Korean relations. In a US–ROK summit in March 2001, President Kim Dae-jung wanted President Bush to endorse his Sunshine Policy toward North Korea, but Bush reacted with skepticism. Regarding Clinton's engagement policy as a failure, the Bush administration even identified North Korea as a part of an "axis of evil" and adopted an aggressive policy based on pressure and sanctions. Due to America's hawkish stance on North Korea, the DPRK government temporarily terminated talks with South Korea. If the United States had continued its engagement policy toward North Korea, inter-Korean relations could have improved significantly. During the Bush administration's first term (2001–2004), the ROK government had difficulty in handling US opposition to the Sunshine Policy. Interestingly, President Roh Moo-hyun was able to have a summit with North Korean leader

Kim Jong-il in October 2007, but only after the Bush government had relaxed its confrontational policy toward North Korea in its second term (Shin 2013, 18).

Newly confrontational era, 2008–2016

Unlike during the previous era, the 2008–2016 period witnessed a sharply worsening relationship between South and North Korea. The frequency of inter-Korean dialogue significantly dropped starting in 2008. As demonstrated in Table 10.1, the two Koreas had held bilateral talks approximately 25 times on average during the 1998–2007 era, but this number decreased to seven during this period. In the previous period, the two governments addressed all five subject areas in their talks, while during the 2008–2015 period, they scarcely dealt with politics, military issues, and socio-economic exchanges. Needless to say, top leaders of the two Koreas held no summits during this confrontational period.

In terms of human exchanges, Figure 10.1 illustrates that the total number of separated families who made reunions plummeted from 19,960 in 2000–2007 to 3,559 in 2008–2015. As viewed in Figure 10.2 and 10.3, the number of South Korean visitors to North Korea shrank drastically, and vice versa. 58,078 South Koreans visited the North in 2007, but this figure dropped to 241 in 2012 and rebounded to 3,531 in 2015. While 1,313 North Koreans visited South Korea in 2005, only four people did so in 2015.

Inter-Korean economic relations also suffered a significant downturn during this period. Thanks to the continual operation of the Kaesong Industrial Complex, the volume of inter-Korean trade increased from about $1.8 billion in 2007 to $2.7 billion in 2015, as shown in Figure 10.4 and Table 10.2. After May 24, 2010, however, South Korea nearly terminated trade with North Korea, except for inter-Korean trade through the KIC. Inter-Korean trade, moreover, stopped due to the shutdown of the industrial park in February 2016. The amount of South Korean aid to North Korea also notably decreased from $305 million in 2007, to $35.3 million in 2010, and to $22.2 million in 2015, as depicted in Figure 10.5.

Furthermore, South Koreans' perception of North Korea deteriorated during this period. Figure 10.6 illuminates that 56.6 percent of South Korean respondents considered the North a cooperative partner in 2007, but this figure continually diminished to 47 percent in 2011 and 35.2 percent in 2015. On the other hand, 11.8 percent of South Korean respondents regarded North Korea as an object for alert in 2007, and this feeling increased to 17.2 percent in 2011 and 23.1 percent in 2015. Compared to the previous era, therefore, the 2008–2016 period saw a comprehensive decline in inter-Korean relations.

A main reason for this worsening inter-Korean relationship was the drastic shift of ROK government's North Korea policy from engagement to a more confrontational approach. In February 2008, new President Lee Myung-bak reversed the engagement policy of the last decade by the Kim Dae-jung and Roh Moo-hyun administrations. President Lee criticized the two previous governments for failing to change North Korean behavior despite a significant amount of economic aid to the North. As noted before, South Korea provided approximately $1.68 billion to North Korea during the 1998–2007 period, but the DPRK did not cease its provocative acts, particularly its first nuclear test and a long-range ballistic missile (Daepodong-2) test in 2006. The Lee administration postulated that North Korea did not feel bound to change its policies, because the ROK government continued to offer economic aid regardless of North Korea's behavior. Given this rationale, the Lee government embraced a new policy initiative, the so-called Denuclearization, Openness and 3000, which highlighted the principle of reciprocity. This new policy posited that if North Korea gave up its nuclear programs, South Korea would "provide assistance to North Korea in cooperation with the international community to help it attain $3,000 in per capita income within 10 years" (Yoon 2008). Thus North Korea's denuclearization became a precondition to economic assistance. The ROK government regarded this new policy as a revised engagement based on the reciprocity principle, but the DPRK regime perceived it as a hostile policy and denounced the Lee government's approach.

In addition, North Korean human rights violations became a grave obstacle to inter-Korean relations. The Lee Myung-bak administration attached great importance to North Korea's human rights atrocities. In an attempt to keep open the channels of dialogue with North Korea, the two previous ROK governments had avoided raising these issues because they would likely anger the DPRK regime. President Lee, however, believed that it was necessary for the ROK government to bring up the issue in order to press for human rights reforms. At the time, the international community often blamed the DPRK regime for seriously violating human rights and refusing to cooperate with the UN Human Rights Commissioner or special investigators (Petrov 2009).

Another key reason for the deteriorated inter-Korean relationship is a series of North Korean provocations taken after the Lee Myung-bak government's adoption of the conditional engagement policy. In March 2008, the DPRK regime began to denounce the Lee government as a "reactionary warmongering clique." In July 2008, a South Korean tourist, Park Wang-ja, was shot to death by a North Korean soldier at the Mt. Geumgang resort. The DPRK denied South Korea's request for a joint investigation about the incident, while defending the shooting as a self-defense measure. This North Korean justification prompted the ROK government to terminate tours to the North. In addition, the DPRK conducted an Unha-2 three-stage rocket test in April 2009 and its second nuclear test in May 2009. This was a clear violation of UN Security Council Resolution 1718, passed after North Korea's first nuclear test. In response to these belligerent acts, the UN Security Council imposed more economic sanctions, including an expanded arms embargo on the DPRK regime in June 2009. Immediately after these punitive acts, North Korea announced that it had begun a uranium enrichment program to produce fuel for a light-water reactor (Agov 2016, 383–4). All of these incidents negatively impacted inter-Korean relations.

The nadir of inter-Korean relations occurred in 2010 due to two military incidents. The first was the sinking of the South Korean corvette *Cheonan* on March 26, the deaths of 46 out of 104 crew members. According to a Joint Civilian-Military Investigation Group, which consisted of experts from the United States, the United Kingdom, Australia, Sweden, and South Korea, the *Cheonan* was sunk by a North Korean torpedo. Based on this conclusion, the Lee Myung-bak government adopted the so-called May 24 Measures, including "a complete ban on navigation by North Korean vessels in South Korea's territorial waters, a suspension of inter-Korean trade and aid to the North, and a ban on South Korean visitors to North Korea" (Ku 2015, 258). The DPRK, which had denied its involvement in the *Cheonan* sinking, also responded with punitive measures, as cutting off all ties with the South except for the operation of the KIC. The second incident was North Korea's shelling on November 23 of Yeonpyeong Island, which is located 12 km off the North Korean coast. This was the first North Korean artillery attack on South Korean territory since the end of the Korean War, and it killed four South Koreans, injured 19, and inflicted substantial property damage. Responding to this aggressive act, the ROK military fired back on DPRK military facilities and conducted formerly scheduled but expanded joint naval exercises with the United States in the Yellow Sea.

It is necessary to note that North Korea's internal power transition played a critical role in further stimulating that nation's provocative actions. After Kim Jong-il suffered stroke in

August 2008, the DPRK regime promptly sought to transfer power to his son, Kim Jong-un. During this process, the DPRK made great efforts to promote the new leader's legitimacy by showing off his military accomplishments, including the launch of a long-range missile, a nuclear test in 2009, and aggressive actions toward South Korea in 2010. For regime security, it was vital for Kim Jong-un to gain strong support from the North Korean military, which was the most powerful institution in the nation. Before he came to power in 1994, Kim Jong-il had adequate time to learn how to rule by serving key positions in the Korean Workers' Party and the North Korean government. However, Kim Jong-un, who was then in the mid-20s, had no actual experience in the political, governmental, and military sectors. The death of Kim Jong-il in December 2011 made it even more imperative for the DPRK to take provocative acts in order to bolster the new leader's political legitimacy and consolidate domestic unity.

On top of this sudden leadership transition, the loosening of North Korea's internal ruling regime, caused by the partial adoption of the market system, provided another motive for its belligerent behavior. Since the early 2000s, the DPRK allowed markets to function within North Korea's communist economic system, because the nation could no longer provide the public with food and other necessary goods. These market activities brought about the emergence of private entrepreneurs and the spread of individualistic propensities among the North Korean public, which contradicted North Korea's communist ideology. This phenomenon created a threat to regime security. In addition, the DPRK has been anxious about regime stability due to increased human and economic exchanges between the two Koreas, primarily triggered by South Korea's engagement policy from 1998–2007 (Kim 2014, 296–9).

Given these fears, the DPRK continued its provocations in the 2010s. In April 2012, North Korea launched a rocket, which may have been a long-range missile test that was banned under UN resolutions. This rocket launch, though failed, led to the annulment of the US–North Korea Leap Day Agreement made on February 29, 2012, in which North Korea promised to suspend nuclear and missile tests in return for receiving food and economic aid from the United States (Panda 2016). In December 2012, the DPRK successfully launched a three-stage rocket, and this was a clear violation of UN resolutions. Responding to these North Korean acts, the UN Security Council in January 2013 adopted another resolution condemning the missile launch and approving harsher sanctions. While criticizing these UN sanctions, North Korea further escalated tensions by conducting a third nuclear test in February 2013. The DPRK also cut off all 14 military hotlines between the two Koreas and ordered its missile units ready to attack the American mainland and South Korea. Moreover, the DPRK declared the annulment of the armistice agreement that had ended the Korean War in 1953 (Ku 2013). In April 2013, North Korea closed entry to the Kaesong Industrial Complex, which was an important symbol of inter-Korean economic cooperation, although it reopened five months later.

Amidst these tensions, ROK President Park Geun-hye (2013–2017) initially took a middle ground between the pro-engagement and hardline stances of her predecessors, given the perception that neither approach has altered North Korean behavior. The first pillar of her approach was to maintain a strong deterrence against Pyongyang's provocations. The second pillar was to focus on "engagement diplomacy based on the principle of *Trustpolitik* with the aim of transforming the atmosphere of suspicion and conflict into one of confidence and cooperation" (Lee and Berger 2015). The pro-active trust building involved Park's promise to implement many inter-Korean initiatives, including the rejuvenation of humanitarian aid to North Korea, the resumption of social and cultural exchanges, the formation of "South-North Exchange and Cooperation Offices" in Seoul and Pyongyang, and the establishment of a peace park in the DMZ. Park also desired to have a summit meeting with the North Korean leader Kim Jong-un. As time went by, however, Park's policy placed more emphasis on changing North Korean behavior through overt pressure than on initiating a mutual trust-building process. A real *Trustpolitik* was not fully implemented, as North Korea continued to take provocative acts, including a landmine explosion that wounded two South Korean soldiers in the DMZ in August 2015 and two additional nuclear tests in January and September 2016. After these incidents, the Park government restarted anti-North Korean propaganda broadcasts for the first time since 2004 and finally shut down the KIC, the symbol of inter-Korean cooperation. It is also important to note that between 2008 and 2016, the ROK's progressive parties and citizens blamed the two conservative governments for further aggravating inter-Korean relations. Those progressives believed that the ROK's more confrontational approaches to North Korea had pushed the DRPK regime to be more aggressive and destabilized the security environment surrounding the Korean Peninsula. This polarization of public opinion in South Korea continued to seriously impede the adoption and implementation of a consistent and effective North Korea policy by ROK governments.

In addition to leadership changes and altered domestic contexts, a significant structural change in East Asia – the intensification of the US–China rivalry – also exerted significant influence on inter-Korean relations. The rise of China has been an important topic of discourse among US pundits since the 1990s. After 2009, this issue assumed new importance as China adopted a more assertive foreign policy, particularly on territorial disputes with Japan and other ASEAN (Association of Southeast Asian Nations) countries, such as the Philippines and Vietnam. Some experts believe that Chinese elites wanted to take advantage of the perceived decline of American power after the serious financial crisis in 2008. Unlike the United States, China was able to handle the recession without major economic disruption due to its increased domestic investment and large foreign currency reserves. Chinese nationalism grew thanks to the successful 2008 Beijing Olympics (Saunders 2014, 160–3). To check and balance growing Chinese power, the United States adopted a so-called pivot to Asia in December 2011. As part of this approach, the United States has strengthened its allied relationships with Japan, Australia, and the Philippines as well as its partnerships with Vietnam, India, and even Myanmar. Despite large defense budget cuts, the United States has maintained strong military presence in the East Asian region and developed strategic doctrines, such as the concept of the Air-Sea Battle. Though rejected by the Donald Trump administration, President Obama tried to balance the powerful Chinese economy by signing the Trans-Pacific Partnership (TPP), a trade agreement with eleven countries in the Asia-Pacific region.

As the US–China rivalry intensified, North Korea gained extra room to maneuver in its foreign policy. The DPRK continued the development of nuclear and missile programs, thus worsening inter-Korean relations. As noted before, UN Security Council has imposed harsh sanctions on North Korea in reaction to the nation's provocative nuclear and missile adventurism. To maximize the efficiency of the sanctions, it has been essential for China, which provides more than 90 percent of oil resources to North Korea, to push the DPRK to give up its provocations. However, the increased US–China rivalry in East Asia has hampered mutual cooperation between the two great powers in handling the North Korean nuclear/missile problem. Although opposing North Korea's provocative behavior, China has no strong incentives to punish its ideological and geostrategic ally, as such action would be harmful to Chinese national interests. China would never allow the DPRK regime to collapse as a result of sanctions, because that could produce a horrible refugee crisis along with the extensive DPRK–China border. As shown by the Syrian refugee crisis, such massive humanitarian crises have severe economic and political ramifications. It is also widely known that China fears a border with a unified Korea in which a pro-American government rules and US military forces are present. Therefore, North Korean leaders, who clearly understand China's stance on the Korean Peninsula, have not been seriously bounded by external pressure, including economic sanctions.

Prospects for Korean reunification

As seen thus far, inter-Korean relations have evolved with significant vacillations since the establishment of the two Koreas in 1948, given dynamic interactions among top leaders, changing domestic conditions, and international structures. This analysis naturally leads to an important question: Is there a high possibility of achieving Korean reunification in the foreseeable future? In addressing this question, this section pays special attention to the following three interrelated facets – the necessity of unification, the methods of unification, and the challenges on the way to unification.

First of all, it would be important to have a broad consensus regarding why Korean reunification is necessary. In March 2014, former President Park Guen-hye mentioned that Korean reunification would bring a bonanza. As such, economic and strategic considerations could be substantial factors for justifying unification. A unified Korea would become an economic giant if the nation could effectively utilize the South's capital and technology as well as the North's cheap labor and rich natural resources (Lee 2015). This enhanced economic power could be converted into military capabilities in the long run, thus helping a unified Korea stand up to powerful neighbors such as China and Japan. On the other hand, some critics might claim that unification could bring a painful outcome to the Korean people, because of its tremendous economic costs estimated to exceed $2.7 trillion, which was larger than Germany's unification expenses (Kim 2015). Despite the significance of these practical considerations, it would be essential to place a great weight on humanitarian and peaceful benefits of Korean reunification (Yoon 2013). As detailed in Chapter 9, a large number of North Koreans have long suffered from the lack of freedom, human rights violations, political oppression, and severe economic hardships. A peaceful reunification would free North Koreans from such harsh suffering. Moreover, successful inter-Korean reconciliation would be able to have a spillover effect in the East Asian region, which has been fraught with historical animosity, mutual distrust, and arms races. A peace-loving, unified Korea could serve as a catalyst for promoting interstate reconciliation between former adversary nations, such as Korea and Japan, as well as China and Japan, thereby contributing to the construction of a peaceful East Asian community.

Second, with these important motives for unification in mind, it appears that there are three ways of achieving Korean reunification – by force, by absorption, or by negotiation. The Vietnamese case falls into the category of unification by force, when communist North Vietnam militarily conquered the capitalist South Vietnam in 1975. North Korea also invaded the South in 1950, but it failed to unify the nation due mainly to the UN intervention led by US forces. After the Korean War, the ROK's first president, Rhee Syngman, supported a march to the North for unification, but he did not actually implement such aggressive policy. Rather, Rhee sought to suppress domestic political opponents and maximize US military aid by heightening tensions on the Korean Peninsula (Jung and Rector 2012). North Korea showed its will to achieve unification by force, but in the current context, such option does not seem feasible to both sides. North Korea has little military and economic capabilities with which to conquer the South, while South Korea has no motive for unification by force, as clearly stipulated in its constitution: "The Republic of Korea shall seek unification and shall formulate and carry out a policy of *peaceful* unification based on the principles of free-dom and democracy."[4] Additionally, the United States and China, the two most influential outside nations on the Korean Peninsula, would not support unification by force. Therefore, such a policy appears to be a remote possibility, except in the cases of a suicidal attack by North Korea caused by power struggle among North Korean elites or preemptive American strikes on North Korea's nuclear facilities, with the subsequent outbreak of an all-out war on the Korean Peninsula.

As shown by German unification in 1990, unification through absorption has been a plau-sible option since the early 1990s. At the time, South Korea ascended to a middle power status based on its rapid economic growth, while North Korea's economic and security con-ditions plunged into darkness. As noted before, North Korea's trade volume plummeted due to the collapse of its long trade partners in the Soviet Union and East European communist nations. President Bill Clinton was at the brink of conducting preemptive airstrikes on North Korea's nuclear facilities in 1994, although the nuclear crisis had a peaceful resolution by former US President Jimmy Carter's mediation. Furthermore, added to this predicament were the sudden death of the founder of North Korea, Kim Il-sung, in July 1994 and a series of natural disasters, such as severe drought and flooding in mid-1990s. Under these harsh circumstances, it was widely believed that the North Korean regime would collapse, and South Korea could take over the North. This scenario, however, did not occur. Kim Jong-il, a son of Kim Il-sung, succeeded in power in 1997, and the regime survived, showing sig-nificant resilience despite horrible economic conditions. South Korea's progressive govern-ments between 1998 and 2007 did not seek unification by absorption. Instead, they helped the DPRK to move toward economic reforms through the Sunshine Policy. The discourse on unification through absorption once more became prevalent in South Korean society when Kim Jong-il had a stroke in August 2008 and suddenly died in December 2011. Many expected that it would be extremely hard for Kim Jong-un to consolidate his power base since he was so young and had little political and military experience. However, Kim Jong-un has sustained his regime since April 2012 while pursuing the advancement of nuclear/missile capabilities and economic development simultaneously. The possibility of a regime collapse in North Korea currently still exists due to continual economic stagnation and deep-ening international economic sanctions caused by the nation's nuclear/missile adventurism. Nevertheless, North Korean regime collapse and subsequent Korean reunification through absorption will not easily take place for the foreseeable future, as long as China continues to place a high strategic value on North Korea and maintains its support for the DPRK regime.

Korean reunification also can be achieved by negotiations between the Korean govern-ments. Since the 1970s, North Korea has proposed to achieve Korean reunification through the formation of a federation, referred to as "Democratic Confederal Republic of *Goryeo*." Prior to this federation stage, the two Koreas would be required to alleviate military ten-sions and increase mutual exchanges and cooperation. As a precondition to this unification formula, however, North Korea requested the withdrawal of US forces from South Korea, the cessation of US–ROK joint military trainings, and the ROK's departure from the US nuclear umbrella. These demands were not acceptable to South Koreans who maintained strong suspicions of North Korea's real intensions (Kim 2014, 351–9). Meanwhile, given South Korea's enhanced economic capabilities, ROK President Roh Tae-woo proposed in 1988 his "Unification Formula for the Korean National Community," which was a three-stage approach to unification – confidence building by cooperation, a confederation with two separate states and governments, and the subsequent establishment of a fully unified government (Koh 2000, 5). Based on this proposal, President Kim Dae-jung supported another three-stage unification formula – the formation of a Korean confederation followed by a federation, and then complete unification. Without having confidence building as a separate stage, Kim intended to realize a de facto unification under a Korean confederation in which the two Koreas could build confidence (Jung and Rector 2012, 498). As mentioned earlier, Roh's and Kim's unification policies brought about actual improvements in inter-Korean relations. Thus this confederal strategy seems the most desirable method toward Korean reunification, as the two Koreas could undertake their own unification initiative through a process that could minimize the risk of military confrontation on the Korean Peninsula. However, it seems necessary to point out the potential difficulty of reaching an agreement regarding unification through negotiations between the two Korean governments. It is hard to imagine that North Korean leaders would accept the South's democracy and capitalism as the basis for a unified Korea. In the same vein, it would be implausible for South Koreans to allow DPRK systems and elites to maintain their roles and privileges after unification. It is also needless to say that the North Korean public, who has experienced acute sufferings from the harsh rule of DPRK leaders, would retaliate against their former leaders in a brutal manner. The ongoing North Korean nuclear/missile standoff with the international community makes it harder for the two Korean governments to move toward unification through negotiations.

Given these three methods of Korean reunification, it is worth pointing out both the internal and external challenges in the way of unification. The first challenge would be the decline of South Koreans' aspiration for unification and the sharply divided public opinion within South Korean society regarding how to handle North Korea. In 2007, 63.8 percent of Korean respondents agreed that unification is *necessary*, and 34.4 percent said that unification is *very necessary*. In 2016, however, these numbers notably decreased to 53.4 percent and 19.5 percent, respectively (Jung et al. 2017, 33). In addition, conservatives place great emphasis on a hardline policy toward North Korea, which includes imposing harsh economic sanctions and strengthening strategic deterrence measures. Conservatives believe that such a hawkish approach could bring about North Korean regime collapse, which would lead to unification by the South's absorption of the North. On the other hand, progressives argue that, prior to political unification, it is essential to reach a de facto unification under which South and North Koreans freely visit each other and conduct business and other daily activities without constraints. To this end, progressives claim that the ROK government should employ an engagement policy toward North Korea rather than maintaining a confrontational approach. Therefore, the diminishing desire for unification and the ideological polarization in terms of the ROK's approach to North Korea and reunification will hinder the formation of effective policy measures and their successful implementation.

As often emphasized, North Korean nuclear and missile adventurism is a serious impediment to peaceful Korean reunification. Many believe that the Kim Jong-un regime will not give up its zeal for nuclear/missile development. As long as this confrontational attitude persists, North Korea could not receive full support from South Korea and the international community in improving its dire economic conditions. As a corollary, the Kim Jung-un regime's *byongjin* policy, which aims at developing nuclear weapons and economic growth simultaneously, cannot move forward. In this circumstance, it would be hard to imagine that the two Koreas could accomplish a peaceful, negotiated transition to unification. Furthermore, it could be extremely dangerous if unification occurs as a result of the North Korean regime collapse in the midst of a power struggle or people's uprisings. This could result in a humanitarian disaster, a refugee crisis, civil war, and unsecured nuclear weapons. The situation could be even more precarious if the Chinese military intervenes in North Korea to stabilize China's southern border (Lind 2015).

Moving beyond these internal elements, external challenges operate to prevent Korean reunification. For peaceful unification, it would be indispensable for Koreans to gain support from the United States and China, the two most influential countries to the Korean Peninsula. A key problem is, however, that the United States and China basically prefer the *status quo* on the Korean Peninsula as opposed to dramatic changes spawned by unification. The United States has concerns over the possibility that a unified Korea would become a pro-Chinese nation for economic reasons and/or counter the US–Japan alliance due to a rise of Korean nationalism based on anti-Japanese sentiment. This could significantly weaken US influence in East Asia vis-à-vis a rising China, thus hampering America's global and regional strategies. In a similar vein, China is concerned about the demise of North Korea caused by unification. The influx of massive numbers of North Korean refugees into Chinese territory could spark serious problems, such as pandemics and societal and economic instability. Moreover, the loss of North Korea as a military ally and strategic buffer could be detrimental to China's national security. China would share a border with a unified Korea strongly influenced by the United States, which has sought an encirclement strategy. China is also concerned by the possibility that US forces could shift their attention to Taiwan, which China considers its own territory, as the need for a US military presence in Korea dwindles with the disappearance of North Korea (Park 2014; Jung 2013). On top of these concerns, the ongoing intensification of the US–China rivalry in the East Asian region will make it harder for Koreans to garner support from those two nations to achieve peaceful unification. To achieve this outcome, therefore, Koreans need political will, diplomatic prudence, and the intellectual capacity to generate a coordinated cooperation from these powerful nations while effectively dealing with a divided ROK domestic public opinion and North Korea's provocative acts.

Conclusion

This chapter has thus far explained the evolution and fluctuations of the relationship between South and North Korea, while examining the roles of top leaders, domestic conditions, and international structures in shaping inter-Korean relations. Despite some occasional thaws, the two Koreas usually maintained an antagonistic relationship until South Korean President Kim Dae-jung was inaugurated in 1998. President Kim Dae-jung's Sunshine Policy and President Roh Moo-hyun's continuous engagement policy toward North Korea brought about considerable changes in inter-Korean relations. During the period from 1998–2007, both President Kim and President Roh held historic summits with North Korean leader, Kim Jong-il. In addition to increased governmental interactions, cultural exchanges skyrocketed primarily due to the opening of the Mt. Geumgang tourist resort and many events initiated by civil society organizations. With South Korea's generous humanitarian support, the two Koreas also launched many joint economic projects. In particular, the development of the KIC played a key role in defusing military tensions between the two Koreas, and it became a symbol of inter-Korean cooperation. However, after conservative forces in South Korea took power in 2008, inter-Korean relations seriously deteriorated due to the ROK governments' hardline policies coupled with North Korea's provocative acts, including nuclear and missile tests and artillery firings.

The newly elected ROK President, Moon Jae-in, has an important but challenging mission to improve the currently deadlocked inter-Korean relations and to lay the groundwork for a peaceful reunification. To achieve these goals, the Moon government needs to strive to build a consensus on North Korea policy among South Koreans, who are sharply divided along ideological stances. It would not be plausible to accomplish such challenging tasks without the formation of consistent North Korea and unification policies based on the wide-ranging public support. As shown above, South Korea's approach to North Korea significantly changed whenever a new government emerged, thus failing to produce successful outcomes. In this regard, the Moon administration needs to establish a special consultative group that consists of both conservative and progressive opinion leaders within South Korea. Although it takes time, Moon could find most reasonable and effective policies through intensive discussions and debates among the group members. In addition, it seems necessary for the Moon administration to take a pro-active stance in dealing with the North Korean problem, rather than sitting on a back seat. As seen in the past experience, the confrontational approach solely based on pressure and sanctions worsened inter-Korean relations and destabilized the Korean Peninsula, because North Korea further accelerated its development of nuclear weapons and missiles. Based on a well-developed strategic roadmap, the Moon government needs to persuade the United States and North Korea to return to a negotiating table, while actively engaging North Korea through economic assistance and cultural exchanges. Having dialogues is a necessary condition for a peaceful resolution of the North Korean problem, although not a sufficient one.

Notes

1 United States Institute of Peace, "Peace Agreements Digital Collection: South-North Joint Declaration," June 15, 2000. Available at www.usip.org/sites/default/files/file/resources/collections/peace_agreements/n_skorea06152000.pdf.
2 United States Institute of Peace, "Peace Agreements Digital Collection: Declaration on the Advancement of South-North Korean Relations, Peace and Prosperity," October 4, 2007. Available at www.usip.org/sites/default/files/file/resources/collections/peace_agreements/n_skorea10042007.pdf.
3 US Department of State, "North Korea." Available at www.state.gov/outofdate/bgn/northkorea/26220.htm.
4 Constitution of the Republic of Korea. Available at http://korea.assembly.go.kr/res/low_01_read.jsp.

References

Agov, Avram. 2016. "Inter-Korean Relations, 1945–2013." In *Routledge Handbook of Modern Korean History*, edited by Michael J. Seth. New York: Routledge.

Armstrong, Charles K. 2005. "Inter-Korean Relations in Historical Perspective." *International Journal of Korean Unification Studies* 14 (2): 1–20.

BBC News. 2003. "S Koreans Charged over Summit Cash." June 25.

BBC News. 2016. "What Is the Kaesong Industrial Complex?" February 10.

Davenport, Kelsey. 2016. "Chronology of U.S.-North Korean Nuclear and Missile Diplomacy." October. Available at: www.armscontrol.org/factsheets/dprkchron.

Heo, Uk, and Terence Roehrig. 2014. *South Korea's Rise: Economic Development, Power, and Foreign Relations*. New York: Cambridge University Press.

Hwang, Eui-gak. 2008. "Inter-Korean Economic Cooperation: The Need for Reciprocity – Does Lopsided Cooperation Continue to Soothe North's Bluffing Mentality?" *International Journal of Korean Studies* 12 (1): 101–26.

Im, Dong-won. 2015. *Peacemaker: Inter-Korean Relations and 25 Years of North Korean Nuclear Issue*. Seoul: Changbi. (in Korean)

Joongang Ilbo. 2003. "Jung Mong-heon, Chairman of Hyundai Asan, Suicidal Death." August 4 (in Korean). Available at: http://news.joins.com/article/210195.

Jung, Geun-sik et al. 2017. *The 2016 Survey of Korean Perception of Unification*. Seoul: Seoul National University.

Jung, Jaeho. 2013. "The Rise of China and Korean Reunification." In *Korean Reunification*, edited by Young-kwan Yoon. Seoul: Seoul National University.

Jung, Jai Kwan, and Chad Rector. 2012. "South Korea's Reunification Dilemmas." *Asian Politics & Policy* 4 (4): 487–505.

Kim, Chang-hee. 2014. *Inter-Korean Relations and the Korean Peninsula: From Conflict and Confrontation Toward Trust*. Seoul: Samusa. (in Korean)

Kim, Subin. 2015. "Korean Unification Costs Would Exceed $2.7 Trillion: Researcher." *NK News*, March 6. Available at: www.nknews.org/2015/03/unification-costs-would-exceed- 2–7-trillion-researcher/.

Kirk, Don. 2002. "Four Killed as North and South Korean Navy Vessels Trade Fire." *New York Times*, June 29. Available at: www.nytimes.com/2002/06/29/world/four-killed-as- north-and-south-korean-navy-vessels-trade-fire.html.

Koh, Yu-hwan. 2000. "Unification Policies of Two Koreas and Outlook for Unity." *Korea Focus* 8 (6): 1–18.

Ku, Yangmo. 2013. "North Korea's Dangerous War Gamble." *Burlington Free Press*, April 25.

Ku, Yangmo. 2015. "Transitory or Lingering Impact? The Legacies of the Cheonan Incident in Northeast Asia." *Asian Perspective* 39 (2): 253–76.

Lee, Chang-sup. 2015. "Reunification Is Neither Jackpot nor Bonanza." *The Korea Times*, February 27. Available at: https://koreatimes.co.kr/www/news/opinon/2015/05/298_152407.html.

Lee, Jae-Bong. 2009. "US Deployment of Nuclear Weapons in 1950s South Korea & North Korea's Nuclear Development: Toward Denuclearization of the Korean Peninsula." *The Asia-Pacific Journal* 7 (3). Available at: http://apjjf.org/-Lee-Jae-Bong/3053/article.html.

Lee, Sangsoo, and Bernt Berger. 2015. "Park's Trustpolitik Challenge." *ISDP Policy Brief 185*, October 12.

Lind, Jennifer. 2015. "Korean Unification: Before the Bonanza." *38 North*, February 12. Available at: http://38north.org/2015/02/jlind021215.

Moon, Chungin, and Seungchan Boo. 2012. "President Kim Dae-jung and the Sunshine Policy: Recasting His Legacies for Peace and Prosperity." *Tongil Yeongu* [Unification Studies] 17 (1): 121–61.

Panda, Ankit. 2016. "A Great Leap to Nowhere: Remembering the US-North Korea Leap Day Deal." *The Diplomat*, February 29.

Park, Kun Young. 2014. *Inter-Korean Relations: Family or Enemy?* Seoul: Hollym.

Petrov, Leonid. 2009. "The Politics of Inter-Korean Economic Cooperation: 1998–2009." *The Asia-Pacific Journal* 7 (3). Available at: http://apjjf.org/-Leonid-Petrov/3190/article.html.

Sanger, David E. 2002. "In North Korea and Pakistan, Deep Roots of Nuclear Barter." *New York Times*, November 24. Available at: www.nytimes.com/2002/11/24/world/threats- responses-alliances-north-korea-pakistan-deep-roots-nuclear-barter.html.

Saunders, Phillip C. 2014. "China's Role in Asia: Attractive or Assertive?" In *International Relations of Asia*, edited by David Shambaugh and Michael Yahuda. New York: Rowman & Littlefield.

Shin, Jongdae. 2013. "North Korea Policy of Kim Dae-jung and Roh Moo-hyun Administrations and Domestic Politics: The Problems Lie with not 'Outside' but 'Inside.'" *Korea and International Politics* 29 (2): 1–35. (in Korean)

Yoon, Duk-min. 2008. "Initiative for 'Denuclearization, Openness and 3000': Tasks and Prospects." *Korea Focus*. Available at: www.koreafocus.or.kr/design2/layout/content_print.asp?group_id=102041.

Yoon, Young-kwan. 2013. "Challenges of Korean Reunification and How to Overcome Them: From Philosophical, Strategic, and Institutional Viewpoints." In *Korean Reunification*, edited by Young-kwan Yoon. Seoul: Seoul National University. (in Korean)

Conclusion

Historical legacies, lingering issues, and future prospects

Jongseok Woo

This book has discussed the historical paths and current dynamics of politics, economy, and foreign relations of North and South Korea, dating back to the opening of the peninsula to the outside world in the late nineteenth century. This concluding chapter presents the issues of domestic politics and foreign relations that the two Koreas currently face. The following section briefly discusses the historical legacies of the twentieth century and the divergent paths to political and economic development taken by North and South Korea. Section two identifies the challenges South Korea currently faces – deepening and broadening its democracy, fostering continued economic development, while building a more equitable and fair society, and designing foreign policies for peace-building on the peninsula and creating an international consensus for peaceful unification of the two Koreas. Section three surveys the ongoing problems for North Korea, which revolve around the seemingly incompatible objectives of regime survival through isolation and armed provocations, on the one hand, and economic development through the termination of economic sanctions, on the other. This chapter closes with a brief discussion about the prospects for peaceful unification of Korea.

Historical legacies and diverging paths of development

At the turn of the twentieth century, the Korean people lost their chance for modern state-building and fell under 36 years of Japanese colonial rule. Japan's departure led to the political division of the Korean Peninsula and the tragic Korean War. The departure of Japanese forces was followed by arrival of two superpowers – the United States and the Soviet Union – which divided the many parts of the world into two political, ideological, economic, and military camps. The superpowers were eager to put their occupied halves of the peninsula under their spheres of influence and establish political systems resembling their own. In the south, nationalist leaders declared the Republic of Korea (or South Korea) with American support; in the North, communist leaders formed the Muscovite communist Democratic People's Republic of Korea with sponsorship from the Soviet Union. For the first time in more than a millennium, the Korean people not only formed two separate political systems but also fought a horrendous war with each other, resulting in the deaths of millions and the utter annihilation of the entire peninsula. Moreover, the Korean War (1950–1953) brought about mutual hostility and hatred with the upcoming generations. After the war, South and North Koreans alike have developed ambivalent and self-conflicting images about the other half. Koreans perceive those in the other nation as Korean compatriots who are destined to live together in a unified country, but they are also arch enemies to confront and fight.

The legacy of the Korean War and ensuing Cold War confrontations largely defined the domestic politics, ideologies, economic systems, and foreign policy strategies of the two Koreas. In South Korea, anti-communism became the governing ideology throughout the Cold War years. Domestically, anti-communism served as an ideological justification for authoritarian rules for Rhee Syngman and subsequent military dictators (and, oftentimes, even democratically elected leaders); opposition to dictators was considered equivalent to being pro-communist or pro-North Korea. Externally, anti-communism fashioned a pro-American foreign policy, so that US–ROK alliance served as the main pillar of South Korea's security policy. Meanwhile, in North Korea, anti-imperialism (defined as being anti-American and anti-Japanese) became one of the mainstays of Kim Il-sung's *Juche* ideology. Kim Il-sung consolidated his dictatorship through massive purges of political opponents in the name of factionalism and ideological impurity and, in that process, created a sense of permanent crisis based on an imminent attack from the United States. In the North and South alike, the Korean War and subsequent confrontations served to consolidate dictatorial regimes based upon mutual hatred.

As opposed to these parallels, however, the two Koreas have established distinct political, ideological, and economic systems that have defined their long-term routes to development. South Korea participated in the American-led camp and adopted a free market economy. Since the 1960s, with continued American economic and security backing, South Korea has experienced an unprecedented economic miracle in its 5,000-year-long history. It took less than two generations for the country to emerge from the ashes of the Korean War to become the 12 largest economy in the world. The economic miracle provided fertile soil for democracy by bringing about urbanization, wealth, higher education, and new lifestyle and culture that promote democratic norms and values. Over three decades of democratic experience, South Korea has established a consolidated and stable democracy and currently stands as one of the finest examples of economic development and democratic governance in the world.

While South Korea has made great strides toward economic prosperity and democracy, its northern counterpart fell under constant crisis that threatened the very survival of the regime. After World War II, North Korea merely copied Moscow-style political, economic, and ideological systems. A decade later, however, Kim Il-sung and his Manchurian guerrilla faction refashioned the country with a political system in which both the party and the military became mere servants to the dictator. Furthermore, Kim's *Juche* ideology (later termed Kimilsungism) became the only principle for every quarter of society and defined North Korea's policy decisions. In particular, main principles of *Juche* – political-economic independence and self-defense – made the Pyongyang regime obsessed with economic autarchy and military expansion that resulted in further economic complications in the post-Cold War period. Without a long-term solution to its problems, North Korea has struggled to survive through policies of further isolation and the development of nuclear weapons and long-range missile systems. With these divergent paths in mind, the ensuing sections discuss the main problems each Korea currently faces.

South Korea: maturing democracy and economy

Challenges to democratic governance

Since pro-democracy movements at the grassroots level toppled decades-long military rule, South Korea has built a consolidated democracy without major interruption. The three-decade-long democratic governance saw four power alternations between conservatives and progressives over roughly ten-year cycles: (1) conservative rule by Roh Tae-woo and Kim Young-sam (1988–1998), (2) progressive rule by Kim Dae-jung and Roh Moo-hyun (1998–2008), (3) conservative rule by Lee Myung-bak and Park Geun-hye (2008–2017), and (4) the progressive Moon Jae-in government (2017–2022). Procedurally speaking, these peaceful power alternations mark an ideal setup for any democratic governance. On closer look, however, the current status of democracy in South Korea reveals several difficult challenges ahead, such as extreme political polarization along regions, generations, and ideologies, rampant political corruption, and individual freedoms that are frequently restricted by the state.

In contrast with the democratic procedures with orderly transitions of power between conservatives and progressives, several indicators reveal signs of crisis in democratic governance in South Korea. One problematic area is a lack of respect for the freedoms and rights of individuals. For instance, ratings by Freedom House demonstrates that, although South Korea has been consistently categorized as "free," specific scores have decreased from 1.5 a decade ago to 2.0 in recent years, with "1" indicating best and "7" worst (Freedom House 2017). A more alarming indicator is the status of press freedom, which Freedom House categorizes as "partly free"; a decade ago, South Korea was "free" in the category. A similar trend is found in the category of internet freedom, which is also "partly free" as of 2016. Although South Korea is one of the most wired countries in the world, individuals' freedom on the internet is limited and often censored by the government. These exemplary scores reveal that the quality of democratic governance has been stagnant or even degenerated over the past decade.

Moreover, as discussed in Chapter 3, the three decades of attempts at democracy have been mired by extreme polarization across regions, ideologies, and generations. Modern day regionalism in South Korea dates back to Park Jung-hee's dictatorship, which actively mobilized regional divisions between his hometown *Yeongnam* and opposition *Honam* for its political hegemony. Regionalism deepened during and after democratization, as three Kims – Kim Young-sam, Kim Dae-jung, and Kim Jong-pil – organized region-based political parties and ran for the presidency. Regional divisions continued to play a major role in post-democratization electoral politics in both parliamentary and presidential elections as the *Yeongnam* region wanted to continue its political hegemony, while the *Honam* region aspires to terminate the regional discrimination.

The regional cleavage overlaps in large part with ideological divisions. Residents in *Yeongnam* have endorsed a more conservative ideology that has close ties with the previous dictatorial regimes, while *Honam* has represented a more progressive ideology. Moreover, while regionalism and ideology play significant roles in electoral politics, generational differences became a newly emerging cleavage in recent elections, especially the 20th National Assembly election in 2016 and the 19th Presidential election in 2017. The younger generation, especially those in their 40s or younger, support progressive parties and candidates, while the older generation, those in their 60s or older, vote for conservative parties and candidates. Political cleavages across regions, ideologies, and generations can be found in most democratic societies. However, the South Korean case reveals their extreme degrees, so that parties and candidates focus on mobilizing these differences rather than having constructive debates about policy agendas. Political leaders' exaggeration of these political, ideological, and regional differences exacerbates the extreme polarization of political society, which in turn makes sound political dialogue extremely difficult.

Another area of troubling concern for South Korea is the level of perceived corruption that has worsened in the recent decade. In 2008, the Transparency International's Corruption Perceptions Index (CPI) ranked the country 40th out of 180 countries surveyed. A decade later, however, South Korea fell to 52th out of 176 countries, making the nation one of the most corrupt members of the Organization for Economic Cooperation and Development (OECD) (Transparency International, various years). Since the first democratically elected Roh Tae-woo government that commenced in 1988, no president has been immune to political corruption. Presidents, families, and/or their political aides have frequently appeared in news stories about corruption and scandal. The more frequent coverage of political corruption by the media may be a sign that the country has grown more transparent, so that corrupt transactions have become difficult to remain secret than in the pre-democratization era. Or, anti-corruption agencies might have become more determined to investigate and prosecute corrupt politicians. If these trends are true, then they are positive signs for democratic governance in South Korea. However, repetitive corruption scandals make citizens disillusioned about democracy, so that their commitment to democratic norms and values may be significantly weakened.

Economic development: growth vs. equality?

South Korea's economic record for the second half of the twentieth century represents the so-called East Asian economic miracle. Against the backdrop of Japanese exploitation during its colonial occupation and the Korean War that completely devastated the entire peninsula, South Korea has achieved an economic miracle by becoming the twelfth largest economy in the world. As illuminated in Chapter 4, South Korea's economic development was due to several internal and external circumstances, such as Koreans' cultural emphasis on education and diligence, state-led industrialization and export-oriented economic policies, and external support from the United States and Japan. Six decades of development has made South Korea into a dynamic economy that boasts a well-educated labor force and first-rate technologies in computer, electronics, and automobile industries, among others. Although it has somewhat slowed in the past decade, and with constant security threats from North Korea, South Korea's economy still presents a model of economic development for many politically and economically undeveloped countries in the world.

However, as much as it has made revolutionary accomplishments in such a short period of time, the South Korean economy exposes numerous challenges that must be overcome before it makes another leap toward a mature developed economy. First of all, as its economic growth owes in large part to the Park Jung-hee's developmental state model, it has also been blamed for many of the structural ills South Korea currently suffers, such as an extreme concentration of wealth within a small number of big businesses, widening inequality, high rates of unemployment, and political corruption, to name a few. A general consensus in the study of political corruption has been that democracy and a free market economy can work together to drastically reduce a country's level of political corruption (Girling 1997; Sandholtz and Koetzle 2000; Aidt 2003). Empirically speaking, most of economically advanced democracies demonstrate low levels of perceived corruption around the world. However, South Korea is an exception to this rule, as it has been democratic for three decades and is ranked 23th out of 180 countries in its economic freedom ranking, according to the Heritage Foundation's Economic Freedom rankings (Heritage Foundation 2017). Contradictorily, political and economic freedoms do not lower South Korea's political corruption.

Another area of troubling concern for South Korea's economy is a widening inequality gap as a result of extreme concentration of wealth within a small number of firms and individuals. The *chaebol*-based economic structure has been an outgrowth of Park Jung-hee style state-led industrialization policies, in which the dictator gave various preferential benefits to a small number of family-owned firms in return for political funds. This *chaebol*-dominant economic system has been the main source of corrupt ties between politics and businesses, as well as an extreme concentration of wealth among these *chaebols*. The recent Park Geun-hye and Choi Soon-sil gate clearly illustrates continuing corrupt ties, in which Lee Jae-yong, the grandson of the founder of Samsung and vice chair of the company, was arrested for paying bribes to Choi Soon-sil, a confidante of the impeached president.

With close political ties, *chaebols* have monopolized the economy. For instance, the five largest *chaebols* accounts for 55.7 percent of South Korea's gross domestic product (GDP) as of 2012. The two largest companies, Samsung and Hyundai, account for more than 33 percent of GDP, although their employees are less than five percent of entire labor force in the country (Business Korea 2014). While these *chaebols* continue to thrive, other medium and small businesses struggle for survival, which creates a widening income gap, as well. Income inequality in South Korea is the worst among the 22 countries in the Asia-Pacific region, with the top 10 percent of the population earning 45 percent of the total income (Kim 2016). A few factors have contributed to the widening inequality gap in South Korea. First, the income gap has widened between workers of big businesses and those of smaller companies. *Chaebols'* industries have continued to thrive, and their workers' income has risen, while small firms struggled to survive and their workers' incomes have remained stagnant. Second, income gaps have widened between regular and non-regular workers. One of IMF-sanctioned reforms in the late-1990s focused on creating a flexible labor market, which dramatically increased the share of non-regular workers in the labor market. While regular workers enjoy higher income, more job security, and other benefits, non-regular workers earn less and struggle with job security. Finally, there has been a growing generational gap between older and younger workers, as young jobseekers find it increasingly difficult to land quality jobs. South Korea's youth-unemployment rate is at all-time high of 12.5 percent, while the overall unemployment rate is 4 percent (Kim 2016).

Many of the social problems South Korea currently faces originate from the *chaebol*-dominant economic structure. A pejorative term, "*Hell Joseon*," symbolically pronounces resulting social problems, such as high suicidal rates, extreme competition, and low birth rates, among others. The South Korean economy has arrived at a critical juncture, and whether it can change, from the existing *chaebol*-oriented economic structure to a more equitable and sustainable one, is uncertain.

Foreign policy challenges

As a strategic center in East Asia, the Korean Peninsula had often been a focal point of major power rivalries for the past two millennia, and therefore, numerous wars have occurred. Since the late nineteenth century, the peninsula was thrust into struggles by major powers, beginning with Sino-Japanese and Sino-Russian wars, and leading to the US–Soviet Cold War confrontation. Territorial division and the Korean War determined the two Koreas' foreign policy strategies thereafter. As a small and poor nation, South Korea depended for survival on the US security commitment, which was not always perceived as dependable. However, South Korea not only survived constant communist threats but also took the offensive by expanding its diplomatic relations with former communist states that had once been Pyongyang's allies. Although South Korea has risen miraculously from the ashes of the Japanese colonial rule and the Korean War to become a notable military and economic power on the global stage, the country's foreign policy is still preoccupied with the growing threat from North Korea.

The foreign policy challenge that haunts South Korea is to deal with the unruly Pyongyang regime that has been muddling through post-Cold War difficulties and has become what Barak Obama once called a "pariah state" in the international community (Malkin 2014). In the past two decades, Seoul has experimented two vastly different approaches – the progressive governments' (Kim Dae-jung's and Roh Moo-hyun's) engagement efforts and the conservative governments' (Lee Myung-bak's and Park Geun-hye's) hostile stances based on strict reciprocity. However, neither strategy proved to be effective enough to change Pyongyang's attitude. Even worse, South Korea's policy toward the north has become a major source of political polarization in the country. The progressive governments' *Sunshine Policy* brought about severe criticism from conservative constituents who advocated a much tougher stance and strict reciprocity against Pyongyang. Successive conservative governments put more pressure on North Korea to cease Pyongyang's armed provocations and WMD (weapons of mass destruction) programs. However, the conservative approaches largely failed to make Pyongyang succumb. Contrariwise, North Korea has responded with rounds of nuclear tests, rocket firings, and armed attacks on South Korea.

The newly elected Moon Jae-in government encounters a challenging foreign policy environment. It needs to resume communications with a North Korea that continues to defy international sanctions on its WMDs, which is likely to limit the Moon government's engagement efforts. At the same time, South Korea has to build an international consensus, especially between the United States and China, over peaceful reunification with North Korea. This task seems to be increasingly difficult due to growing rivalry and tensions between the two superpowers over various regional and global issues. An equally important mission for President Moon is to escape from previous governments' North Korean policies that have polarized South Korean society.

North Korea: beyond regime survival

The logic of political survival

The 7th Party Congress, held on May 6–9, 2016, proclaimed completion of the hereditary succession and consolidation of Kim Jong-un's leadership. The previous 6th Party Congress, held in 1980, declared the succession from Kim Il-sung to Jong-il. North Korea went 36 years between party gatherings mainly due to a lack of policy successes that the regime could propagandize. In this sense, the 7th Party Congress was an ambitious declaration that North Korea has overcome difficulties and is ready to usher in a new era of power and prosperity. Contrary to the popular 'collapsist' forecast that predicted an imminent regime collapse in Pyongyang, Kim Jong-il and his son, Jong-un, have managed to survive multiple challenges from several quarters of North Korean society. How could it survive, and at what cost? Can Kim Jong-un steer his nation into the next stage of socialist utopia that his grandfather and his *Juche* ideology proclaimed a half century ago?

As discussed in Chapter 6, Kim Jong-il's military-first (*Songun*) politics was at the heart of North Korea's regime survival in the post-Cold War and post-Kim Il-sung eras. In the mid-1990s, North Korea faced multiple challenges that directly threatened the very survival of the regime, such as economic and diplomatic isolation, natural disasters, an ensuing nationwide famine, and massive defections by North Koreans to China and South Korea. After his father's death, Kim Jong-il declared military-first politics as his governing slogan in which the Korean People's Army (KPA) rather than the Korean Workers Party (KWP) emerged as the vanguard of the *Juche* revolution and guarantor of the Kim regime. The KPA expanded its national defense role into traditionally non-military areas of socio-economic development and protector of the dictator. Military-first politics brought about a massive expansion of the KPA's influence at the expense of the KWP's political supremacy, and a major portion of resources were invested in the military and defense-related sectors. As the selectorate theory of authoritarianism illustrates, Kim Jong-il distributed scarce resources to his key inner circle through massive promotions and provisions of goods, such as comfortable housing, luxury goods, and honors, in order to secure their unconditional allegiance (Mesqueta et al. 2003; Byman and Lind 2010).

At the same time, Kim Jong-il employed various coup-proofing tactics at both the institutional and personnel levels. He compartmentalized major political institutions so that inter-institutional coordination became impossible, and inter-institutional communication was made possible only through Kim himself. By separating other government institutions from the KWP's supervision, Kim exercised authority over all of the political institutions, as they engaged in inter-institutional competition for loyalty to him (McEachern 2010). In parallel with inter-institutional competition, Kim Jong-il also designed a delicate system of checks and balances among key elites in the party and the military. He appointed geriatric party leaders to leadership positions in government organizations, albeit without real political power, and he gave real decision-making power to second- or third-ranking officers. Due to this personnel appointment system, official rankings within Pyongyang's governmental hierarchy do not always correctly reflect the real power structure.

In a sense, Kim Jong-il's political survival was largely due to his decades-long political experience and ability to command the power-wielding institutions and key leaders in the party and the military. This suggests that Kim Jong-il's highly personalistic ruling style does not transfer to young and inexperienced Kim Jong-un's leadership style. This point partly explains why Kim Jong-un attempted to demote the KPA's political influence and restore the KWP's authority of the pre-military-first politics era. The KWP's political rise, and the KPA's relative decline, was the centerpiece of the young and inexperienced leader's strategy to consolidate power through partisan institutions such as the Central Committee of the KWP, the Politburo (and Standing Committee), and the Central Military Commission. Such power rebalancing accompanied significant generational changes in the party and the cabinet, as almost a half of the personnel in the above-mentioned partisan institutions turned over. In this respect, the current Kim Jong-un regime has made efforts to reject his father's military-first politics.

Survived but . . .

Military-first politics enabled the survival of the Kim Jong-il and Kim Jong-un regimes from internal and external challenges. Internally, military-first politics prevented coup attempts at the elite-level or anti-Kim movements at the grassroots level from emerging out of the dire economic crisis in which millions starved to death or left the country. Externally, military-first politics was the driving force for the defense buildup and advancement of WMDs that intended to deter a possible military attack from the United States. While it allowed regime survival from multiple challenges, military-first politics could by no means become a long-term solution for the poverty-stricken country. In foreign policy, military-first politics generated offensive and oftentimes adventurous actions against its enemies. Against South Korea, it conducted several low-intensity armed attacks, and against the United States, it continues brinkmanship with nuclear detonations and firings of long-range missiles.

Ultimately, military-first politics made North Korea completely isolated from the outside world, and it remains a most secretive society to most outsiders. Due to severe economic sanctions, inter-Korean economic cooperation is not likely to resume any time soon. The Kaesong Industrial complex was shut down in February 2016 after North Korea's nuclear detonation and missile launching. The Mount Kumgang tour program closed in 2008 after a female South Korean tourist was shot dead by a North Korean soldier. The complete cessation of inter-Korean economic cooperation made North Korea ever more dependent on China. According to an estimate by the Korea Trade-Investment Promotion Agency (KOTRA 2016), the volume of Sino-North Korean trade accounted for 91.3 percent of North Korea's foreign trade in 2015. North Korea's dependence on China must make Pyongyang's leaders feel extremely perturbed, as it will ultimately put them under expanded Chinese influence. Furthermore, the growing economic dependence creates a discrepancy between *Juche*'s principle of self-reliance or independence and North Korea's increasing reliance on China.

Kim Jong-un acutely understands the challenges his country faces, which makes him eager for extensive economic reforms to improve his people's living conditions. The above-mentioned 7th Party Congress placed much emphasis on the leader's desire for economic development, identifying the cabinet (and not the KPA) as the "headquarters of the national economy" and expressing his willingness to give extensive management rights to enterprises (Woo 2016, 7). Kim Jong-un specified his economic reform plans through the announcement of a five-year strategy for economic development. This is an important sign of change occurring in North Korea, as the leader acknowledged that improving living standards was his responsibility and is the basis of his regime's legitimacy. It has been more than two decades since the Pyongyang government significantly cut provisions of basic necessities to the people. The emerging market system at the grassroots level, called *Jangmadang*, replaced the government's role in the recent decade. In any dictatorial regime, the only *raison d'être* for regime legitimacy is to satisfy the people's material necessities, which North Korea has called *gangseongdaeguk, or* "a powerful and prosperous nation."

Regardless of the Kim regime's aspiration to implement economic reforms, its route to economic development will be rocky and uncertain at best due to its *byongjin* policy that simultaneously pursues nuclear weapons and economic development. On the one hand, Pyongyang's WMD programs might have assured the Kim family's regime security. On the other hand, its nuclear weapons brought about severe economic sanctions and continues to limit North Korea's economic development. Kim Jong-un is at crossroads in choosing either nuclear weapons and continuing isolation, or giving up nuclear weapons and focusing on economic prosperity. The Kim Jong-un regime cannot acquire both.

Road to peaceful reunification

The divided Korean Peninsula remains the last bastion of Cold War confrontations that have been resolved in other parts of the world over the past three decades. The two Koreas demonstrate striking disparities between the economically prosperous and democratic South and the economically backward and repressive North. Divided Korea has continued to be a major source of instability and tension in East Asia, as the legacy of the Korean War and ensuing confrontations have dominated inter-Korean relations. Moreover, the Korean problem is truly an international issue in which world's major powers are deeply involved, including the United States, China, Russia, and Japan. Because of this, unification of the Korean Peninsula requires consensus at both the domestic and international levels. At first, Seoul and Pyongyang must find a way to reduce military tensions and expand political, economic, cultural exchanges before arriving at a peaceful unification. Toward that purpose, the two Koreas can go back to two previous inter-Korean agreements declared at the June 15th North–South Joint Declaration in 2000 and confirmed at the October 4th North–South Declaration in 2007. The two nations had agreed to expand economic, social, and cultural exchanges, and to work toward peaceful Korean unification. Internationally, the two Koreas should make efforts to persuade the surrounding powers, especially the United States and China, that the peaceful unification of Korea will not harm, but uphold their own national interests.

References

Aidt, Toke S. 2003. "Economic Analysis of Corruption: A Survey." *Economic Journal* 113 (491): 632–52.

Business Korea. 2014. "Economic Concentration: Samsung, Hyundai Motor More than 33% of Korea's GDP." Available at: www.businesskorea.co.kr/english/news/money/2937-economic-concentration-samsung-hyundai-motor-more-33-korea%E2%80%99s-gdp.

Byman, Daniel, and Jennifer Lind. 2010. "Pyongyang's Survival Strategy: Tools of Authoritarian Control in North Korea." *International Security* 35 (1): 44–74.

Freedom House. 2017. "Freedom in the World." Various years. Available at: https://freedomhouse.org/report/freedom-world/freedom-world-2017.

Girling, John. 1997. *Corruption, Capitalism, and Democracy*. New York: Routledge.

Heritage Foundation. 2017. "2017 Index of Economic Freedom." Available at: www.heritage.org/index/.

Kim, Jae-won. 2016. "Korea Worst in Income Inequality in Asia." *Korea Times*, March 16. Available at: www.koreatimes.co.kr/www/news/biz/2016/03/488_200524.html.

Korea Trade-Investment Promotion Agency, Republic of Korea. 2016. "2015 Annual Report on North Korea's Foreign Trade" (in Korean). Available at: https://news.kotra.or.kr/user/globalBbs/kotranews/11/globalBbsDataView.do?setIdx=249&dataIdx=151201.

Malkin, Bonnie. 2014. "Barak Obama Says North Korea Is a 'Pariah State.'" *The Telegraph*, April 26. Available at: www.telegraph.co.uk/news/worldnews/barackobama/10789626/Barack-Obama-says-North-Korea-is-a-pariah-state.html.

McEachern, Patrick. 2010. *Inside the Redbox: North Korea's Post-Totalitarian Politics*. New York: Columbia University Press.

Mesqueta, Bruce B., Alastair Smith, Randolph M. Siverson, and James D. Morrow. 2003. *The Logic of Political Survival*. Cambridge, MA: MIT Press.

Sandholtz, Wayne, and William Koetzle. 2000. "Accounting for Corruption: Economic Structure, Democracy, and Trade." *International Studies Quarterly* 44 (1): 31–50.

Transparency International (various years). "Corruption Perceptions Index." Available at: www.transparency.org/research/cpi/.

Woo, Jongseok. 2016. "The 7th Party Congress in Pyongyang: Institutional Adjustments, Policy Priorities, and Future Prospects." *RINSA Forum* 44: 5–8.

Index

Page numbers in *italic* indicate a figure and page numbers in **bold** indicate a table.